HISTORY OF THE SIEGE OF BOSTON

A Da Capo Press Reprint Series

THE ERA OF THE AMERICAN REVOLUTION

GENERAL EDITOR: LEONARD W. LEVY
Brandeis University

HISTORY OF THE
SIEGE OF BOSTON,
AND OF THE
BATTLES OF LEXINGTON,
CONCORD, AND BUNKER HILL

By Richard Frothingham

DA CAPO PRESS • NEW YORK • 1970

A Da Capo Press Reprint Edition

This Da Capo Press edition of the
History of the Siege of Boston
is an unabridged republication of the sixth edition
published in Boston in 1903.

Library of Congress Catalog Card Number 77-115680
SBN 306-71932-0

Published by Da Capo Press
A Division of Plenum Publishing Corporation
227 West 17th Street, New York, N. Y. 10011
All Rights Reserved

Manufactured in the United States of America

HISTORY OF THE SIEGE OF BOSTON

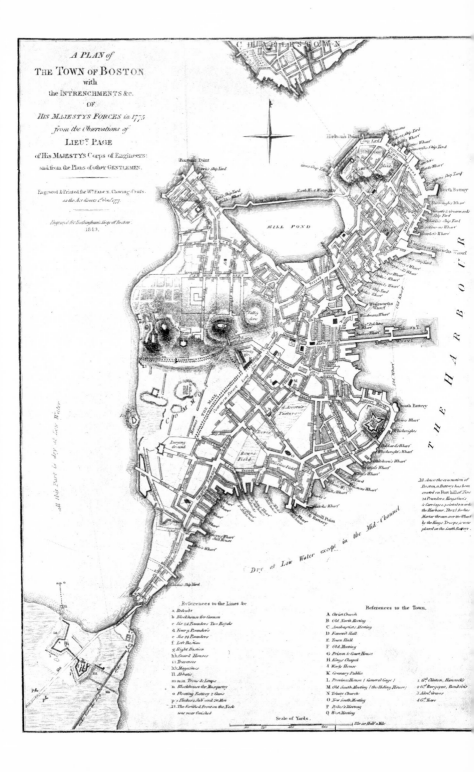

A PLAN of
THE TOWN OF BOSTON
with
the INTRENCHMENTS &c.
OF
HIS MAJESTYS FORCES in 1775
from the Observations of
LIEUT. PAGE
of His Majestys Corps of Engineers:
and from the Plans of other GENTLEMEN.

Engraved & Printed for Wm. FADEN, Charing-Cross,
as the Act directs 1st Octr. 1777.

Engraved for Frothingham's Siege of Boston.
1849.

CHARLES TOWN

MILL POND

THE HARBOUR

Dry at Low Water except in the Mid-Channel

all this Part is dry at Low Water

M. since the evacuation of
Boston, a Battery has been
erected on Fort hill of Nine
24 Pounders, Kingstons's
& Carriages, pointed towards
the Harbour. The 13 Inches
Mortar thrown over the Wharf
by the Kings Troops, is now
placed in the South Battery.

References to the Lines &c
a Redoubt
b Blockhouse for Cannon
c Six 24 Pounders Two Royals
d Four 9 Pounders
e Six 24 Pounders
f Left Bastion
g Right Bastion
h Guard Houses
i Traverses
k Magazines
l Abbatis
m m m Trous de Loup
n Blockhouse for Musquetry
o Floating Battery 2 Guns
p 2 Flatters Salt and 20 Men
13 The Fortified Front on the Neck
was near finished

References to the Town.
A Christ Church
B Old North Meeting
C Anabaptists Meeting
D Fanueil Hall
E Town Hall
F Old Meeting
G Prison & Court House
H Kings Chapel
J Work House
K Granary Public
L Province House (General Gage)
M Old South Meeting (the Riding House)
N Trinity Church
O New South Meeting
P Brles's Meeting
Q West Meeting

1 Genl. Clinton, Hancocks
2 Genl. Burgoyne, Bowdoins
3 Adml. Graves
4 Genl. Howe

Scale of Yards.

SSe or Half a Mile

HISTORY

OF THE

SIEGE OF BOSTON,

AND OF THE

BATTLES OF LEXINGTON, CONCORD.

AND

BUNKER HILL.

ALSO, AN ACCOUNT OF THE

BUNKER HILL MONUMENT.

WITH ILLUSTRATIVE DOCUMENTS.

BY

RICHARD FROTHINGHAM.

SIXTH EDITION.

BOSTON:

LITTLE, BROWN, AND COMPANY.

1903.

PREFACE.

The preparation of a History of Charlestown led to large collections relative to the military transactions that occurred, in 1775 and 1776, in the vicinity of Boston. The greater part of them, however, could not be properly used in a publication of so local a character; and as no work had been issued containing a full narrative of these interesting events, it was concluded to prepare the present volume. It will be found to contain little of general history, and no more of the civil history of Boston than appeared to be necessary to show its relation to the patriot party at the commencement of hostilities.

Time and labor have been freely spent in searching for original documents for this work. Hence, much of the narrative has been drawn from contemporary manuscripts, and nearly all of it from contemporary authorities. Less scepticism as to tradition, and the admission of a larger portion of personal anecdote, might have made it more amusing, but it would have been less reliable. No statement has been made without being warranted by authority believed to be good, and no opinion has been expressed which a careful scrutiny of evidence did not seem to authorize. Ample time, also, has been taken in the labor of arrangement, and hence haste will not be pleaded in extenuation of error. It will only be remarked, that while there has been diligent search for facts, a careful endeavor has been made to state them fairly and exactly.

The author takes pleasure in expressing grateful acknowledgments to the many friends who have aided or encouraged his humble labors. He will always remember their courtesy and kindness. He is specially indebted to President Jared Sparks, Hon. James Savage, and George Ticknor, Esquire, for valuable assistance. The librarians of various public institutions have rendered every facility in making researches Such attention is alike cheering and gratifying to the inquirer.

This volume has been written under sentiments of grateful veneration for the memory of the men who sacrificed so much, and who struggled so nobly, in behalf of American Liberty. May it contribute something to perpetuate the story of their heroism and suffering, and to foster a desire to emulate their virtues and patriotism.

December, 1849.

The volume has been revised for this new edition, and a few correc tions, mostly verbal, have been made.

Charlestown, February, 1851.

In this third edition a few errors have been corrected, and a few facts and authorities added, — one, in the Appendix, being a Letter relative to the Battle of Bunker Hill.

Charlestown. December 2, 1872.

CONTENTS.

CHAPTER I. — COLONIAL POLITICS.

CHAPTER II. — LEXINGTON AND CONCORD.

CHAPTER III. — THE SIEGE OF BOSTON.

CHAPTER IV. — BUNKER HILL BATTLE.

CHAPTER V. — BUNKER HILL BATTLE.

CHAPTER VI. — BUNKER HILL BATTLE.

CHAPTER VII. — BUNKER HILL BATTLE.

CHAPTER VIII. — THE SIEGE OF BOSTON.

CHAPTER IX. — THE SIEGE OF BOSTON.

CHAPTER X. — THE SIEGE OF BOSTON.

CHAPTER XI. — THE SIEGE OF BOSTON.

CHAPTER XII. — THE SIEGE OF BOSTON.

CHAPTER XIII. — THE SIEGE OF BOSTON.

THE BUNKER HILL MONUMENT.

APPENDIX.

ILLUSTRATIONS.

MAPS AND ILLUSTRATIONS.

THE PLAN OF BOSTON, by Lieut. Page, was published in England, in 1777. It is the only plan of Boston, of much value, of the publications of 1775. It contains many names not on the last edition of Price's plan, which is entitled, "A New Plan of the Great Town of Bos. ton, in New England, in America; with the many Additional Buildings and New Streets, to the year 1769." Page's plan is curious, as it shows the streets and principal places in the last year Boston was under British authority, and the intrenchments erected by the British troops. This is the first American engraving of this plan. It is of the same size as the engraving of 1777, and as nearly as possible a fac-simile of it.

THE PLAN OF BUNKER HILL BATTLE is by the same person — the groundwork being from an actual survey by the celebrated British engineer, Capt. Montresor. It is the only plan of Charlestown of so early a date. It is on the same scale as that published by Felton and Parker, in 1848, and the plans will be found to agree as to Main-street, Bunker Hill-street and other streets. The engraving for this work is the first American engraving. It is of the same size as the British engraving, and as to the outlines — streets, houses, trees, fences, line of fire and lettering — is an exact copy. It will be observed that the hills are not named correctly — Bunker Hill should be Breed's Hill. This plan was first published in 1776 or 1777, and the plate of it, with a few alterations in the lettering, was used by Stedman, in 1794, — without, however, any credit being given either to Montresor or Page. A plan was also made by Henry D'Berniere, a British officer. This was first engraved in this country, in 1818, for the Analectic Magazine. The ground plan is not so correct as Page's. I have seen an old MS. copy of this, slightly varying in the streets from the engraving. This plan forms the basis of Colonel Swett's plan of the battle.

THE PLAN OF BOSTON AND ITS ENVIRONS was prepared from several plans. Various maps of this vicinity were published during the Revolution. A curious one appeared in England, in 1775, entitled, "The Seat of War in New England, by an American Volunteer, with the Marches of several Corps sent by the Colonies towards Boston." It is on one sheet of imperial paper, and was published by R. Sayer and J. Bennett, Sept. 2, 1775. This map contains a plan of Boston and of Boston harbor; also, a picture of the battle of Bunker Hill. It represents the town on fire, and the British columns, with colors, marching to the attack. The map represents the New Hampshire troops coming by the way of Andover, Wilmington and Woburn; the Connecticut troops, by way of Providence; and Washington and "the New York Grenadiers" (!) by the way of Worcester. It is more curious than valuable. The Philadelphia Ledger (Aug. 19, 1775) contains an advertisement of a map taken "by the most skilful draughtsman in all America." This was Roman's Map of the Seat of Civil War in America. It is inscribed to John Hancock. It has a rude view of the lines on Boston Neck, and a "Plan of Boston and its Environs." A curious map of Boston and its environs was published, in 1776, at Paris, by "Ch. de Beaurain, Geographer to his Majesty." It purports to be copied from a British plan, — probably from a plan drawn by an engineer in Boston, in October, 1775, and (March, 1776) published "by a nobleman." This plan also is curious, but not correct. Other smaller plans also appeared, in various publications. Lieut. Page prepared a map of "Boston, its Environs and Harbor, with the Rebels' Works," &c., from his own observations and the plans of Capt. Montresor. This was published in England, by William Faden, in 1777. It is valuable as to the harbor, but incorrect as to the country. Henry Pelham published in 1777, a large map of Boston and its environs, dedicated to Lord George Germaine, which is by far the most accurate of the maps of the environs. The plan in Dr. Gordon's History was evidently compiled from Page's for the harbor, and from Pelham's for the country. This was copied by Marshall.

THE VIEW OF CHARLESTOWN is copied from an original MS. of 1775, and communicated by Henry Stevens, Esq.

THE VIEW OF THE LINES ON BOSTON NECK is taken from one of the British prints of 1777.

THE PLAN OF THE FORT ON BUNKER HILL is taken from Lieut. Carter's letters, written mostly from Charlestown Heights, during the siege, and published in England, in 1781.

THE REPRESENTATION OF THE PINE-TREE FLAG is from the French map of Boston and environs.

THE SIEGE OF BOSTON.

CHAPTER I.

THE New England colonists always claimed the liberties of Englishmen. They brought with them the principles that the people are the fountain of political power, and that there can be no just taxation without representation; and contended for the right of applying these principles according to their wants. They brought with them, also, that republican spirit which animated the English Puritans, and their early ideal was the establishment of civil commonwealths on the basis of Christian principles. To their vision, this form was a divine institution, the government of angels in heaven, and which ought to be that of men upon earth. It was instituted by God himself in the Holy Scriptures, whereby any nation might enjoy all the ends of government in the best manner.[1] Hence the New England communities became republican in form, while they had for their "quickening spirit, equal rights, freedom of thought and action, and personal independence."[2]

It was this spirit, and the bold application of these principles, that made the colonists, so far as their internal policy was concerned, virtually independent; while, so far as their external politics were concerned, their allegiance to the crown did not include an admission of the supremacy of Parliament. In fact, they regarded themselves as capable of organizing

---

[1] Eliot's Christian Commonwealth, Preface, 1650   [2] John Q. Adams, in Mass. Hist. Coll., vol. 29, p. 210.

local governments, contracting alliances with each other, coining money, making war, and concluding peace. The institutions that grew up, shaped in a great measure as experience dictated, were admirably adapted to strengthen and develop a love of liberty united to a respect for law. The almost continual struggles with the aborigines and the French served as an invaluable school in which to learn the discipline, and to become inured to the dangers, of a military life; while schools, and colleges, and churches, maintained with wonderful perseverance, nurtured an equally invaluable intelligence and public virtue. Persons and property were secure, and labor was less burdened with restriction, and more free to reap a fair reward, than it was in any country in the world. In a word, there grew up a system of local administration well suited to the condition of a rising people, united to a general organization, capable, in any emergency, of affording it protection. The colonists, in the enjoyment of so large a measure of individual freedom, developed in a remarkable degree the resources of the country, and increased surprisingly its commercial and political importance.

This progress, which ought to have been regarded in Great Britain with pride and pleasure, was beheld with jealousy and apprehension; — with jealousy, lest the industrial enterprise of the colonists should compete too successfully with that of the mother country; and with apprehension, lest their rising importance should invite them to assert political independence. These feelings were strengthened by the representations made of their condition by agents of the ministry and by royal governors. Quarry's memorial in 1703 affords a striking illustration of these reports. "Commonwealth notions," he wrote, "improve daily; and if it be not checked, in time the rights and privileges of British subjects will be thought by them to be too narrow." Various measures were recommended to check these ideas. Sagacious royalists saw the republican tendencies of the prevailing system of local government,— the Congregationalism in the churches, the town organizations, the local assemblies, — whose influence reached the roots and fibres of the social system; and it is worthy of remark, that their recommendations reached the foundation of this tendency.

Randolph in 1685, Quarry in 1703, Hutchinson in 1773, advised an interference with the towns, and the adoption of .he policy of centralization. Other recommendations were made, and commercial regulations were established, which bore with monstrous injustice on their rising manufactures and trade. The colonists, however, had enjoyed their social and political advantages too long to relinquish them without a struggle. They determined to retain their admirable system of local government, and to keep free from foreign taxation. They claimed the right to go on in the path of freedom and progress they with so much toil and treasure had laid open. Why should a country, clothed by the God of nature with all his highest forms of magnificence and grandeur, be governed by an island of the Old World? Why should it be impeded in its career by manacles thrown about its giant limbs by the selfishness of its parent?[2] The tyrannical revenue laws were never fully submitted to; and if they were not openly opposed, it was because they were not rigidly enforced.

The British ministry, dissatisfied with so easy an allegiance, resolved, after the conclusion of the treaty of Aix La Chapelle, (1748,) to adopt a more stringent policy with respect to the colonies, by enforcing the revenue laws, and asserting the principle of British supremacy. They introduced into Parliament a bill which proposed to sweep away the colonial charters without the form of legal judgment, and which authorized the king's instructions to be enforced as law. This bill excited great alarm, and was successfully resisted by the agents of the colonies.[3] War again broke out with France, and William Pitt, who was opposed to this policy, became prime minister. This great statesman resigned in 1761, and the Grenville ministry subsequently renewed it. In consequence of this, politics became the chief concern of almost every local community.

[1] Hutchinson, March 10, 1773, wrote, " Is there any way of compelling Boston to be a corporation, by depriving them of their present privileges, and not suffering any acts of the town ? The charter of New York city might be a good pattern. Can no restraint be laid on the other towns, from acting in any other affairs than such as immediately concern them respect-ively ? " [2] Smyth's Lectures, vol. II., p. 357. [3] Minot's Massachusetts vol. I , p. 147.

In opposition to this policy, and in behalf of commercial freedom, James Otis made (1761) his memorable speech on writs
of assistance. The idea was entertained, at this period, that
an American empire was close at hand. It was deduced from
the ratio of the increase of population in the colonies, their
great natural resources, free spirit, deliverance from danger
from the French, and the adoption of the restrictive policy of
the ministry. It is not the purpose of these pages, however
to dwell on political events further than as they were the immediate occasion of the commencement of hostilities. In 1765
the ministry determined to enforce the supremacy of Parliament by a system of internal taxation. Hence the stamp act,
and the opposition to it; its repeal, and the wild joy of the
colonists. But the claim was still asserted, that Parliament
had the right to bind the colonies in all cases whatsoever; and,
to enforce it, other acts were passed, bearing upon all of them,
and calling forth in all general opposition and counteracting
measures.

In Massachusetts, for nearly a century and a half, there had
been a steady and healthy development of free principles.
The people manifested it in the early struggles for their charters, in their resistance to the greedy tyranny of Andros, and
in the subsequent political controversies between the liberty-
men and the prerogative-men. Hence, during the ten years
of strong reasoning, and firm resolve, and eloquent appeal —
from 1764 to 1774 — the acts judged unconstitutional, and
contrary to natural and chartered rights, met in this colony
with the most determined opposition. It was carried on by
men of the Puritan stock, who had in them the earnestness,
singleness of heart, and ready devotion, of the olden time, and
who believed that Divine Providence had appointed them to
develop and defend a rational liberty. There was no compromise, by such men, with duty. Hence, in dealing with
the small tax on tea, when no other course remained, they
did not hesitate to destroy the obnoxious herb. Hutchinson
writes, " This was the boldest stroke that had been struck in
America." It was done after deliberate council, was the work
of no common mob, was welcomed through the colonies by
the ringing of bells and other signs of joy, and was defended

as a measure of political necessity. Ministerial wisdom devised as a punishment the Boston Port Bill, which was signed March 31, 1774, and went into effect on the first day of June. The execution of this measure devolved on Thomas Gage, who arrived at Boston May 13, 1774, as Captain General and Governor of Massachusetts. He was not a stranger in the colonies. He had exhibited gallantry in Braddock's defeat, and aided in carrying the ill-fated general from the field. He had married in one of the most respectable families in New York, and had partaken of the hospitalities of the people of Boston. His manners were pleasing. Hence he entered upon his public duties with a large measure of popularity. But he took a narrow view of men and things about him. He had no sympathy with the popular ideas, and no respect for those who advocated them. In his eyes, the mass of the people were "a despicable rabble," without the ability to plan or the courage to fight, and their leaders were oily demagogues governed by a selfish ambition; and it was beyond his comprehension, how, in a time of prosperity, when trade was good, when food was cheap and taxes were light, such a community could run the chance of ruin out of devotion to principle. His instructions required him to compel "a full and absolute submission" to the rigorous laws of Parliament; and to this end he was, if it should be considered necessary, authorized to employ with effect the king's troops.[1] This was a harsh duty

---

[1] The Earl of Dartmouth, in a letter to Governor Gage, dated April 9, 1774, after urging the duty of "mild and gentle persuasion," says : "At the same time, the sovereignty of the king, in this Parliament, over the colonies, requires a full and absolute submission ; and his majesty's dignity demands, that until that submission be made, the town of Boston, where so much anarchy and confusion have prevailed, should cease to be the place of the residence of his governor, or of any other officer of government who is not obliged by law to perform his functions there." After dwelling on the "criminality" of those who aided in the proceedings in Boston during the months of November and December, 1773, the letter says : "The king considers the punishment of these offenders as a very necessary and essential example to others of the ill consequences that must follow from such open and arbitrary usurpatios as tend to the subversion of all government," &c. The instructions of the Treasury Board, dated March 31, are equally rigorous, and looked to a complete prostration of the commerce of Boston.

to perform; but, making every allowance for its character, General Gage proved as a civilian and a soldier unfit for his position. He was arrogant in the discharge of his office, and to downright incapacity he added gross insincerity in his intercourse with the people.

General Gage, on the seventeenth of May, landed at the Long Wharf, and was received with much parade. Members of the Council and House of Representatives, and some of the principal inhabitants of the town, with the company of cadets, escorted him to the Council Chamber, amid salutes from the batteries of the town and of the shipping. In King-street, the troop of horse, the artillery company, the grenadiers, and several companies of militia, saluted him as he passed. About noon his commission was proclaimed in form, and a proclamation was read by the high sheriff, continuing all officers in their places. It was answered by three huzzas from the concourse of people, by three vollies of small arms, and a discharge of cannon by the artillery. The governor then received the compliments of his friends, reviewed the militia, and was escorted to Faneuil Hall, where "an elegant dinner," loyal toasts, and animating festivity, closed the ceremonies. He then repaired to the Province House, the place of his residence.[1]

General Gage held a consultation with Governor Hutchinson, the admiral, and the commissioners of the customs, in relation to putting the Port Bill in force. All agreed in the manner of doing it. The officials left the town, the admiral stationed his ships, and on the first day of June the act went into effect. It met with no opposition from the people, and hence there was no difficulty in carrying it into rigorous execution. "I hear from many," the governor writes, "that the act has staggered the most presumptuous;" "the violent party men seem to break, and people fall off from them." Hence he looked for submission; but Boston asked assistance from the other colonies, and the General Court requested him to appoint a day of fasting and prayer. The loyalists felt uneasy at the absence of the army.[2] "Many are impatient," Gen-

---

[1] Journals of the day. [2] In 1767, an addition was first made to the number of men who commonly formed the garrison of Castle William. On the

eral Gage writes, May 31, "for the arrival of the troops; and
I am told that people will then speak and act openly, which
they now dare not do." Hence a respectable force was soon
concentrated in Boston. On the 14th June, the 4th or king's
own regiment, and on the 15th, the 43d regiment, landed at
the Long Wharf, and encamped on the common. Additional
transports with troops soon arrived in the harbor, and on the
4th and 5th of July, the 5th and 38th regiments landed at the
Long Wharf. Lord Percy was among the officers of this arrival. At this time the governor had a country seat at Danvers. On the 6th of August the 59th regiment arrived from
Halifax, and during the following week landed at Salem, and
there encamped.[1] Additional troops were ordered from New
York, the Jerseys, and Quebec. These measures, General
Gage writes, give spirits to one side, and throw a damp on
the other. "Your lordship will observe, that there is now an
open opposition to the faction, carried on with a warmth and
spirit unknown before, which it is highly proper and necessary
to cherish and support by every means; and I hope it will not
be very long before it produces very salutary effects."[2]

The Boston Port Bill went into operation amid the tolling
of bells, fasting and prayer, the exhibition of mourning emblems, and every expression of general and deep sympathy.
It bore severely upon two towns, Boston and Charlestown,
which had been long connected by a common patriotism.
Their laborers were thrown out of employment, their poor
were deprived of bread, and gloom pervaded their streets.
But they were cheered and sustained by the large contributions sent from every quarter for their relief, and by the noble
words that accompanied them. The mission of this law, how-

1st of October, 1768, a body of seven hundred, covered by the fleet, landed
in Boston, and with charged muskets marched to the common, amid the
sullen silence of the people. In November following, parts of the 64th and
65th regiments joined them. Collisions with the inhabitants followed, and
then the tragedy of the fifth of March, 1770. This occasioned the removal
to the castle. Here they remained until the ministry resolved to subdue
Massachusetts by arms.

[1] Newell's Diary. [2] The letters of Lord Dartmouth and General Gage, or
rather extracts from them, were published in the Parliamentary Register of
1775.

ever, was rather to develop an intense fraternal feeling, to promote concert of action and a union of the colonies, than to create a state of open war. The excitement of the public mind was intense; and the months of June, July, and August, were characterized by varied political activity. Multitudes signed a solemn league and covenant against the use of British goods. The breach between the whigs and loyalists daily became wider. Patriotic donations from every colony were on their way to the suffering towns. Supplies for the British troops were refused; and essays demonstrated that the royal authority had ceased, and that the people, being in a state of nature, were at liberty to incorporate themselves into an independent community. It was while the public mind was in this state of excitement, that other acts arrived, which General Gage was instructed to carry into effect.

The British Parliament had passed two acts,[1] virtually repealing the charter of Massachusetts, entitled "An Act for the better regulating the government of the Province of Massachusetts Bay," and "An Act for the more impartial administration of justice in said Province." The first law provided that the councillors, which were chosen by the representatives annually, should be appointed by the king, and should serve according to his majesty's pleasure; that the judges, sheriffs, and other civil officers, should be appointed by the governor, or, in his absence, the lieutenant-governor; that juries should be summoned by the sheriffs; and that town-meetings, except the annual ones of March and May, and other public meetings, should not be held without the permission of the governor. The other act provided that offenders against the laws might be carried to other colonies or to England for trial. These arbitrary acts went to the root of the political system that had grown with the growth and had strengthened with the strength of Massachusetts. They undermined those fundamental principles which formed its basis. They struck down customs,

---

[1] The bill for regulating the government passed the House of Commons May 2, 1774, yeas 239, nays 64; the House of Lords, May 11, yeas 92, nays 20. The bill for the administration of justice passed the House of Commons May 6, 1774, yeas 127, nays 24; the House of Lords, May 18, yeas 43, nays 12. Both bills were approved May 20.

which, in a century and a half's practice, had grown into rights. They invaded the trial by jury; and what was scarcely less dear to the colonists, they prohibited public meetings, and thus, it was said, "cut away the scaffolding of English freedom." The issue, no longer one of mere taxation, involved the gravest questions as to personal rights. The freeman was required to become a slave. It was the attempted execution of these laws that became the immediate occasion of the commencement of hostilities between the American colonists and Great Britain.

Copies of these acts were received early in June,[1] and were immediately circulated through the colonies. General Gage did not receive them officially until the 6th of August, and with them a letter of instructions from the government. Lord Dartmouth hoped these new laws would have "the good effect" to give vigor to the civil authority, "to prevent those unwarrantable assemblings of the people for factious purposes, which had been the source of so much mischief," and to secure an impartial administration of justice; and he instructed the governor, at all hazards, to put them in force. Not only the dignity and reputation of the empire, but the power and the very existence of the empire, depended upon the issue; for if the ideas of independence once took root, the colonial relation would be severed, and destruction would follow disunion. It was actual disobedience, and open resistance, that had compelled coercive measures. With this imperative order there came a nomination of thirty-six councillors. General Gage lost no time in attempting to carry these laws into execution. Twenty-four of the council immediately accepted. The first meeting of such of the members as could be collected was held on the 8th; and a meeting of the whole was called on the 16th. Judges, also, proceeded immediately to hold courts, and sheriffs to summon juries, under the authority of the new acts. The momentous question of obedience now came up. Should Massachusetts submit to the new acts? Would the other colonies see, without increased alarm, the humiliation of Massachusetts?

[1] June 2, Captain Williamson, in 36 days from Bristol, (arrived) with copy of another cruel act of Parliament. — Newell's Ms. Diary.

This was the turning point of the Revolution. It did not find the patriots unprepared. They had an organization beyond the reach alike of proclamations from the governors, or of circulars from the ministry. This was the committees of correspondence, chosen in most of the towns in legal town-meetings, or by the various colonial assemblies, and extending throughout the colonies. Their value was appreciated by the patriots, while their influence was dreaded by the crown. His majesty had formally signified his disapprobation of their appointment;[1] but the ministers of state corresponded with their colonial officials and friends; and why should it be thought unreasonable or improper for the agents of the colonists to correspond with each other ? The crisis called for all the wisdom of these committees. A remarkable circular from Boston, addressed to the towns, (July, 1774,) dwelt upon the duty of opposing the new laws: the towns, in their answers, were bold, spirited, and firm, and echoed the necessity of resistance. Nor was this all. The people promptly thwarted the first attempts to exercise authority under them. Such councillors as accepted their appointments were compelled to resign, or, to avoid compulsion, retired into Boston. At Great Barrington, (August, 1774,) the judges, on attempting to hold courts, were driven from the bench, and the Boston people were gravely advised to imitate the example.[2] At length the committee of Worcester suggested a meeting of various committees, to conclude upon a plan of operation to be adopted through the province,[3] and requested the Boston committee to call it. Accordingly, a meeting of delegates from the committees of the counties of Worcester, Essex, and Middlesex, and of the committee of correspondence of Suffolk, was held on the 26th of August, 1774, at Faneuil Hall. It was first resolved that

[1] Governor Hutchinson, in his message to the General Court, January 26, 1774, said : " I am required to signify to you his majesty's disapprobation of the appointment of committees of correspondence, in various instances, which sit and act during the recess of the General Court." [2] A paper, in stating this fact, says : Here is now an example for you, inhabitants of Suffolk ! An infant county, hardly organized, has prevented the session of a court on the new system of despotism. [3] " A county congress " was suggested at a Boston town-meeting, August 9, and the committee of correspondence authorized to appoint delegates to it. — Records.

certain officers of the crown, — such as judges, and justices, and officers of courts, — were, by the act for the better regu lation of the government, rendered unconstitutional officers; and then a committee was raised, to report resolutions proper to be adopted on so alarming an occasion. The meeting then adjourned to the next day. On the 27th, this meeting considered the report of its committee, and adopted it. Its preamble declares that the new policy of the ministry formed a complete system of tyranny; that no power on earth had a right, without the consent of this province, to alter the minutest tittle of its charter; that they were entitled to life, liberty, and the means of sustenance, by the grace of Heaven, and without the king's leave; and that the late act had robbed them of the most essential rights of British subjects. Its resolves declare : 1. That a Provincial Congress is necessary to counteract the systems of despotism, and to substitute referee committees in place of the unconstitutional courts; and that each county will act wisely in choosing members, and resolutely executing its measures. 2. That, previous to the meeting of such congress, the courts ought to be opposed. 3. That officers attempting to hold them, or any others attempting to execute the late act, would be traitors cloaked with a pretext of law. 4. That all persons ought to separate from them. — laborers ought to shun their vineyards, and merchants ought to refuse to supply them with goods. 5. That every defender of the rights of the province, or of the continent, ought to be supported by the whole county, and, if need be, by the province. 6. That, as a necessary means to secure the rights of the people, the military art, according to the Norfolk plan, ought to be attentively practised. Such was the bold determination of what may not be inaptly termed the executive of the patriot party. I know of no more important consultation of this period,[1] or one that was followed by more momentous action. These resolves, reflecting as they did the deep convictions of the majority of the people, were carried out to the

[1] This meeting does not appear to have been public. I have not met with a single allusion to it in print, either in the newspapers or in the histories The proceedings, from Mss. in the rich cabinet of the Mass. Hist. Society with the ca.l, are in the Appendix.

letter. The result was, a Provincial Congress, hostile preparation, a clash of arms, and a general rising of the people.

To the people of Middlesex County belongs the honor of
taking the lead in carrying out the bold plan resolved upon in
Faneuil Hall. A convention, consisting of delegates from every
town and district in it, chosen at legal town-meetings, assembled at Concord on the 30th of August. It numbered one hundred and fifty, and constituted a noble representation of the
character and intelligence of this large county. The members felt that they were dealing with "great and profound
questions," — their own words, — at a stage when judicious
revolutionary action, rather than exciting language, was required. Their report and resolves are pervaded by the deep
religious feeling that runs through the revolutionary documents of New England, and are remarkable for their firmness,
moderation, and strength. After reviewing the late acts, they
say, "To obey them would be to annihilate the last vestiges
of liberty in this province, and therefore we must be justified
by God and the world in never submitting to them." Actu-
ated by "a sense of their duty as men, as freemen, and as
Christian freemen," they resolved that every civil officer, acting under the new acts, "was not an officer agreeable to the
charter, therefore unconstitutional, and ought to be opposed."
They concluded in the following lofty strain: "No danger
shall affright, no difficulties shall intimidate us; and if, in
support of our rights, we are called to encounter even death,
we are yet undaunted, sensible that he can never die too soon
who lays down his life in support of the laws and liberties of
his country." Memorable words for men to utter, who led at
Lexington, Concord, and Bunker Hill! Proceedings worthy
to have emanated from these world-renowned battle-grounds.[1]

The governor, meantime, kept a watchful eye on these
movements. He resolved to use his troops to disperse public
meetings, and to protect the courts; and made his first attempt
at Salem. A meeting was called in this town, August 20, by
printed handbills from the committee of correspondence, and

[1] These proceedings were published at length in the journals of the time.
A copy was officially sent to Congress, then in session at Philadelphia, where
they were much applauded.

the object was to elect delegates to a county convention to be holden at Ipswich. On the 23d of August, General Gage issued a proclamation, forbidding all persons from attending this meeting, "or any other not warranted by law," as they would be chargeable with all the ill consequences that might follow, and must "answer them at their utmost peril." The inhabitants, however, assembled on the 24th, according to the notice. By request, the committee waited on General Gage, who ordered them to dissolve the meeting. The committee began to argue the legality of the assembly. "I came to execute the laws, not to dispute them," replied Gage. A detachment of troops was ordered to disperse the meeting; but while the committee were in consultation, the people transacted their business and adjourned, and the discomfited governor gratified his resentment by arresting those who called the unlawful assembly.

The next attempt of General Gage indicated his intention to secure the cannon and powder of the province, and thus disarm the people. In Charlestown, on Quarry Hill, was a magazine, — the powder-house, — where it was customary to store powder belonging to the towns and the province. Owing to the lowering aspect of public affairs, the towns, in August, withdrew their stock, which left only that belonging to the province. This fact was communicated to General Gage by William Brattle, of Cambridge, when it was determined to remove the remainder of the powder to Castle William. Accordingly, on the first day of September, in the morning about sunrise, Lieutenant-Colonel Maddison, and two hundred and sixty troops, embarked in thirteen boats at Long Wharf, Boston, landed at Temple's Farm, (The Ten Hills,) crossed over Winter Hill to the powder-house, and carried the powder, two hundred and fifty half-barrels, on board the boats. Meantime a detachment went to Cambridge, and carried away two field-pieces, lately procured for the regiment of that place. The party then proceeded to Castle William.

The report of this affair, spreading rapidly, excited great indignation. The people collected in large numbers, and many were in favor of attempting to recapture the powder and cannon. Influential patriots, however, succeeded in turning their attention in another direction. They were persuaded to remain quiet on this day, and on the next day, September 2, to carry into effect the resolves of the convention of Middlesex County, so far as related to officers who were exercising authority under the new acts. Accordingly, under the sanction and direction of members of the committees of correspondence of Boston, Charlestown, and Cambridge, the people repaired in a body to the residence of Lieutenant-Governor Oliver, and obliged him to resign his office. The resignation of other important officers, who had accepted appointments or executed processes, was procured. General Gage was wisely advised by his adherents not to use force to disperse this meeting, and thus, unmolested, it acted in a revolutionary manner almost within gun-shot of his batteries. Meantime the fact of the removal of the powder became magnified into a report that the British had cannonaded Boston, when the bells rang, beacon-fires blazed on the hills, the neighbor colonies were alarmed, and the roads were filled with armed men hastening to the point of supposed danger.

These demonstrations opened the eyes of the governor to the extent of the popular movement, and convinced him of the futility of endeavoring to protect the courts by his troops. He left Salem for Boston, to attend the Superior Court, Aug. 30th, and with the intention of sending a detachment to protect the judges in holding a court at Worcester; but his council hesitated as to the propriety of weakening his forces by division. It would be to tempt their destruction. "The flames of sedition," he writes, September 2, "had spread universally throughout the country beyond conception;" and he assured Lord Dartmouth that "civil government was near its end;" that the time for "conciliation, moderation, reasoning, was over," and that nothing could be done but by forcible means; that Connecticut and Rhode Island were as furious as Massachusetts; that the only thing to be done was to secure the friends of government in Boston, to reinforce the troops, and act as circumstances might require. "I mean, my lord," he adds, "to secure all I can by degrees; to avoid any bloody crisis as long as possible, unless forced into it by themselves, which may happen." But as it was resolved "to stem the torrent, not yield to it," he frankly told the minister "that a very respectable force should take the field."

This was the period of transition from moral suasion to physical force. General Gage saw no hope of procuring obedience but by the power of arms; and the patriot party saw no safety in anything short of military preparation. Resistance to the acts continued to be manifested in every form. On the ninth of September the memorable Suffolk resolves were adopted, going to the same length with those of Middlesex; and these were succeeded by others in other counties equally bold and spirited. These resolves were approved by the Continental Congress, then in session. Everywhere the people either compelled the unconstitutional officers to resign, or opposed every attempt to exercise authority, whether by the governor or by a constable.[1] They also made every effort to transport ammunition and stores to places of security. Cannon and muskets were carried secretly out of Boston.[2] The guns were taken from an old battery at Charlestown, where the navy yard is. This was difficult to accomplish, for any unusual noise in the battery might be heard on board of a ship of war which lay opposite to it. But a party of patriots, mostly of Charlestown, removed the guns silently at night, secreted them in the town for a few days, and eluding a strict search made for them by British officers, carried them into the country.

General Gage immediately began to fortify Boston Neck.

A letter from Boston states :"The distress occasioned to the town by that indiscriminating act which, by shutting up the port of Boston, involves the innocent equally with the guilty, seems to be entirely absorbed by what is thought a greater evil, the act for regulating, or rather altering, the constitution and government of the province, regardless of their long-enjoyed charter privileges. As this affects the whole province, and deprives them of what they hold most dear, the temper of the people is raised to the highest pitch of enthusiasm, and their behavior borders upon distraction."

[2] Newell writes, September 15 :"Last night all the cannon in the North Battery were spiked up. It is said to be done by about one hundred men, who came in boats, from the men of war in the harbor. September 17 : Last night the town's people took four cannon from the gun-house very near the common. September 20 : Some cannon removed by the men-of-war's men from the mill-pond."

This added intensity to the excitement. The inhabitants became alarmed at so ominous a movement; and, on the 5th of September, the selectmen waited on the general, represented the public feeling, and requested him to explain his object. The governor stated in reply, that his object was to protect his majesty's troops and his majesty's subjects; and that he had no intention to stop up the avenue, or to obstruct the free passage over it, or to do anything hostile against the inhabitants. He went on with the works, and soon mounted on them two twenty-four pounders and eight nine pounders. Again, on the 9th, the selectmen called on him, and represented the growing apprehension of the inhabitants. The fortress at the entrance of the town, they said, indicated a design to reduce the metropolis to the state of a garrison. In a written reply, General Gage repeated his former assurances, and characteristically remarked, that as it was his duty, so it should be his endeavor, to preserve the peace and promote the happiness of every individual, and recommended the inhabitants to cultivate the same spirit. On the next day a committee from the Suffolk convention waited on him. They represented that the prevailing ferment was caused by his seizing the powder at Charlestown, by his withholding the stock in the Boston magazine from its legal proprietors, by his new fortification, and by the insults of his troops to the people. General Gage's reply is dated September 12. He admits instances of disorder in the troops, but appeals to their general good behavior, and concludes : "I would ask what occasion there is for such numbers going armed in and out of town, and through the country in a hostile manner? Or why were the guns removed privately in the night from the battery at Charlestown? The refusing submission to the late acts of Parliament I find general throughout the province, and I shall lay the same before his majesty." The patriots were never at a loss for words; and on receiving this, they promptly presented an address to the governor, recapitulating his hostile acts, and requesting him, in his purposed representation, to assure his majesty, "That no wish of independency, no adverse sentiments or designs towards his majesty or his troops now here, actuate his good subjects in this colony; but

that their sole intention is to preserve pure ai d inviolate those
rights to which, as men, and English Americans, they are
justly entitled, and which have been guaranteed to them by
his majesty's royal predecessors." Dr. Warren, in presenting
to General Gage this address, remarked, "That no person had,
so far as he had been informed, taken any steps that indicated
any hostile intention, until the seizing and carrying off the
powder from the magazine in the County of Middlesex." [1]

All eyes now centred on Boston. It was filled with the
spirit of the olden time, — the spirit of the indomitable men,
pure in life and strong in faith, who founded it, and who
reared it for the abode of civil independence as well as for
religious liberty. In every period of its history it had been
jealous of its rights. It had grown up in the habitual exercise of them, and had been quick to discern their infringe-
ment. It had dared to depose Andros for his tyranny, and
it was early and decided in its opposition to the claim of parliamentary supremacy. For years it had been alive with the
kindling politics of the age, and stood boldly prominent as
the advocate of the patriot cause. It was regarded by the
Whigs as the great representative of liberty. It was regarded
by the Tories as the grand focus of rebellion. [2] Hence the
British administration made it feel the full weight of British
power, and expected by crushing the spirit of Boston to crush
the spirit of disobedience in the colonies.

The great natural features of the metropolis of Massachusetts, at this time, were almost unchanged. The original

---

[1] The General Congress remonstrated on these fortifications. General
Gage, October 20, in his reply, says : "Two works of earth have been
raised at some distance from the town, wide of the road, and guns put in
them. The remains of old works, going out of the town, have been strengthened, and guns placed there likewise." The documents are in the newspapers of this period.

[2] General Gage, Aug. 27, 1774, wrote to Lord Dartmouth : — It is agreed
that popular fury was never greater in this province than at present, and it
has taken its rise from the old source at Boston, though it has appeared first
at a distance. Those demagogues trust their safety in the long forbearance
of government, and an assurance that they cannot be punished. They chicane,
elude, openly violate, or passively resist the laws, as opportunity serves ; and
opposition to authority is of so long standing, that it is become habitual.

peninsula, with its one broad avenue by land to connect it
with the beautiful country by which it was surrounded, had
sufficiently accommodated its population, without much alteration of the land, or without much encroachment on the sea.
Beacon Hill, and its neighboring eminences, now so crowded
with splendid mansions, were then pasture grounds, over
which grew the wild rose and the barberry.   Copp's Hill,
one of the earliest spots visited by the Pilgrims, and Fort
Hill, memorable as the place where Andros and his associates were imprisoned, were also of their original height.
Much of Boston, now covered by piles of brick and busy
streets, was then overflowed by the tide, or was parceled out
in gardens and fields.   It would require, however, too much
space to dwell on its topography, or its municipal affairs, or
to describe the change that enterprise and wealth, under the
benign influence of freedom, have wrought in its appearance.

Its government, however, exercised too powerful a political
influence to be passed over without remark.   Its form was
simple, and peculiar to New England.   No common law originally authorized it; and so widely did it differ from that of
the municipal corporations of England, that Andros (1686)
declared there was no such thing as a town in all the country.   At first the inhabitants of the towns managed their
affairs in general meeting, but soon chose " the seven men,"
or " the selectmen," to act as an executive body.   The General Court in 1636 recognized the towns, and defined their
powers.   Such was their origin.   In Boston the selectmen
were at first chosen for six months; but after a few elections,
for a year.   The general town affairs were decided in general
meetings of the citizens.   So important were these little local
assemblies regarded, that the absentee from them was fined;
so free were they, that in them — the General Court ordered,
1641 — any man, whether inhabitant or foreigner, might
make any motion or present any petition; so wide was the
range of subjects discussed by them, that the debates ran
from a simple question of local finance to general questions
of provincial law and human rights; so great was their political effect, that the credit has been assigned them of having
commenced the American Revolution.   The hand votes of the

citizens in them were equal, and "this apparent equality in the decisions of questions taught every man, practically, the greatest principle of a republic, that the majority must govern."[1] "The people," Tudor well remarks, "were the subjects of a distant monarch, but royalty was merely in theory with them."[2]

The population of Boston was about seventeen thousand. A marked peculiarity of it was its homogeneous character. It was almost wholly of English extraction; and, during the preceding century, it had gradually increased from its own stock. It had few foreigners — few even of English, Irish, or Scotch. It was an early remark in relation to it, that it wore so much the aspect of an English town, that a Londoner would almost think himself at home at Boston. Strangers praised its generous hospitality. "I am arrived," a traveller[3] writes, "among the most social, polite, and sensible people under heaven, — to strangers, friendly and kind, — to Englishmen, most generously so." Its inhabitants, by their industry, enterprise and frugality, generally had acquired a competence. There was no hopeless poverty; there were few of large wealth; and none were separated by privileges from the rest of the community. The common school[4] had made deep its

---

[1] Tudor's Otis, p. 446. [2] Ib., p. 444. [3] A physician, November 8, 1774, describes Boston as follows : —"In this land of bustling am I safe arrived, among the most social, polite and sensible people under heaven, — to strangers, friendly and kind, — to Englishmen, most generously so. Much have I travelled, and much have I been pleased with my excursions. This is a fine country, for everything that can gratify the man or please the fancy. War, that evil, looks all around us ; the country expect it, and are prepared to die freemen, rather than live what they call slaves. The patriots here are, in general, men of good sense, and high in the cause. I have been introduced to General Gage and the Tories — to Hancock and the Whigs. I find myself a high son — that is the strongest side at present. How long I shall stay here is uncertain. Much have I been entreated to settle here as physician ; and was peace and unanimity once more established, I should prefer this place to any I ever saw. The town is finely situated, very considerable, and well worth preserving. If hostile measures take place, I believe it will fall a sacrifice." [4] In May, 1773, the South Grammar School had 130 scholars ; North, 59 ; South Writing, 220 ; North Writing, 250 : Writing School, Queen-street, 264.

mark of common brotherhood; and in the public meeting, in
the social circle, in the varied walks of life, men met as equals
in the race of enterprise or of ambition. The Province
House — still standing — was the centre of fashion; and the
polished circle that moved in it shed abroad the influence of
manners characterized by the urbanity of the olden time.
The attention paid to education and religion, and the activity
of the printing presses, indicate the value placed on the higher
interests of a community. The general thrift was shown in
the air of comfort spread over the dwellings, the elegance of
many private mansions, and the number of public buildings.
One fact is worthy of remark. Notwithstanding the political
excitement that continued for ten years, with hardly an intermission; notwithstanding the hot zeal of the sons of liberty,
the bitter opposition of as zealous loyalists, the presence of
the military, the firing upon the people, the individual collisions with the soldiers, "throughout this whole period of
ferment and revolution, not a single human life was taken by
the inhabitants, either by assassination, popular tumult, or
public execution."[1]

The prosperity of Massachusetts never had been greater,
and it never had felt less the ordinary burdens of society. It
was, as to commerce, the envy of the other colonies. "In no
independent state in the world," Hutchinson writes, "could
the people have been more happy."[2] Boston, more than any
other town, represented this prosperity. Its relative importance, when compared with the cities and towns of the other
colonies, was far greater than it is at the present day; and it
was pronounced the most flourishing town in all British
America. A glance at the ship-yards marked on the map
will indicate the direction of a large portion of its industry;
a thousand vessels, cleared in a single year from its port,[3] will
indicate the activity of its trade. It was not only the metropolis of Massachusetts and the pride of New England, but it
was the commercial emporium of the colonies. It could
assert, without much exaggeration, that its trade had been an

[1] Tudor's Life of Otis, p. 451.   [2] Hutchinson, vol. 3, p. 351.   [3] Price's
Map, 1769.

essential link in that vast chain of commerce which had raised New England to be what it was, the southern provinces to be what they were, the West India Islands to their wealth, and the British empire to its height of opulence, power, pride and splendor.[1]

To enumerate the services and to sketch the characters of the patriots who won for Boston a world-wide renown, would require a volume. I can do little more than indicate their fields of labor. The foremost of them, James Otis, so vehement and wild in his support of liberty that the British called him mad, of such pure patriotism and spirit-stirring eloquence that the people hung upon his words with delight, had accomplished his great pioneer work; and his fine genius, by a savage blow from an enemy, had become a wreck. Samuel Adams, a kindred spirit, who best represents the sternness, the energy, the puritanism of the Revolution, was commencing his career as a member of the Continental Congress, and had begun to manage its factions, by the simple wand of integrity of purpose, with the same success with which he gathered about him the strong men of Boston. " All good men," George Clymer writes in 1773, " should erect a statue to him in their hearts." John Adams, ardent, eloquent, learned in the law, ready with his tongue or his pen to defend the boldest measures as necessary, whether the destruction of the tea or the obstruction of a court, was in the same Congress continuing a brilliant service. There, too, was John Hancock, whose mercantile connections, social position, lavish hospitality and large wealth, made up an influence in favor of the Whig cause, when influence was invaluable. Joseph Warren, skilful as a physician, of a chivalrous spirit and of fascinating social qualities, beloved as a friend and of judgment beyond his years, seeing as clearly as any other the great principles of the contest, and representing as fully as any other the fresh enthusiasm of the Revolution, was working laboriously in the committee of correspondence, in the

---

[1] Vote of Boston, May 18, 1774. Town Records. The population of New York was about 21,000 ; the population of Massachusetts, in 1775, was estimated at 352,000 ; that of the colony of New York at 238,000.

Boston committee of safety, in the committee on donations, in the provincial committee of safety, and in the Provincial Congress. Josiah Quincy, jr., the Boston Cicero, devoted to the patriot cause, profound in the conviction that his countrymen would be required to seal their labors with their blood, was on a confidential mission to England, — being destined, on his return, to yield up his pure spirit in sight of the native land which he loved so much and for which he labored so well. Thomas Cushing, of high standing as a merchant, of great amenity of manner, of large personal influence, was a delegate to the Continental Congress. So widely was his name known in England, from its being affixed to public documents, that Dr. Johnson remarked, in his ministerial pamphlet, that one object of the Americans was to adorn Cushing's brows with a diadem. James Bowdoin, as early as 1754 one of the members of the General Court, was still of such fresh public spirit as to be one of the leading politicians; and though not so ardent as some of his associates, yet his sterling character gave him great influence, while he was none the less attached to the Whig cause, and none the less obnoxious to the royal governor. Benjamin Church, a respectable physician, of genius and taste, who had made one of the best of the "massacre" orations, was working in full confidence with the patriots, though his sun was destined to set in a cloud. Nathaniel Appleton was active on various boards, and his name is affixed to some of the most patriotic letters that went from the donation committee. William Phillips, one of the merchant princes, irreproachable as a man, for thirty years deacon of the Old South, was serving on various boards, and contributed money in aid of the cause with the same liberality with which, subsequently, he contributed to aid the cause of education. Oliver Wendell, of liberal education, of uncommon urbanity of manner and integrity of character, at this time in mercantile life, though subsequently a judge, was one of the selectmen and one of the committee of correspondence. John Pitts, of large wealth and of large influence, was a zealous patriot, one of the Provincial Congress, and on other boards. James Lovel, the schoolmaster, of fair reputation as a scholar, was an efficient patriot and

was destined to severe suffering on account of his political
course.   William Cooper, the town-clerk forty-nine years, the
brother of Dr. Cooper, who lived a long and useful life, was
one of the most fearless and active of the Whigs.   William
Molineaux, a distinguished merchant, an ardent friend to the
country, whose labors had proved too much for his constitution, had just died.   Paul Revere, an ingenious goldsmith, as
able to engrave a lampoon as to rally a caucus, was the
ready confidential messenger of the patriots and the great
leader of the mechanics.   Benjamin Austin, a long time in
public life and in responsible offices; Nathaniel Barber, an
influential citizen; Gibbens Sharpe, a deacon of Dr. Eliot's
church, one of the zealous and influential mechanics; David
Jeffries, the town treasurer, a useful citizen and active patriot; Henry Hill, wealthy, of great kindness of heart, and
greatly beloved; Henderson Inches, afterwards filling offices
of high trust with great fidelity; Jonathan Mason, a deacon
of one of the churches, one of the opulent merchants, of solid
character and great influence; Timothy Newell, one of the
deacons of the Brattle-street church; William Powell, of
large wealth and of great usefulness; John Rowe, also rich,
enterprising and influential; John Scollay, of much public
spirit, energetic and firm, — all these, and others equally
deserving, were actively employed on various committees and
in important and hazardous service.   They were not the men
to engage in a work of anarchy or of revolution.   In fact,
strictly speaking, their work was not revolutionary.   There
were no deep-seated political evils to root out.   There was no
nobility taking care of the masses, no inferior order hating a
nobility; no proud hierarchy in the church, no grinding mo-
nopoly in the state.   But there was a social system based on
human equality, new in the world, with its value tested by
new results.   Hence the patriots did not aim to overturn, but
to preserve.   They asked for the old paths.   They claimed
for their town its ancient rights — for the colony its ancient
liberties.   To them freedom did not appear as the instigator
of license, but as the protector of social order and as the guardian genius of commercial enterprise and of moral progress.

To their praise be it said, that they counted ease and luxury and competence as nothing, so long as were denied to them the rights enjoyed by their ancestors.

The labors of the Boston divines deserve a grateful remembrance. Some of them, distinguished by their learning and eloquence, were no less distinguished by their hearty opposition to the designs of the British administration. This opposition had been quickened into intense life by the attempts made from time to time to create a hierarchy in the colonies. The Episcopal form of worship was always disagreeable to the Congregationalists; but it was the power that endeavored to impose it on which their eyes were most steadily fixed. If Parliament could create dioceses and appoint bishops, it could introduce tithes and crush heresy. The ministry entertained the design of sending over a bishop to the colonies; and controversy, for years, ran high on this subject. So resolute, however, was the opposition to this project, that it was abandoned. This controversy, John Adams[1] says, contributed as much as any other cause to arouse attention to the claims of Parliament. The provisions of the Quebec act were quoted with great effect; and what had been done for Canada might be done for the other colonies. Hence, few of the Congregational clergy took sides with the government, while many were zealous Whigs; and thus the pulpit was often brought in aid of the town-meeting and the press. Of the Boston divines, none had been more ardent and decided than Jonathan Mayhew, one of the ablest theologians of his day; but he died in 1766. Dr. Charles Chauncy, Dr. Samuel Cooper, Dr. Andrew Eliot, Dr. Samuel Mather, Reverends John Lathrop, John Bacon, Simeon Howard, Samuel Stillman, were of those who took the popular side. They were the familiar associates and the confidential advisers of the leading patriots; but by virtue of their office, they were not less familiar or less confidential with wide circles of every calling in life, who were playing actively and well an important part, and without whose hearty coöperation the labors of even leading patriots

[1] Letter, December 2, 1815. The spirit of the time is well represented in a plate in the Political Register of 1769.

An Attempt to land a Bishop in America.

Engraved for Frothingham's History

would have been of little avail. At a time when the pristine reverence for the ministers had hardly declined into respect, who shall undervalue the influence such men threw into the scale, in giving intensity to zeal and firmness to resolution, and thus strengthening the tone of public opinion? They gave the sanction of religion — the highest sanction that can fill the human breast — to the cause of freedom, the holiest cause that can prompt human effort. They nurtured the idea in the people that God was on their side; and that power, however great, would be arrayed in vain against them. No wonder that, in the day of Lexington, there were men who went to the field of slaughter with the same solemn sense of duty with which they entered the house of worship.[1]

No description of Boston will be just, that does not make honored mention of Boston mechanics. It was freedom of labor that lay at the bottom of a century's controversy, and none saw it more clearly, or felt it more deeply; for it was the exercise of this freedom, — the industry, skill, and success of the American mechanics, — that occasioned the acts of the British Parliament, framed to crush the infant colonial manufactures. The Boston mechanics, as a general thing, were the early and steady supporters of the patriot cause. No temptation could allure them, no threats could terrify them, no Tory argument could reach them. In vain did the loyalists endeavor to tamper with them. "They certainly carry all before them," a letter says. As the troops thickened in Boston, some living in town, and some from the country, without much thought, accepted the chance to work on barracks for their accommodation. It did not, however, last long. "This morning," Newell writes, September 26, 1774, "all the carpenters of the town and country that were employed in building barracks for the soldiery left off work at the barracks."

---

[1] A Tory letter, dated Boston, September 2, 1774, says : "Some of the ministers are continually in their sermons stirring up the people to resistance ; an instance of which lately happened in this neighborhood, where the minister, to get his hearers to sign some inflammatory papers, advanced that the signing of them was a material circumstance to their salvation ; on which they flew to the pen with an eagerness that sufficiently testified their belief in their pastor."

British gold could not buy Boston labor. "New England holds out wonderfully," a letter in September says, "notwithstanding hundreds are already ruined, and thousands half starved." Loyalists from abroad were astonished at such obstinacy. Gage was disappointed and perplexed by this refusal. It was one of the disappointments that met him at every turn. "I was premature," he writes Lord Dartmouth, October 3, 1774, "in telling your lordship that the Boston artificers would work for us. This refusal has thrown us into difficulties." He sent to New York for workmen. The Boston mechanics, through their committee, sent a letter expressing their confidence "that the tradesmen of New York would treat the application as it deserved." The governor at length was successful in getting mechanics from New York and other places, to work for him. The patriotic mechanics of Boston were doomed to a long season of trial and suffering.

The patriots carried on their political action by public meetings, by committees, by social clubs, and through the press.

The right of public meeting was always dear to New England; and the local assemblies of the towns were used with immense efficiency by the patriots of the Revolution. Here dangerous political measures were presented to the minds of the citizens. Here public opinion was concentrated, sternly set against oppression, and safely directed in organized resistance. Great town-meetings were those in Boston, where Samuel Adams was the moderator; where James Otis, John Adams, and Josiah Quincy, jr., were the orators; where liberty was the grand inspiration theme; and where those to respond to the burning words were substantial, intelligent men, in earnest about their rights! The government[1] had long

---

[1] Governor Gage summoned the selectmen to meet at the Province House, August 13, when he abruptly handed them the clause about town-meetings, and read it to them. He was going out of town; and if a meeting was wanted, he would allow one to be called, if he should judge it expedient. The selectmen told him they had no occasion for calling a meeting — they had one alive. The governor looked serious, and said "He must think of that. By thus doing they could keep the meetings alive for ten years." The selectmen replied that the provincial law would be the rule of their conduct; when the governor stated that he was determined to enforce the act of Parliament, and they must be answerable for any bad consequences. — Boston Records:

felt their effect, and dreaded their influence. This was the reason why the regulating act prohibited them after the first of August, and why Governor Gage summoned the selectmen to the Province House to tell them that he should enforce the act. The selectmen remarked that they should be governed by the law of the province. Now, the clause framed to strangle free speech was clear enough as to prohibition, but was silent as to adjournment. Hence, the source of the seditious mischief, which the British ministry expected this clause would dry up, continued as prolific as ever. Hence, meetings called before the first of August were kept alive for weeks and months; and they might be kept alive, remarked Gage, for years. The governor and his advisers were puzzled. They dared not order the troops to stop them; and to their infinite annoyance, the patriots continued to thunder in the forum. The people flocked in crowds to Faneuil Hall, a place redolent with the blossoming of young America. When this overflowed, the resort was to the Old South Church, which hence has not inaptly been called the Sanctuary of Freedom. But in case an obnoxious office was to be resigned, or a patriotic agreement was to be entered into, or a public measure was to be lampooned, the concourse flocked to Liberty Tree, where, agreeably to previous notice, the invisible genius of the place had displayed the satirical emblems, or procured table, paper, and pens. It was a fine large old elm, near the Boylston Market. A staff ran through it, reaching above it, on which a flag was displayed, and an inscription was put on it, stating that it was pruned by order of the Sons of Liberty in 1766. All processions saluted it as an emblem of the popular cause. No wonder it put the royal governors in mind of Jack Cade's Oak of Reformation.[1]

The labors of the town-officers and of the committees, at this time, were arduous and important. The selectmen confined their labors chiefly to municipal concerns, though they often met with the committee of correspondence. At a crisis when so much depended on the good order of the town, their

Boston Gazette, August 15. General Gage, September 2, writes of this clause in the act: No persons I have advised with can tell what to do with it.

[1] Governor Bernard's letter, June 16, 1773.

services were required to be unusually energetic and judicious
A committee of safety was chosen, to devise measures for the
alarming emergency.   A large and respectable committee was
appointed to receive the contributions sent from abroad, and
distribute them among the citizens.   This was called the
Donation Committee, which was in communication with patriots from every colony from Canada to Georgia, and even
from the western parts of Virginia; and the letters, in reply
to those they received, contain descriptions of the sufferings
of the inhabitants, and express gratitude for the relief.   The
committee of correspondence, however, was the great executive of the patriot party, — the mainspring of its movements.
It had long acted the part of a faithful sentinel on the watch-
tower.   It promptly framed important news from abroad, or
important action at home, into hand-bills, and despatched them
to local committees, to be laid before the town-meetings of a
hundred communities.   It was the great counsellor of the
Whigs.   Besides meeting with the selectmen, it often summoned the committees of the neighboring towns[1] for consultation.   In this way this admirable machinery was kept in
constant play.   Thus measures that might startle the timid
by their boldness were carefully weighed in their inception,
and concert of action with other towns was secured.[2]

[1] One of the notices is as follows :

"Gentlemen, — Our enemies proceed with such rapidity, and execute
their measures so successfully, by the assistance of enemies in this and the
neighboring towns, that we are constrained to request your presence and
advice immediately.   Matters of such extreme importance now claim your
attention, that the least delay may prove fatal.   We therefore entreat your
company at Fanueil Hall, at five o'clock this afternoon, with such committees in your neighborhood as you can influence to attend on so short a
notice.   We are your friends and fellow-countrymen,

"NATH'L APPLETON,
"Per order of the Committee of Correspondence.
"Boston, Tuesday, September 27, 1774.
"The Committee of Correspondence of Charlestown."

[2] The Committee of Safety chosen July 26, 1774, were : James Bowdoin,
Samuel Adams, John Adams, John Hancock, William Phillips, Joseph Warren, Josiah Quincy.

The Selectmen chosen March, 1774, were : John Scollay, John Hancock

Boston was literally full of clubs and caucuses, which were used with great effect to secure unity of action. Here town politics were freely talked over, and political measures were determined upon. A club of leading patriots, mostly lawyers and merchants — such as Adams, Otis, and Molineaux — were accustomed to meet at private dwellings, often at William Cooper's house in Brattle-square. John Adams has given a good idea of the conviviality as well as of the gravity of their meetings. The mechanics had their clubs. One of them often met at the Green Dragon Tavern. One of their important duties at this time was to watch the movements of the troops and the Tories. "We were so careful," Paul Revere writes, "that our meetings should be kept secret, that every time we met every person swore upon the Bible that he would not discover any of our transactions but to Messrs. Hancock, Adams, Doctors Warren, Church, and one or two more." The engine companies were larger clubs, some of which had written agreements to "aid and assist" the town "to the utmost of their powers" in opposing the acts of Parliament. The most celebrated of these clubs, however, were three caucuses, — the North End Caucus, the South End Caucus, and the Middle District Caucus. They were rather societies than the public meetings understood by this term at the present time. They agreed whom they would support for town officers, whom they would name on committees, what instructions they would pass, what important measures they would carry out. Thus the

Timothy Newell, Thomas Marshall, Samuel Austin, Oliver Wendell, John Pitts ; Town Clerk, William Cooper ; Town Treasurer, David Jeffries.

The Donation Committee were: Samuel Adams, John Rowe, Thomas Boylston, William Phillips, Joseph Warren, John Adams, Josiah Quincy, jr., Thomas Cushing, Henderson Inches, William Molineaux, Nathaniel Appleton, Fortesque Vernon, Edward Proctor, John White, Gibbins Sharpe, William Mackay, Thomas Greenough, Samuel Partidge, Benjamin Austin, Jonathan Mason, John Brown, James Richardson, Thomas Crafts, jr., Henry Hill, Joshua Henshaw, jr., David Jeffries.

The Committee of Correspondence chosen 1772 were : James Otis, Samuel Adams, Joseph Warren, Dr. Benjamin Church, William Dennie, William Greenleaf, Joseph Greenleaf, Thomas Young, William Powell, Nathaniel Appleton, Oliver Wendell, John Sweetser, Josiah Quincy, jr., John Bradford, Richard Boynton, William Mackay, Nathaniel Barber, Caleb Davis, Alexander Hill, William Molineaux, Robert Pierpont.

North End Caucus — the original records of which are before
me — voted, October 23, 1773, that they "would oppose with
their lives and fortunes the vending of any tea" that might
be sent by the East India Company. Again, on the 2d of
November, after appointing a committee of three to wait on
the committee of correspondence and desire their attendance,
and another committee of three to invite John Hancock to
meet with them, the caucus voted that the tea shipped by
the East India Company should not be landed. A good understanding was kept up with the other two caucuses, and committees of conference were often appointed to communicate
their proceedings and desire a concurrence.[1]

---

[1] The records of the North End "caucos" extend from March 23, 1772,
to May 17, 1774. On the first leaf is the memorandum, "Began 1767 —
records lost." On the cover, under the date of March 23, there is a list of
sixty persons, probably the members of the caucus. The Adamses, Warren,
Church and Molineaux, were members : but the names of Hancock, Bowdoin, or Cushing, are not on the list. On the 3d of November, a committee was chosen to get a flag for Liberty Tree.

The clubs, however, were of earlier date than 1767. I am indebted to
Hon. C. F. Adams for the following extracts from the diary of his grand-
father, John Adams, in relation to their meetings :

"Boston, Feb. 1, 1763. — This day learned that the Caucus Club meets at
certain times in the garret of Tom Dawes, the adjutant of the Boston regiment. He has a large house, and he has a movable partition in his garrett,
which he takes down, and the whole club meet in one room. There they
smoke tobacco till you cannot see from one end of the garret to the other.
There they drink flip, I suppose, and there they choose a moderator, who puts
questions to the vote regularly ; and selectmen, assessors, collectors, war-
dens, firewards, and representatives, are regularly chosen before they are
chosen in the town. Uncle Fairfield, Story, Ruddock, Adams, Cooper, and
a *rudis indigestaque moles* of others, are members. They send committees
to wait on the Merchant's Club, and to propose and join in the choice of men
and measures. Captain Cunningham says they have often solicited him to go
to these caucuses, — they have assured him benefit in his business, &c.

Dec. 23, 1765. — Went into Mr. Dudley's, Mr. Dana's, Mr. Otis's office,
and then to Mr. Adams's, and went with him to the Monday night club.
There I found Otis, Cushing, Wells, Pemberton, Gray, Austin, two Waldos,
Inches, (Dr. Parker ?) and spent the evening very agreeably. Politicians all
at this club.

Jany. 15, 1766. — Spent the evening with the Sons of Liberty at their
own apartment in Hanover-square, near the Tree of Liberty. It is a compt-
ing room in Chase and Speakman's distillery — a very small room it is

The press was used by the patriots with great activity and effect. The Boston Gazette and the Massachusetts Spy were the principal Whig journals, of the five weekly newspapers printed this year in Boston. The Gazette had for a long time been the main organ of the popular party ; and it was through its columns that Otis, the Adamses, Quincy, and Warren, addressed the public. In fact, no paper on the continent took a more active part in politics, or more ably supported the rights of the colonies. Its tone was generally dignified, and its articles were often elaborate. The Massachusetts Spy was more spicy, more in the partisan spirit, less scrupulous in matter, and aimed less at elegance of composition than at clear, direct, and efficient appeal. In two years after its establishment it had the largest circulation of any paper in New England. Its pungent paragraphs annoyed the loyalists. The soldiers at home threatened its editor with tar and feathers, — the Tories abroad burnt him in effigy. The boldness, firmness, and ability of these journals did invaluable service to the cause of freedom. The Tories acknowledged the effect of them. "The changes," says the Tory Massachusettensis, "have been rung so often upon oppression, tyranny, and slavery, that, whether sleeping or waking, they are continually vibrating in our ears." They are yet vibrating in the world.[1]

John Avery, distiller or merchant, of a liberal education ; John Smith, the brazier ; Thomas Crafts, the painter ; Edes, the printer ; Stephen Cleverly, the brazier ; Chase, the distiller ; Joseph Field, master of a vessel ; Henry Bass, George Trott, jeweller, were present. I was invited by Crafts and Trott to go and spend an evening with them and some others. Avery was mentioned to me as one. I went, and was very civilly and respectfully treated by all present. We had punch, wine, pipes and tobacco, biscuit and cheese, &c. I heard nothing but such conversation as passes at all clubs among gentlemen about the times. No plots, no machinations. They chose a committee to make preparations for grand rejoicings upon the arrival of the news of the repeal of the Stamp Act."

[1] The five newspapers printed in Boston, in 1774, were as follows : The Boston Evening Post, on Monday mornings. It was first an evening paper. It was printed by Thomas and John Fleet. This journal contained many articles from the pens of the Whigs, but it appears also to have been employed by the government. The Boston News-Letter was published by Margaret Draper, widow of Richard Draper, and her partner, Robert Boyle,

The patriots did not carry their measures without opposition. The Revolution was no unanimous work; and the closer it is studied, the more difficult and more hazardous it will be found to have been. In Boston, the opposition, the Tories, were respectable in number, and strong in character and ability. General Gage expected much from them;[1] for though they were comparatively inactive when he arrived, yet he was assured that, after his troops were concentrated so as to afford them protection, many would come out boldly for the government who had been intimidated by "the faction." One of the last rallies of the Tory party — one of their strongest contests with the Whigs — was at a town-meeting held in June, when one of their number made a motion to censure and annihilate the committee of correspondence. They were patiently heard in support of it, — Samuel Adams leaving the chair, and mingling in the debate. No reports of town-meeting speeches are extant; but the Tory speaker would be bold and vehement against this busy committee. "This is the foulest, subtlest, and most venomous serpent that ever issued from the eggs of sedition. It is the source of the rebellion. I saw the small seed when it was implanted; it was as a grain of mustard. I have watched the plant until it has become a great tree; the vilest reptiles that crawl upon the earth are concealed at the root; the foulest birds of the air rest upon its branches. I now would induce you to go to work immediately with axes and hatchets, and cut it down, for a two-fold reason : — because it is a pest to society, and lest it be felled suddenly by a stronger arm, and crush its thou-

---

in Newbury-street. They separated before the commencement of hostilities, when John Howe became her partner, and remained in business with her until the British troops left Boston, when the News-Letter ended. It was the only paper printed in Boston during the siege. The chief organ of the government party was the Massachusetts Gazette and Boston Post-Boy and Advertiser, published by Mills and Hicks. It was patronized by the officers of the crown, and attracted the most notice from the Whigs. The Boston Gazette and Country Journal was printed by Benjamin Edes and John Gill. The Massachusetts Spy was printed by Isaiah Thomas. — Thomas' History of Printing.

[1] See Gage's Letter, on page 7.

sands in the fall." [1] And great must have been the patriot, Samuel Adams, in reply to such a strain. He was not only the father, but he was the soul, of this committee; and his deepest feelings would be aroused to defend it. "On such occasions," John Adams writes, "he erected himself, or rather nature seemed to erect him, without the smallest symptom of affectation, into an upright dignity of figure and gesture, and gave a harmony to his voice, which made a strong impression on spectators and auditors, — the more lasting for the purity, correctness, and nervous elegance of his style." The meeting began in Faneuil Hall, and it ended in the Old South. The committee, instead of being annihilated, were thanked for their patriotic action. One hundred and twenty-nine of the citizens made their protest against the proceedings. An opposition that could muster so strong was one not to be despised. "A number of the better sort of people," General Gage writes, July 5, "attended town-meeting in Boston with a design to make a push to pay for the tea, and annihilate the committee of correspondence, but they were outvoted by a great number of the lower class."

The Tories were severe in their condemnation of the patriot cause, and confident of the power of Great Britain to crush it. "The annals of the world," Massachusettensis says, "have not yet been deformed with a single instance of so unnatural, so causeless, so wanton, so wicked a rebellion." Should hostilities commence, "New England would stand recorded a singular monument of human folly and wickedness." Then nothing short of a miracle could gain the patri-

---

[1] Massachusettensis. Edition 1819, pp. 159, 165.

This was by far the ablest of the Tory writers. Trumbull says it was the last combined effort of Tory wit and argument to write down the Revolution. Hence in McFingal the poet writes :

> Did not our Massachusettensis
> For your conviction strain his senses ;
> Scrawl every moment he could spare
> From cards and barbers and the fair ;
> Show, clear as sun in noon-day heavens,
> You did not feel a single grievance ;
> Demonstrate all your opposition
> Sprung from the eggs of foul sedition ?

ots one battle, and hence there was but one step between them
and ruin. The Tory descriptions of the men "whose ambition wantonly opened the sources of civil discord" were
equally severe. They were called "the faction," consisting
of "calves, knaves, and fools," and not numbering "a fourth
part of the inhabitants." Their motives were described as
the most selfish and unworthy. The majority were "an
ignorant mob, led on and inflamed by self-interested and
profligate men." "The town-meeting was the hot-bed of
sedition." Incessant were the sneers in the British journals and
pamphlets against "the Boston saints."   "The venerable
forefathers of the loyal saints of Boston" were rebels when
they deposed Andros, and "their hopeful progeny" were rebels against George III.   Long had the Bostonians cherished
a desire of independence : "Many years' observation has convinced me," one in 1774 writes, "that the Bostonians wanted
to throw off the authority of Great Britain."   The merchants
were characterized as smugglers, and "the smugglers were the
main body of the patriots."   "The merchants," a Boston letter says, "form a part of those seditious herds of fools and
knaves which assemble on all important occasions in Faneuil
Hall, in the House of Representatives, or in the Council
Chamber, at Boston ; in which places, with the most sanctified
countenances, they preface their wise and learned harangues,
and their treasonable votes and resolves, with humbly beseech-
ing the Almighty to stand forth the champion of rebellion."
"The generality of young Bostonians are bred up hypocrites
in religion, and pettifoggers in law."   In a word, Boston was
represented as the seat of all the opposition to the ministry ;
and this opposition was represented as confined to "the faction" in Boston.   "The demons of folly, falsehood, madness,
and rebellion, seem to have entered into the Boston saints,
along with their chief, the angel of darkness."   These phrases
may be thought unworthy to be introduced here.   But it was
the information that was sent to England concerning the
character, motives, and extent of the patriot party; and it was
the information on which the British ministry chose to rely.[1]

[1] These phrases are taken from the newspapers, and a sharply written
pamphlet, entitled " Letters, &c.," " Humbly inscribed to the very loyal and

How vivid would be the picture of Boston in this eventfu period, — of its hopes and fears, of its intense mental life, — could the daily news be given as it was spoken in groups in the streets, or in the social gathering; and could the feelings with which it was received be realized! Eagerly would the inhabitants devour up each new report. "Samuel Adams writes that things go on in the Continental Congress, without any motion of our members, as perfectly to his liking as if he were sole director." "John Adams writes, there is a great spirit in the Congress, and that we must furnish ourselves with artillery, and arms, and ammunition, but avoid war if possible — if possible." "The members of our General Court, though Gage dissolved them, mean to stick to the charter, and have resolved themselves into a Provincial Congress." "Their proceedings are carried on in secret; but Dr. Warren says, the debates are worthy of an assembly of Spartans or ancient Romans, and their votes are worthy of a people determined to be free." "Our friends abroad say that Great Britain is determined to force the regulating act down our throats, and that the people have too generally got the idea that Americans are all cowards and poltroons." "Josiah Quincy, jr., writes for us to prepare for the worst, for it is a serious truth in which our friends there are all agreed, that our countrymen must seal their cause with their blood." "Our old Louisburg soldiers laugh at the newly erected fortifications, and say they are mud walls in comparison with what they have subdued; and that, if necessary, they would regard them no more than a beaver dam." "Our woollen manufactory is getting along finely, and has just turned out a large quantity

truly pious Doctor Samuel Cooper, pastor of the Congregational Church in Brattle-street." "Boston : Printed by order of the selectmen, and sold at Donation Hall, for the benefit of the distressed patriots, 1775."

The London Chronicle, 1774, thus describes the patriots, after the Port Bill had arrived : "The faction of Boston are now in the same condition that all people feel themselves in after having committed some signal outrage against the laws ; at first they support one another by talking over their spirited exertions, and praising each other's bravery ; but these vain notions soon evaporate, and the dread of punishment takes possession of their minds, upon which they become as low-spirited and dastardly as they were before outrageous and overbearing."

of baizes, and we see that we can make any kind of linens or woollens." "Mrs. Cushing says she hopes there are none of us but would sooner wrap ourselves in sheep-skins and goat-skins than buy English goods of a people who have insulted us in such a scandalous manner."[1] "Two of the greatest military characters of the age are visiting this distressed town, — General Charles Lee, who has served in Poland, and Colonel Israel Putnam, whose bravery and character need no description." "The collectors have begun to pay the public moneys to the people's treasurer; and the king's treasurer, Gray, gives notice (October 31) that he shall soon issue his distress warrant to collect the taxes from the constables and collectors." "Peters, the Tory minister, writes (September 28) that six regiments, with men-of-war, are coming over; and as soon as they come hanging work will go on, and that destruction will begin at the seaport towns, and that the lintel sprinkled on the side-posts will preserve the faithful." "Last week, at the field-day at Marblehead, the regiment did not fire a single volley, nor waste a kernel of powder." "Another regiment of red-coats marched proudly up King-street to-day, music playing, colors flying, bayonets gleaming, and encamped on the common." "John Adams says that the great Virginia orator, Patrick Henry, on being told that it was Major Hawley's opinion that 'We must fight, and make preparation for it,' solemnly averred, 'I am of that man's mind.'" Such phrases now are mere words. Then they were things. And as they went into happy homes, they made the father

[1] This expression is taken from a Ms. letter written by the wife of Thomas Cushing, then in Congress, dated Boston, September 21, 1774. She writes: "My spirits were very good until one Saturday, riding into town, I found the Neck beset with soldiers, the cannon hoisted, — many Tories on the Neck, and many more going up to see the encampment with the greatest pleasure in their countenances, which, I must confess, gave a damp to my spirits which I had not before felt. But I hope the rod of the wicked wont always rest upon us, and that the triumph will be but short. None of our friends think of moving themselves or house furniture at present. When it is necessary, I doubt not I shall have many good friends to advise and assist me. I hope there are none of us but what would sooner wrap themselves in sheep and goat-skins than buy English goods of a people who have insulted them in such a scandalous manner."

thoughtful and solemn, and the mother's heart throb with intenser anxiety. It was felt that the shadows in the horizon were not to pass away as the summer cloud, but were lengthening and deepening, and gathering with angry portent. They heralded the coming of that terrible calamity, civil war.

While such was the mental life of Boston, how changed had become its material aspect! How still its streets, how deserted its wharves, how dull its marts! The Port Bill not only cut off its foreign trade, but the whole of its domestic trade by water. Did a lighter attempt to land hay from the islands, or a boat to bring in sand from the neighboring hills, or a scow to freight to it lumber or iron, or a float to land sheep, or a farmer to carry marketing over in the ferry-boats, the argus-eyed fleet was ready to see it, and prompt to capture or destroy.[1] Not a raft or a keel was allowed to approach the town with merchandise. Many of the stores, especially all those on Long Wharf, were closed. In a word, Boston had fairly entered on its season of suffering. Did its inhabitants expostulate on the severity with which the law was carried out, the insulting reply was, that to distress them was the very object of the bill. As though the deeper the iron entered into the soul, the sooner and the more complete would be the submission. Citizens of competence were reduced to want; the ever hard lot of the poor became harder. To maintain order and preserve life, at so trying a season, called for nerve and firmness. Work was to be provided when there was no demand for the products of labor, and relief was to be distributed according to the circumstances of the applicants. The donation committee sat every day, Sundays excepted, to distribute the supplies. An arrangement was made with the selectmen, by which a large number were employed to repair and pave the streets, and hundreds were employed in brick-yards laid out on the Neck.[2] Manufactories

---

[1] Boston Gazette, October 17, 1774.   [2] Report of the donation committee. One seventh of all the contributions were assigned to Charlestown. The letters of this committee are among the Mss. in the cabinet of the Mass. Hist. Society. Contributions continued to be received in Boston until the commencement of hostilities ; they were also made for the poor of Boston a long time afterwards.

of various kinds were established; the building of vessels and of houses and setting up blacksmith-shops were among the projects started. The means to carry on all this business were derived from the contributions. This forced labor, however, ill compared with that voluntary activity which had so long characterized the metropolis; and a visiter to it, during the gloomy winter of 1774—5, would have seen little of that commerce which had raised "the great town" to its high prosperity.

All eyes then were fixed on Boston; and until its evacuation, it continued to be regarded with warm sympathy, with intense interest, and at times with fearful apprehension. A hostile fleet surrounded it without, a formidable military were assembling within. Tents covered its fields, cannon were planted on its eminences, and troops daily paraded in its streets. Thus, in addition to the destruction of its trade, it wore the aspect, and became subject to the vexations, of a garrisoned place. It was cheerful only to the adherents of the British ministry, for it was the only spot in Massachusetts where the governor was in authority, and where the laws of Parliament were in force. Hence, those repaired to it for protection who had become obnoxious to the people by their zeal in behalf of the government. Hence, General Gage, his crown-appointed councillors, and the official functionaries, were obliged to live in a town in which the dignity of his Britannic majesty required that not one of them should reside.[1] Hence, the custom-house was of necessity located in a port from which the British Parliament had proscribed all trade. Boston received from every quarter assurances of support. Salem spurned the idea of rising on the ruins of its neighbor; Marblehead generously offered the inhabitants the use of its wharves; the Provincial Congress and the Continental Congress recommended contributions for its relief; donations of money, clothing, and provisions, continued to pour into it; while visions of the better days in store for it cheered patriot hearts. "I view it," Mrs. Adams writes, "with much the same sensations that I should the body of a departed friend;— as having only put off its present glory to rise finally to a more

[1] See Dartmouth's letter to Gage, p. 5.

happy state." [1] Boston, on its part, did not falter in its course, nor did it relax its efforts. Its committees, in replies to letters that tendered aid and sympathy from abroad, sent out words full of reliance on the right, and of confidence in an ultimate triumph ; and its town-meetings continued their patriotic action. Boston (September 22, 1774) instructed its representatives to adhere to the old charter, — "to do nothing that could possibly be construed into an acknowledgement" of the regulating act; and if the legislature should be dissolved, to join in a Provincial Congress, and act in such manner as "most likely to preserve the liberties of all America." [2] It pursued steadily the course laid out for it,[3] that of patient suffering. Hence it became so quiet, that the royal officers

---

[1] Mrs. Adams dates this letter, Boston Garrison, 22d September, 1774. — Letters, p. 19. [2] Boston Records.

[3] The patriots were occasionally cheered by a song. The following is copied from the Essex Gazette of October 25, 1774 : —

LIBERTY SONG.
Tune — Smile Britannia.

I.

Ye sons of freedom, smile !
America unites ;
And friends in Britain's isle
Will vindicate our rights ;
In spite of Ga—s hostile train,
We will our liberties maintain.

II.

Boston, be not dismayed,
Tho' tyrants now oppress ;
Tho' fleets and troops invade,
You soon will have redress :
The resolutions of the brave
Will injured Massachusetts save.

III.

The delegates have met ;
For wisdom all renowned ;
Freedom we may expect
From politics profound.
Illustrious Congress, may each name
Be crowned with immortal fame !

IV.

Tho' troops upon our ground
Have strong entrenchments made,
Tho' ships the town surround,
With all their guns displayed,
'T will not the free-born spirit tame,
Or force us to renounce our claim.

V.

Our Charter-Rights we claim,
Granted in ancient times,
Since our Forefathers came
First to these western climes :
Nor will their sons degenerate,
They freedom love — oppression hate.

VI.

If Ga—e should strike the blow,
We must for Freedom fight,
Undaunted courage show,
While we defend our right ;
In spite of the oppressive band
Maintain the freedom of the Land.

ascribed it to fear and to submission.[1] But the patriots saw in this calmness, this forbearance, this absence of tumult, a high and necessary duty. It was such moderation and firmness that made the cause of Boston the cause of the other colonies. Its praise was in the midst of every village, and in the mouth of every patriot. "We think it happy for America," Charlestown, with prophetic accuracy, wrote to Boston, "that you are placed in the front rank of the conflict; and with gratitude acknowledge your vigilance, activity, and firmness in the common cause, which will be admired by generations yet unborn."[2]

The Boston patriots had warned their fellow-countrymen that the new acts could not fail to "bring on a most important and decisive trial."[3] Though the day of this trial had come, though it had been resolved to resist at all hazards the execution of these acts, yet they were anxious to postpone, until it was absolutely necessary, a collision with the British troops, and had agreed upon a plan for this purpose.[4] Before a contest took place, they hoped to receive the assurance that other colonies would make common cause with Massachusetts. In this hope they were not disappointed. Governor Gage was astonished to witness the spread of the union spirit, — that so many "should interest themselves so much in behalf of Massachusetts." "I find," he writes September 20, 1774, "they have some warm friends in New York and Philadelphia," and "that the people of Charleston (S. C.) are as mad as they are here." Again, on the 25th, he writes : "This province is supported and abetted by others beyond the conception of most people, and foreseen by none. The disease was believed to have been confined to the town of Boston, from whence it might have been eradicated, no doubt, without a great deal of

[1] An officer, November 3, 1774, says :"The faction in Boston is now very low. Believe me, all ranks of people are heartily tired of disorder and confusion ; and as soon as the determination of Great Britain to despise their resolves and petitions is known, all will be very quiet."

[2] Hist. Charlestown, 300.   [3] See the remarkable letter of Boston, dated July 26, 1774, written when these acts were "every day expected."

[4] Dr. Warren, August 27, 1774, writes : "As yet we have been preserved from action with the soldiery, and we shall endeavor to avoid it until we see that it is necessary, and a settled plan is fixed on for that purpose."

trouble, and it might have been the case some time ago; but now it is universal, — there is no knowing where to apply a remedy."

Governor Gage issued writs, dated September 1, convening the General Court at Salem on the 5th of October, but dissolved it by a proclamation dated September 28, 1774. The members elected to it, pursuant to the course agreed upon resolved themselves into a Provincial Congress. This body, on the 26th of October, adopted a plan for organizing the militia, maintaining it, and calling it out when circumstances should render it necessary. It provided that one quarter of the number enrolled should be held in readiness to muster at the shortest notice, who were called by the popular name of minute-men. An executive authority — the Committee of Safety — was created, clothed with large discretionary powers; and another, called the Committee of Supplies. On the 27th Jedediah Preble, (who did not accept,) Artemas Ward, and Seth Pomeroy, were chosen general officers; and on the 28th, Henry Gardner was chosen treasurer of the colony, under the title of Receiver-General. Among the energetic acts of this memorable Congress, was one authorizing the collection of military stores. It dissolved December 10. The committee of safety, as early as November, authorized the purchase of materials for an army, and ordered them to be deposited at Concord and Worcester. These proceedings were denounced by General Gage, in a proclamation dated November 10, as treasonable, and a compliance with them was forbidden. In a short time the king's speech and the action of Parliament were received, which manifested a firm determination to produce submission to the late acts, and to maintain "the supreme authority" of Great Britain over the colonies. General Gage regarded this intelligence as having "cast a damp upon the faction," and as having produced a happy effect upon the royalist cause. However, a second Provincial Congress (February 1 to 16, 1775) renewed the measures of its predecessor; and gave definiteness to the duties of the committee of safety, by "empowering and directing" them (on the 9th of February) to assemble the militia whenever it was required to resist the execution of the two acts, for altering the government and the administration of justice. At the same time it appointed two additional generals, John Thomas and William Heath, and made it the duty of the five general officers to take charge of the militia when called out by the committee of safety, and to "effectually oppose and resist such attempt or attempts as shall be made for carrying into execution by force" the two acts. In a spirited address, Congress appealed to the towns for support. It urged that, when invaded by oppression, resistance became "the Christian and social duty of each individual;" and it enjoined the people never to yield, but, with a proper sense of dependence on God, defend those rights which Heaven gave them, and no one ought to take from them.[1]

The conviction was fast becoming general that force only could decide the contest. Stimulated and sustained by such a public opinion, the committees of safety and supplies were diligent, through the gloomy months of winter, in collecting and storing at Concord and Worcester materials for the maintenance of an army. The towns, which had done so fearlessly and so thoroughly the necessary preparatory work of forming and concentrating political sentiment, came forward now to complete their patriotic action by voting money freely to arm, equip, and discipline "Alarm List Companies." Citizens of every calling appeared in their ranks. To be a private in them was proclaimed by the journals to be an honor; to be chosen to office in them, to be a mark of the highest distinction. In Danvers the deacon of the parish was elected captain of the minute-men, and the minister his lieutenant. These minute-men were trained often — the towns paying the expense; when the company, after its field exercises, would sometimes repair to the meeting-house to hear a patriotic sermon, or partake of an entertainment at the town-house, where zealous "Sons of Liberty" would exhort them to prepare to fight bravely for God and their country. Such was the dis-

[1] Journals of the Provincial Congress. Of this Congress Joseph Warren wrote, November 21, 1774—"About two hundred and sixty members were present. You would have thought yourself in an assembly of Spartans, or ancient Romans, had you been a witness to the ardor which inspired those who spoke upon the important business they were transacting."

ciplme, — so free from a mercenary spirit — so full of inspiring
influences, — of the early American soldiery. And thus an
army, in fact, was in existence, ready, at a moment's call, for
defensive purposes, to wheel its isolated platoons into solid
phalanxes; while it presented to an enemy only the opportunity of an inglorious foray upon its stores.[1]

In the mean time troops continued to arrive in Boston. On
the 17th of November the whole force consisted of eleven
regiments, and the artillery. In December five hundred
marines landed from the Asia. At this time nearly all the
regiments which had been ordered from Quebec, New York,
and the Jerseys, had arrived. Mechanics had been brought
from abroad to build barracks for their accommodation during
the winter, and they were all under cover. "Our army," a
British officer writes, December 26, 1774, "is in high spirits;
and at present this town is pretty quiet. We get plenty of provisions, cheap and good in their kind; we only regret that
necessity obliges us to enrich, by purchasing from a set of
people we would wish to deprive of so great an advantage.
Our parade is a very handsome one; three hundred and seventy men mount daily, and more are expected soon; a field
officer's guard of one hundred and fifty men, at the lines on
the Neck. The army is brigaded. The first brigadier-general, Earl Percy; major of brigade, Moncreiff; second brigadier, Pigott; major of brigade, Small; third brigade, Jones;

[1] Many paragraphs of similar character to the following appear in the
journals :

"On the 2d of this instant the minute-company of the town of Lunenburg,
consisting of fifty-seven able-bodied men, appeared in arms on the parade, at
10 o'clock, A. M., and after going through the several military manœuvres,
they marched to a public-house, where the officers had provided an elegant
dinner for the company, a number of the respectable inhabitants of the town,
and patriotic ministers of the towns adjacent. At two o'clock, P. M., they
marched in military procession to the meeting-house, where the Rev. Mr.
Adams delivered an excellent sermon, suitable to the occasion, from Psalm
xxvii. 3. The whole business of the day was performed with decency,
order, and to the satisfaction of a very large number of spectators. On the
day following, the freeholders and other inhabitants of the town assembled in
legal town-meeting, and voted £100, L. M., for the purpose of purchasing
fire-arms with bayonets, and other implements of war, agreeable to the advice of the late Provincial Congress."— Essex Gazette, January 17, 1775.

major of brigade, Hutchinson." Another officer, in a letter written a month previous, shows what the army thought of their antagonists. " As to what you hear of their taking arms to resist the force of England, it is mere bullying, and will go no further than words; whenever it comes to blows, he that can run the fastest will think himself best off: believe me, any two regiments here ought to be decimated if they did not beat, in the field, the whole force of the Massachusetts province; for though they are numerous, they are but a mere mob, without order or discipline, and very awkward at handling their arms."

CHAPTER II.

Firmness of the Patriots. Policy of General Gage. Movements of the
British Troops. Expedition to Concord. Gathering of the Minute-men.
Retreat of the British Troops.

THE Massachusetts patriots were never more determined to
resist the new acts of Parliament, and were never more confident in their ability to maintain their ground, than on the
commencement of the new year. The north and the south
had counselled and acted together in the memorable First
Continental Congress, and it had been demonstrated that one
purpose animated the colonies. This Congress, alsc, had
approved of the stand which Massachusetts had resolved to
make against Great Britain. Still, up to this time, a vast
majority of the patriots of the other colonies looked rather to
non-importation and non-consumption, than to a resort to arms,
as a means of obtaining redress. And the fear was entertained and expressed, that Massachusetts, smarting under
accumulated wrong, might break the line of a prudent opposition, and rashly plunge into civil war. Hence the leading
patriots of this colony were so desirous, that when a collision
did take place, the British troops should be clearly the aggressors. Besides, delay would enable them to increase their
means to carry on so great a contest; while every new act of
aggression, every attempt to compel submission, would tend to
unite all in a common cause. By such a policy, they hoped,
in the trial which they felt was coming, to secure the coöperation of the other colonies.

General Gage, for more than three months, put this policy
to a severe test. He had tried every means "to spirit up
every friend to the government," and yet his plans had been
most adroitly thwarted, and he could see no other course to
take but to disarm the colonists. This policy had been suggested by Lord Dartmouth,[1] but General Gage frankly informed

---

[1] Gage's letter, December 15, 1774   He writes, — " Your lordship's idea

the minister that it was not practicable without a resort to force, and without being master of the country. As early as November 2, 1774, Gage wrote that he was confident, to begin with an army twenty thousand strong would, in the end, save Great Britain blood and treasure. [1] He had now — January, 1775 — only a force of about thirty-five hundred. Yet, as the excitement of the preceding summer had passed away, he regarded the aspect of affairs as favorable for the work of disarming and of intimidating. Hence, on the 18th of January, 1775, he wrote to Lord Dartmouth that it was the opinion of most people, "If a respectable force is seen in the field, the most obnoxious of the leaders seized, and a pardon proclaimed for all others, government will come off victorious, and with less opposition than was expected a few months ago." [2] And this was the policy — to be followed by such momentous results — that General Gage now proceeded to carry out.

He saw a gleam of hope in an application he received, about this time, from Marshfield. General Timothy Ruggles, the great leader of the loyalists, proposed the formation of associations throughout the colony, with constitutions binding those who signed them to oppose, at the risk of life, the acts of all unconstitutional assemblies, such as committees and congresses. In January, a large number of the people of Marshfield signed one of these constitutions, and thus formed a "Loyal Association." It was reported that the patriots of Plymouth had determined to make them recant, and hence the associators applied to General Gage for protection. He was gratified with this request, and accordingly, January 23, 1775, he sent Captain Balfour, with about a hundred men and three hundred stand of arms, to Marshfield. The troops were joyfully received by the loyalists, and were comfortably accom-

---

of disarming certain provinces would doubtless be consistent with prudence and safety, but it neither is or has been practicable without having recourse to force, and being master of the country."

[1] This phrase will not be found in the Parliamentary Register of 1775. It was copied by President Sparks, from the original. — Sparks' Washington vol. III., p. 506.

[2] Sparks' Washington, vol. III., **p. 507.**

modated. They preserved exact discipline, found none to attack them, and did not molest the inhabitants. The Marshfield associators, and their friends, made formal addresses of acknowledgment to General Gage and Admiral Graves, for the timely protection that had been granted, and received from both, in return, sufficiently gracious replies. General Gage was satisfied with the good effect of this movement, and hoped that similar applications would be made from other places. The patriot journals, with better judgment, regarded such expeditions as having a tendency to irritate and alarm the people.[1] The detachment remained at Marshfield until the memorable nineteenth of April.

The next attempt of the troops was made at Salem, where a few brass cannon and gun-carriages were deposited. Colonel Leslie, with a detachment of the army, on Sunday, February

---

[1] General Gage made this affair the subject of a letter to Lord Dartmouth, dated January 27, which was read in Parliament, March 8. He assured the ministry that he often had information from the country that the people of the towns were becoming more divided.

The following version of this affair, extracted from Rivington's New York Gazette of February 9, 1775, well shows the tone in which the Tories were accustomed to write of the patriots. It is in a letter from Marshfield. "Two hundred of the principal inhabitants of this loyal town, insulted and intimidated by the licentious spirit that unhappily has been prevalent amongst the lower ranks of people in the Mass. government, having applied to the governor for a detachment of his majesty's troops, to assist in preserving the peace, and to check the insupportable insolence of the disaffected and turbulent, were happily relieved by the appearance of Capt. Balfour's party, consisting of one hundred soldiers, who were joyfully received by the loyalists. Upon their arrival, the valor of the minute-men was called forth by Adam's crew ; they were accordingly mustered, and, to the unspeakable confusion of the enemies of our happy constitution, no more than twelve persons presented themselves to bear arms against the Lord's anointed. It was necessary that some apology should be made for the scanty appearance of their volunteers, and they colored it over with a declaration, that ' had the party sent to Marshfield consisted of half a dozen battalions, it might have been worth their attention to meet and engage them ; but a day would come, when the courage of their minute host would be able to clear the country of all their enemies, howsoever formidable in numbers.' The king's troops are very comfortably accommodated, and preserve the most exact discipline ; and now, every faithful subject to his king dare freely utter his thoughts, drink his tea, and kill his sheep, as profusely as he pleases."

26, 1775, was sent to seize them. He landed at Marblehead in the afternoon, while the people were at meeting. His object being suspected, intelligence was immediately sent to Salem. The warlike materials were on the north side of the North Bridge, which was built with a draw to let vessels pass, and which, before Colonel Leslie reached it, had been hoisted. He ordered it to be lowered; but the people refused, saying, "It is a private way, and you have no authority to demand a passage this way." Colonel Leslie then determined to pass the river in two large gondolas that lay near. But their owners jumped in and began to scuttle them. A few of the soldiers tried to prevent this; a scuffle ensued, some were pricked with bayonets, and thus blood was shed. Things were proceeding to extremities, when the Rev. Mr. Barnard, a clergyman of Salem, interfered, and a compromise was effected. The people consented to lower the bridge, and Colonel Leslie pledged his honor not to march more than thirty rods beyond it. The troops, having done this, returned unmolested; but the alarm spread; the minute-men began to assemble; and one company from Danvers arrived just as the British were leaving town. Thus the good sense of an intelligent British officer, and the influence of a few leading citizens, rather than the want of spirit in the people, prevented Salem from being the Lexington of the Revolution; for had Col. Leslie, instead of negotiating, decided to force his way over the bridge, a collision must have occurred. This circumstance, probably, occasioned the report in England, that in Salem "the Americans had hoisted their standard of Liberty." [1]

[1] Gentleman's Magazine, 1775. Essex Gazette. Trumbull, in M'Fingal, notices this expedition. After describing its arrival at Marblehead, he writes, —

> " Through Salem straight, without delay,
>   The bold battalion took its way ;
>   Marched o'er a bridge, in open sight
>   Of several Yankees armed for fight ;
>   Then, without loss of time or men,
>   Veered round for Boston back again,
>   And found so well their projects thrive,
>   That every soul got home alive."

The pacific policy of the patriots was further severely tried by the bearing of the British troops. Their conduct had been in general orderly,[1] and no disposition had been manifested by

[1] The anxiety of the leading patriots to keep Boston free from the mob spirit is seen in the private letters of this period. They endeavored to live as peaceable as possible with the troops. Still riots would occur. At a town-meeting, November 7, 1774, it was voted, as the governor had assured the town that he would do all in his power to secure peace and good order, that the town would exert its best endeavors to effect the same purpose. The meeting voted to recommend to the selectmen to increase the watch to twelve men, to patrol the streets the whole night; to recommend to the justices of the peace to exert their authority promptly for the observance of the laws, and to recommend masters of families to restrain their children and servants from going abroad after nine o'clock in the evening. Taverners and retailers were also enjoined to strictly conform to the laws of the province as to disorderly persons.

It was in accordance with this policy, probably, that so little is heard of the Boston military at this period. Mills and Hicks' Register of 1775 gives the names of the military corps of the town : 1. The Governor's Troop of Horse Guards, David Phipps captain, with the rank of colonel. 2. The Ancient and Honorable Artillery Company, William Bell captain. 3. The Boston Regiment, John Erving colonel, John Leverett lieut.-colonel, Thomas Dawes major. 4. The Grenadier Company, Major Dawes captain, Joseph Pierce lieut., with the rank of captain, Henry Knox lieutenant. 5. The Train attached to the Boston Regiment, Adino Paddock captain. 6. The Train belonging to the Suffolk First Regiment, Lemuel Robinson captain. 7. The Train belonging to the Suffolk 2d Regiment, Francis Barker captain. 8. The Train belonging to the Suffolk 3d Regiment, Eliphalet Pond captain. At the South Battery was a company, Jeremiah Green captain. At the North Battery, another company, Nathaniel Barber captain.

There had been, also, an Independent Company of Cadets, of which John Hancock was the commander. He was dismissed by Governor Gage, shortly after his arrival. The corps met, August 14, 1774, and appointed a committee to wait on the governor at Salem and return to him their standard, " as they had almost unanimously disbanded themselves." The committee, on the next day, delivered the standard accordingly, and told him, " They no longer considered themselves the Governor's Independent Company."

Early in 1775, the Ancient and Honorable, on a parade day, were refused admittance to the common, and Major Bell marched the company to Copp's Hill. Some years after, a question arose as to who owned this hill. At a town-meeting some one said, " The Ancient and Honorable." Col. Jackson, their treasurer, was questioned, who stated that a mortgage upon it to them had long since run out, and they took possession of it in 1775. The moderator, Col. Thomas Dawes, inquired of Major Bell — " Why did you march

the officers to bring about a collision. But in March so marked
was their change of behavior, that it indicated an intention to
provoke a quarrel. On the anniversary of the memorable
fifth of March, Dr. Warren delivered the customary oration
at the Old South Meeting-house, before a crowded audience.
About forty British officers were present, who, at its conclusion, hissed and were otherwise insulting in their bearing.
On the 9th, a citizen of Billerica, Thomas Ditson, jr., on the
pretence that he was tempting a soldier to desert, was tarred
and feathered, fastened in a chair on a truck, and drawn
through the streets, surrounded by a party of officers and soldiers of the 47th regiment, under Colonel Nesbit. On this
occasion, the tune of Yankee Doodle was played in derision.
The sixteenth of March, on the recommendation of the Provincial Congress, was observed as a day of fasting and prayer,
when the people of the west part of Boston were annoyed by
a party of the Fourth, or King's own Regiment. As the
congregation were assembling, two marquee tents were pitched
within a few yards of the meeting-house; and during the
service, they were disturbed by the noise of drums and fifes.
On the 17th, Colonel Hancock's house, near the common, was
assaulted and his fence hacked, by a party, who otherwise
behaved abusively. During this period, the patriots were

your company to Copps Hill?" "I was prohibited from entering the common, and conceiving this hill to be the property of the company, I marched
them there as a place no one had a right to exclude them from." Colonel
Dawes again asked — "Suppose British soldiers had forbidden your entrance?" "I would have charged bayonets and forced my way, as surely
as I would have forced my way into my dwelling-house, if taken possession
of by a gang of thieves." Col. William Tudor then remarked, "The hill
belongs to that company." The mortgage was afterwards discharged. —
Snow's Boston, p. 106.

Major Paddock lost his pieces, the Whigs carrying them off in the night.
They first carried off two, and though the other two were put under guard,
they carried them off also. This made the officers mad. They said "They
believed the devil got them away, for it was not half an hour ago they
had their hands on them."—Ms. Letter. On the 23rd of February, the committee of safety requested Dr. Warren to confer with the company formerly
under the command of Major Paddock, to know how many could be depended
on, officers and men, "when the constitutional army of the province should
take the field."

making every effort to carry into the country military stores; and on the 18th, the Neck guard seized 13,425 musket cartridges and a quantity of balls, in doing which, they severely abused a teamster. In the evening, a party of officers, heated with liquor, committed excesses in the streets, and attacked the Providence coach. These insults irritated and inflamed the people.[1]

Other movements, however, created more alarm. The committees of safety and supplies had deposited large quantities of military stores at Concord, under the care of Colonel James Barrett. It was rumored, in March, that General Gage was determined to destroy them; and as early as the 14th of this month, the committee of safety voted to place a guard over them. On the 15th, its clerk, John Pigeon, was directed to establish a nightly watch, and to arrange for teams to be in readiness to carry them, on the shortest notice, to places of safety. Couriers also were engaged in Charlestown, Cambridge, and Roxbury, to alarm the country. These precautions were rendered still more necessary by the movements of General Gage. He sent officers in disguise to make sketches of the roads, and to ascertain the state of the towns. On the 20th of March, Captain Brown and Ensign D'Bernicre, of the British army, visited Concord, and subsequently presented a narrative of what they saw to the governor.[2] Vigilant patriots watched them narrowly. Bodies of troops, also, occasionally marched into the country.[3] On the 30th, the first brigade, about eleven hundred men, marched out towards Jamaica Plains, but without baggage or artillery. They did much damage in throwing down stone walls. "Great numbers," Dr. Warren writes, "completely armed, collected in the neighboring towns; and it is the opinion of many, that had they marched eight or ten miles, and attempted to destroy any magazines, or abuse the people, not a man of them would

---

[1] Letter of S. Adams; Ditson's Deposition in the newspapers of 1775; Letter, Boston, March 22, 1775; Gordon, vol. i., p. 319.

[2] Bernicre's narrative. [3] The Provincial Congress, sitting at Cambridge, February 10, appointed Messrs. Devens, Watson, Gardner, Howe, and Batchelor, a committee to observe the motion of the troops said to be on the road to this town.

have returned to Boston."[1] Smaller parties went out over Charlestown Ferry, and marched through Roxbury into Boston.

While things thus wore a hostile aspect at home, intelligence was received from Great Britain that the ministry were determined to force the colonists to obedience. There the Americans were looked upon as cowards, whom British redcoats would look into submission. Five regiments, it was said, would march from one end of the continent to the other. "The senator," Gordon writes, "holds this language in the senate, and the general at the head of an army. It passes for a maxim, and it is thought scepticism to doubt it."[2] Additional coercive measures were proposed in Parliament; additional troops were announced to be on their way to Boston. The generals Howe, Clinton, and Burgoyne, of established reputation for courage and conduct, were ordered to join General Gage; and British journals announced that the army would take the field. A speech made in Parliament by General Burgoyne, February 27, 1775, while he was under orders, shows the feelings with which the generals accepted their commands. He was convinced that the cause of Great Britain was just, and that the claims of the colonists were chimerical. "Is there," he asked, "a man in England, — I am sure there is not an officer or soldier in the king's service, —

---

[1] Life Arthur Lee, vol. II., 266. Gordon, vol. I., 320. The following notice of the Boston committee of correspondence shows how vigilant this committee was : —

> Boston, March 30, 1775.

Gentlemen, — The alarming manœuvre of a large detachment of the army is the reason of our desiring your attendance at our chamber in Faneuil Hall to-morrow, at ten o'clock, A. M., in order to determine upon measures of safety. The wisdom of the joint committees has been very conspicuous. The fullest exertion of the same wisdom is absolutely necessary at this excited time. We therefore desire your punctual attendance.

> We are, gentlemen,
>   Your friends and countrymen.
>   Signed, by order of the committee
>   of correspondence of Boston,
>   WILLIAM COOPER, Clerk.

To Committee of Correspondence for Charlestown.

[2] Gordon, vol. I., 316.

who does not think the Parliamentary rights of Great Britain a cause to fight for — to bleed and die for?" While there was a charm in the very wanderings and dreams of liberty that disarmed an Englishman's anger, yet the existence of the constitution and the country depended on bringing the Americans to submission.[1] The insulting and warlike tenor of this news, however, only made the patriots firmer. They presented, at this period of intense anxiety, a noble spectacle. It was the awful pause between the resolution and the act. They had determined to resist, and yet had not been obliged to strike. Gordon remarks of Massachusetts : its people were "in a state of nature, and yet as still and peaceable as ever they were when government was in full vigor;" royal authority was suspended, and yet individual security was everywhere enjoyed; the Tory had but to keep his temper and observe a neutrality, and he was safe in person and property.[2] Strange as it may appear, this very order was ascribed to the presence of the British troops. How different, however, was the great spirit that animated and supported the patriots! "The people," Cushing writes, "are not dismayed. Should the administration determine to carry into execution the late acts by military force, they will make the last appeal. They are determined life and liberty shall go together." The resolve and the language of the patriots were : "America must and will be free. The contest may be severe, — the end will be glorious. We would not boast, but we think, united and prepared as we are, we have no reason to doubt of success, if

---

[1] Parliamentary Register, 1775.

[2] Gordon, I., 291. The patriots were severely provoked by the conduct of the Tories. The course of a prominent citizen of Rowley affords a good instance of their manner of speech. Among the charges against him were :—

" Your saying you wished Boston was laid in ashes.

" Your speaking reproachfully of the most respectable gentlemen of Boston.

" Your saying our General Court acted like fools ; and that the town of Boston was the means of all those troubles.

" Your saying you wished that these laws were put in execution, and that we were in lordships."

The patriots required him to make a proper confession. Another citizen, equally loud-mouthed, the town voted " was not worthy of any public notice." — Essex Gazette.

we should be compelled to make the last appeal; but we mean not to make that appeal until we can be justified in doing it in the sight of God and man."[1]

Each day, however, it became more and more evident that this last appeal was at hand. Intelligence of the reinforcements on their way to Boston was published in the journals of April 4th. Also the declaration of the Parliament to the king, that the opposition to legislative authority in Massachusetts constituted rebellion; and the "solemn assurances" of the king to the Parliament, that " the most speedy and effectual measures" should be taken to put the rebellion down. This news elated the confident Tories; it depressed the timid Whigs; but the firm friends of liberty avowed themselves ready for the struggle.[2] "Nothing is now talked of"—Stiles writes, April 4—"but immediately forming an American army at Worcester, and taking the field with undaunted resolution."[3] The Provincial Congress met the crisis, and the demand of public opinion, by energetic measures. On the 5th, it adopted rules and regulations for the establishment of an army; on the 7th, it sent a circular to the committees of correspondence, "most earnestly recommending" them to see to it that "the militia and minute-men" be found in the best posture of defence, whenever any exigence might require their aid, but at whatever expense of patience and forbearance, to act only on the defensive; on the 8th, it resolved to take effectual measures to raise an army, and to send delegates to Rhode Island, New Hampshire, and Connecticut, to request their coöperation; on the 13th, it voted to raise six companies of artillery, pay them, and keep them constantly in exercise; on the 14th, it advised the removal of the citizens of Boston into the country; on the 15th, it appointed a day of fasting and prayer, and adjourned to the 10th of May.[4] The committees of safety and supplies — 14th to 19th — were busy in preparing for immediate hostilities, — establishing a train of artillery, making powder into cartridges, removing cannon to places of safety, and distributing the military supplies.[5]

---

[1] Dr. Warren utters this noble language in a letter dated April 3, 1775.
[2] Stiles' Diary. [3] Ib. [4] Journals of Provincial Congress.
[5] The committee of safety were: John Hancock, Joseph Warren, Benja

These preparations must have been well known ; indeed, they could not be concealed. Many of the people of Boston had already moved into the country. Early in April many more left the town. A continuance in it became hazardous for the leading patriots. The governor might make it a prison, and hold its citizens hostages for the good order of the province ; or he might send them to England, to be mocked with a trial for alleged political offences. However, many who had taken a prominent part in opposition to the government — among them Dr. Warren — remained, but a great number left the town. Samuel Adams and John Hancock, then attending the Provincial Congress, were persuaded to remain at the house of Rev. Jonas Clark, of Lexington. Meantime General Gage made every exertion to purchase supplies for camp service ; the patriots made every exertion to anticipate him, and to cut off his supplies, both in Massachusetts and in New York. The troops, also, became still more proud in their bearing, and still more insulting in their conduct. Thus hourly did things assume a more hostile appearance ; "nothing was wanting," writes Gordon, "but a spark, to set the whole continent in a flame."[1]

General Gage, after receiving a small reinforcement, had, in the middle of April, about four thousand men in Boston. He resolved, by a secret expedition, to destroy the magazines collected at Concord. This measure was neither advised by his council nor by his officers. It was said that he was worried into it by the importunities of the Tories; but it was undoubtedly caused by the energetic measures of the Whigs. His own subsequent justification was, that when he saw an assembly of men, unknown to the constitution, wresting from him the public moneys and collecting warlike stores, it was

min Church, Richard Devens, Benjamin White, Joseph Palmer, Abraham Watson, Azor Orne, John Pigeon, William Heath, and Thomas Gardner.

The committee of supplies were : Elbridge Gerry, David Cheever, Benjamin Lincoln, Moses Gill, Benjamin Hall.

These committees usually met together for the transaction of business. On the 17th of April they adjourned from Concord, to meet at " Mr Wether by's, at Menotomy."

[1] Gordon, I., 321.

alike his duty and the dictate of humanity to prevent the calamity of civil war by destroying these magazines.[1] His previous belief was, that, should the government show a respectable force in the field, seize the most obnoxious patriot leaders, and proclaim a pardon for others, it would come off victorious.

On the 15th of April, the grenadiers and light infantry, on the pretence of learning a new military exercise, were relieved from duty; and at night, the boats of the transport ships which had been hauled up to be repaired were launched and moored under the sterns of the men of war. These movements looked suspicious to the vigilant patriots, and Dr. Warren sent intelligence of them to Hancock and Adams, who were in Lexington. It was this timely notice that induced the committee of safety to take additional measures for the security of the stores in Concord, and to order (on the 17th) cannon to be secreted, and a part of the stores to be removed to Sudbury and Groton.

On Tuesday, April 18, General Gage[2] directed several officers to station themselves on the roads leading out of Boston, and prevent any intelligence of his intended expedition, that night, from reaching the country. A party of them, on that day, dined at Cambridge. The committees of safety and supplies, which usually held their sessions together, also met that day, at Wetherby's Tavern, in Menotomy, now West

---

[1] Gage's letter to Trumbull, May 3, 1775. Hence Trumbull, in M'Fingal, writes of this " mercy " of Gage : —

> " But mercy is, without dispute,
>   His first and darling attribute ;
>   So great, it far outwent and conquered
>   His military skill at Concord.
>   There when the war he chose to wage,
>   Shone the benevolence of Gage ;
>   Sent troops to that ill-omened place
>   On errands mere of special grace ;
>   And all the work he chose them for,
>   Was to prevent a civil war."

[2] Several valuable pamphlets have been published relative to the events of the 19th of April. A notice of the most important will be found in the Appendix.

Cambridge. Mr. Gerry and Colonels Orne and Lee, of the members, remained to pass the night. Mr. Devens and Mr. Watson rode in a chaise towards Charlestown, but soon meeting a number of British officers on horseback, they returned to inform their friends at the tavern, waited there until the officers rode by, and then rode to Charlestown. Mr. Gerry immediately sent an express to Hancock [1] and Adams, that "eight or nine officers were out, suspected of some evil design," which caused precautionary measures to be adopted at Lexington.[2]

[1] The messenger sent to Hancock and Adams took a by-path, and delivered his letter. Hancock's reply to Gerry, while it bears marks of the haste with which it was written, is also characterized by the politeness which neither haste nor danger could impair. " Lexington, April 18, 1775. Dear Sir : I am much obliged for your notice. It is said the officers are gone to Concord, and I will send word thither. I am full with you that we ought to be serious, and I hope your decision will be effectual. I intend doing myself the pleasure of being with you to-morrow. My respects to the committee. I am your real friend, JOHN HANCOCK." — Austin's Life of Gerry, vol. I., p. 68.

[2] Rev. Jonas Clark alludes to three different messages received at Lexington, on the evening and night of April 18 : 1. A verbal one ; 2, a written one from the committee of safety, in the evening ; 3, between twelve and one, an express from Dr. Warren. Revere's narrative accounts for the last message. I found among the papers of Richard Devens, of Charlestown, — for a liberal use of which I am indebted to David Devens, Esq., — the following memorandum, without a date, but evidently written about this period, which, in connection with Gerry's express, will account for both of the previous messages. " On the 18th of April, '75, Tuesday, the committee of safety, of which I was then a member, and the committee of supplies, sat at Newell's tavern, (the records of the committee of safety say Wetherby's,) at Menotomy. A great number of British officers dined at Cambridge. After we had finished the business of the day, we adjourned to meet at Woburn on the morrow, — left to lodge at Newell's, Gerry, Orne, and Lee. Mr. Watson and myself came off in my chaise at sunset. On the road we met a great number of B. O. (British officers) and their servants on horseback, who had dined that day at Cambridge. We rode some way after we met them, and then turned back and rode through them, went and informed our friends at Newell's. We stopped there till they came up and rode by. We then left our friends, and I came home, after leaving Mr. Watson at his house. I soon received intelligence from Boston, that the enemy were all in motion, and were certainly preparing to come out into the country. Soon afterward, the signal agreed upon was given ; this was a lanthorn hung out in the upper window of the tower of the N. Ch., (North Church) towards Charlestown. I then

Richard Devens, an efficient member of the committee of safety, soon received intelligence that the British troops were in motion in Boston, and were certainly preparing to go into the country. Shortly after, the signal agreed upon in this event was given, namely, a lanthorn hung out from the North Church steeple in Boston, when Mr. Devens immediately despatched an express with this intelligence to Menotomy and Lexington. All this while General Gage supposed his movements were a profound secret, and as such in the evening communicated them in confidence to Lord Percy. But as this nobleman was crossing the common, on his way to his quarters, he joined a group of men engaged in conversation, when one said, " The British troops have marched, but will miss their aim !" " What aim ?" inquired Lord Percy. " Why, the cannon at Concord." He hastened back to General Gage with this information, when orders were immediately issued that no person should leave town.[1] Dr. Warren, however, a few minutes previous, had sent Paul Revere and William Dawes into the country. Revere, about eleven o'clock, rowed across the river to Charlestown, was supplied by Richard Devens with a horse, and started to alarm the country.[2] Just outside of Charlestown Neck, he barely escaped capture by British officers; but leaving one of them in a clay-pit, he got to Medford, awoke the captain of the minute-men, gave the alarm on the road, and reached the Rev. Jonas Clark's house in safety, where, the evening before, a guard of eight men had been stationed to protect Hancock and Adams. It was mid-

sent off an express to inform Messrs. Gerry, &c., and Messrs. Hancock and A., (Adams) who I knew were at the Rev. Mr. ——, (Clark's) at Lexington, that the enemy were certainly coming out. I kept watch at the ferry to watch for the boats till about eleven o'clock, when Paul Revere came over and informed that the T. (troops) were actually in the boats.* I then took a horse from Mr. Larkin's barn, and sent him ——.* I procured a horse and sent off P. Revere to give the intelligence at Menotomy and Lexington. He was taken by the British officers before mentioned, before he got to Lexington, and detained till near day."

[1] Stedman's History, I., p. 119.   [2] Revere's Narrative. This interesting paper was not written until 1798. It varies but slightly from the memorandum of Devens, which certainly is a prior authority. Devens errs in stating that Revere was taken before he arrived at Lexington.

night as Revere rode up and requested admittance. William Monroe, the sergeant, told him that the family, before retiring to rest, had requested that they might not be disturbed by noise about the house. "Noise!" replied Revere, "you'll have noise enough before long — the regulars are coming out!" He was then admitted. Mr. Dawes, who went out through Roxbury, soon joined him. Their intelligence was, "That a large body of the king's troops, supposed to be a brigade of twelve or fifteen hundred, had embarked in boats from Boston, and gone over to Lechmere's Point, in Cambridge, and it was suspected they were ordered to seize and destroy the stores belonging to the colony, then deposited at Concord." [1]

The town of Lexington, Major Phinney writes, is "about twelve miles north-west of Boston, and six miles south-east of Concord. It was originally a part of Cambridge, and previous to its separation from that town was called the 'Cambridge Farms.' The act of incorporation bears date March 20, 1712. The inhabitants consist principally of hardy and independent yeomanry. In 1775, the list of enrolled militia bore the names of over one hundred citizens. The road leading from Boston divides near the centre of the village in Lexington. The part leading to Concord passes to the left, and that leading to Bedford to the right of the meeting-house, and form two sides of a triangular green or common, on the south corner of which stands the meeting-house, facing directly down the road leading to Boston." At the right of the meeting-house, on the opposite side of Bedford road, was Buckman's tavern.[2]

About one o'clock the Lexington alarm-men and militia were summoned to meet at their usual place of parade, on the common; and messengers were sent towards Cambridge for additional information. When the militia assembled, about two o'clock in the morning, Captain John Parker, its commander, ordered the roll to be called, and the men to load with powder and ball. About one hundred and thirty were now assembled with arms. One of the messengers soon returned with the report that there was no appearance of troops on the roads; and the weather being chilly, the men, after being on

[1] William Monroe's Deposition ; Revere's Narrative ; Clark's **Account.**
[2] Phinney's History, p. 10

parade some time, were dismissed, with orders to appear again
at the beat of the drum. They dispersed into houses near the
place of parade — the greater part going into Buckman's tavern. It was generally supposed that the movements in Boston
were only a feint to alarm the people.[1]

Revere and Dawes started to give the alarm in Concord,
and soon met Dr. Samuel Prescott, a warm patriot, who agreed
to assist in arousing the people. While they were thus engaged, they were suddenly met by a party of officers, well
armed and mounted, when a scuffle ensued, during which
Revere was captured; but Prescott, by leaping a stone wall,
made his escape. The same officers had already detained
three citizens of Lexington, who had been sent out the preceding evening to watch their movements. All the prisoners,
after being questioned closely, were released near Lexington;
when Revere rejoined Hancock and Adams, and went with
them towards Woburn, two miles from Mr. Clark's house.[2]

While these things were occurring, the British regulars
were marching towards Concord. Lieutenant-colonel Smith,
at the head of about eight hundred troops, — grenadiers, light
infantry, and marines, — embarked about ten o'clock at the
foot of Boston Common, in the boats of the ships of war.
They landed, just as the moon arose, at Phipps Farm, now
Lechmere Point, took an unfrequented path over the marshes,
where in some places they had to wade through water, and
entered the old Charlestown and West Cambridge road. No
martial sounds enlivened their midnight march; it was silent,
stealthy, inglorious. The members of the "rebel congress"

[1] Gordon's Account and Depositions of 1775 ; Clark.   [2] Revere and
Gordon.

Hancock and Adams, whose safety was regarded as of the utmost importance, were persuaded to retire to the then 2d precinct of Woburn, to the
house occupied by Madam Jones, widow of Rev. Thomas Jones, and Rev.
Mr. Marett, which is now standing in Burlington, and occupied by Rev.
Samuel Sewell. Dorothy Quincy accompanied her intended husband —
Hancock. Here, at noon, they had just sat down to an elegant dinner, when
a man broke suddenly in upon them with a shriek, and they believed the
regulars were upon them. Mr. Marett then piloted Adams and Hancock
along a cart-way to Mr. Amos Wyman's house, in a corner of Billerica,
where they were glad to dine off of cold salt pork and potatoes, served in a
wooden tray. — Letter of Rev. Samuel Sewell.

arose from their beds at the tavern in Menotomy, to view them. They saw the front pass on with the regularity of veteran discipline. But when the centre was opposite the window, an officer and file of men were detached towards the house. Messrs. Gerry, Orne, and Lee, half dressed as they were, then took the hint and escaped to an adjoining field, while the British in vain searched the house.[1]

Colonel Smith had marched but few miles, when the sounds of guns and bells gave evidence that, notwithstanding the caution of General Gage, the country was alarmed. He detached six companies of light infantry, under the command of Major Pitcairn, with orders to press forward and secure the two bridges at Concord, while he sent a messenger to Boston for a reinforcement. The party of officers who had been out joined the detachment, with the exaggerated report that five hundred men were in arms to oppose the king's forces. Major Pitcairn, as he advanced, succeeded in capturing every one on the road until he arrived within a mile and a half of Lexington meeting-house, when Thaddeus Bowman succeeded in eluding the advancing troops, and galloping to the common, gave the first certain intelligence to Captain Parker of their approach.[2]

It was now about half-past four in the morning. Captain Parker ordered the drum to beat, alarm guns to be fired, and Sergeant William Monroe to form his company in two ranks a few rods north of the meeting-house. It was a part of "the constitutional army," which was authorized to make a regular and forcible resistance to any open hostility by the British troops; and it was for this purpose that this gallant and devoted band, on this memorable morning, appeared on the field. Whether it ought to maintain its ground, or whether it ought to retreat, would depend upon the bearing and numbers of the regulars. It was not long in suspense. At a short distance from the parade-ground, the British officers, regarding the American drum as a challenge, ordered their troops to halt, to prime and load, and then to march forward in double-quick time. Meantime sixty or seventy of the militia had collected,

---

[1] Gage's Account; Austin's Life of Gerry, 169. [2] Gage's Account; Phinney's History.

and about forty spectators, a few of whom had arms. Captain Parker ordered his men not to fire unless they were fired upon. A part of his company had time to form in a military position facing the regulars ; but while some were joining the ranks, and others were dispersing, the British troops rushed on, shouting and firing, and their officers — among whom was Major Pitcairn — exclaiming, " Ye villains! ye rebels! disperse!" " Lay down your arms !" " Why don't you lay down your arms?" The militia did not instantly disperse, nor did they proceed to lay down their arms. The first guns, few in number, did no execution. A general discharge followed, with fatal results.[1]

[1] Gordon's Letter, May 17, 1775 : Clark's Narrative : Depositions of 1775.

Dr. John Warren, in his Ms. diary, — for which, and for other courtesies, I am indebted to his son, Dr. John C. Warren, — writes, April 19, 1775 : " Some dispersed, but a few continued in a military position ; on seeing which, Major Pitcairn, upon the plea of some person snapping a gun," &c. Gordon also says " a few continued in their military position." This agrees with Bernicre's (British) account, which says : Major Pitcairn cried out for the militia " to throw down their arms and disperse, which they did not do ; he called out a second time, but to no purpose," &c. Gordon also gives the details of a person, just before the firing, " offering to fire, but the piece flashed in the pan without going off."

Stiles, in his Ms. diary, gives the following interesting relation of Major Pitcairn's own version of the beginning of the firing : —

1775, August 19. —"Major Pitcairn, who was a good man in a bad cause, insisted upon it, to the day of his death, that the colonists fired first ; and that he commanded not to fire, and endeavored to stay and stop the firing after it began : but then he told this with such circumstances as convince me that he was deceived, though on the spot. He does not say that he saw the colonists fire first. Had he said it, I would have believed him, being a man of integrity and honor. He expressly says he did not see who fired first ; and yet believed the peasants began. His account is this : That riding up to them, he ordered them to disperse ; which they not doing instantly, he turned about to order his troops to draw out so as to surround and disarm them. As he turned, he saw a gun in a peasant's hand, from behind a wall, flash in the pan without going off ; and instantly, or very soon, two or three guns went off, by which he found his horse wounded, and also a man near him wounded. These guns he did not see ; but believing they could not come from his own people, doubted not, and so asserted, that they came from our people, and that thus they began the attack. The impetuosity of the king's troops was such, that a promiscuous, uncommanded, but general fire took place, which Pitcairn could not prevent ; though he struck his staff or sword downwards with all earnestness, as the signal to forbear or cease firing."

A few of the militia who had been wounded, or who saw others killed or wounded by their side, no longer hesitated, but returned the fire of the regulars. Jonas Parker, John Monroe, and Ebenezer Monroe, jr., and others, fired before leaving the line; Solomon Brown and James Brown fired from behind a stone wall; one other person fired from the back door of Buckman's house; Nathan Monroe, Lieutenant Benjamin Tidd, and others, retreated a short distance and fired.[1] Meantime the regulars continued their fire as long as the militia remained in sight, killing eight and wounding ten. Jonas Parker, who repeatedly said he never would run from the British, was wounded at the second fire, but he still dis-

---

[1] This account is not more than just to Lexington. The contemporary evidence of this return fire is too positive to be set aside. In the counter manifesto to Gage's proclamation, prepared in June, 1775, which was not published at the time, it is said that the British, "in a most barbarous and infamous manner, fired upon a small number of the inhabitants, and cruelly murdered eight men. The fire was returned by some of the survivors, but their number was too inconsiderable to annoy the regular troops, who proceeded on their errand, and upon coming up to Concord," &c. &c. I copy from Ms. in Mass. Archives. Gordon, May 17, 1775, says that James Brown informed him, that "being got over the wall, and seeing the soldiers fire pretty freely, he fired upon them, and some others did the same." Deposition Number 8, of 1775, is clear : — "About five o'clock in the morning we attended the beat of our drum, and were formed on the parade. We were faced towards the regulars, then marching up to us, and some of our company were coming to the parade with their backs towards the troops; and others on the parade began to disperse, when the regulars fired on the company, before a gun was fired by any of our company on them." The great point was as to who fired first. Clark says : — "So far from firing first upon the king's troops, upon the most careful inquiry, it appears, that but very few of our people fired at all, and even they did not fire till, after being fired upon by the troops, they were wounded themselves," &c. Phinney's History contains the details, with depositions, which, as to the main fact, are supported by the authorities of 1775. All the British accounts state that the fire was returned, or rather they state that it was begun, by the militia. This last assertion, made in Gage's hand-bill, (see Appendix,) was contradicted. Much controversy took place about it, and the Provincial Congress account was prepared in reference to it. As late as May 3, 1776, a London journal says : — "It is whispered that the ministry are endeavoring to fix a certainty which party fired first at Lexington, before hostilities commenced, as the Congress declare, if it can be proved that American blood was first shed, it will go a great way towards effecting a reconciliation on the most honorable terms."

charged his gun, and was killed by a bayonet. "A **truer** heart did not bleed at Thermopylæ."[1] Isaac Muzzy, Jonathan Harrington, and Robert Monroe, were also killed on or near the place where the line was formed. "Harrington's was a cruel fate. He fell in front of his own house, on the north of the common. His wife at the window saw him fall, and then start up, the blood gushing from his breast. He stretched out his hands towards her, as if for assistance, and fell again. Rising once more on his hands and knees, he crawled across the road towards his dwelling. She ran to meet him at the door, but it was to see him expire at her feet."[2] Monroe was the standard bearer of his company at the capture of Louisburg. Caleb Harrington was killed as he was running from the meeting-house, after replenishing his stock of powder; Samuel Hadley and John Brown, after they had left the common; Asahel Porter, of Woburn, who had been taken prisoner by the British, as he was endeavoring to effect his escape.[3] The British suffered but little; a private of the 10th regiment, and probably one other, were wounded, and Major Pitcairn's horse was struck.[4] Some of the provincials retreated up the road leading to Bedford, but most of them across a swamp to a rising ground north of the common. The British troops formed on the common, fired a volley, and gave three huzzas in token of their victory.[5] Colonel Smith, with the remainder of the troops, soon joined Major Pitcairn, and the whole detachment marched towards Concord, about six miles distant, which it reached without further interruption. After it left Lexington six of the regulars were taken prisoners.

Concord was described in 1775, by Ensign Berniere, as follows: It "lies between two hills, that command it entirely. There is a river runs through it, with two bridges over it. In summer it is pretty dry. The town is large, and contains a church, jail, and court-house; but the houses are not close together, but in little groups." The road from Lexington entered Concord from the south-east. along the side of a hill,

---

[1] Everett's Lexington Address.   [2] Ib.   [3] Phinney's History.   [4] Gage's account.   [5] Phinney and Clark.

which commences on the right of it about a mile below the village, rises abruptly from thirty to fifty feet above the road, and terminates at the north-easterly part of the square. The top forms a plain, which commands a view of the town. Here was the liberty pole. The court-house stood near the present county-house. The main branch of the Concord river flows sluggishly, in a serpentine direction, on the westerly and northerly side of the village, about half a mile from its centre. This river was crossed by two bridges, — one called the Old South Bridge — the other, by the Rev. William Emerson's, called the Old North Bridge. The road beyond the North Bridge led to Colonel James Barrett's, about two miles from the centre of the town.[1]

Dr. Samuel Prescott, whose escape has been related, gave the alarm in Lincoln and Concord. It was between one and two o'clock in the morning when the quiet community of Concord were aroused from their slumbers by the sounds of the church bell. The committee of safety, the military officers, and prominent citizens, assembled for consultation. Messengers were despatched towards Lexington for information; the militia and minute-men were formed on the customary parade-ground near the meeting-house; and the inhabitants, with a portion of the militia, under the able superintendence of Colonel Barrett, zealously labored in removing the military stores into the woods and by-places for safety. These scenes were novel and distressing; and among others, Reverend Wil-

---

[1] "There were at this time in this vicinity," Shattuck writes, "under rather imperfect organization, a regiment of militia, and a regiment of minute-men. The officers of the militia were, James Barrett, colonel; Ezekiel Howe, of Sudbury, lieutenant-colonel; Nathan Barrett and George Minot, of Concord; Joseph Robbins, of Acton; John Moore, of Bedford; Samuel Farrar, of Lincoln; and Moses Stone and Aaron Hayes, of Sudbury, captains. The officers of the minute-men were, Abijah Pierce, of Lincoln, colonel; Thomas Nixon, of Framingham, lieutenant-colonel; John Buttrick, of Concord, major; Jacob Miller, of Holliston, second major; Thomas Hurd, of East Sudbury, adjutant; David Brown and Isaac Davis, of Acton; William Smith, of Lincoln; Jonathan Wilson, of Bedford; John Nixon, of Sudbury, captains. There were also two small companies of horse, — one in Concord and one in Sudbury, — but they were out among the foot companies at this time." — History of Concord.

liam Emerson, the patriotic clergyman, mingled with the people, and gave counsel and comfort to the terrified women and children.

Reuben Brown, one of the messengers sent to obtain information, returned with the startling intelligence that the British regulars had fired upon his countrymen at Lexington, and were on their march for Concord.[1] It was determined to go out to meet them.[2]   A part of the military of Lincoln, -- the minute-men, under Captain William Smith, and the militia, under Captain Samuel Farrar, — had joined the Concord people; and after parading on the common, some of the companies marched down the Lexington road until they saw the British two miles from the centre of the town. Captain Minot, with the alarm company, remained in town, and took possession of the hill near the liberty pole.[3]   He had no sooner gained it, however, than the companies that had gone down the road returned with the information that the number of the British was treble that of the Americans. The whole then fell back to an eminence about eighty rods distance, back of the town, where they formed in two battalions.[4] Colonel Barrett, the commander, joined them here, having previously been engaged in removing the stores. They had scarcely formed, when the British troops appeared in sight at the distance of a quarter of a mile, and advancing with great celerity, — their arms glittering in the splendor of early sunshine. But little time remained for deliberation. Some were in favor of resisting the further approach of the troops; while others,

[1] Nathan Barrett and others, April 23, 1775, state, that they assembled "in consequence of an information that a number of regular troops had killed six of our countrymen at Lexington." See also depositions of John Hoar and others, of the same date. Emerson says: "We were the more cautious to prevent beginning a rupture with the king's troops, as we were then uncertain what had happened at Lexington, and knew (not) that they had began the quarrel there by firing upon our people, and killing eight men upon the spot." To emphasize "uncertain" and "had began," will make this harmonize with the depositions. Colonel Baldwin says in his diary that he heard the firing at Lexington, saw the men lay dead on the field, and then pressed on to Concord.

[2] Reverend William Emerson's Account, an excellent contemporary authority, part of it not discovered until 1835.   [3] Emerson and Ripley.   [4] Emerson; Clark's Narrative.

more prudent, advised a retreat and a delay until further rein·
forcements should arrive. Colonel Barrett ordered the militia
to retire over the North Bridge to a commanding eminence
about a mile from the centre of the town.[1]

The British troops then marched into Concord in two divisions; one by the main road, and the other on the hill north
of it, from which the Americans had just retired. They were
posted in the following manner. The grenadiers and light
infantry, under the immediate command of Colonel Smith,
remained in the centre of the town. Captain Parsons, with
six light companies, about two hundred men, was detached to
secure the North Bridge and to destroy stores, who stationed
three companies, under Captain Laurie, at the bridge, and
proceeded with the other three companies to the residence of
Colonel Barrett, about two miles distant, to destroy the magazines deposited there. Captain Pole, with a party, was sent,
for a similar purpose, to the South Bridge.[2] The British met
with but partial success in the work of destruction, in consequence of the diligent concealment of the stores. In the centre
of the town they broke open about sixty barrels of flour,
nearly half of which was subsequently saved; knocked off
the trunnions of three iron twenty-four pound cannon, and
burnt sixteen new carriage-wheels and a few barrels of
wooden trenchers and spoons. They cut down the liberty
pole, and set the court-house on fire, which was put out, however, by the exertions of Mrs. Moulton. The parties at the
South Bridge, and at Colonel Barrett's, met with poor success.
While engaged in this manner, the report of guns at the North
Bridge put a stop to their proceedings.[3]

The British troops had been in Concord about two hours.
During this time the minute-men from the neighboring towns
had been constantly arriving on the high grounds, a short distance from the North Bridge, until they numbered about four
hundred and fifty.[4] They were formed in line by Joseph
Hosmer, who acted as adjutant. It is difficult, if not impossible, to ascertain certainly what companies were present thus
early in the day. They came from Carlisle, from Chelmsford,

[1] Ripley; Emerson; Depositions of 1775. [2] British Account. [3] Emerson;
Shattuck's History; Clark's Narrative. [4] Ripley's History.

from Westford, from Littleton, and from Acton. The minute-men of Acton were commanded by Captain Isaac Davis, a brave and energetic man. Most of the operations of the British troops were visible from this place of rendezvous, and several fires were seen in the middle of the town. Anxious apprehensions were then felt for its fate. A consultation of officers, and of prominent citizens, was held. It was, probably, during this conference that Captain William Smith, of Lincoln, volunteered, with his company, to dislodge the British guard at the North Bridge.[1] Captain Isaac Davis, as he returned from it to his ranks, also remarked, "I have n't a man that 's afraid to go." The result of this council was, that it was expedient to dislodge the guard at the North Bridge.[2] Colonel Barrett, accordingly, ordered the militia to march to it, and to pass it, but not to fire on the king's troops unless they were fired upon. He designated Major John Buttrick to lead the companies to effect this object. Lieutenant-colonel Robinson volunteered to accompany him. On the march, Major Buttrick requested Colonel Robinson to act as his superior, but he generously declined.

It was nearly ten oclock in the morning, when the provincials, about three hundred in number,[3] arrived near the river. The company from Acton was in front, and Major Buttrick, Colonel Robinson, and Captain Davis, were at their head. Captains David Brown, Charles Miles, Nathan Barrett, and William Smith, with their companies, and also other companies, fell into the line. Their positions, however, are not precisely known.[4] They marched in double file, and with trailed

---

[1] Massachusetts Archives: "Lincoln, November, 1776. This may certify, that Captain William Smith, of Lincoln, in the County of Middlesex, appeared on Concord parade early in the morning of April 19, 1775, with his company of minute-men ; was ordered to leave his horse by the field officer, and take post on an adjacent hill, — the British troops possessing the North Bridge. He voluntarily offered, with his company, to endeavor to dislodge them, leaving his horse at the tavern ; by which means, on their retreat, the horse, &c., were carried off, with one of their wounded men. JOHN BUTTRICK, Major."

[2] William Smith's Petition, 1775. Gordon's Letter, May 17, 1775. [3] Depositions of 1775. [4] Ripley's History. See on the Acton company Adams' Address. Gordon says this company made the front.

arms.[1] The British guard, under Captain Laurie, about one hundred in number, were then on the west side of the river; but on seeing the provincials approach, they retired over the bridge to the east side of the river, formed as if for a fight, and began to take up the planks of the bridge.[2] Major Buttrick remonstrated against this, and ordered his men to hasten their march. When they had arrived within a few rods of the bridge, the British began to fire upon them. The first guns, few in number, did no execution; others followed with deadly effect. Luther Blanchard, a fifer in the Acton company, was first wounded; and afterwards Captain Isaac Davis and Abner Hosmer, of the same company, were killed.[3] On seeing the fire take effect, Major Buttrick exclaimed, "Fire, fellow-soldiers! for God's sake, fire!" The provincials then fired, and killed one and wounded several of the enemy. The fire lasted but few minutes. The British immediately retreated, in great confusion, towards the main body, — a detachment from which was soon on its way to meet them. The provincials pursued them over the bridge, when one of the wounded of the British was cruelly killed by a hatchet.[4] Part of the provincials soon turned to the left, and ascended the

---

[1] Letter in Concord paper, 1824. [2] Depositions of 1775.

[3] The evidence in relation to the firing is as follows. Emerson says: "We received the fire of the enemy in three several and separate discharges of their pieces, before it was returned by our commanding officer." Clark says: "Upon the provincials' approach towards the bridge, Captain Laurie's party fired upon them, killed Captain Davis and another man dead upon the spot, and wounded several others. Upon this, our militia rushed on,"&c. Gordon says, that Mr. Emerson saw the firing, and "was very uneasy till he found that the firing was returned." Colonel James Barrett, and four others, testify, (1775,) that two of the militia were killed, and several wounded, before the fire was returned. Captain Nathan Barrett, and twenty-three others, say, that "when we got near the bridge they fired on our men, first three guns, one after the other, and then a considerable number more; upon which, and not before, we fired upon the regulars, and they retreated," — without saying that any were killed. Adams, in his Centennial, discusses this question with acuteness.

[4] This barbarous deed gave rise to the British charge, that the Americans scalped the wounded, and cut off their ears. Mr. Emerson gave Gordon an account of it at the time, with great concern for its having happened. It was the act of a young man, who killed the soldier as he was attempting to get up.

hill on the east of the main road, while another portion
returned to the high grounds, carrying with them the remains

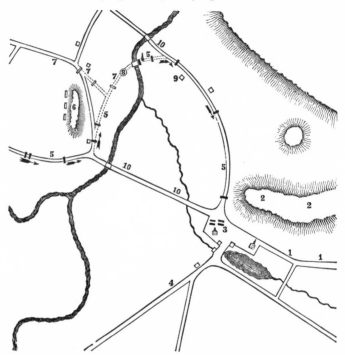

of the gallant Davis and Hosmer.   Military order was broken,
and many, who had been on duty all the morning and were

[1] Lexington road.

[2] Hill and high lands where the liberty pole stood.

[3] Centre of the town, and main body of the British.

[4] Road to the South Bridge.

[5] Road to the North Bridge, and to Colonel Barrett's, two miles from the
centre of the town.

[6] High grounds a mile north of the meeting-house, where the militia
assembled.

[7] Road along which they marched to dislodge the British at North Bridge.

[8] Spot where Davis and Hosmer fell.

[9] Reverend Mr. Emerson's house.

[10] Bridges and roads made in 1793, when the old roads, with dotted lines,
were discontinued.

Arrow.   Return of Captain Parsons, after the firing at the North Bridge.

hungry and fatigued, improved the time to take refreshment. Meantime, the party under Captain Parsons — who was piloted by Ensign D'Berniere — returned from Captain Barrett's house, re-passed the bridge where the skirmish took place, and saw the bodies of their companions, — one of which was mangled. It would have been easy for the provincials to have cut them off. But war had not been declared ; and it is evident that it had not been fully resolved to attack the British troops.   Hence, this party of about one hundred were allowed, unmolested, to join the main body.   Colonel Smith concentrated his force, obtained conveyances for the wounded, and occupied about two hours in making preparations to return to Boston, — a delay that nearly proved fatal to the whole detachment.[1]

While these great events[2] were occurring at Lexington and Concord, the intelligence of the hostile march of the British troops was spreading rapidly through the country ; and hundreds of local communities, animated by the same determined and patriotic spirit, were sending out their representatives to the battle-field.   The minute-men, organized and ready for action, promptly obeyed the summons to parade.   They might wait, in some instances, to receive a parting blessing from their minister, or to take leave of weeping friends ;[3] but in all the

---

The time occupied by the British troops was nearly as follows : Left Boston at half-past ten, P. M., on the 18th, (British accounts,) — arrived at Lexington at half-past four, A. M., on the 19th, (Gordon,) — halted twenty minutes, (Phinney,) — arrived at Concord at seven, (Barrett's deposition, 1775, "about an hour after sunrise,") — the firing at the bridge was between nine and ten, (Brown's diary, in Adams, and deposition No. 18, 1775, "nearly ten,") — the troops left Concord at twelve, (British accounts, Clark,) — they met Percy's brigade at two, (British letters,) — arrived at Charlestown at sunset.

[2] Samuel Adams heard the volley of musketry at Lexington that commenced the war of the revolution.   It was in view of the inevitable train of consequences that would result from this, that he exclaimed, " O, what a glorious morning is this ! "

[3] King's Danvers Address, p. 11.   In Dedham, besides the minute-men, there was a company of veterans who had been in the French wars.   On the alarm reaching this town, they assembled on the green in front of the church, where Reverend William Gordon stood on the steps, and invoked the blessing of Heaven on their enterprise.   " The gray-headed warriors then began their

roads leading to Concord, they were hurrying to the scene of
action.   They carried the firelock that had fought the Indian,
and the drum that beat at Louisburg; and they were led by
men who had served under Wolfe at Quebec.   As they drew
near the places of bloodshed and massacre, they learned that,
in both cases, the regulars had been the aggressors, — "had
fired the first," — and they were deeply touched by the slaughter of their brethren.[1]   Now the British had fairly passed the
Rubicon.   If any still counselled forbearance, moderation,
peace, the words were thrown away.   The assembling bands
felt that the hour had come in which to hurl back the insulting charges on their courage that had been repeated for years,
and to make good the solemn words of their public bodies.
And they determined to attack on their return the invaders
of their native soil.

Colonel Smith, about twelve o'clock, commenced his march
for Boston.   His left was covered by a strong flank guard that
kept the height of land that borders the Lexington road, leading to Merriam's Corner; his right was protected by a brook ;
the main body marched in the road.   The British soon saw
how thoroughly the country had been alarmed.   It seemed,
one of them writes, that "men had dropped from the clouds,"
so full were the hills and roads of the minute-men.   The provincials left the high grounds near the North Bridge and went
across the pastures known as "the great fields," to Bedford
road.   Here the Reading minute-men, under Major Brooks,
afterwards Governor Brooks, joined them; and a few minutes
after, Colonel William Thompson, with a body of militia from
Billerica and vicinity, came up.   It is certain, from the diaries
and petitions of this period, that minute-men from other towns
also came up in season to fire upon the British while leaving
Concord.

Rev. Mr. Foster, who was with the Reading company,
relates the beginning of the afternoon contest in the following
manner: "A little before we came to Merriam's Hill, we
discovered the enemy's flank guard, of about eighty or one

march, leaving the town, almost literally, without a male inhabitant below
the age of seventy and above that of sixteen." — Haven's Historical Address.

[1] Tay's petition.

hundred men, who, on their retreat from Concord, kept that
height of land, the main body in the road. The British troops
and the Americans, at that time, were equally distant from
Merriam's Corner. About twenty rods short of that place, the
Americans made a halt. The British marched down the hill,
with very slow but steady step, without music, or a word
being spoken that could be heard. Silence reigned on both
sides. As soon as the British had gained the main road, and
passed a small bridge near that corner, they faced about
suddenly, and fired a volley of musketry upon us. They
overshot; and no one, to my knowledge, was injured by the
fire. The fire was immediately returned by the Americans,
and two British soldiers fell dead, at a little distance from each
other, in the road, near the brook." [1]

The battle now began in earnest, and as the British troops
retreated, a severe fire was poured in upon them from every
favorable position. Near Hardy's Hill, the Sudbury company,
led by Captain Nathaniel Cudworth,[2] attacked them, and there
was a severe skirmish below the Brooks tavern, on the old
road, north of the school-house. The woods lined both sides
of the road which the British had to pass, and it was filled
with the minute-men. "The enemy," says Mr. Foster, "was
now completely between two fires, renewed and briskly
kept up. They ordered out a flank guard on the left, to
dislodge the Americans from their posts behind large trees, but
they only became a better mark to be shot at." A short and
sharp battle ensued. And for three or four miles along these
woody defiles the British suffered terribly. Woburn had
" turned out extraordinary;" it sent out a force one hundred
and eighty strong, " well armed and resolved in defence of the
common cause." Major Loammi Baldwin, afterwards Colonel Baldwin, was with this body. At Tanner Brook, at
Lincoln Bridge, they concluded to scatter, make use of the
trees and walls as defences, and thus attack the British. And
in this way they kept on pursuing and flanking them.[3] In
Lincoln, also, Captain Parker's brave Lexington company
again appeared in the field, and did efficient service. " The

<hr />

[1] Ripley's History. [2] Mass. Archives. [3] Tay's Petition and Baldwin's
Diary. I am indebted to George R. Baldwin, Esq., for the Ms. Diary.

enemy," says Colonel Baldwin, "marched very fast, and left many dead and wounded, and a few tired." Eight were buried in Lincoln grave-yard. It was at this time that Captain Jonathan Wilson, of Bedford, Nathaniel Wyman, of Billerica, and Daniel Thompson, of Woburn, were killed.

In Lexington, at Fiske's Hill, an officer on a fine horse, with a drawn sword in his hand, was actively engaged in directing the troops, when a number of the pursuers, from behind a pile of rails, fired at him with effect. The officer fell, and the horse, in affright, leaped the wall, and ran towards those who had fired. It was here that Lieut-col. Smith was severely wounded in the leg. At the foot of this hill, a personal contest between James Hayward, of Acton, and a British soldier took place. The Briton drew up his gun, remarking, "You are a dead man!" "And so are you!" answered Hayward. The former was killed. Hayward was mortally wounded, and died the next day.[1]

The British troops, when they arrived within a short distance of Lexington meeting-house, again suffered severely from the close pursuit and the sharp fire of the provincials. Their ammunition began to fail, while their light companies were so fatigued as to be almost unfitted for service. The large number of wounded created confusion, and many of the troops rather ran than marched in order. For some time the officers in vain tried to restore discipline. They saw the confusion increase under their efforts, until, at last, they placed themselves in front, and threatened the men with death if they advanced. This desperate exertion, made under a heavy fire, partially restored order. The detachment, however, must have soon surrendered, had it not, in its extreme peril, found shelter in the hollow square of a reinforcement sent to their relief.[2]

[1] Shattuck; Foster; Essex Gazette; Ripley.

[2] British accounts admit that the position of Colonel Smith, when Percy joined him, was very critical. Lieut. Carter, in his letters, says: "The consequences must have proved far more serious, had not a brigade, under the command of Lord Percy, marched to our support." Other accounts admit that the detachment must have surrendered. These accounts err as much in making the numbers of the provincials too large, as some of the American accounts do in making them too small. Thus, one letter says, April 30: "It

General Gage received, early in the morning, a request from Colonel Smith for a reinforcement. About nine o'clock he detached three regiments of infantry and two divisions of marines, with two field-pieces, under Lord Percy, to support the grenadiers and light infantry. Lord Percy marched through Roxbury, to the tune of Yankee Doodle, to the great alarm of the country. To prevent or to impede his march, the selectmen of Cambridge had the planks of the Old Bridge, over which he was obliged to pass, taken up; but instead of being removed, they were piled on the causeway on the Cambridge side of the river. Hence, Lord Percy found no difficulty in replacing them so as to admit his troops to cross. But a convoy of provisions was detained until it was out of the protection of the main body. This was captured at West Cambridge. According to Gordon, Rev. Dr. Payson led this party. David Lamson, a half Indian, distinguished himself in the

was thought there were about six thousand at first, and at night double that number." Another letter says: "The rebels were monstrous numerous, and surrounded us on every side; when they came up we gave them a smart fire, but they never would engage us properly." Another says: "As we came along, they got before us, and fired at us out of the houses, and killed and wounded a great number of us, but we levelled their houses as we came along." Bernicre says that Captain Laurie was attacked "by about fifteen thousand rebels," and yet "they let Captain Parsons, with his company, return, and never attacked us."

The Conduct of the American War states: "Lieutenant-colonel Smith's party would have been destroyed had not Lord Percy joined him, and even he was almost too late, from two stupid blunders we committed. The general ordered the first brigade under arms at four in the morning; these orders, the evening before, were carried to the brigade major's; he was not at home; the orders were left; no inquiry was made after him; he came home late; his servant forgot to tell him there was a letter on his table; four o'clock came; no brigade appeared; at five o'clock an express from Smith, desiring a reinforcement, produced an inquiry; the above discovery was made; at six o'clock part of the brigade got on the parade; there they waited, expecting the marines; at seven, no marines appearing, another inquiry commenced; they said they had received no orders; it was asserted they had; in the altercation it came out that the order had been addressed to Major Pitcairn, who commanded the marines, and left at his quarters, though the gentlemen concerned in this business ought to have recollected that Pitcairn had been despatched the evening before, with the grenadiers and light infantry, under Lieut-col. Smith. This double mistake lost us from four till nine o'clock, the time we marched off to support Col. Smith."

affair. Percy's brigade met the harassed and retreating troops about two o'clock, within half a mile of the Lexington meeting-house. "They were so much exhausted with fatigue," the British historian, Stedman, writes, "that they were obliged to lie down for rest on the ground, their tongues hanging out of their mouths, like those of dogs after a chase." The field-pieces from the high ground below Monroe's tavern played on the provincials, and for a short period there was, save the discharge of cannon, a cessation of battle. From this time, however, the troops committed the most wanton destruction. Three houses, two shops and a barn, were laid in ashes in Lexington; buildings on the route were defaced and plundered, and individuals were grossly abused.

At this time, Dr. Warren and General Heath were active in the field, directing and encouraging the militia. General Heath was one of the generals who were authorized to take the command when the minute-men should be called out. On his way to the scene of action, he ordered the militia of Cambridge to make a barricade of the planks of the bridge, take post there, and oppose the retreat of the British in that direction to Boston. At Lexington, when the minute-men were somewhat checked and scattered by Percy's field-pieces, he labored to form them into military order. Dr. Warren, about ten o'clock, rode on horseback through Charlestown. He had received by express intelligence of the events of the morning, and told the citizens of Charlestown that the news of the firing was true. Among others, he met Dr. Welsh, who said, "Well, they are gone out." "Yes," replied the Dr., "and we'll be up with them before night."

Lord Percy had now under his command about eighteen hundred troops, of undoubted bravery and of veteran discipline. He evinced no disposition, however, to turn upon his assailants, and make good the insulting boasts of his associates. After a short interval of rest and refreshment, the British recommenced their retreat. Then the provincials renewed their attack. In West Cambridge the skirmishing again became sharp and bloody, and the troops increased their atrocities. Jason Russell, an invalid and a non-combatant, was barbarously butchered in his own house. In this town a mother was killed while nursing her child. Others were driven from their dwellings, and their dwellings were pillaged. Here the Danvers company, which marched in advance of the Essex regiment, met the enemy. Some took post in a walled enclosure, and made a breastwork of bundles of shingles; others planted themselves behind trees on the side of the hill west of the meeting-house. The British came along in solid column on their right, while a large flank guard came up on their left. The Danvers men were surrounded, and many were killed and wounded.[1] Here Samuel Whittemore was shot and bayoneted, and left for dead. Here Dr. Eliphalet Downer, in single combat with a soldier, killed him with a bayonet. Here a musket ball struck a pin out of the hair of Dr. Warren's earlock.[2] The wanton destruction of life and property that marked the course of the invaders, added revenge to the natural bravery of the minute-men. "Indignation and outraged humanity struggled on the one hand; veteran discipline and desperation on the other."[3] The British had many struck in West Cambridge, and left an officer wounded in the house still standing at the railroad depot.[4]

[1] Address of Hon. D. P. King. [2] Heath's Memoirs. [3] Hon. Edward Everett.

[4] Dr. Eliot remarks of Dr. Warren, — " At the battle of Lexington he was, perhaps, the most active man in the field. His soul beat to arms, as soon as he learnt the intention of the British troops." He said to the last person with whom he conversed in Boston, near the ferry, just as he was about crossing, in reply to a question about the political aspect : " Keep up a brave heart. They have begun it — that either party could do ; and we 'll end it — that only one can do." A poem was printed in Boston, 1781, by John Boyle, entitled, " An Eulogium on Major-general Joseph Warren, by a Columbian." After describing the march of the troops to Concord, the alarm, the retreat, and the rescue by Lord Percy, the author thus describes the feats on the " Plain," at West Cambridge :

> " Again the conflict glows with rage severe,
> And fearless ranks in combat mixt appear.
> Victory uncertain ! fierce contention reigns,
> And purple rivers drench the slippery plains.
> Column to column, host to host oppose,
> And rush impetuous on their adverse foes,
> When lo ! the hero Warren from afar
> Sought for the battle, and the field of war.

The British troops took the road that winds round Prospect Hill. When they entered this part of Charlestown their situation was critical. The large number of the wounded proved a distressing obstruction to their progress, while they had but few rounds of ammunition left. Their field-pieces had lost their terror. The main body of the provincials hung closely on their rear; a strong force was advancing upon them from Roxbury, Dorchester, and Milton; while Colonel Pickering, with the Essex militia, seven hundred strong, threatened to cut off their retreat to Charlestown.[1] Near Prospect Hill the fire again became sharp, and the British again had recourse to their field-pieces. James Miller, of Charlestown, was killed here. Along its base, Lord Percy, it is stated, received the hottest fire he had during his retreat. General Gage, about sunset, might have beheld his harassed troops, almost on the run, coming down the old Cambridge road to Charlestown Neck, anxious to get under the protection of the guns of

> From rank to rank the daring warrior flies,
> And bids the thunder of the battle rise.
> Sudden arrangements of his troops are made,
> And sudden movements round the plain displayed.
> Columbia's Genius in her polished shield
> Gleams bright, and dreadful o'er the hostile field !
> Her ardent troops, enraptured with the sight,
> With shock resistless force the dubious fight.
> Britons, astonished, tremble at the sight,
> And, all confused, precipitate their flight.

[1] Dr. Welsh, who was on Prospect Hill when the British went by, saw Colonel Pickering's regiment on the top of Winter Hill, near the front of Mr Adams' house, the enemy being very near in Charlestown road. Washington writes, May 31, 1775 : " If the retreat had not been as precipitate as it was, — and God knows it could not well have been more so, — the ministerial troops must have surrendered, or been totally cut off. For they had not arrived in Charlestown, (under cover of their ships,) half an hour, before a powerful body of men from Marblehead and Salem was at their heels, and must, if they had happened to be up one hour sooner, inevitably have intercepted their retreat to Charlestown." — Sparks' Washington, vol. II., p. 407.

Dr. Welsh says that cannon fired occasionally. The troops kept up a steady fire. A Ms. letter of Mr. W. B. Shedd states that in a house now in Somerville, at the foot of Prospect Hill, a regular was found, on the return of the inmates, laying across the draw of a secretary, dead, having been shot through the window as he was pilfering.

the ships of war. The minute-men closely followed, but when they reached the Charlestown Common, General Heath ordered them to stop the pursuit.

Charlestown, throughout the day, presented a scene of intense excitement and great confusion. It was known early in the morning that the regulars were out. Rumors soon arrived of the events that had occurred at Lexington. The schools were dismissed, and citizens gathered in groups in the streets.[1] After Dr. Warren rode through the town, and gave the certain intelligence of the slaughter at Lexington, a large number went out to the field, and the greater part who remained were women and children. Hon. James Russell received, in the afternoon, a note from General Gage, to the effect, that he had been informed that citizens had gone out armed to oppose his majesty's troops, and that if a single man more went out armed, the most disagreeable consequences might be expected. It was next reported, and correctly, that Cambridge Bridge had been taken up, and that hence the regulars would be obliged to return to Boston through the town. Many then prepared to leave, and every vehicle was employed to carry away their most valuable effects. Others, however, still believing the troops would return the way they went out, determined to remain, and in either event to abide the worst. Just before sunset the noise of distant firing was heard, and soon the British troops were seen in the Cambridge road. The inhabitants then rushed towards the Neck. Some crossed Mystic River, at Penny Ferry. Some ran along the marsh, towards Medford. The troops, however, soon approached the town, firing as they came along. A lad, Edward Barber, was killed on the Neck. The inhabitants then turned back into the town, panic-struck. Word ran through the crowd that

[1] The late Dr. Prince, of Salem, used to relate, that as he was standing with a party of armed men at Charlestown Neck, a person enveloped in a cloak rode up on horseback, inquired the news, and passed on ; but he immediately put spur to his horse, and the animal started forward so suddenly as to cause the rider to raise his arms, throw up the cloak, and thus reveal a uniform. The men instantly levelled their guns to fire, when Dr. Prince struck them up, exclaiming, "Don't fire at him — he is my friend Small, a fine fellow." It was Major Small, an express from the army, who got safe into Boston.

"The Britons were massacring the women and children!"
Some remained in the streets, speechless with terror; some ran
to the clay-pits, back of Breed's Hill, where they passed the
night. The troops, however, offered no injury to the inhabitants. Their officers directed the women and children, half-
distracted with fright, to go into their houses, and they would
be safe, but requested them to hand out drink to the troops.
The main body occupied Bunker Hill, and formed a line
opposite the Neck. Additional troops also were sent over
from Boston. The officers flocked to the tavern in the square,
where the cry was for drink. Guards were stationed in various parts of the town. One was placed at the Neck, with
orders to permit no one to go out. Everything, during the
night, was quiet.[1] Some of the wounded were carried over
immediately, in the boats of the Somerset,[2] to Boston. General Pigot had the command in Charlestown the next day,
when the troops all returned to their quarters.

The Americans lost forty-nine killed, thirty-nine wounded,
and five missing.[3] A committee of the Provincial Congress

[1] Of the notices of the arrival of the troops in Charlestown, I select the
following. The Salem Gazette, April 25, says : The consternation of the
people of Charlestown, when our enemies were entering the town, is inex-
pressible ; the troops, however, behaved tolerably civil, and the people have
since nearly all left the town. Stiles, in his diary, April 24, 1775, writes :
" In the afternoon of the same day, by order of General Gage, a proclamation was read to the inhabitants of Charlestown, purporting that he would lay
that town in ashes if they obstructed the king's troops." Clark says : The
firing continued, " with but little intermission, to the close of the day, when
the troops entered Charlestown, where the provincials could not follow them,
without exposing the worthy inhabitants of that truly patriotic town to their
rage and revenge." Jacob Rogers' petition gives a minute detail of the
town during the evening.

[2] On the 14th of April, the Somerset man-of-war, of sixty-four guns, was
hauled into Charles River, and now lays between the ferry ways. — Essex
Gazette, April 18.

[3] Several lists of the killed and wounded were published in the journals of
the day. One of them was corrected by John Farmer, and was published
in the Mass. Hist. Collections, vol. xviii. I have added a few names.

Lexington. — Killed, Jonas Parker, Robert Monroe, Samuel Hadley, Jonathan Harrington, jr., Isaac Muzzy, Caleb Harrington, John Brown, Jedediah Monroe, John Raymond, Nathaniel Wyman, 10. Wounded, John
Robbins, Solomon Pierce, John Tidd, Joseph Comee, Ebenezer Monroe, jr.,

estimated the value of the property destroyed by the ravages of the troops, to be — in Lexington, £1761 15s. 5d.; in Concord, £274 16s. 7d.; in Cambridge, £1202 8s. 7d. Many petitions of persons who engaged the enemy on this day are on file. They lost guns or horses, or suffered other damage. The General Court indemnified such losses.

Thomas Winship, Nathaniel Farmer, Prince Estabrook, Jedediah Monroe, Francis Brown, 10.

Concord. — Wounded, Charles Miles, Nathan Barrett, Abel Prescott, jr., Jonas Brown, George Minot, 5.

Cambridge. — Killed, William Marcy, Moses Richardson, John Hicks, Jason Russell, Jabez Wyman, Jason Winship, 6. Wounded, Samuel Whittemore, 1. Missing, Samuel Frost, Seth Russell, 2.

Needham. — Killed, John Bacon, Elisha Mills, Amos Mills, Nathaniel Chamberlain, Jonathan Parker, 5. Wounded, Eleazer Kingsbury, —— Tolman, 2.

Sudbury. — Killed, Josiah Haynes, Asahel Reed, 2. Wounded, Joshua Haynes, jr., 1.

Acton. — Killed, Isaac Davis, Abner Hosmer, James Hayward, 3. Wounded, Luther Blanchard, 1.

Bedford. — Killed, Jonathan Wilson, 1. Wounded, Job Lane, 1.

Woburn. — Killed, Daniel Thompson, Asahel Porter, 2. Wounded, George Reed, Jacob Bacon, —— Johnson, 3.

Medford. — Killed, Henry Putnam, William Polly, 2.

Charlestown. — Killed, James Miller, Edward Barber, 2.

Watertown. — Killed, Joseph Coolidge, 1.

Framingham. — Wounded, Daniel Hemminway, 1.

Dedham. — Killed, Elias Haven, 1. Wounded, Israel Everett, 1.

Stow. — Wounded, Daniel Conant, 1.

Roxbury. — Missing, Elijah Seaver, 1.

Brookline. — Killed, Isaac Gardner, 1.

Billerica. — Wounded, John Nichols, Timothy Blanchard, 2.

Chelmsford. — Wounded, Aaron Chamberlain, Oliver Barron, 2.

Salem. — Killed, Benjamin Pierce, 1.

Newton. — Wounded, Noah Wiswell, 1.

Danvers. — Killed, Henry Jacobs, Samuel Cook, Ebenezer Goldthwait, George Southwick, Benjamin Deland, Jotham Webb, Perley Putnam, 7. Wounded, Nathan Putnam, Dennis Wallace, 2. Missing, Joseph Bell, 1

Beverly. — Killed, Reuben Kennison, 1. Wounded, Nathaniel Cleves, Samuel Woodbury, William Dodge, 3d, 3.

Lynn. — Killed, Abednego Ramsdell, Daniel Townsend, William Flint, Thomas Hadley, 4. Wounded, Joshua Felt, Timothy Monroe, 2. Missing, Josiah Breed, 1.

Total. — Killed, 49. Wounded, 39. Missing, 5. = 93.

The British lost seventy-three killed, one hundred and seventy-four wounded, and twenty-six missing, — the most of whom were taken prisoners. Of these, eighteen were officers, ten sergeants, two drummers, and two hundred and forty were rank and file. Lieutenant Hall, wounded at the North Bridge, was taken prisoner on the retreat, and died the next day. His remains were delivered to General Gage. Lieutenant Gould was wounded at the bridge, and taken prisoner, and was exchanged, May 28, for Josiah Breed, of Lynn. He had a fortune of £1900 a year, and is said to have offered £2000 for his ransom. The prisoners were treated with great humanity, and General Gage was notified that his own surgeons, if he desired it, might dress the wounded.

In Lexington, the anniversary of the battle was appropriately noticed for several years. In 1776, Rev. Jonas Clark delivered the sermon, which was printed. Seven sermons, by Reverends Samuel Cook, 1777, Jacob Cushing, 1778, Samuel Woodward, 1779, Isaac Morrill, 1780, Henry Cummings, 1781, Phillips Payson, 1782, and Zabdiel Adams, in 1783, were also published. The Legislature granted four hundred dollars to build a monument in this town; and hence the one erected in 1779 states it was erected by the town, "under the patronage, and at the expense, of the commonwealth," to the memory of the eight men who fell at the fire of the British troops. It is of granite, twenty feet high, stands near the place where they were killed, and bears an inscription written by Rev. Jonas Clark. In 1825, Major Elias Phinney prepared a history of the battle, and in 1835, Hon. Edward Everett delivered an oration on the anniversary.

In Concord, a monument has been erected near the place where the two soldiers, who were killed on the bridge, were buried. In 1824, the Bunker Hill Monument Association appropriated five hundred dollars to build one in this town; and at its suggestion, the corner stone, in 1825, was laid, with great parade. Sixty of the survivors joined in the celebration. Hon. Edward Everett delivered the address. Subsequently this association pledged one thousand dollars more for the purpose of securing the completion of this monument

In 1827, Dr. Ripley and others published "A History of the Fight at Concord."

In Danvers, on Monday, April 20, 1835, the corner-stone was laid of a monument to the memory of seven of its citizens, who fell on that day. General Gideon Foster, one of the survivors, made the address at the site of the monument, in which he stated that over a hundred of his townsmen went with him to the field this day. A procession proceeded to the church, where an address was delivered by Hon. Daniel P. King.

In West Cambridge, a monument was erected, June 24, 1848, over the remains of twelve of the patriots slain on this day, — the names of only three of whom, belonging to what is now West Cambridge, are known, viz: Jason Russell, Jason Winship, and Jabez Wyman. The twelve were buried in a common grave. Their remains were disinterred, and placed in a stone vault, now under the monument, April 22, 1848. This is a simple granite obelisk, nineteen feet in height, enclosed by a neat iron fence. It was done by the voluntary contributions of the citizens of West Cambridge.[1]

The work so worthy of commemoration — THE COMMENCEMENT OF THE WAR OF THE AMERICAN REVOLUTION — cannot be satisfactorily accounted for, without taking into view previous effort. Nothing is clearer than that it obeyed the great law of production. It was the result of labor. It took the people years of deliberation to arrive at the point of forcible resistance; and after this point had been reached, it took months of steady preparation to meet such a crisis worthily. This crisis did not come unexpected, nor was it left to shift for itself when it did come. The leading patriots were not quite so dull and rash as to leave this unprovided for. They were men of sound common sense, who well discerned the signs of the times. If they trusted to the inherent goodness of their cause, they also looked sharp to have their powder dry. Individual volunteers, it is true, appeared on this day in the field. But still the power that was so successful against a body of British veterans of undoubted bravery, finely officered and

---

[1] Hon. James Russell, Ms. letter, who took a prominent part in this patriotic work.

finely disciplined, that twice put them in imminent peril of
entire capture, was not an armed mob, made up of individuals,
who, on a new-born impulse, aroused by the sudden sound of
the tocsin, seized their rusty firelocks, and rushed to the
"tented field." But it was an organized power, made up of
militia who had associated themselves — often by written
agreements — to meet such an exigence; who had been disciplined [1] to meet it, who were expected to meet it, and who
had been warned [2] that it was close at hand. They were the
minute-men. It is enough to say, that they came so near up
to their own ideal of hazardous duty, and to the high expectation of their fellow-patriots, as to win praise from friend and
foe. [3] They did a thorough, a necessary, and an immortal
work. They should have the credit of it. This battle should
be called THE BATTLE OF THE MINUTE-MEN.

The effect of the news of the commencement of hostilities,
both in the colonies and in Great Britain, was very great.

In the colonies the intelligence spread with wonderful rapidity. In almost every community in New England, on its
reception, the minute-men rushed to arms. Hundreds of the
muster-rolls — thousands of individual accounts of the soldiers of the revolution — date from "The Lexington Alarm."
And the same spirit prevailed out of New England. Nothing
could exceed the shock which it gave to the public mind. To
detail, however, the manner in which it was received throughout the colonies, would be foreign to the purpose of this
work. In every quarter the people assembled, and prepared
to join their brethren of Massachusetts in defence of their liberties. [4]

---

[1] The discipline described, pages 42—3, continued to this day. Thus
Rev. Mr. Emerson, March 13, at a review in Concord, preached to the
minute-men. Rev. Mr. Marett writes in his diary, April 4 : Rode to Reading, and heard Mr. Stone preach a sermon to the minute-men. On the 19th,
he writes : Fair, windy, and cold.

[2] See the order of the Provincial Congress, page 54. [3] "Lord Percy said
at table, he never saw anything equal to the intrepidity of the New England
minute-men." — Remembrancer, vol. i., 111.

[4] It was the battle of Lexington that elicited, in North Carolina, the Meck-
lenburg County series of Resolves, about which so much has been written.
This Proceeding is alluded to in the journals of the time. Thus the Penn-

In Massachusetts the leading patriots regarded it to be important to present, as early as possible, an accurate account of the events of the day to the people of England. The Provincial Congress, which was immediately summoned, appointed, on the day of its meeting, April 22, a committee to take depositions in relation to the transactions of the troops in their route to and from Concord. On the next day Doctor Church, Mr. Gerry, and Mr. Cushing, were appointed a committee to draw up a "narrative of the massacre." The committee on depositions, on the 23d and 25th of April, held sessions at Concord and Lexington, and took a large number of affidavits. On the 25th, a letter was read in Congress, urging the expediency of sending an account immediately to England. On the 26th, a committee, consisting of the president, Doctor Warren, Mr. Freeman, Mr. Gardner, and Colonel Stone, were chosen to prepare a letter to the colonial agent. This committee, on the same day, reported the letter, and an account of the battle, addressed "To the Inhabitants of Great Britain;" and the committee of supplies was ordered to send these papers, with others in preparation, to England. This committee engaged the Hon. Richard Derby,[1] of Salem, to fit out his vessel as a packet. This vessel arrived in London on the 29th of May, and carried, besides the official papers, copies of the Essex Gazette, containing the published accounts of the events of the day. The address,

sylvania Ledger, November 4, 1775, contains Governor Martin's proclamation, which reviews it, and denounces it. The point of actual forcible resistance had been reached in Massachusetts nine months previous. To go further back, the bold Abington resolves of 1770, declaring acts of Parliament "a mere nullity," produced a great effect through the colonies. They were a virtual declaration of independence. Other towns were equally bold.

[1] The order to Captain Derby was as follows: — In Committee of Safety, April 27, 1775. Resolved, That Captain Derby be directed, and he hereby is directed, to make for Dublin, or any other good port in Ireland, and from thence to cross to Scotland or England, and hasten to London. This direction is given, that so he may escape all cruisers that may be in the chops of the channel, to stop the communication of the provincial intelligence to the agent. He will forthwith deliver his papers to the agent on reaching London. J. WARREN, Chairman. P. S. — You are to keep this order a profound secret from every person on earth.

after a brief relation of the battle, and of the outrages of the troops, stated, that these "marks of ministerial vengeance had not yet detached us from our royal sovereign ;" that the colonists were still ready to "defend his person, family, crown, and dignity ;" that they would not tamely submit to the persecution and tyranny of this cruel ministry, but, appealing to Heaven for the justice of their cause, they were determined to die or be free ; and in closing said, that in a constitutional connection with the mother country, they hoped soon to be altogether a free and happy people.[1] In the letter to the agent, he is requested to have the papers printed, and dispersed through every town in England. Accordingly, on the day after the arrival of Captain Derby, the address was printed and circulated, and gave the first intelligence of the battle of Lexington and Concord to the British public.

The news was astounding. The government had information of the state of things in America that was accurate, but it refused to credit it. Speeches were made in Parliament portraying the consequences of political measures with a foresight and precision that to-day appear wonderful, but the ministry listened to them with dull ears. It preferred to rely on representations from the colonies, made by adherents of the government blinded by passion or swayed by interest, or on language in Parliament dictated by ignorance or pride, which described the great patriot party as a mere faction, and the colonists as cowards, and five thousand regulars as invincible. Hence, they looked to see their imposing military and naval preparations strike fear into "a rude rabble," and produce submission. Such ignorance and expectation were shared by the British nation. How great, then, was the astonishment to hear that a collection of country people, hastily assembled, had compelled the veterans of England to retreat to their strong holds ! The news agitated London to its centre. It engrossed the attention of all classes. It seemed not merely improbable, but almost incredible.

On learning the intelligence, the government, which had received no despatches, issued the following card : —

---

[1] This address appeared in the London Chronicle for May 27—30.

" Secretary of State's Office, Whitehall, May 30, 1775.

"A report having been spread, and an account having been printed and published, of a skirmish between some of the people in the province of the Massachusetts Bay, and a detachment of his majesty's troops, it is proper to inform the public, that no advices have as yet been received in the American department of any such event.

"There is reason to believe that there are despatches from General Gage on board the Sukey, Capt. Brown, which, though she sailed four days before the vessel that brought the printed accounts, is not yet arrived."

Arthur Lee immediately issued the following note : — [1]

"TO THE PUBLIC.

"*Tuesday, May* 30, 1775.

"As a doubt of the authenticity of the account from Salem, touching an engagement between the king's troops and the provincials, in the Massachusetts Bay, may arise from a paragraph in the Gazette of this evening, I desire to inform all those who wish to see the original affidavits which confirm that account, that they are deposited at the Mansion House, with the right honorable the Lord Mayor, for their inspection.

"ARTHUR LEE,

"*Agent for the House of Representatives of the Massachusetts Bay.*"

General Gage's despatches did not arrive until eleven days after the arrival of Captain Derby. The excitement on their reception increased. The clamor against the ministers grew louder, because it was presumed that they concealed the official accounts, and intended to keep the people in ignorance. As soon, however, as General Gage's report reached Whitehall, on the 10th of June, it was published. This account was severely criticised in the journals, while Lord Dartmouth, in

---

[1] This note was published in the London Chronicle for June 1, 1775 Some of the affidavits appear in full in this number. The original papers are now in Harvard College Library. Captain Derby declined to go to Lord Dartmouth's office. Mr. De Berdt communicated to the minister the details. ' He was too much affected to say much," writes Mr. De Berdt.

a letter to General Gage, dated July 1, hesitates to approve of the step, which was certainly warranted, if not expressly commanded, in his previous despatches, and which was only carrying out his idea of disarming the province.[1] " I am to presume that the measure of sending out a detachment of troops to destroy the magazines at Concord was taken after the fullest consideration of the advantages on the one hand, and hazards on the other, of such an enterprise, and of all the probable consequences that were to result from it. It is impossible for me to reflect upon this transaction, and upon all its consequences, without feelings, which, although I do not wish to conceal them, it is not necessary for me to express; but I believe every man of candor will agree with me in opinion, that, let the event be what it may, the rashness and rebellious conduct of the provincials on this occasion evince the necessity, and will manifest to all the world the justice, of the measures which the king has adopted for supporting the constitution, and in which his majesty will firmly persevere."

The excitement was not allayed by the publication of the official despatches. The ministry, in virtually asking a suspension of judgment until their arrival, evidently hoped that the American narrative might prove fictitious, or at least might be exaggerated. Gage's account, however, substantially agreed with it. It admitted that a people who had been represented as " too cowardly ever to face the regulars," had attacked the king's troops: it admitted the galling annoyance,

----

[1] Extracts from Lord Dartmouth's letters to General Gage, already given, show how positive were the instructions sent to direct the conduct of the governor. In a letter, dated April 15, 1775, on its way to Boston when the battle was fought, Lord Dartmouth says : " It would appear necessary and expedient, that all fortifications should be garrisoned by the king's troops, or dismantled and destroyed ; that all cannon, small arms, and military stores of every kind, that may be either in any magazine, or secreted for the purpose of aiding the rebellion, should also be seized and secreted ; and that the persons of such as, according to the opinion of his majesty's attorney and solicitor general, have committed themselves in acts of treason and rebellion, should be arrested and imprisoned." This letter authorized General Gage to offer a reward for the apprehension of the patriot leaders, and a pardon to those who should return to obedience. Hence, the subsequent proclamation of General Gage.

and that many were killed and wounded. I have only room
for a single specimen of the sharp strictures these despatches
elicited. "Let us," says one of them, "accompany the army
in its return, and we find them met by Lord Percy, at Lexington, with 'sixteen companies and the marines, amounting
in all to about twelve hundred men, with two pieces of cannon. We have now almost the whole army that was collected
at Boston, under so active a leader as Lord Percy, with the
assistance of Colonel Smith and Major Pitcairn, 'doing everything (so says the Gazette) that men could do,' and two pieces
of cannon. We may expect that not a man of the unheaded
poltroon provincials will be left alive. Not quite so bad. The
Gazette tells us, dryly, that 'the rebels were for a while dispersed.' They were so dispersed, however, that 'as soon as
the troops resumed their march,' (not their flight,) they began
again to fire on them, and continued it during the whole of
fifteen miles' march, 'by which means several were killed
and wounded.' If this was not a flight, and if Lord Percy's
activity was not in running away, I should be glad to know
where were the flanking parties of this army on its march,
with all this light infantry? Would any commanding officer
suffer such an enemy to continue killing and wounding his
troops, from stone walls and houses, if it was not a defeat and
flight?"[1]

Such was the effect, in the colonies and in England, of this
manifestation of the resolute spirit that animated the American
patriots. Those who stood in the breach at the breaking of
this day of blood at Lexington, those who joined in battle and
died honorably facing the foe at Concord, those who so gal-

---

[1] One hundred pounds sterling were contributed in England for the relief
of those who were wounded in this battle, and of the widows and children
of those who were slain. This was paid to a committee of the Massachusetts Assembly, by Dr. Franklin, in the following October.

Stedman, a British historian, remarks : "The conduct of Colonel Smith,
in this unfortunate expedition, was generally censured ; but Lord Percy
gained on this occasion, what he afterwards uniformly sustained, great reputation as an active, brave, and intelligent officer." A British journal says :
" He was in every place of danger, and came off unhurt." He had, how
ever, a narrow escape. A musket ball struck one of the buttons of his
waistcoat.

lantly pursued the flying veterans, deserve the tribute of grateful admiration.[1] Their efforts were in behalf of the cause of the freedom of America, and their success was typical of its final triumph. It is this that clothes their valor on this remarkable day with such beauty and dignity. " In other circumstances," Dr. Dwight writes, " the expedition to Concord, and the contest which ensued, would have been merely little tales of wonder and woe, chiefly recited by the parents of the neighborhood to their circles at the fireside, commanding a momentary attention of childhood, and calling forth the tear of sorrow from the eyes of those who were intimately connected with the sufferers. Now, the same events preface the history of a nation, and the beginning of an empire; and are themes of disquisition and astonishment to the civilized world." [2]

[1] Hon. Edward Everett's Concord Address, 53.
[2] Dwight's Travels, I., p. 387.

LEXINGTON MONUMENT.

BOSTON
With its Environs
in 1775 & 1776.

Engraved for Frothingham's History.

Scale of Miles

REFERENCES.
1 State House & King Street.
2 Town Hall, Dock Square.
3 Old South Meeting House.
4 Beacon Hill.
5 Fort Hill.
6 Copp's Hill.
7 Fort on Noddle's I. erected after Boston was evacuated.

NAHANT BAY

DEER I.

Pullen Point

Hospital I.

Ramsford or

NANTASKET ROAD

Gallops

Nicks Mate

Western Channel

Speckele

Ft. Strasbury

Castle I.

Shirley Pt.
Falling Pt.

Apple I.

Bird Island

CHELSEA

Winnisimet

Wood, Aldersborn & Medford

Road to Winnisimet

Ferry to Winnisimet

Hancock's Wharf

Long Wharf

South Battery

NODDLE I.

MALDEN N.

Maiden R.

to Medford R.

Powder Ho.

Cobble Hill

Willis's

Charles River

CHARLESTOWN

Breed's Hill

Bunker Hill

Mill

Floating Battery

DORCHESTER FLATS

Am. Battery

Dorchester Pt.

Nook Hill

Am. Fortified Hill

Castle Pt.

DORCHESTER

DORCHESTER NECK

Dorchester Lines

Boston Neck

BOSTON

Barracks

Fox Hill

Powder Ho.

Roxbury

ROXBURY

Meeting Ho.

George Tavern

Burying Ho.

Am. Right wing

Road to Providence & Rhode I.

Redoubt

Swamp

American Right wing

Redoubt

Muddy River

BROOKLINE

Am. Battery

Cedar Am. Battery

Brookline Fort

Charles River

3 Gun Battery

2 Gun Battery

Central

Redoubt

Mill Cove

Roxbury

Gen. Thomas Right wing

Washington's Head Quarters

Barracks

CAMBRIDGE or Newtown

Camp

2 Reserve

Reserve

Wright

Camp

Prospect Hill

Winter Hill

Charlestown Lines

Gen. Lee's

American Lines

Prospect Hill

Redoubt

Cobble Hill

Ten Hills

From Lexington & Concord

Gen. Lee's

Powder Magazine Winter Hill

Ft. No. 3

Redoubt

Mystic or Medford R.

CHAPTER III.

Gathering of an Army. Proceedings of Massachusetts, New Hampshire, Connecticut, Rhode Island. The American Army. Skirmishes. The British Army. Resolve to fortify Bunker Hill.

THE intelligence of the breaking out of hostilities was immediately followed by circulars from the Massachusetts committee of safety, calling out the militia. One addressed to the towns, dated April 20, urged them " to hasten and encourage, by all possible means, the enlistment of men to form an army," and to send them forward without delay. "Our all," it reads, "is at stake. Death and devastation are the certain consequences of delay. Every moment is infinitely precious. An hour lost may deluge your country in blood, and entail perpetual slavery upon the few of our posterity that may survive the carnage."[1] Another circular, addressed to the other New England colonies, (April 26,) applied for as many troops as could be spared, to march forthwith to the assistance of Massachusetts.[2] One spirit, however, animated the country. Companies of minute-men and individual volunteers rushed from every quarter to the seat of hostilities; and, joining the intrepid bands that fought the British troops on their way from Concord, commenced the memorable siege of Boston.[3]

The committee of safety and the general officers had an arduous task, to keep so large a body of men together, and to provide for them; and until there were regular enlistments, there was, unavoidably, much confusion. General Heath continued to issue orders until the arrival of General Ward, in the afternoon of April 20, who then took the command. Other general officers were early on the ground. At the first council of war (April 20) there were present, Generals Ward, Heath, and Whitcomb; Colonels Bridge, Frye, James Pres-

---

[1] Journals of Provincial Congress, p. 518. [2] Ib., p. 254. [3] Stiles, in his Ms. Diary, writes that, on Friday, April 21, an American army of 20,000 men was assembled.

cutt, William Prescott, Bullard, and Barrett; and Lieutenant-colonels Spaulding, Nixon, Whitney, Mansfield, and Wheelock. On this day Colonel William Prescott was ordered to the command of a guard of five companies, — two of which were posted on Charlestown road, one towards Phipps' Farm, one towards Menotomy, (West Cambridge,) and the remainder at other points. On the next day the guards were posted in the same manner; but Colonels Prescott, Learned, and Warner, were ordered to march their regiments to Roxbury, to join General Thomas.[1]

The army was soon joined by General Israel Putnam, and Colonels John Stark and Paul Dudley Sargent, who rendered valuable service in this trying season. On the 22d, Colonel Stark was ordered to march to Chelsea, with three hundred men, to defend the inhabitants. But no public character had more influence than Dr. Warren. He was judicious, as well as zealous and energetic. "He did wonders," Dr. Eliot writes, "in preserving order among the troops;" and at a time when there was extreme difficulty in maintaining discipline. The alarm of the people was still great. Many of the inhabitants of Cambridge had left their homes; and a general order of the 22d threatened punishment to any soldier who should injure property. At this date many of the regiments were at Waltham and Watertown; but on the 26th, they were ordered to march forward to Cambridge. On the 27th, Mr. Huntington, of Connecticut, writes, that General Ward was in Roxbury, and General Putnam commanded in Cambridge, "with too much business on their hands." At this time Colonel Stark was in Medford. In a short time each colony made separate provision for its troops, — enlisting men, establishing their pay, supplying them with provisions, and appointing and commissioning their officers.[2]

Before this, however, could be done, many of the minute-men, after a few days' continuance before Boston, returned home, — some to look after their private affairs, and others to make permanent arrangements to join the army. This left some of the avenues into the country but slightly guarded. Gordon writes, that "during the interval between their return

[1] Ward's Orderly Book.   [2] Mass. Archives; Orderly Books.

and the provincials' resorting afresh to the place of rendezvous, the land entrance into and out of the town, by the Neck,
was next to unguarded. Not more than between six and
seven hundred men, under Colonel Robinson, of Dorchester,
were engaged in defending so important a pass, for several
days together. For nine days and nights the colonel never
shifted his clothes, nor lay down to sleep; as he had the
whole duty upon him, even down to the adjutant, and as
there was no officer of the day to assist. The officers, in
general, had left the camp, in order to raise the wanted number of men. The colonel was obliged, therefore, for the time
mentioned, to patrol the guards every night, which gave him
a round of nine miles to traverse." [1]

The inhabitants of Boston, by the order of General Gage,
were now cut off from intercourse with the country, and consequently were suddenly deprived of their customary supplies
of provisions, fuel, and necessaries of life. This exposed them
to great distress. Civil war, in all its complicated horrors,
was at their doors, — the sundering of social ties, the burning
of peaceful homes, the butchery of kindred and friends, — and
all was uncertainty respecting their own fate. It was amidst
such scenes, when the metropolis was surrounded by multitudes of armed men, exasperated to the last degree by the
recent destruction and massacre, that General Gage requested
an interview with the selectmen. He did not feel safe in his
position. He was apprehensive that the people without would
attack the town, that the inhabitants within would join them,
and that this combination would prove too much for his troops.
He represented to the selectmen that such an attack might
result in unhappy consequences to the town; but that he
would do no violence to it, provided the inhabitants would conduct peaceably. An understanding to this effect was entered

---

[1] Gordon's History, I., 349. General Ward wrote, April 24, 1775, to
the Provincial Congress, as follows : " Gentlemen, — My situation is such,
that if I have not enlisting orders immediately, I shall be left all alone. It is
impossible to keep the men here, except something be done. I therefore
pray that the plan may be completed, and handed to me this morning, that
you, gentlemen of the Congress, issue orders for enlisting men. I am, gentlemen, yours, &c., A. WARD."

into between the general and the selectmen. A town-meeting was held on the 22d of April, at which Hon. James Bowdoin presided, when the arrangement was confirmed by a vote of the citizens. After instructing a committee to confer with General Gage in relation to opening a communication with the country, the meeting adjourned to the next day, Sunday, at ten o'clock.

The meeting was held, according to the adjournment, on Sunday, when the committee reported that General Gage, after a long conference, agreed: "That upon the inhabitants in general lodging their arms in Faneuil Hall, or any other convenient place, under the care of the selectmen, marked with the names of the respective owners, that all such inhabitants as are inclined might depart from the town, with their families and effects, and those who remain might depend on his protection; and that the arms aforesaid, at a suitable time, would be returned to the owners." The town voted to accept these proposals. A committee waited upon the general with the vote, who, in addition, promised to request the admiral to lend his boats to facilitate the removal; and to allow carriages to pass and repass for this purpose. He likewise promised that the poor should not suffer from want of provisions, and requested that a letter might be written to Dr. Warren, to the effect: "That those persons in the country who might incline to remove into Boston with their effects, might have liberty to do so without molestation." The town voted unanimously to accede to these conditions, and to request the inhabitants to deposit their arms promptly with the selectmen.[1]

---

[1] Proceedings of the Town of Boston. This arrangement was made with the sanction and advice of the committee of safety. It sent the following letter to the inhabitants: Cambridge, April 22, 1775. Gentlemen, — The committee of safety being informed that General Gage has proposed a treaty with the inhabitants of the town of Boston, whereby he stipulates that the women and children, with all their effects, shall have safe conduct without the garrison, and their men also, upon condition that the male inhabitants within the town shall, on their part, solemnly engage that they will not take up arms against the king's troops within the town, should an attack be made from without, — we cannot but esteem those conditions to be just and reasonable; and as the inhabitants are in danger from suffering from want of provisions, which, in this time of general confusion, cannot be conveyed into the

This arrangement, which appears to have been as earnestly desired by the British commander as it was by the distressed inhabitants, was carried out, for a short time, in good faith. On the 27th of April the people delivered to the selectmen 1778 fire-arms, 634 pistols, 973 bayonets, and 38 blunderbusses; and on the same day it was announced in a town-meeting, that General Gage had given permission to the inhabitants to remove out of town, with their effects, either by land or by water; and applications for passes were to be made to General Robertson. Accordingly, thousands applied for passes, and hundreds immediately removed to the country, taking with them their valuable effects.[1] The Provincial Congress met the liberality of General Gage with appropriate measures: they resolved (April 30) that any inhabitants inclining to go into Boston should be permitted to do so; and officers to give them permits were stationed at the Sign of the Sun, in Charlestown, (at the Neck,) and at Mr. Greaton's house, in Roxbury. The number unable to bear the expense of removal, and of supporting themselves, was estimated at five thousand; and the Congress ordered that the several towns should provide for them, according to their population, — delicately resolving that such inhabitants should not, in future, be considered as the poor of the several towns.

But this removal became so general as to alarm the Tories, and to give uneasiness to the British commander. The former were prompt in this crisis to manifest their loyalty. On the day of the battle about two hundred, merchants and traders, sent their names in to General Gage, and offered to arm as volunteers in his service. The offer was thankfully accepted. The corps was enrolled under General Ruggles, and was immediately put on duty. This treaty, however,

town, we are willing you shall enter into and faithfully keep the engagement aforementioned, said to be required of you, and to remove yourselves, and your women, children, and effects, as soon as may be. We are, &c.

[1] I have one of the original passes given by General Gage. It shows that everything but arms and ammunition was allowed to pass: — Boston, April, 1775. Permit ——, together with —— family, consisting of —— persons, and —— effects, to pass —— between sunrise and sunset. By order of his Excellency the Governor. No arms nor ammunition is allowed to pass.

caused great excitement among them. They remonstrated against the bad policy of the measure. They explained the "pernicious tendency of such an indulgence." They regarded the presence of the inhabitants as necessary to save the town from assault and from conflagration. For several days no answer was given by General Gage. They then threatened to lay down their arms, and to leave the town. The importunity of interest or fear proved too strong for a treaty obligation with "rebels." This agreement, on various pretexts, was shamefully violated. Obstructions were thrown in the way of a removal. "All merchandise was forbid," says a letter, May 21; "after a while all provisions were forbid; and now all merchandise, provisions, and medicine. Guards were appointed to examine all trunks, boxes, beds, and everything else to be carried out." None but the patriots, the Tories alleged, would be in favor of removing; and when they had removed, and had carried their property away, the town would be set on fire; merchandise carried out would strengthen the rebels in their resistance, and hence this ought to be retained. At length passes were refused; and many who obtained them were obliged to leave their property, which deprived them of their accustomed resources for living. Besides, in a variety of instances, the passports were so framed that families were cruelly divided; wives were separated from their husbands, children from their parents, and the aged and sick from their relations and friends, who wished to attend and comfort them. The general was very averse to allow women and children to leave Boston, as he thought they contributed to its safety, and prevented his being attacked. Numbers of the poor and the helpless — some infected with the small-pox — were sent out. It was in vain that the selectmen, the inhabitants, and the Provincial Congress, remonstrated against this bad faith on the part of the British commander. It occasioned severe and just denunciations in the documents of the time.[1]

---

[1] Proceedings of Town of Boston; Mass. Com. Safety; Journals of the time; Gordon's History, I., 354. It will be seen that the idea of burning the town is referred by General Howe in his speech to his army before the Bunker Hill battle. A letter from Boston, dated April 23, says : — "On

The distresses of the inhabitants of Charlestown also were great. The British troops, on the 20th of April, crossed over the ferry to Boston. But the peculiar situation of the town, added to the threats of the British commander, created the belief that its fate was sealed. Hence the greater part of its inhabitants removed out of it with their effects. A guard was stationed at the Neck, and no one was allowed, without a pass,[1] to go into it. So deserted had it become, that early in June a petition to the Provincial Congress represented that there remained but few, who, by their extreme poverty, were wholly unable to do anything toward removing themselves from the "extreme hazardous situation" they were in, and that it was "truly deplorable." After reminding the Congress that their distress flowed from the same causes as that of their brethren of Boston, the petitioners requested that the same disposition might be made of the poor, by sending them to the interior towns. This, accordingly, was done. Charlestown, in a short time, was nearly deserted. A few of its citizens went into it to look after their effects, or to plant their gardens, or to mow their grass; but so general was the belief that it would be

Wednesday last about two hundred merchants and traders, friends to government, sent in their names to the general, offering to take up arms as volunteers at his service, which he thankfully accepted of. Everything here is in great confusion. We hourly expect an attack." A British paper, September 14, says of the removal : — " The bad policy of the measure excited great commotions among the gentlemen volunteers, under the command of General Ruggles. They explained to the general the pernicious tendency of such an indulgence ; and not receiving a distinct answer for some days, they threatened to lay down their arms, and leave the town. This spirited exertion of the volunteers at last compelled the general to detain all the effects and merchandise of the rebel emigrants, except their household furniture."

May 12. — The inhabitants of Boston are permitted to come out, but very slow ; numbers are not permitted to come out on any terms. The distress of the inhabitants, on account of provisions, is shocking indeed. — Newspaper.

[1] May 6. — General Orders. — That the commanding officer of the guard at Charlestown permit no person to go into Charlestown with any provisions whatever, with or without a pass.

May 13. — Ordered, That Captain Isaac Foster be permitted to carry provisions into Charlestown, for the benefit only of such persons as have moved out of Boston, and are going into the country, and our friends in said town — Ward's Orderly Book.

destroyed,[1] that, on the 17th of June, not more than one or two hundred remained, out of a population of between two and three thousand.

In the mean time the several colonies, with noble despatch, adopted measures for the general defence. In Massachusetts, the Provincial Congress assembled at Concord, April 22, and on the next day, Sunday, resolved that an army of thirty thousand was necessary for the defence of the country. It resolved to raise, as the proportion of this colony, thirteen thousand six hundred troops. In the plan for its organization, fifty-nine men were to form a company, and ten companies a regiment; and to promote rapid enlistments, those who raised companies or regiments were promised commissions to command them. Artemas Ward was appointed commander-in-chief; John Thomas, lieutenant-general; and Richard Gridley, the chief engineer. Congress took measures — April 30 — to raise a train of artillery, but it was not fully organized when the battle of Bunker Hill took place. Indeed, so slowly did the work of general organization go on, that General Ward, in a letter to Congress, May 19, stated, that to save the country, "it was absolutely necessary that the regiments be immediately settled, the officers commissioned, and the soldiers mustered." Even his own commission had not been issued. On this day Congress adopted the form of one for the commander, and passed orders relative to the ranks of the regiments and the officers. The settlement of the ranks of the officers, however, was referred to a future time. It also revised the powers of the committee of safety, and clothed

---

[1] A midshipman on board of the Nautilus man-of-war, then lying at Boston, about May, 1775, writes : " My situation here is not very pleasant, for I am stationed in an open boat, at the mouth of Charles River, to watch the Americans, who are busily employed in making fire-stages, to send down the stream to burn our ships. I have command of six men, and a six-pounder is fixed to the bow of our boat, which we are to fire to alarm the camp and fleet, as soon as we observe the fire-stages. The inhabitants of Boston are delivering up their arms, and leaving the town. The Somerset, of 74 guns, lays between Boston and Charlestown, which are only separated by a channel about a mile broad, and our ship lays about half a mile above her ; and if she sees a particular signal hung out, she is to fire on Charlestown." — Remembrancer, vol. I., 111

this body with full authority to direct the movements of the army. The work of organization then went on more rapidly, though it was far from being complete when the battle of Bunker Hill was fought.[1]

The New Hampshire troops were peculiarly situated. They assembled at Medford, where the field officers, April 26, held a meeting, and advised the men to enlist in the service of the Massachusetts colony. They also recommended Colonel John Stark to take the charge of them until the Provincial Congress of New Hampshire should act.[2] This was accordingly done. The New Hampshire Congress, May 20, voted to raise two thousand men, adopted those that had already enlisted, and voted that "the establishment of officers and soldiers should be the same as in the Massachusetts Bay."[3] They were organized into three regiments, and placed (May 23) under the command of Nathaniel Folsom, with the rank of brigadier-general. Two regiments were organized previous to the battle of Bunker Hill, under Colonels John Stark and James Reed. On the 2d of June, General Folsom ordered Colonel Reed to collect his companies, — part of which were at Medford, under Colonel Stark, — and "put himself under the command of General Ward, until further order." On the 13th of June, by order of Ward, this regiment, fully officered, took post at Charlestown Neck.[4] Colonel Enoch Poor was appointed to command the third regiment, which, however, did not arrive at the camp until after June 17. Nor did General Folsom arrive at Cambridge until June 20.

[1] Journals of Provincial Congress ; Mass. Archives. The committee of safety, elected May 18, were : — John Hancock, Joseph Warren, Benjamin Church, Benjamin White, Joseph Palmer, Richard Devens, Abraham Watson, John Pigeon, Azor Orne, Benjamin Greenleaf, Nathan Cushing, Samuel Holten, Enoch Freeman. On the next day Congress enlarged the powers of this committee. They had authority to call out the militia, to nominate officers to the Congress, to commission them, and to direct the operations of the army.

[2] Mass. Archives, where are the records of this meeting. [3] Journals of New Hampshire Provincial Congress. [4] Reed's letter, Ms., in New Hampshire Archives. Difficulties occurred in organizing the regiments. On the 31st of May, Colonel Stark was ordered to repair to Exeter, to receive the orders of the Congress. After General Folsom was appointed, Stark refused for a short time, to obey his orders.

Connecticut was so prompt in its action, that, a few days after the nineteenth of April, it had but few towns not represented in the army. A large portion of these minute-men soon returned to their homes. That colony voted, April 26, to raise six thousand men, and organized them into six regiments, of ten companies each, — one hundred men constituting a company. Joseph Spencer, with the rank of brigadier-general, was the senior officer in command,[1] who arrived with one regiment early in May, and took post at Roxbury.[2] Captain John Chester's fine company formed part of it. Another regiment, commanded by Israel Putnam, with the rank of brigadier-general, was stationed at Cambridge. The sixth regiment was under Colonel Samuel Holden Parsons; two companies of which — his own and Chapman's — were ordered, June 7, to the camp, and subsequently, one other, Captain Coit's; the remainder of it being stationed, until after the battle of Bunker Hill, at New London.[3] The disposition of these troops was directed by a "committee of war," which supplied them with ammunition and provisions.

The Rhode Island Assembly, April 25, voted to raise fifteen hundred men, to constitute "an army of observation," and ordered it to "join and coöperate with the forces of the neighboring colonies."[4] This force was organized into three regiments, of eight companies each, under Colonels Varnum, Hitchcock, and Church, and placed under the command of Nathaniel Greene, with the rank of brigadier-general.[5] One of the companies was a train of artillery, and had the colony's field-pieces. General Greene, on arriving at the camp, Jamaica Plains, found his command in great disorder; and it was only by his judicious labors, and great personal influence, that it was kept together.[6] In the rules and regulations for the government of this force, it is called "The Rhode Island

---

[1] Hinman's War of the Revolution, p. 547. [2] Trumbull's Memoirs. [3] Records of the Council of War. A company is also named, under Captain Perit. The general officers were also captains. Thus General Putnam was brigadier-general, colonel of a regiment, and captain of a company.

[4] The act is in Force's Archives, vol. ii., p. 390. [5] Proceedings of Rhode Island Assembly. [6] General Greene's letter, June 2. "Several companies had clubbed their muskets, in order to return home." Colonel Varnum's regiment had not, June 2, arrived in camp.

army." They provide that "all public stores, taken in the enemy's camp or magazines," should be "secured for the use of the colony of Rhode Island."[1] It was not until June 28 that this colony passed an act putting its troops under the orders of the general of the combined army.[2]

The official returns of the army, until the arrival of General Washington, are so defective and inaccurate, that it is impossible to ascertain, with precision, its numbers. The "grand American army,"[3] as it is called in the newspapers, consisted of about sixteen thousand men. Massachusetts furnished about 11,500, Connecticut 2300, New Hampshire 1200, Rhode Island 1000. It was so peculiarly constituted, each colony having its own establishment, supplying its troops with provisions[4] and ammunition, and directing their disposition, that its only element of uniformity was the common purpose that called it together. General Ward was authorized to command only the Massachusetts and New Hampshire forces, though the orders of the day were copied by all the troops; and a voluntary obedience, it is stated, was yielded to him by the whole army, as the commander-in-chief. Nor was it until after the experience of the battle of Bunker Hill, that the committee of war of Connecticut, to remedy the evils of the want of "a due subordination," and "of a general and commander-in-chief," instructed Generals Spencer and Putnam to yield obedience to General Ward, and advised the colonies of Rhode Island and New Hampshire to do the same respecting

[1] Article xxviii. [2] The preamble reads, — " Whereas, it is absolutely necessary, for the well-governing and exerting the force of an army, that the same should be under the direction of a commander-in-chief."

[3] We have the pleasure to inform the public that the grand American army is nearly completed. Great numbers of the Connecticut, New Hampshire, and Rhode Island troops are arrived ; among the latter is a fine company of artillery, with four excellent field-pieces. — Essex Gazette, June 8.

[4] Connecticut Assembly. Force's Archives, vol. ii., 418. The New Hampshire regiments were first enlisted under the authority of Massachusetts. Hence a general order of April 27 directs : " That the Hampshire troops be supplied with provisions in the same manner, by Mr. Commissary Pigeon, as the Massachusetts troops are supplied, until further orders." — Ward's Orderly Book. On the 8th of June, the New Hampshire committee of safety authorized large purchases for the troops. — Mss.

their troops.[1]   This measure indicates the confusion that existed, as to rank, among the officers of the different colonies.   In addition to this want of subordination, so vital to success in military operations, the army was inadequately supplied with bayonets, powder, horses, clothing, and tents or commodious barracks.   No measure of bravery or of patriotism could make up, in a day of trial, for such deficiencies.[2]

But this ill-appointed army was not entirely unprepared for an encounter.   Some of its officers, and not a few of the privates, had served in the French wars, — an invaluable military school for the colonies; a martial spirit had been excited in the frequent trainings of the minute-men, while the habitual use of the fowling-piece made these raw militia superior to

---

[1] Force's Archives, ii., 1039.   " On motion of the difficulties the army are and must be under, for want of a general and commander-in-chief of the whole body, raised by different colonies, &c., and a due subordination," &c. The news of the Bunker Hill battle arrived June 18, about 10 o'clock. — Ib.

[2] It is stated in an inscription on the " Adams " cannon, one of the Ancient and Honorable artillery pieces, that " four cannon constituted the whole train of field artillery possessed by the British colonies of North America at the commencement of the war, on the 19th of April, 1775." — Tudor's Otis, p. 456.   This is certainly doing injustice to the foresight of the patriots. They did not throw down the gauntlet to Great Britain so rashly as this.   In the committee of safety, and in the newspapers, previous to April 19, there are frequent allusions to cannon of various calibre, — to two-pounders, to six-pounders, both iron and brass.   Also to mortars.   I have not met with a statement of the number on hand previous to the 19th of April.   On the 18th of April, however, the committee order thirty-three rounds of round-shot and grape-shot, with powder, to be lodged " with each of the twelve field-pieces belonging to the province."   There were then, certainly, twelve field-pieces, besides other cannon and mortars, in Massachusetts alone.   On the 29th, a report states there were in Cambridge one six-pounder, six three-pounders ; and in Watertown, sixteen pieces of artillery.

In the Mass. Hist. Coll., vol. i., p. 232, there is the following account of stores in Massachusetts, April 14, 1775 : — Fire-arms, 21,549 ; pounds of powder, 17,441 ; of ball, 22,191 ; flints, 144,699 ; bayonets, 10,108 ; pouches, 11,979.   Shattuck's Concord, p. 97, contains extracts from a document found among Colonel Barrett's papers, which shows that no small progress had been made in collecting material for an army and its support, previous to the 19th of April.   Among the items are 20,000 pounds of musket balls and cartridges, 15,000 canteens, 17,000 pounds salt fish, 35,000 pounds of rice, and large quantities of beef, pork, a great number of tents, working tools, &c.

veteran troops in aiming the musket. They were superior to them, also, in character, being mostly substantial farmers and mechanics, who had left their homes and pursuits, not for want of employment or to make war a trade, but because they were animated by a fresh enthusiasm for liberty. The British general paid dearly for despising such preparation.

The army, also, reposed great confidence in its officers. If it be true that this, in some cases, was bestowed on men unworthy of it, still no occasion had arisen to prove it, and they were the free choice of the men. Many in high command had been tried in important civil and military service, and had that influence over their fellow-men that ever accompanies character. Ward had served under Abercrombie, was a true patriot, had many private virtues, and was prudent and highly esteemed; Thomas was an excellent officer, of a chivalrous spirit and noble heart, and was much beloved; Putnam, widely known, not less for his intrepid valor than for his fearless and energetic patriotism, was frank and warm-hearted, and of great popularity; Pomeroy had fought well at Louisburg, where Gridley had won laurels as an accomplished engineer; Prescott, in the French war, had exhibited great bravery, and military skill of a high order; and Stark, hardy, independent, brave, was another of these veterans. This list might easily be extended. Officers of such experience constituted no mean element of efficiency.

The histories of this period do not describe the colors under which the troops of the several colonies took the field. Was there a common flag? If so, was it the old New England ensign? As early as 1686 there are notices of such a flag. A representation of one in 1701 is simply an English ensign, with a quarter divided into four by a cross, and having in one of the corners the figure of a pine tree. This tree was a favorite emblem of Massachusetts. It appears, for instance, on its coin. It is more probable, however, that there was no common flag thus early, but that the troops of each colony marched into the camp under their own local flag. Thus a letter, April 23, 1775, says of the Connecticut troops: "We fix on our standards and drums the colony arms, with the motto, '*qui transtulit sustinet*' round it in letters of gold, which we construe thus : 'God, who transplanted us hither, will support us.'" [1]

While thus war was settling down over Massachusetts, and nothing but resistance was thought of by its patriots, hopes of peace and reconciliation still existed in other colonies. At this time an embassy and letter, sent by the Assembly of Connecticut to General Gage, excited no small uneasiness, and drew forth some of the most remarkable documents of the time. The committee appointed to confer with the British general were Dr. Johnson and Colonel Wolcott. The object of this mission — to procure a suspension of hostilities — met with a decided rebuke from the Massachusetts patriots. After holding, on the 1st of May, a conference with the embassy, the committee of safety sent a strong letter to Governor Trumbull, in which they frankly express their uneasiness at the proposed cessation of hostilities. This letter is dated Cambridge, May 2, 1775, and gives a striking picture of the firmness and designs of the patriots. "We fear," it says, "that our brethren in Connecticut are not even yet convinced of the cruel designs of administration against America, nor thoroughly sensible of the miseries to which General Gage's army have reduced this wretched colony." After a description of the country, the letter goes on : "No business but that of war is either done or thought of in this colony. No agreement or compact with General Gage will in the least alleviate our distress, as no confidence can possibly be placed in any assurance he can give to a people he has deceived in the matter, taking possession of and fortifying the town of Boston, and whom he has suffered his army to attack in the most inhuman and treacherous manner. Our relief must now arise from driving General Gage, with his troops, out of the country, which, with the blessing of God, we are determined to accomplish, or perish in the attempt; as we think an honorable death in the field, whilst fighting for the liberties of all America, far preferable to being butchered in our own houses, or to be reduced to an ignominious slavery. We must entreat that

---

[1] In 1774 there are frequent notices of " union flags" in the newspapers, but I have not met with any description of the devices on them. Thus Liberty Tree had its flag, and there were flags flying from the tops of the liberty poles

our sister colony, Connecticut, will afford, immediately, all possible aid, as at this time delay will be attended with all that fatal train of events which would follow from an absolute desertion of the cause of American liberty. Excuse our earnestness on this subject, as we know that upon the success of our present contest depend the lives and liberties of our country and succeeding generations." A letter of similar import was also sent by the Provincial Congress. Governor Trumbull, in patriotic replies to these letters, dispelled the fears that were entertained of Connecticut.

No important military operations, on either side, took place until the Bunker Hill battle. Both parties endeavored to secure the stock on the islands in the harbor. This occasioned several skirmishes, which afforded the uncommon spectacle of hostile parties engaged in conflict on land and water. The Americans were generally successful. These skirmishes proved of essential service to them. They elated their spirits, accustomed them to face danger, and inspired them with confidence.[1] They talked of attacking General Gage, and of burning his ships. "It is not expected," Dr. Warren writes, May 16, "he will sally out of Boston at present; and if he does, he will but

[1] The songs of the day well exhibit the prevailing spirit. The following is copied from the New England Chronicle, May 18, 1775 : —

A SONG.
To the tune of " The Echoing Horn."

HARK ! 'tis FREEDOM that calls, come, Patriots, awake !
    To arms, my brave Boys, and away :
'Tis Honor, 'tis Virtue, 'tis Liberty calls,
    And upbraids the too tedious Delay.
What Pleasure we find in pursuing our Foes,
    Thro' Blood and thro' Carnage we'll fly ;
Then follow, we'll soon overtake them, Huzza !
    The Tyrants are seized on, they die.

Triumphant returning, with Freedom secured,
    Like MEN, we'll be joyful and gay, —
With our Wives and our Friends we will sport, love and drink,
    And lose the Fatigues of the Day.
'Tis Freedom alone gives a Relish to Mirth,
    But Oppression all Happiness sours ;
It will smooth Life's dull Passage, 'twill slope the Descent,
    And strew the Way over with Flowers.

gratify thousands who impatiently wait to avenge the blood of their murdered countrymen." "Danger and war are become pleasing, and injured virtue is now aroused to avenge herself."

The Americans began in May to build fortifications. The directions in the orderly books are not sufficiently precise, however, to determine their locality. Thus, on the 3d of May, a party of two hundred privates and officers, under Colonel Doolittle, were ordered on fatigue; the directions for the work to be done were to be given by Mr. Chadwick, engineer. On the next day, a party of four hundred and fifty were ordered on similar duty, under Colonel Frye. Most probably these works were at Cambridge. At this early period, no works were commenced either on Prospect Hill, or Winter Hill, though General Putnam was earnestly in favor of fortifying the former.

A Continental Congress had been appointed to convene at Philadelphia on the 10th of May. On the 3d, the Provincial Congress addressed to this body a letter on the condition of the colony. It suggested that a powerful army, on the side of America, was the only measure left to stem the rapid progress of a tyrannical ministry, and to put an immediate end to the ravages of the troops; and expressed the greatest confidence in the wisdom and ability of the continent to support Massachusetts, so far as it should be necessary to support the common cause of the American colonies. On the 15th, the Provincial Congress sent an express — Dr. Church — with another letter, containing an application to the Continental Congress for advice in relation to the assumption of civil government, and also suggesting to Congress the propriety of that body's taking the regulation and general direction of the army.

The passage into the country, through Roxbury, was inadequately defended, and in the early part of this month was a matter of great anxiety. The committee of safety wrote to the government of Connecticut, May 4, that it was their earnest and pressing desire that it would send three or four thousand men of their establishment to Massachusetts immediately, to enable the committee "to secure a pass of the greatest importance" to the common interests, and of which the enemy would certainly take possession as soon as their reinforcements arrived. "If they once gain possession," the committee say, "it will cost us much blood and treasure to dislodge them; but it may now be secured by us, if we had a force sufficient, without any danger." A similar letter was sent to Rhode Island.[1]

On the 5th, the Provincial Congress resolved that General Gage, by recent proceedings, had "utterly disqualified himself to serve this colony as a governor, and in every other capacity; and that no obedience ought, in future, to be paid, by the several towns and districts in this colony, to his writs for calling an assembly, or to his proclamations, or any other of his acts or doings; but that, on the other hand, he ought to be considered and guarded against, as an unnatural and inveterate enemy to this country."

On the 9th of May, strong apprehensions were entertained of a sally from Boston. A council of war requested of the committee a force of two thousand men, to reinforce the troops at Roxbury. The committee ordered the officers of the ten nearest towns to muster immediately one half of the militia, and all the minute-men, and march forthwith to Roxbury. Messages from Boston stated that the British were certainly preparing for a capital stroke. At this time, General Thomas had but seven hundred men under his command. His post included a high hill visible from Boston. To deceive the British as to his force, "the general," says Gordon, "continued marching his seven hundred men round and round the hill, and by this means multiplied their appearance to any who were reconnoitring them at Boston." The committee ordered on this day the colonels of the regiments to repair to Cambridge with the men they had enlisted.

On the 13th, in the afternoon, all the troops at Cambridge, except those on guard, marched, under General Putnam, into Charlestown. They were twenty-two hundred in number, and their line of march was made to extend a mile and a half.

---

[1] A letter from Rhode Island, May 4, 1775. says: "We have various accounts from Boston, almost every hour; but what is most to be depended on is, that the Mohawks are determined to stand by us. There are about thirty now at the camp."

They went over Bunker Hill, and also over Breed's Hill, came out by Captain Henly's still-house, and passed into the main street by the fish-market, near the old ferry, where Charles River Bridge is. They then returned to Cambridge.[1] It was done to inspire the army with confidence. Though they went within reach of the guns of the enemy, both from Boston and the shipping, no attempt was made to molest them.

On the 17th a party of Americans fired upon a barge near Wheeler's Point, and it was supposed killed two of the enemy. Expecting an attack, a detachment of four hundred, under Colonel Henshaw, Majors Bigelow and Baldwin, occupied Lechmere's Point. They formed in ambush in the wood near it, near the causeway. General Ward visited the men about five o'clock, and reconnoitred the island. No skirmish, however, occurred.[2] The British, about this time, occasionally fired upon the Americans from the shipping.[3]

On the 21st, Sunday morning, two sloops and an armed schooner sailed from Boston to Grape Island, with a party of the troops, to take off a quantity of hay stored there. The troops landed on the island, and began to put the hay on board the sloops. The people of Weymouth and the neighborhood were alarmed by the ringing of bells and firing of guns; and General Thomas, on being informed of the landing, ordered three companies to assist them. The people assembled on the point of land next to the island, but the distance was too great for small arms to do execution. Their fire, however, was returned from the ships. After some hours, a flood tide enabled the people to float a lighter and a sloop, when a party went on board and landed on the island. The British then left, and the Americans set fire to about eighty tons of hay, burnt the barn, and brought off the cattle. Mrs. Adams, in writing of this affair to her husband, says: "You inquire of me who were at the engagement at Grape Island. I may say

---

[1] Baldwin's Diary.   [2] Ibid.   [3] Ibid.

May the 17th there was a great fire in Boston, commencing at a barrack on Treat's Wharf, which burnt twenty-seven stores, one shop, and four sheds. General Gage had appointed new captains to the engine companies, and the engine men took offence at it. Hence, the engines were badly served.

with truth all of Weymouth, Braintree, Hingham, who were able to bear arms, and hundreds from other towns within twenty, thirty, and forty miles of Weymouth. Both your brothers were there; your younger brother, with his company, who gained honor by their good order that day. He was one of the first to venture on board a schooner, to land upon the island."

The next skirmish was dwelt upon with great exultation throughout the colonies. The committee of safety had directed the live stock to be driven from the islands. On Saturday, May 27, a detachment was ordered to drive it from Hog and Noddle's Islands, lying near Chelsea, the passage to which, at low tide, was covered by about three feet of water. About eleven A. M. a party went from Chelsea to Hog Island, and thence to Noddle's Island, to drive off the stock. They were observed by the British, who, to prevent this, despatched a schooner, a sloop, and forty marines. The party, however, burnt a barn full of salt hay, an old farm-house, killed three cows and fifteen horses, and sent a few horses and cows to Hog Island. At this time they were fired on from the vessels, and by a large party of marines, who put off in boats from the men-of-war; and they retreated to a ditch, lay there in ambush, until they obtained a chance to fire on the marines, when they killed two and wounded two. They then retreated to Hog Island, and were joined by the remainder of the detachment. The stock was first driven off, — between three and four hundred sheep and lambs, cows, horses, &c., — and then the Americans formed on Chelsea neck, during which, the British fired from the vessels, from the barges fixed with swivels, and from Noddle's Island. The Americans sent for a reinforcement. About three hundred men and two pieces of cannon arrived about nine o'clock. General Putnam now commanded the party; and Dr. Warren, to encourage the men, served as a volunteer. General Putnam hailed the schooner, offering the men good quarters if they would submit, who answered this summons with two cannon shot. This was immediately returned by the Americans, and a sharp fire on both sides continued until eleven o'clock, when the fire of the schooner ceased. The men had abandoned her, and towards

morning she got aground upon the ferry ways. A party consisting of Isaac Baldwin and twelve men, about day-break,
after taking out her guns and sails, and other articles, burnt
her, under a fire from the sloop. In the morning—Sunday—
the firing on both sides was renewed,—by the British from
Noddle's Island Hill, and the sloop. The sloop was so much
disabled that she was obliged to be towed off by the boats.
After a few shots had been exchanged between the party at
Chelsea and the marines on Noddle's Island, the firing ceased.
The Americans did not lose a man, and had only four wounded.
The loss of the enemy was reported at twenty killed and fifty
wounded. This was probably exaggerated. The Americans
captured, besides clothes and money, twelve swivels, and four
four-pound cannon. This affair was magnified into a battle,
and the gallantry of the men engaged in it, and the bravery
of General Putnam, elicited general praise. The news of it,
arriving in Congress just as it was choosing general officers,
influenced the vote of Putnam for major-general, which was
unanimous.[1]

On the 30th of May, a party of Americans went to Noddle's Island again, burnt the mansion-house of Mr. Williams,
and drove off the stock, consisting of between five and six
hundred sheep and lambs, twenty head of cattle and horses.
On the 31st, at night, a party under Colonel Robinson removed about five hundred sheep and thirty head of cattle
from Pettick's Island. On the night of June 2, Major Greaton
took from Deer Island about eight hundred sheep and lambs,
and a number of cattle. He captured, also, a barge belonging
to one of the men-of-war, with four or five prisoners.

In June, the Provincial Congress was occupied with long
and earnest debates in relation to the expediency of fitting out
armed vessels. It was evidently regarded as a daring act to
defy the proud navy of England. Contests, however, had
already occurred on the sea. On the 5th of May, Captain
Linzee, of the Falcon, captured two provincial sloops at
Bedford. He intended to send them to Martha's Vineyard,
and freight sheep to Boston. But the Bedford people fitted

---

[1] Journals of the Day ; Baldwin's Diary ; Ms. Letters.

out two sloops, with thirty men, and re-took the captured vessels, with fifteen men on board. In the action three of the Falcon's crew were wounded, one of them mortally. Thirteen prisoners were sent to Cambridge. On June 11th, an action occurred off Machias, where Jeremiah O'Brien captured the Margaretta, after a severe combat He brought his prisoners to Watertown. The plantation committee immediately appointed O'Brien to command the Liberty, when he made other prizes.[1] Admiral Graves had ordered the British cruisers to capture every provision vessel, and several had been seized. On the 7th of June the Provincial Congress first acted on the subject of a navy. It is curious to notice the caution with which it moved. It appointed a committee " to consider the expediency of establishing a number of small armed vessels, to cruise on our sea coasts, for the protection of our trade, and the annoyance of our enemies : and that the members be enjoined, by order of Congress, to observe secrecy in the matter." On the 8th, this committee was ordered to sit forthwith. On the 10th, an addition was made to it. On the 11th, in a proposed address to the Continental Congress, it apprised that body of the proposition under discussion to fit out armed vessels. The committee reported on the 12th. On the 13th, the report was considered, and postponed till three o'clock, when the committees of safety and supplies were notified. A very long debate on the report then took place, and the further consideration of it postponed until the following Friday. The battle of Bunker Hill prevented further proceeding. Nothing beyond building a few boats appears to have been done until after this period, — among them, barges called "fire-boats." [2]

On the 6th of June an exchange of prisoners took place. "Between twelve and one," the Essex Gazette says, "Dr.

[1] Williamson's Maine, 2, **431**. He writes the name of the British vessel, Margranetto. Cooper calls this action the Lexington of the seas.

[2] On the 30th of April, the selectmen of Medford were directed by the committee of safety to take a party of men to Charlestown Neck, launch the " fire-boats" there, and carry them up Mystic River, or such other place as they might judge to be safe from the men-of-war's boats. This agrees with the British letter, on page 98.

Warren and Brigadier-general Putnam, in a phaeton, together
with Major Dunbar and Lieutenant Hamilton, of the 64th, on
horseback; Lieut. Potter, of the marines, in a chaise; John
Hilton, of the 47th, Alexander Campbell, of the 4th, John
Tyne, Samuel Marcy, Thomas Parry, and Thomas Sharp, of
the marines, wounded men, in two carts, — the whole escorted
by the Wethersfield company, under the command of Captain
Chester, — entered the town of Charlestown, and marching
slowly through it, halted at the ferry, when, upon a signal
being given, Major Moncrief landed from the Lively, in order
to receive the prisoners, and see his old friend, General Putnam. Their meeting was truly cordial and affectionate. The
wounded privates were soon sent on board the Lively; but
Major Moncrief and the other officers returned with General
Putnam and Dr. Warren to the house of Dr. Foster, where an
entertainment was provided for them. About three o'clock,
a signal was made by the Lively that they were ready to
deliver up our prisoners; upon which, General Putnam and
Major Moncrief went to the ferry, where they received Messrs.
John Peck, James Hews, James Brewer, and Daniel Preston,
of Boston; Messrs. Samuel Frost and Seth Russell, of Cambridge;[1] Mr. Joseph Bell, of Danvers; Mr. Elijah Seaver, of
Roxbury, and Cæsar Augustus, a negro servant of Mr. Tileston, of Dorchester, who were conducted to the house of Captain Foster, and there refreshed; after which, the general and
major returned to their company, and spent an hour or two in
a very agreeable manner. Between five and six o'clock,
Major Moncrief, with the officers that had been delivered to
him, were conducted to the ferry, where the Lively's barge
received them; after which, General Putnam, with the prisoners who had been delivered to him, &c., returned to
Cambridge, escorted in the same manner as before. The
whole was conducted with the utmost decency and good
humor; and the Wethersfield company did honor to themselves, their officers, and their country. The regular officers
expressed themselves as highly pleased: those who had been
prisoners politely acknowledged the genteel, kind treatment

[1] Some of these were prisoners of war, taken on the 19th of April. See
the list, p. 81.

they had received from their captors; the privates, who were all wounded men, expressed in the strongest terms their grateful sense of the tenderness which had been shown them in their miserable situation, — some of them could only do it by their tears. It would have been to the honor of the British arms, if the prisoners taken from us could with justice have made the same acknowledgment."

On the 12th of June General Gage issued his memorable proclamation — arrogant in its tone, and grossly insulting to the people. It commenced in the following strain : "Whereas the infatuated multitudes, who have long suffered themselves to be conducted by certain well known incendiaries and traitors, in a fatal progression of crimes against the constitutional authority of the state, have at length proceeded to avowed rebellion, and the good effects which were expected to arise from the patience and lenity of the king's government have been often frustrated, and are now rendered hopeless, by the influence of the same evil counsels, it only remains for those who are intrusted with the supreme rule, as well for the punishment of the guilty as the protection of the well-affected, to prove that they do not bear the sword in vain." It declared martial law; pronounced those in arms and their abettors "to be rebels and traitors," and offered pardon to such as should lay down their arms or "stand distinct and separate from the parricides of the constitution," — "excepting only from the benefit of such pardon Samuel Adams and John Hancock, whose offences are of too flagitious a nature to admit of any other consideration than that of condign punishment." This document only served to exasperate the people. The Massachusetts Congress prepared a counter proclamation, which was not, however, issued. This paper war was stopped by the important operations of the field.[1]

The rumors that the British troops intended to make a sally

---

[1] The indignation which this proclamation excited is well shown in one of Mrs. Adams' letters. She writes, June 15, 1775, to her husband, John Adams : "Gage's Proclamation you will receive by this conveyance. All the records of time cannot produce a blacker page. Satan, when driven from the regions of bliss, exhibited not more malice. Surely the father of lies is superseded. Yet we think it the best proclamation he could have issued.'

out of Boston were not without foundation. General Gage
was advised to occupy Charlestown Heights and Dorchester
Heights, — both of them military positions of the greatest
importance; and he postponed offensive operations only until
he should receive the expected reinforcements. At length
they had mostly arrived; and also the Generals Howe, Clinton, and Burgoyne.[1] The army, complete, it was said, would
amount to ten thousand men.[2] It was in high spirits, in a
high state of discipline,[3] well provided with officers, and portions of it were inured to hard service. It continued to entertain a low opinion of its antagonists. Its commanders would
hardly allow that they were in a state of siege by so ill-
appointed a force as the raw militia that had gathered in their
neighborhood. General Gage, however, but gave vent to
wounded pride, when, in his proclamation — June 12 — he
said that " the rebels" added "insult to outrage," as " with a
preposterous parade of military arrangement, they affected to
hold the army besieged." Hence he determined to enlarge
his quarters, and no doubt intended to penetrate into the

[1] These generals arrived in the Cerberus, May 25. The following appeared
in the newspapers just before the battle of Bunker Hill : —"When the three
generals, lately arrived, were going into Boston, they met a packet coming
out, bound to this place, (Newport,) when, we hear, General Burgoyne
asked the skipper of the packet — ' What news there was ?' And being
told that Boston was surrounded by 10,000 country people, asked — ' How
many regulars there were in Boston ?' and being answered about 5000, cried
out, with astonishment, ' What ! ten thousand peasants keep five thousand
king's troops shut up ! Well, let *us* get in, and we 'll soon find elbow-
room.' Hence this phrase, " Elbow-room," was much used all through the
revolution. General Burgoyne is designated by Elbow-room in the satires
of the time. It is said that he loved a joke, and used to relate, that after
his Canada reverses, while a prisoner of war, he was received with great
courtesy by the Boston people, as he stepped from the Charlestown ferry-
boat ; but he was really annoyed when an old lady, perched on a shed above
the crowd, cried out at the top of a shrill voice : " Make way, make way —
the general's coming ! Give him elbow-room !"   [2] Letter, June 18.

[3] A British general order, on the 14th of June, after minute directions as
to drilling and firing, directs that non-commissioned officers, drummers, and
privates, shall " have their hair cut uniformly close in the front," leaving as
much as " will appear the most becoming and smart, and to wear it uniformly
clubbed behind ; and the commanding officer expects to see the men always
exceedingly well and smoothly powdered." — Waller's Orderly Book.

country. The letters of the officers continued to be as boast-
ful and as confident as ever. They regarded the idea that
such a body of British veterans could be successfully resisted,
to be as preposterous as the idea was that they were really
besieged. They expected to be able to conquer their rustic
enemies as easily as, at home, they could scatter a mob.
Even the experience of the nineteenth of April was lost upon
them. They expected to see the same militia, who had
fought so bravely from behind stone walls, run like sheep in
the open field.

Reports of the designs of the British commander found
their way to the American camp, and measures were planned
to counteract them. The committee of safety and the council
of war appointed a joint committee to reconnoitre, especially,
the heights of Charlestown. Their report, May 12, recommended the construction of a breastwork near the Red House,
near the road leading to the McLean Asylum; another opposite, on the side of Prospect Hill; a redoubt on the top of the
hill where the guard-house stood, Winter Hill, to be manned
with three or four nine-pounders; and a strong redoubt on
Bunker Hill, provided with cannon, to annoy the enemy either
going out by land or by water. "When these are finished,"
the committee say, "we apprehend the country will be safe
from all sallies of the enemies in that quarter." [1] This report
was referred to the council of war.

The council of war accepted the report so far as to author-

<hr>

[1] Journals of Provincial Congress, p. 543. This report was signed by
Benjamin Church, chairman of the sub-committee from the committee of
safety, and William Henshaw, chairman of a committee from the council of
war. Colonel Henshaw, in a letter written to Governor Brooks, (in 1818,)
gives the following relation : — "General Ward, the fore part of May,
requested Colonel Gridley, Mr. Richard Devens, one of the committee of
safety in Charlestown, and self, to view the heights from the camp in Charlestown. We did so, and made a written report as follows, viz : 1. To build
a fort on Prospect Hill. 2. To proceed to Bunker Hill and fortify it. 3. To
Breed's Hill and do the same." — Worcester Magazine, vol. ii., p. 126.
Colonel Henshaw, however, most probably refers to the written report in the
text. He was not correct in his recollection. It was not Breed's Hill that he
recommended, — but Bunker Hill, Winter Hill, and Prospect Hill. There
was no guard-house at this time on Breed's Hill.

ize the construction of a part of these works. But on the most important measure, that of occupying Bunker Hill, there was much difference of opinion. General Putnam, Colonel Prescott, and other veteran officers, were strongly in favor of it, and chiefly to draw the enemy out of Boston on ground where he might be met on equal terms. They urged that the army wished to be employed, and that the country was growing dissatisfied with its inactivity.[1] They felt great confidence in the militia. "The Americans," Putnam said, "were not afraid of their heads, though very much afraid of their legs; if you cover these, they will fight forever."[2] Generals Ward and Warren were among those who opposed it, and chiefly because the army was not in a condition, as it respected cannon and powder, to maintain so exposed a post; and because it might bring on a general engagement, which it was neither politic nor safe to risk.[3] It was determined to take possession of Bunker Hill, and also of Dorchester Heights, but not until the army should be better organized, more abundantly supplied with powder, and better able to defend posts so exposed.[4]

The contemplated operations of General Gage, however, brought matters to a crisis. He fixed upon the night of June 18, to take possession of Dorchester Heights. Authentic advice of this was communicated — June 13 — to the American commanders. The committee of safety, on the same day, ordered the general to procure an immediate return of the state and equipments of the several regiments. On the 15th, it resolved to recommend to the Provincial Congress to provide for an immediate augmentation of the army, and to order that the militia of the colony hold themselves ready to march on the shortest notice. Also, that it issue a general recommendation to the people to go to meeting armed, on the Lord's day, in order to prevent being thrown into confusion. The committee of safety then passed, on the same day, the following resolve : —

"Whereas, it appears of importance to the safety of this colony, that possession of the hill called Bunker's Hill, in Charlestown, be securely kept and defended; and also, some

---

[1] Ms. Memoir, by Daniel Putnam. [2] Gov. Brooks. [3] Daniel Putnam. Gray's Ms. Letter, July 12, 1775.

In Committee of Safety

Cambridge June 15: 1775

Whereas it appears of Importance to the Safety of this Colony, that possession of the Hills called Bunkers hills in Charlestown be securely kept, and defended; and also some one hill or hills on Dorchester be likewise Secured. Therefore

unanimously

Resolved, that it be recommended to the Council of War, that the abovementioned Bunkers hill be maintained, by sufficient force being posted there, and as the particular Situation of Dorchester neck is unknown to this Committee they advise that the Council of War pursue such steps respecting the same, as to them shall appear to be, for the Security of this Colony.

Benja: White Chairman

one hill or hills on Dorchester Neck be likewise secured : therefore, resolved, unanimously, that it be recommended to the council of war, that the above mentioned Bunker's Hill be maintained, by sufficient forces being posted there ; and as the particular situation of Dorchester Neck is unknown to this committee, they advise that the council of war take and pursue such steps, respecting the same, as to them shall appear to be for the security of this colony."

The committee then appointed Colonel Palmer and Captain White to join with a committee from the council of war, and proceed to the Roxbury camp for consultation ; also to communicate the above resolve to the council. To secure secrecy, this important resolve was not recorded until the nineteenth of June.

At this time but comparatively small progress had been made in building fortifications. Breastworks had been thrown up in Cambridge, but no works had been commenced on Prospect Hill, or on Winter Hill. A breastwork had been also thrown up on the Cambridge road, near the base of Prospect Hill. The army was posted nearly in the following manner. The right wing, under General Thomas, was at Roxbury; and consisted of about four thousand Massachusetts troops, the Rhode Island forces under General Greene at Jamaica Plains, and the greater part of General Spencer's regiment of Connecticut troops. General Thomas had three or four artillery companies with field-pieces, and a few heavy cannon. General Ward's head quarters were at Cambridge, where the centre division of the army was stationed. It consisted of fifteen Massachusetts regiments; the battalion of artillery, hardly organized, under Colonel Gridley; and General Putnam's regiment, with other Connecticut troops. They were quartered in the colleges, in the church, and in tents. Most of the Connecticut troops were at Inman's Farm; part of Little's regiment was at the tavern in West Cambridge; Patterson's regiment was at the breastwork, near Prospect Hill; and a large guard was at Lechmere's Point. There were in Cambridge, it is stated, (probably incorrectly,) but four companies of artillery with field-pieces. Of the left wing of the army three companies of Gerrish's regiment were at

Chelsea ; Stark's regiment was at Medford ; and Reed's regiment was at Charlestown Neck, with sentinels reaching to Penny Ferry (Malden Bridge) and Bunker Hill.[1]

The peninsula of Charlestown is situated opposite to the north part of Boston, and is separated from it by Charles River. It is about a mile in length from north to south, and

[1] The return nearest in date to the battle, that I have been able to find, of the troops at Cambridge, is the following, dated June 9, and entitled, " Return of the Army at Cambridge."

Regiments.	Privates.	Regiments.	Privates.
Whitcomb, . . .	470	Frye, ...	493
Brewer, . . .	318	Scammon, . . .	396
Nixon, ...	224	Prescott, . . .	456
Little, ...	400	Gerrish, . . .	421
Mansfield, . . .	345	Woodbridge, . .	242
Gridley, (artillery,) .	370	Ward, . . .	449
Bridge, ...	315	Gardner, . . .	425
Doolittle, . . .	308	Patterson, . . .	422
			6063
		Drummers, &c., .	1581
			7644

A Return of Colonel Gridley's battalion, dated June 16, gives but an imperfect view of it. The captains and the number of men were : Edward Crafts, 44 ; Joseph Chadwick, 24 ; Edward Burbeck, 25 ; Thomas Wait Foster, 43 ; Thomas Pierce, 47 ; Samuel Gridley, 49 ; John Popkin, 49 ; Samuel R. Trevett, 37 ; John Wiley, 52 ; John Callender, 47. A large portion of their arms are returned as unfit for service. The cannon are not named.

The regiments stationed at Roxbury were those of Thomas, Learned, Fellows, Cotton, Walker, Read, Danielson, Brewer, Robinson — 93 companies, 3992 men.

Colonel Swett, in his history of the battle of Bunker Hill, mentions another regiment, under Colonel Sergeant, of New Hampshire. This officer took out beating orders, on the condition, that if he succeeded in raising a regiment, and the New Hampshire colony would not accept of it, that it should be established in the Massachusetts service. On the 9th of June he had but four companies at head quarters, but had a few more men enlisted in New Hampshire. A committee recommended that these companies should be discharged from the service of Massachusetts. Some of the companies enlisted by Colonel Sergeant appear in the rolls of Stark's and Reed's regiments. I do not find his name among the returns of the army until after the 17th of June, when he had the command of a Massachusetts regiment. It appears from his own letter, see Chapter VI., that he was on duty on the 17th of June

its greatest breadth, next to Boston, is about half a mile, whence it gradually becomes narrower until it makes an isthmus, called the Neck, connecting it with the main land. The Mystic River, about half a mile wide, is on the east side ; and on the west side is Charles River, which here forms a large bay, — a part of which, by a dam stretching in the direction of Cobble Hill, is a mill-pond. In 1775 the Neck, an artificial causeway, was so low as to be frequently overflowed by the tides. The communication with Boston was by a ferry, where Charles River Bridge is, and with Malden by another, called Penny Ferry, where Malden Bridge is. Near the Neck, on the main land, there was a large green, known as The Common. Two roads ran by it, — one in a westerly direction, as now, by Cobble Hill, (McLean Asylum,) Prospect Hill, Inman's Woods, to Cambridge Common ; the other in a northerly direction, by Ploughed Hill, (Mount Benedict,) Winter Hill, to Medford, — the direct road to West Cambridge not having been laid out in 1775. Bunker Hill begins at the isthmus, and rises gradually for about three hundred yards, forming a round, smooth hill, sloping on two sides towards the water, and connected by a ridge of ground on the south with the heights now known as Breed's Hill. This was a well known public place, — the name "Bunker Hill" being found in the town records, and in deeds, from an early period. Not so with "Breed's Hill," for it is not named in any description of streets previous to 1775. This tract of land was called after the owners of the pastures into which it was divided, rather than by the common name of Breed's Hill. Thus, Monument-square was called Russell's Pasture ; Breed's Pasture lay further south ; Green's Pasture was at the head of Green-street.[1] The easterly and westerly sides of this height were

---

[1] This hill is called Green's Hill in a British description of the town in 1775. It has been often remarked that Breed's Hill has been robbed of the glory that justly belongs to it. It should be remembered, however, that the rail fence was at the base of Bunker Hill, and if not the great post of the day, here a large part of the battle was fought. Besides, the name Breed' Hill will not do near so well for patriotic purposes. Thus, in the " Declaration of Independence," a poem, the author writes : —

> Dun clouds of smoke ! avaunt ! — Mount Breed, all hail !
> There glory circled patriot Warren's head.

steep; on the east side, at its base, were brick-kilns, clay-pits, and much sloughy land; on the west side, at the base, was the most settled part of the town.   Moulton's Point, a name coeval with the settlement of the town, constituted the south-east corner of the peninsula.   A part of this tract formed what is called, in all the accounts of the battle, "Morton's Hill."   Bunker Hill was one hundred and ten feet high, Breed's seventy-five feet, and Morton's Hill thirty-five feet.   The principal street of the peninsula was Main-street, which extended from the neck to the ferry.   A highway from sixteen feet to thirty feet wide ran over Bunker Hill to Moulton's Point, and one connecting with it wound round the heights now known by the name of Breed's Hill.   The easterly portions of these hills were used chiefly for hay ground and pasturing; the westerly portions contained fine orchards and gardens.

CONCORD MONUMENT.

Mystery Hill

Charlestown

Bunker Hill

Moulton's Point

Breed's Hill

Narrow Pass

A VIEW OF CHARLES TOWN, AND THE BACK GROUND, AS FAR AS THE NARROW PASS,

Taken from the Beacon Hill.

CHAPTER IV.

Breed's Hill Fortified.   Cannonade of the British.   The Landing at Charlestown.

ON Friday, the sixteenth of June, the commanders of the
army, in accordance with the recommendation of the committee of safety, took measures to fortify Bunker Hill.[1]   Orders
were issued for Prescott's, Frye's, and Bridge's regiments, and
a fatigue party of two hundred Connecticut troops, to parade
at six o'clock in the evening, with all the intrenching tools in
the Cambridge camp.   They were also ordered to furnish
themselves with packs and blankets, and with provisions for
twenty-four hours.   Also, Captain Samuel Gridley's company of artillery, of forty-nine men and two field-pieces, was

[1] The narrative of the Bunker Hill battle, in the text, is the result of as
critical a collation of the authorities as I am able to make.   A chronological
notice of the principal of them will be found in the Appendix.   All of them
have been consulted.   Great caution is necessary in using the material which
controversy on this subject has elicited.   It is but just to remark, however,
that many of the depositions of the soldiers harmonize remarkably with each
other, and with contemporary material.

I am indebted to Colonel Samuel Swett for permission to take copies of
his manuscripts.   The authorities cited as Gov. Brooks, Joseph Pearce, and
Ebenezer Bancroft, are statements chiefly taken by him.   He states (Notes
to his History, p. 3) that any person may take copies of any documents in
his possession.

A memoir of the battle, prepared by the late Judge William Prescott, the
son of Colonel Prescott, and in his own hand-writing, is often quoted.   The
high character of the author, and his rare opportunity for obtaining information, unite to render this an invaluable authority.   I am indebted to President
Jared Sparks for this manuscript, and other material.   Col. Prescott's account of the action, also an important authority, will be found in the Appendix.

The testimony on some points is perplexing and conflicting ; and though
I have endeavored to frame the narrative without partiality or prejudice, yet
I submit it with great diffidence , and will only add, that I feel incapable of
intentionally disparaging the services of any of the patriot band who bore a
part in this great work.

ordered to parade.   The Connecticut men, draughted from
several companies, were put under the gallant Thomas Knowlton, a captain in General Putnam's regiment.[1]

The detachment was placed under the command of Colonel
William Prescott, of Pepperell, who had orders in writing, from
General Ward, to proceed that evening to Bunker Hill, build
fortifications to be planned by Col. Richard Gridley, the chief
engineer, and defend them until he should be relieved, — the
order not to be communicated until the detachment had passed
Charlestown Neck.[2]   The regiments and fatigue party ordered
to parade would have constituted a force of at least fourteen
hundred; but only three hundred of Prescott's regiment, a
part of Bridge's, and a part of Frye's under Lieut.-col. Bricket,
the artillery, and the two hundred Connecticut troops, were
ordered to march.[3]   Hence the number may be fairly estimated
at twelve hundred.[4]   It was understood that reinforcements
and refreshments should be sent to Colonel Prescott on the
following morning.[5]

This detachment paraded on Cambridge Common at the
time appointed; and after a fervent and impressive prayer by
President Langdon, of Harvard College, it commenced, about
nine o'clock, its memorable march for Charlestown.   Colonel
Prescott was at its head, arrayed in a simple and appropriate
uniform, with a blue coat and a three-cornered hat.[6]   Two
sergeants, carrying dark lanterns, were a few paces in front
of him, and the intrenching tools, in carts, in the rear.   Col.
Gridley accompanied the troops.   They were enjoined to
maintain the strictest silence, and were not aware of the object
of the expedition until they halted at Charlestown Neck.
Here Major Brooks joined them; and, probably, General Put-

---

[1] The committee of safety account says: "Orders were issued that a
detachment of one thousand men should that evening march," &c.   Fenno's
Orderly Book, June 16, says: "Frye's, Bridge's, and William Prescott's
regiments to parade this evening, at six o'clock, with all the intrenching tools
in this encampment."   Chester's letter says 200 Connecticut men were
called for. — Letter July 22.

[2] Judge Prescott's Memoir; Gordon, vol. I., p. 362; Martin's Relation
[3] Prescott's Letter.   [4] This was the estimate of the Mass. Provincial Con
gress.   Col. Prescott says, "about one thousand."   [5] Brooks.   [6] El'is'
Oration.

nam[1] and another general. Here Captain Nutting, with his company and ten of the Connecticut troops, was ordered to proceed to the lower part of the town as a guard.[2] The main body then marched over Bunker Hill, and again halted for some time. Here Colonel Prescott called the field officers around him, and communicated his orders.[3] A long consultation took place in relation to the place to be fortified. The veteran Colonel Gridley, and two generals, one of whom was General Putnam, took part in it. The order was explicit as to Bunker Hill, and yet a position nearer Boston, now known as Breed's Hill, seemed better adapted to the objects of the expedition, and better suited the daring spirit of the officers. It was contended, however, that works ought not to be commenced at this place until Bunker Hill had been fortified, in order to cover, in case of necessity, a retreat. The moments were precious, and the engineer strongly urged the importance of a speedy decision. On the pressing importunity of one of the generals, it was concluded to proceed to Breed's Hill.[4]

[1] Judge Prescott states that General Putnam did not head the detachment from Cambridge to Bunker Hill, nor march with it. Some of the soldiers state that he rode up at the Neck.

[2] Abel Parker; Brooks; Cleaveland. [3] Brooks says the troops halted at the foot of Breed's Hill.

"Colonel Prescott had determined never to be taken alive. A few months before the battle, while he commanded a regiment of minute-men, his brother-in-law, Colonel Willard, was at his house; and endeavoring to dissuade him from the active part he was taking against the king's government, among other things suggested, that if he should be found in arms against it, his life and estate would be forfeited for treason. He replied : ' I have made up my mind on that subject. I think it probable I may be found in arms, but I will never be taken alive. The Tories shall never have the satisfaction of seeing me hanged.' He went on to the heights with that resolution." — Judge Prescott's Memoir.

[4] The order was explicit as to Bunker Hill, and the committee of safety account says, " by some mistake," Breed's Hill was marked out for the intrenchment. In Gray's letter, July 12, 1775, it is stated, " that the engineer and two generals went on to the hill at night, and reconnoitred the ground ; that one general and the engineer were of opinion we ought not to intrench on Charlestown Hill (Breed's Hill) till we had thrown up some works on the north and south ends of Bunker Hill, to cover our men in their retreat, if that should happen; but on the pressing importunity of the other general officer, it was consented to begin as was done." That the best posi

At the same time it was determined that works should be
erected on Bunker Hill.   When the detachment reached
Breed's Hill, the packs were thrown off, the guns were
stacked, Colonel Gridley marked out the plan of a fortification, tools were distributed, and about twelve o'clock the men
began to work.   Colonel Prescott immediately detached Captain Maxwell, of his own regiment, and a party, with orders
to patrol the shore in the lower part of the town, near the old
ferry, and watch the motions of the enemy during the night.[1]
General Putnam, after the men were at labor, returned to
Cambridge.[2]

Anxious to the patriot laborers were the watches of that
star-light night.   The shore in Boston, opposite to them, was
belted by a chain of sentinels, while nearer still, British men-
of-war were moored in the waters around them and commanded the peninsula.   The Falcon was off Moulton's Point;
the Lively lay opposite the present navy yard; the Somerset
was at the ferry; the Glasgow was near Cragie's Bridge;
and the Cerberus, and several floating batteries, were within
gunshot.   This proximity to an enemy required great caution;
and a thousand men, accustomed to handling the spade,
worked with great diligence and silence on the intrenchments;[3] while the cry of "All's well," heard at intervals

tion was Breed's Hill, Judge Prescott says, was "Colonel Gridley's opinion,
and the other field officers who were consulted, — they thought it came within his (Prescott's) orders.   There was not then the distinction between Bunker Hill and Breed's that has since been made."   Colonel Swett remarks
there could be no mistake, and that the account meant to say, delicately, the
order to fortify Bunker Hill was not complied with.

It has been doubted whether General Putnam was on the ground during
the night.   Gray's letter does not give the names of the two generals, it is
true, but in Stiles' Diary, June 20, in Major Jackson's Diary, June 16,
(Swett's notes, p. 21,) and in the newspapers of the day, Putnam is named
as going on at night.   The testimony of some of the soldiers is positive.
Thus Judge Grosvenor, in letters dated April 18, 1818, and March 29, 1825,
says that he was present when ground was broken.   Judge Prescott states,
that though he did not march with the troops, he might be present at the
consultation.

[1] William Taylor's Letter; J. Pearce; Depositions.   [2] Swett, p. 21.

[3] Martin says, about a thousand were at work, and that "the men dug in
the trenches one hour, and then mounted guard and were relieved."

through the night by the patrols, gave the assurance that they were not discovered.[1] Colonel Prescott, apprehensive of an attack before the works were in such a condition as to cover the men, went down twice to the margin of the river with Major Brooks to reconnoitre, and was delighted to hear the watch on board the ships drowsily repeat the usual cry.[2] The last time, a little before daylight, finding everything quiet, he recalled the party under Maxwell to the hill.[3]

The intrenchments, by the well-directed labor of the night, were raised about six feet high, and were first seen at early dawn, on the seventeenth of June, by the sailors on board the men-of-war. The captain of the Lively, without waiting for orders, put a spring on her cable and opened a fire on the American works;[4] and the sound of the guns, breaking the calmness of a fine summer's morning, alarmed the British camp, and summoned the population of Boston and vicinity to gaze upon the novel spectacle. Admiral Graves almost immediately ordered the firing to cease;[5] but, in a short time, it was renewed, by authority, from a battery of six guns and howitzers, from Copp's Hill, in Boston, and from the shipping.[6] The Americans, protected by their works, were not at first injured by the balls, and they kept steadily at labor, strengthening the intrenchments, and making inside of them platforms of wood and earth, to stand upon when they should be called upon to fire.[7]

[1] Brooks; Pearce; Josiah Cleaveland was one of the Connecticut men detached to the shore, and states that he heard the British sentinels at intervals all night. [2] Judge Prescott's Memoir. [3] Brooks; Taylor; Pearce.

" Colonel Prescott was often heard to say, after the battle, that his great anxiety that night was to have a screen raised, however slight, for his men before they were attacked, which he expected would be early in the morning as he knew it would be difficult, if not quite impossible, to make raw troops. however full of patriotism, to stand in an open field against artillery and well-armed and well-disciplined soldiers. He therefore strenuously urged on the work, and every subaltern and private labored with spade and pickaxe, without intermission, through the night, and until they resumed their muskets near the middle of the next day. Never were men in worse condition for action, — exhausted by watching, fatigue, and hunger, — and never did old soldiers behave better." — Judge Prescott's Memoir.

[4] Fenno's Ms. Orderly Book. [5] British Letter, June 25. [6] Ibid, with Gage's official account. [7] Ms. Petitions, 1775; Israel Hunt.

Early in the day, a private[1] was killed by a cannon ball, when some of the men left the hill. To inspire confidence, Colonel Prescott mounted the parapet and walked leisurely around it, inspecting the works, giving directions to the officers, and encouraging the men by approbation, or amusing them with humor. One of his captains, understanding his motive, followed his example while superintending the labors of his company. This had the intended effect. The men became indifferent to the cannonade, or received the balls with repeated cheers. The tall, commanding form of Prescott was observed by General Gage, as he was reconnoitring the Americans through his glass, who inquired of Councillor Willard, near him, "Who the person was who appeared to command?" Willard recognized his brother-in-law. "Will he fight?" again inquired Gage. "Yes, sir; he is an old soldier, and will fight as long as a drop of blood remains in his veins!" "The works must be carried," was the reply.[2]

As the day advanced the heat became oppressive. Many of the men, inexperienced in war, had neglected to comply with the order respecting provisions,[3] while no refreshments had arrived. Hence there was much suffering from want of food and drink, as well as from heat and fatigue; and this

---

[1] Asa Pollard, of Billerica, of Stickney's company, Bridge's regiment. A subaltern informed Col. Prescott, and asked what should be done. "Bury him," he was told. "What!" said the astonished officer, "without prayers?" A chaplain insisted on performing service over the first victim, and gathered many soldiers about him. Prescott ordered them to disperse. The chaplain again collected his audience, when the deceased was ordered to be buried. — Swett's History.

[2] Brooks; Israel Hunt; Prescott's Memoir. The British Annual Register, 1775, says, "the Americans bore this severe fire with wonderful firmness, and seemed to go on with their business as if no enemy had been near." The following are the vessels that took part in the cannonade during the day. The position of the Cerberus is not stated.

Somerset,	68 guns,	520 men.	Captain	Edward Le Cras.
Cerberus,	36 "			"	Chads.
Glasgow,	24 "	130 "		"	William Maltby.
Lively,	20 "	130 "		"	Thomas Bishop.
Falcon,				"	Linzee.
Symmetry,	20 "				

[3] Brooks' Statement.

produced discontent and murmurs. The officers urged Col. Prescott to send a request to General Ward for them to be relieved by other troops. The colonel promptly told them, in reply, that he never would consent to their being relieved. " The enemy," he said, " would not dare to attack them; and if they did, would be defeated : the men who had raised the works were the best able to defend them : already they had learned to despise the fire of the enemy : they had the merit of the labor, and should have the honor of the victory." [1]

Soon after this, the enemy were observed to be in motion in Boston. General Gage had called a council of war early in the morning. As it was clear that the Americans were gaining strength every hour, it was the unanimous opinion that it was necessary to change the plan of operations that had been agreed upon, and drive them from their newly erected works, though different views prevailed as to the manner in which it should be attempted. It is said that Gen. Clinton, and a majority of the council, were in favor of embarking a force at the common, in Boston, and under the protection of their batteries, landing in the rear of the Americans, at Charlestown Neck, to cut off their retreat. General Gage opposed this plan as unmilitary and hazardous. It would place his force between two armies, — one strongly fortified, and the other superior in numbers, — and thus expose it to destruction.[2] It was decided to make the attack in front, and orders were immediately issued for the troops to parade. It was the consequent preparation, — dragoons galloping from their places of encampment, and the rattling of artillery carriages, — that was observed at the American lines. Colonel Prescott, about

[1] Brooks' Statement ; Swett's History ; Prescott's Memoir. [2] British Account, 1775 ; Ms. Letter.

A royalist in Boston at this time used to relate, that knowing the British officers were in consultation at the Province House, on the morning of this day, he called there to learn their intentions. Immediately after the arrangements had been made for the attack, he met in the front yard an officer by the name of Ruggles, who warmly inveighed against the decision of the other officers. " It would cost many lives to attack in front ; but the English officers would not believe the Americans would fight." Ruggles advised the attack to be made in the rear, and thus cut off a retreat and prevent a reinforcement. — Ms. letter.

nine o'clock, called a council of war. The officers represented that the men, worn down by the labors of the night, in want even of necessary refreshments, were dissatisfied, and in no condition for action, and again urged that they should be relieved, or, at least, that Colonel Prescott should send for reinforcements and provisions. The colonel, though decided against the proposition to relieve them, agreed to send a special messenger to General Ward for additional troops and supplies. The officers were satisfied, and Major John Brooks, afterwards Governor Brooks, was despatched for this purpose to head quarters, where he arrived about ten o'clock.[1]

General Ward, early in the morning, had been urged by General Putnam[2] to send reinforcements to Colonel Prescott, but was so doubtful of its expediency that he ordered only one third of Stark's regiment to march to Charlestown;[3] and after receiving the message by Major Brooks, he refused to weaken further the main army at Cambridge, until the enemy had more definitely revealed his intentions. He judged that General Gage would make his principal attack at Cambridge, to destroy the stores.[4] The committee of safety, then in session, was consulted. One of its most active members, Richard Devens, strongly urged that aid should be sent, and his opinion partially prevailed. With its advice, General Ward, about eleven o'clock, ordered the whole of the regiments of Colonels Stark and Read, of New Hampshire, to reinforce Colonel

---

[1] Governor Brooks' Statement. Judge Prescott's Memoir refers only to one consultation of Colonel Prescott with his officers; Governor Brooks states that there were two councils of war, the last at nine o'clock. Martin's relation, though confused, confirms the statement that Prescott was reluctant to send for reinforcements; and Brown's letter agrees with Prescott's Memoir as to the discontent of the men.

Judge Prescott states that the colonel despatched two men, in the course of the forenoon, to head quarters — the last Major Brooks. " For greater expedition," Col. Swett says, " he was directed to take one of the artillery horses; but the order was vehemently opposed by Capt. Gridley, who feared for the safety of his pieces. Prescott then directed him to proceed on foot."

[2] Grosvenor, Daniel Putnam, and others, state that General Putnam repaired to the heights early in the morning, but returned to Cambridge to urge on provisions and reinforcements. — See Swett's History, p. 24.

[3] Stark's Letter.   [4] Analectic Magazine, 1818.   Gov. Brooks

Prescott.[1] Orders, also, were issued for the recall of the companies stationed at Chelsea.[2]

During the forenoon a flood tide enabled the British to bring three or four floating batteries to play on the intrenchments, when the fire became more severe. The men-of-war at intervals discharged their guns, — the Glasgow, one account states, continued to fire all the morning.[3] The only return made to this terrific cannonade was a few ineffectual shot from a cannon in a corner of the redoubt.[4] About eleven o'clock the men had mostly ceased labor on the works; the intrenching tools had been piled in the rear, and all were anxiously awaiting the arrival of refreshments and reinforcements. No works, however, had been commenced on Bunker Hill, regarded as of great importance in case of a retreat. General Putnam who was on his way to the heights when Major Brooks was going to Cambridge, rode on horseback to the redoubt, "and told Colonel Prescott" — as General Heath first relates the circumstance — "that the intrenching tools must be sent off,

---

[1] Stark; Brooks; Dearborn. [2] Swett.

On this day the Provincial Congress, convened at Watertown, held sessions morning and afternoon. The committee of safety, in session at Cambridge, issued an order to the selectmen of the towns to send all the town stocks of powder instantly to Watertown. The committee of supplies, by David Cheever, on this day, sent a letter to the committee of safety, stating, That exclusive of thirty-six half barrels of powder received from the governor and council of Connecticut, there were only in the magazine twenty-seven half barrels, and that no more could be drafted from the towns without exposing them more than they would consent to.

The committee of safety, on this day, asked, also, for " four of the best riding horses," to bring quick intelligence to head quarters. The committee of supplies replied, that they had no horses at present, but what were unfit for use, or were wanted for the expresses of that committee. " We have received," says the letter, " but ten out of the twenty-eight horses ordered by Congress to be delivered us, and are informed that those left behind are some of the best. Pray take them, if to be found, unless detained by the generals. We have sent to procure four, which shall be sent as soon as possible."

[3] Fenno's Orderly Book ; British Letter. [4] Winslow ; J. Pearce ; Clarke. The latter, in his pamphlet, states that cannon were fired, " to the infinite terror and danger of the inhabitants " of Boston, and that it was in consequence of this insult that General Gage determined to attack the redoubt.

or they would be lost : the colonel replied, that if he sent any
of the men away with the tools, not one of them would return :
to this the general answered, they shall every man return.   A
large party was then sent off with the tools, and not one of
them returned : in this instance the colonel was the best judge
of human nature."¹ A large part of the tools were carried
no further than Bunker Hill, where, by General Putnam's
order, the men began to throw up a breastwork. Most of
the tools fell into the hands of the enemy.

In the mean time General Gage had completed his preparations to attack the intrenchments. He ordered the ten oldest
companies of grenadiers and light-infantry, (exclusive of two
regiments, the 35th and 49th, just arrived,) and the 5th and
38th regiments, to parade at half-past eleven o'clock, with
ammunition, blankets, and provisions, and march by files to
the Long Wharf. The 52d and 43d regiments, with the
remaining companies of grenadiers and light-infantry, received
similar orders to parade and march to the North Battery. At
the same time the 47th regiment and 1st battalion of marines
were directed to proceed to the battery after the former should
embark, and there await orders. The remainder of the troops
were directed to hold themselves in readiness to march at a
moment's warning. The strictest attention to discipline was
enjoined. Whoever should quit the ranks, or engage in plun-

¹ Heath's Memoirs, p. 19. This is the only instance of a collision of General Putnam with Colonel Prescott that appears in the authorities. The
depositions often contain stories of the intrenching tools, and much has been
written about them in connection with General Putnam. Joseph Pearce, in
1818, stated, "Putnam, before we saw the British on the water, came and
said the tools ought to be carried off. Came on a horse. I expected to see
him knocked off." E. Bancroft, in a Ms. letter, December 7, 1824, says :
After ten o'clock General Putnam " rode up to us at the fort, and says, ' My
lads, these tools must be carried back,' and turned and rode away. An order
was never obeyed with more readiness. From every part of the line within
hearing volunteers ran, and some picked up one, some two shovels, mattocks,
&c., and hurried over the hill." Heath is too severe on the party who carried the tools to Bunker Hill. Some of them fought well at the rail fence,
and some state that they went back to the redoubt. It is probable that this
incident is the origin of the impression of some of the soldiers, who stated,
over forty years after, that Putnam rode off the field with pick-axes, spades
tents or tent-poles, on his horse !

der, was threatened with execution without mercy.[1] This force was put under the command of General Howe, who had under him Brigadier-general Pigot, and some of the most distinguished officers in Boston. He was ordered to drive the Americans from their works.[2]

About twelve o'clock the several regiments marched through the streets of Boston to their places of embarkation, and two ships of war moved up Charles River to join the others in firing on the works. Suddenly the redoubled roar of the cannon announced that the crisis was at hand. The Falcon and the Lively swept the low grounds in front of Breed's Hill, to dislodge any parties of troops that might be posted there to oppose a landing; the Somerset and two floating batteries at the ferry, and the battery on Copps Hill, poured shot upon the American works; the Glasgow frigate, and the Symmetry transport, moored further up Charles River, raked the Neck.[3] The troops embarked at the Long Wharf and at the North Battery; and when a blue flag was displayed as a signal, the fleet, with field-pieces in the leading barges, moved towards Charlestown. The sun was shining in meridian splendor; and the scarlet uniforms, the glistening armor, the brazen artillery, the regular movement of the boats, the flashes of fire, and the belchings of smoke, formed a spectacle brilliant and imposing. The army landed in good order at Moulton's Point, about one o'clock, without the slightest molestation, and immediately formed in three lines. General Howe, after

[1] This account is taken from Adjutant Waller's (British) Orderly Book. A British letter, June 25, states that the troops embarked "at the Long Wharf, and at the North Battery." [2] Stedman's History, vol. i., p. 126 I prefer the authority of the orderly book, and of contemporaries, in relation to the embarkation, to others.

[3] Joseph Pearce stated: "It was the heaviest cannonade previous to the landing." A Boston letter, June 25, says: "The landing was covered by a heavy fire from the Lively and another man-of-war stationed off the North Battery, a large sloop and two floating batteries at Charlestown Ferry, the battery from Copps Hill, a transport mounting twenty guns, lying a little higher up, and the Glasgow man-of-war." A British letter, June 23, states: "At the landing several attempted to run away, and five actually took to their heels to join the Americans, but were presently brought back, and two of them were hung up in terrorem to the rest."

reconnoitring the American works, applied to General Gage for a reinforcement; and, while waiting for it to arrive, many of his troops quietly dined. It proved to many a brave man his last meal.

When the intelligence of the landing of the British troops reached Cambridge, there was suddenly great noise and confusion. The bells were rung, the drums beat to arms, and adjutants rode hurriedly from point to point, with orders for troops to march and oppose the enemy.[1] General Ward reserved his own regiment, Patterson's, Gardner's, and part of Bridge's regiments, to be prepared for any attack on Cambridge, but ordered the remainder of the Massachusetts forces to Charlestown.[2] General Putnam ordered on the remainder of the Connecticut troops.[3] Colonel Gardner's regiment was directed to march to Patterson's station, opposite Prospect Hill. A large part of these forces, owing to various causes, failed to reach the lines.

[1] Chester's letter, July 22, 1775, gives a life-like picture of what fell under his own observation, when the news arrived of the landing. "Just after dinner, on Saturday, 17th ult., I was walking out from my lodgings quite calm and composed, and all at once the drums beat to arms, and bells rang, and a great noise in Cambridge. Captain Putnam came by on full gallop. 'What is the matter?' says I. 'Have you not heard?' 'No.' 'Why, the regulars are landing at Charlestown,' says he, 'and father says you must all meet, and march immediately to Bunker Hill to oppose the enemy.' I waited not, but ran and got my arms and ammunition, and hasted to my company, (who were in the church for barracks,) and found them nearly ready to march. We soon marched, with our frocks and trousers on over our other clothes, (for our company is in uniform wholly blue, turned up with red,) for we were loth to expose ourselves by our dress; and down we marched." I had from Jesse Smith, of Nixon's regiment, a similar description of the sudden alarm at Cambridge. Simeon Noyes, 1825, states, "The bell was ringing; our adjutant, Stephen Jenkens, rode up and hallooed, 'Turn out! turn out! the enemy's all landed at Charlestown!'" [2] Swett.

[3] Chester. Letter dated Cambridge, June 19, 1775, signed by John Chester and Samuel B. Webb, and addressed to Joseph Webb, has interesting facts. They state, "About one o'clock we that were at Cambridge heard that the regulars were landing"—and they "were ordered to march directly down to the fort." Mss. See p. 415.

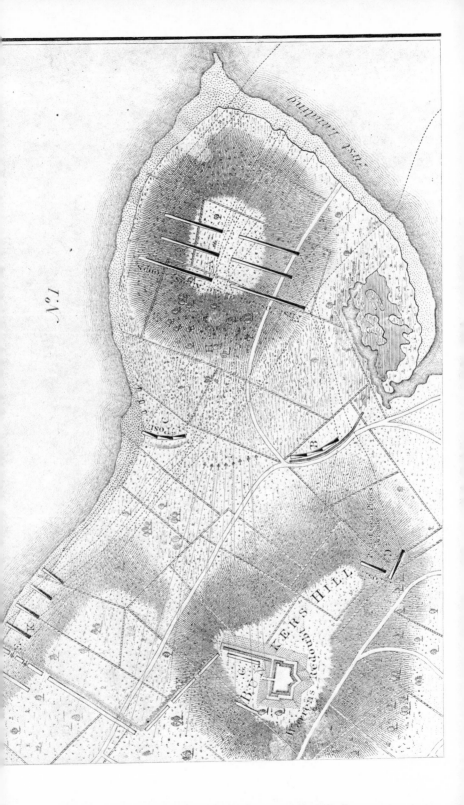

CHAPTER V.

The Battle of Bunker Hill.   The Burning of Charlestown.   The Retreat of
the Americans.

ABOUT two o'clock in the afternoon intense anxiety prevailed
at the intrenchments on Breed's Hill.   The patriot band who
raised them had witnessed the brilliant landing of the British
veterans, and the return of the barges to Boston.   They saw
troops again filling the boats, and felt not without apprehension that a battle was inevitable.   They knew the contest
would be an unequal one, — that of raw militia against the
far-famed regulars, — and they grew impatient for the promised reinforcements.   But no signs appeared that additional
troops were on the way to support them, and even the supply
of refreshments that reached them was so scanty that it served
only to tantalize their wants.[1]   It is not strange, therefore, the
idea was entertained that they had been rashly, if not treach-
erously, led into danger, and that they were to be left to their
own resources for their defence.   This idea, however, must
have been dispelled, as characters who had long been identified with the patriot cause, who were widely known and
widely beloved, appeared on the field, and assured them that
aid was at hand.   Such, among others, were Generals Warren
and Pomeroy, who took stations in the ranks as volunteers.
The enthusiastic cheers with which they were greeted indicated how much their presence was valued.   General Putnam

[1] Some of the depositions state that barrels of beer arrived.   Ms. petitions
of 1775 state that teams were impressed to carry on provisions.   Peter
Brown, a private, June 25, 1775, wrote to his mother : " The danger we
were in made us think there was treachery, and that we were brought here
to be all slain.   And I must and will venture to say there was treachery,
oversight, or presumption, in the conduct of our officers."

Warren said that 2000 reinforcements would be down in twenty minutes —
ne came by them.   Said he came to promote or encourage a good cause. — J.
Pearce

also, who had the confidence of the whole army, again rode
on, about this time, with the intention of remaining to share
their labors and peril. He continued in Charlestown through
the afternoon, giving orders to reinforcements as they arrived
on the field, cheering and animating the men, and rendering
valuable service.

The movements of the British, along the margin of Mystic
River, indicated an intention of flanking the Americans, and
of surrounding the redoubt. To prevent this, Col. Prescott
ordered the artillery, with two field-pieces, and Capt. Knowlton with the Connecticut troops, to leave the intrenchments,
march down the hill, and oppose the enemy's right wing.[1]
Captain Knowlton took a position near the base of Bunker
Hill, six hundred feet in the rear of the redoubt, behind a
fence, one half of which was stone, with two rails of wood.
He then made, a little distance in front of this, another parallel line of fence, and filled the space between them with the
newly cut grass lying in the fields.[2] While Captain Knowlton's party was doing this, between two and three o'clock,
Colonel John Stark, with his regiment, arrived at the Neck,
which was then enfiladed by a galling fire from the enemy's
ships and batteries. Captain Dearborn, who was by the side
of the colonel, suggested to him the expediency of quickening
his step across; but Stark replied, "One fresh man in action is
worth ten fatigued ones," and marched steadily over.[3] General Putnam ordered part of these troops to labor on the works
begun on Bunker Hill, while Colonel Stark, after an animated
address to his men, led the remainder to the position Captain
Knowlton had taken, and they aided in extending the line of
the fence breastwork to the water's edge, by throwing up a
stone wall on the beach.[4] Colonel Reed left the Neck, and

---

[1] Chester's Letter, Prescott's.   [2] Chester is minute on this point, and
says this movement from the redoubt was made by order of "our officers in
command." Grosvenor says, General Putnam ordered Knowlton to this
position. Judge Winthrop, N. A. Review, July, 1818, saw Putnam here
just previous to the first attack ; and Simeon Noyes, 1825, says he rode up
to the company he was in, and said : " Draw off your troops here, ' pointing
to the rail fence, " and man the rail fence, for the enemy 's flanking of us
fast." [3] Dearborn. [4] Wilkinson.

marched over Bunker Hill, and took position near Colonel Stark, at the rail fence.[1]

The defences of the Americans, at three in the afternoon, were still in a rude, unfinished state. The redoubt on the spot where the monument stands was about eight rods square. Its strongest side, the front, facing the settled part of the town, was made with projecting angles, and protected the south side of the hill. The eastern side commanded an extensive field. The north side had an open passage-way. A breastwork, beginning a short distance from the redoubt, and on a line with its eastern side, extended about one hundred yards north towards a slough. A sally-port, between the south end of the breastwork and the redoubt, was protected by a blind. These works were raised about six feet from the level of the ground, and had platforms of wood, or steps made of earth, for the men to stand on when they should fire. The rail fence has been already described. Its south corner was about two hundred yards, on a diagonal line, in the rear of the north corner of the breastwork. This line was slightly protected; a part of it, however — about one hundred yards — between the slough and the rail fence, was open to the approach of infantry. It was the weakest part of the defences. On the right of the redoubt, along a cartway, a fence was made similar to the one on the left. The redoubt and breastwork constituted a good defence against cannon and musketry, but the fences were hardly more than the shadow of protection.[2]

These defences were lined nearly in the following manner. The original detachment, under Colonel Prescott, except the

[1] Reuben Kemp ; Wilkinson's Memoirs, vol. i., 845.

[2] Page's and Bernier's Plans ; Committee of Safety Account ; Depositions ; Swett's History, pp. 20, 27 ; Dearborn's Account. Some who were in the battle state that the diagonal line between the breastwork and rail fence was entirely without protection, — others state that it was slightly protected. Page represents the same defence as at the rail fence ; Bernier has here three angular figures, which, though not explained on the plan, indicate defences. Chester's letter confirms the statement in the text, and the British plans.

In a report in Mass. Archives, Captain Aaron Brown is named as having " behaved very gallantly, — erected the platforms, and behaved with courage and good conduct in the whole affair."

Connecticut troops, were at the redoubt and breastwork. They were joined, just previous to the action, by portions of Massachusetts regiments, under Colonels Brewer, Nixon, Woodbridge, Little, and Major Moore, and one company of artillery — Callender's. General Warren took post in the redoubt. Captain Gridley's artillery company, after discharging a few ineffectual shot from a corner of the redoubt towards Copp's Hill,[1] moved to the exposed position between the breastwork and rail fence, where it was joined by the other artillery company, under Captain Callender. Perkins' company, of Little's regiment, and a few other troops, Captain Nutting's company — recalled from Charlestown after the British landed — and part of Warner's company, lined the cartway on the right of the redoubt. The Connecticut troops, under Captain Knowlton, the New Hampshire forces, under Colonels Stark and Reed, and a few Massachusetts troops, were at the rail fence. General Putnam was here when the action commenced, and General Pomeroy, armed with a musket, served here as a volunteer. Three companies — Captain Wheeler's, of Doolittle's regiment, Captain Crosby's, of Reed's regiment, and a company from Woodbridge's regiment — were stationed in Main-street, at the base of Breed's Hill, and constituted the extreme right of the Americans. Though this statement may be in the main correct, yet, such is the lack of precision in the authorities, that accuracy cannot be arrived at.[2] The

---

[1] Seven or eight shot, — one went through an old house, another through a fence, and the rest stuck in the face of Copp's Hill. — Letter, July 5.

[2] It is not possible to ascertain, from the known authorities, precisely the number of reinforcements that arrived on the field either before the action commenced, or in season to engage the enemy. Colonel Swett states, that previous to the action, Colonels Brewer, Nixon, Woodbridge, and Major Moore, " brought on their troops, each about 300 men ; " also, that " Colonel Little arrived with his troops," and that Callender's artillery and Ford's company, of Bridge's regiment, arrived. The accounts of Little's regiment will serve to show the want of precision on this point. It consisted, (Ms. returns,) June 15, of 456 men ; one company was in Gloucester, one in Ipswich, one at Lechmere's Point, and some at West Cambridge. Three companies — Perkins', Wade's, and Warner's — probably marched on, under their colonel. They scattered, and part went to the redoubt, part to the cartway south of it, part to the breastwork, and some to the rail fence, (Ms. depositions.) One company, Lunt's, (Ms. depositions, and Swett, p. 46,)

Massachusetts reinforcements, as they came on to the field, appear to have marched to the redoubt, and were directed to take the most advantageous positions. In doing this, parts of regiments, and even companies, that came on together, broke their ranks, divided, and subsequently fought in various parts of the field, in platoons or as individuals, rather than under regular commands.

Meantime, the main body of the British troops, formed in brilliant array at Moulton's Point, continued to wait quietly for the arrival of the reinforcements. It was nearly three o'clock when the barges returned. They landed at the Old Battery, and at Mardlin's ship-yard, near the entrance to the navy-yard, the 47th regiment, the 1st battalion of marines, and several companies of grenadiers and light-infantry.[1] They, or the most of them, did not join the troops at Moulton's Point, but marched directly towards the redoubt. There had now landed about three thousand troops.[2]

General Howe, just previous to the action, addressed his army in the following manner : —

"Gentlemen, — I am very happy in having the honor of commanding so fine a body of men : I do not in the least doubt but that you will behave like Englishmen, and as becometh good soldiers.

"If the enemy will not come from their intrenchments, we must drive them out, at all events, otherwise the town of Boston will be set on fire by them.

"I shall not desire one of you to go a step further than where I go myself at your head.

"Remember, gentlemen, we have no recourse to any resources if we lose Boston, but to go on board our ships, which will be very disagreeable to us all."[3]

Before General Howe moved from his first position, he sent

did not arrive until near the close of the battle. Similar confusion exists in the accounts of other regiments.

[1] Stedman's History ; Gage's Account ; Letter, June 25, 1775.   [2] Gordon says "near 3000 ; " contemporary Mss. say 3300.

[3] Clark's Narrative. Clark was a lieutenant in the marines. He says, after giving this address : "We then began to proceed to action, by marching with a quick step up the precipice that led to the provincial army "

our strong flank guards, and directed his field-pieces to play on the American lines.   The fire from Copp's Hill, from the ships, and from the batteries, now centred on the intrench- ments;[1] while a furious cannonade and bombardment from Boston occupied the attention of the right wing of the Amer- ican army, at Roxbury.[2]   The fire upon the lines was but feebly returned from Gridley's and Callender's field-pieces. Gridley's guns were soon disabled, and he drew them to the rear.   Capt. Callender, alleging that his cartridges were too large for his pieces, withdrew to Bunker Hill.   Here he met General Putnam, who ordered him to return.   Callender returned; but soon left his post, and was soon deserted by his men.[3]   About this time, Capt. Ford's company, of Bridge's regiment, came on to the field, and, at the pressing request of General Putnam, drew the deserted pieces to the rail fence.   Meantime Colonel Prescott detached Lieut.-col. Robin- son and Major Woods, each with a party, to flank the enemy. Both behaved with courage and prudence.   No details, how- ever, are given of their service.   Capt. Walker, with a few men, probably of one of these parties, met with the British near the navy-yard, and fired from the cover of buildings and fences. On being driven in, he passed with a few of the party to their right flank, along the margin of Mystic River, where he was wounded and taken prisoner.   The greater part of his men, under a heavy fire, succeeded in regaining the redoubt.[4]

The general discharge of artillery was intended to cover the advance of the British columns.   They moved forward in two divisions, — General Howe with the right wing, to penetrate the American line at the rail fence, and cut off a retreat from

---

[1] Page's Plan; Mass. Committee of Safety; Swett's History.   Fenno's Orderly Book says: " The fire of three ships, three batteries, several field- pieces, a battery on Copp's Hill, from six different directions, all centred on the intrenchments."

[2] General Heath says, Memoirs, p. 20, " A furious cannonade and throw- ing of shells took place at the lines on Boston Neck against Roxbury, with intent to burn that town; but although several shells fell among the houses, and some carcasses near them, the balls went through some."   One man only was killed.

[3] Account of Callender, in the Boston Centinel, 1818; B. Pierce; Israel Hunt. Report, 1775.   [4] James Varnum; E. Bancroft; Prescott's Letter.

the redoubt, — General Pigot with the left wing, to storm the
breastwork and redoubt.[1] The artillery, after playing a short
time, ceased, and General Howe was told that twelve pound
balls had been sent with which to load six-pounders, when

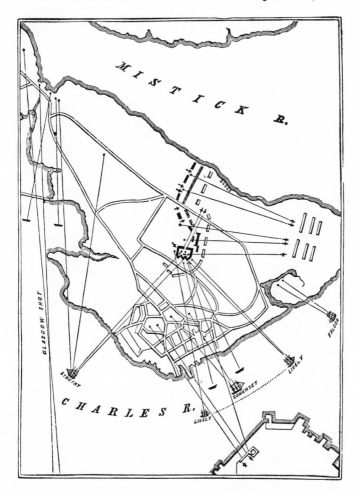

he ordered the pieces to be charged with grape. In advancing,
however, the artillery was soon impeded by the miry ground
at the base of the hill, and took post near the brick-kilns,

[1] Page; Bernier; Gage. "The assault was made on the whole front.'
Stedman, 1, 129.

whence its balls produced but little effect.[1] The troops moved
forward slowly, for they were burdened with knapsacks full
of provisions, obstructed by the tall grass and the fences, and
heated by a burning sun; but they felt unbounded confidence
in their strength, regarded their antagonists with scorn, and
expected an easy victory.[2] The Americans coolly waited their
approach. Their officers ordered them to reserve their fire
until the British were within ten or twelve rods, and then to
wait until the word was given.[3] "Powder was scarce, and
must not be wasted," they said; "Fire low;" "Aim at the
waistbands;" "Wait until you see the white of their eyes;"
"Aim at the handsome coats;" "Pick off the commanders."[4]

General Pigot's division consisted of the 5th, 38th, 43d,
47th, 52d regiments, and the marines, under Major Pitcairn.
The 38th first took a position behind a stone wall, and being
joined by the 5th, marched up the hill. The 47th and the
marines moved from the battery where they landed directly
towards the redoubt. The 43d and 52d advanced in front of
the breastwork. The troops kept firing as they approached
the lines.[5] When Colonel Prescott saw the enemy in motion,
he went round the works to encourage the men, and assured
them that the red coats would never reach the redoubt if they
would observe his directions.[6] The advancing columns, how-

---

[1] Bernier. The letter in the Conduct of the War says: "The wretched
blunder of the over-sized balls sprung from the dotage of an officer of rank in
that corps, who spends his whole time in dallying with the school-master's
daughters."

[2] Stedman, I., 128. "Let us take the bull by the horns," was the phrase
of some great men among us, as we marched on. — Conduct of the War.
A British account states of the fences: "These posts and rails were too
strong for the columns to push down, and the march was so retarded by
the getting over them, that the next morning they were found studded with
bullets, not a hand's breadth from each other."

[3] Mass. Committee of Safety Account. [4] These phrases occur frequently
in the depositions, the same one being often ascribed to different officers.
Philip Johnson states of Putnam: "I distinctly heard him say, 'Men, you
are all marksmen—don't one of you fire until you see the white of their
eyes.'"

[5] I follow mostly Page's plan: Gage's account is confused as to the movements of his regiments; Bernier differs in some points from Page.

[6] Judge Prescott's Memoir

ever, having got within gunshot, a few of the Americans could not resist the temptation to return their fire, without waiting for orders. Prescott indignantly remonstrated at this disobedience, and appealed to their often expressed confidence in him as their leader; while his officers seconded his exertions, and some[1] ran round the top of the parapet and kicked up the guns. At length the British troops reached the prescribed distance, and the order was given to fire; when there was a simultaneous discharge from the redoubt and breastwork, that did terrible execution on the British ranks. But it was received with veteran firmness, and for a few minutes was sharply returned. The Americans, being protected by their works, suffered but little; but their murderous balls literally strewed the ground with the dead and wounded of the enemy. General Pigot was obliged to order a retreat, when the exulting shout of victory rose from the American lines.[2]

General Howe, in the mean time, led the right wing against the rail fence. The light-infantry moved along the shore of Mystic River, to turn the extreme left of the American line, while the grenadiers advanced directly in front.[3] The Americans first opened on them with their field-pieces (Callender's) with great effect, some of the discharges being directed by Putnam;[4] and when the advancing troops deployed into line, a few, as at the redoubt, fired without waiting for the word, when Putnam hastened to the spot, and threatened to cut down the next man who disobeyed.[5] This drew the enemy's fire, which they continued with the regularity of troops on parade; but their balls passed over the heads of the Americans. At length the officers gave the word, when the fire

---

[1] Brooks; J. Pearce; E. Bancroft.

[2] The British account, in the Conduct of the War, says, "On the left Pigot was staggered, and actually retreated by orders : great pains have been taken to huddle up this matter."

[3] Page's and Bernier's Plans. [4] Hunt; Wade; Swett. [5] R. Kemp; Swett.

"Our officers ordered our men not to fire till the word was given. Lieutenant Dana tells me he was the first man that fired, and that he did it singly and with a view to draw the enemy's fire, and he obtained his end fully, without any damage to our party." — Chester's Letter.

from the American line was given with great effect. **Many**
were marksmen, intent on cutting down the British officers;
and when one was in sight, they exclaimed, "There! See
that officer!" "Let us have a shot at him!"—when two or
three would fire at the same moment. They used the fence
as a rest for their pieces, and the bullets were true to their
message. The companies were cut up with terrible severity,
and so great was the carnage, that the columns, a few
moments before so proud and firm in their array, were disconcerted, partly broken, and then retreated. Many of the
Americans were in favor of pursuing them, and some, with
exulting huzzas, jumped over the fence for this purpose, but
were prevented by the prudence of their officers.[1]

And now moments of joy succeeded the long hours of toil,
anxiety, and peril. The American volunteer saw the veterans
of England fly before his fire, and felt a new confidence in
himself. The result was obtained, too, with but little loss
on his side.[2] Colonel Prescott mingled freely among his
troops, praised their good conduct, and congratulated them on
their success. He felt confident that another attack would
soon be made, and he renewed his caution to reserve the fire
until he gave the command. He found his men in high spirits,
and elated by the retreat. In their eyes the regulars were no
longer invincible. General Putnam rode to Bunker Hill and
to the rear of it, to urge on reinforcements. Some had arrived

---

[1] Chester; Dearborn; Capt. Mann, of Reed's regiment, in his excellent
account, (Ms.,) agrees with Chester: "During the engagement, a portion
of the company twice passed the fence huzzaing, supposing, at the time, that
we had driven the enemy."

A British letter, July 5, 1775, says: "Our light-infantry were served up
in companies against the grass fence, without being able to penetrate;—indeed,
how could we penetrate? Most of our grenadiers and light-infantry, the
moment of presenting themselves, lost three fourths, and many nine tenths of
their men. Some had only eight and nine men a company left; some only
three, four, and five." Another British letter says: "It was found to be
the strongest post that was ever occupied by any set of men."

[2] Judge Prescott's Memoir:— "Colonel Prescott said they (the British)
had commenced firing too soon, and generally fired over the heads of his
troops; and as they were partially covered by the works, but few were killed
or wounded."

at Charlestown Neck, but were deterred from crossing it by the severe fire that raked it. Portions of regiments had reached Bunker Hill, where they scattered. Colonel Gerrish was here, and confessed that he was exhausted. General Putnam endeavored to rally these troops. He used entreaty and command, and offered to lead them into action, but without much effect. It is doubtful whether any considerable reinforcement reached the line of defence during the short interval that elapsed before a second attack was made by the British troops.[1]

General Howe in a short time rallied his troops, and immediately ordered another assault. They marched in the same order as before, and continued to fire as they approached the lines. But, in addition to the previous obstacles, they were obliged to step over the bodies of their fallen countrymen.[2] The artillery did more service on this attack. It moved along the narrow road, between the tongue of land and Breed's Hill, until within three hundred yards of the rail fence, and nearly on a line with the breastwork, when it opened a severe fire to cover the advance of the infantry. The American officers, grown confident in the success of their manœuvre, ordered their men to withhold their fire until the enemy were within five or six rods of the works.[3]

Charlestown, in the mean time, had been set on fire; — in the square by shells thrown from Copps Hill, and in the easterly part by a party of marines from the Somerset. As the buildings were chiefly of wood, the conflagration spread with great

[1] " In the interval between the first and second attack of the British on our lines, he (General Putnam) rode back to Bunker Hill, and in the rear of it, to urge on reinforcements." — " Found part of Gerrish's regiment there, with their colonel." — Daniel Putnam's Letter, Oct. 19, 1825, Ms., confirmed by Samuel Basset, 1818, and others. " The men that went to intrenching over night were in the warmest of the battle, and by all accounts they fought most manfully. They had got hardened to the noise of cannon ; but those that came up as recruits were evidently most terribly frightened, many of them, and did not march up with that true courage that their cause ought to have inspired them with." — Chester's Letter.

[2] It was surprising to see how they would step over their dead bodies, as though they had been logs of wood. — Rivington's Gazette.   [3] Swett's History ; Committee of Safety.

rapidity. And now ensued one of the greatest scenes of war that can be conceived. To fill the eye, — a brilliantly appointed army advancing to the attack and storming the works, supported by coöperating ships and batteries; the blaze of the burning town, coursing whole streets or curling up the spires of public edifices; the air above filled with clouds of dense black smoke, and the surrounding hills, fields, roofs and steeples, occupied by crowds of spectators: to fill the ear, — the shouts of the contending armies, the crash of the falling buildings, and the roar of the cannon, mortars and musketry: to fill the mind, — the high courage of men staking not only their lives, but their reputation, on the uncertain issue of a civil war, and the intense emotions of the near and dear connections standing in their presence; and, on the other side, the reflection that a defeat of the regulars would be a final loss to British empire in America.[1] And yet, in strange contrast to this terrific scene, the day was calm and clear, — nature in its beauty and repose smiling serenely upon it all, as if in token of the triumphant end of the great conflict.

The burning of the town neither intimidated the Americans nor covered the attack on their lines. The wind directed the

[1] Burgoyne's Letter: Hon. Daniel Webster, in N. American Review, vol. VII., p. 226. The descriptions of this terrific scene are numerous. " A complication of horror and importance beyond anything that ever came to my lot to witness." — Burgoyne. " Sure I am nothing ever has or can be more dreadfully terrible than what was to be seen or heard at this time. The most incessant discharge of guns that ever was heard with mortal ears," &c. — Letter, June 24.

The eulogy on General Warren, already quoted, contains the following : —

> " Amazing scene ! what shuddering prospects rise !
> What horrors glare beneath the angry skies !
> The rapid flames o'er Charlestown's height ascend, —
> To heaven they reach ! urged by the boisterous wind.
> The mournful crash of falling domes resound,
> And tottering spires with sparkles seek the ground.
> One general burst of ruin reigns o'er all ;
> The burning city thunders to its fall !
> O'er mingled noises the vast ruin sounds,
> Spectators weep ! earth from her centre groans !
> Beneath prodigious unextinguished fires,
> Ill-fated Charlestown welters and expires.

smoke so as to leave a full view of the approach of the British columns,[1] which kept firing as they advanced. Colonels Brewer, Nixon, and Buckminster were wounded, and Major Moore was mortally wounded. In general, however, the balls of the British did but little execution, as their aim was bad, and the intrenchments protected the Americans. At length, at the prescribed distance, the fire was again given, which, in its fatal impartiality, prostrated whole ranks of officers and men. The enemy stood the shock, and continued to advance with great spirit; but the continued stream of fire that issued from the whole American line was even more destructive than before.[2] General Howe, opposite the rail fence, was in the hottest of it. Two of his aids, and other officers near him, were shot down, and at times he was left almost alone.[3] His officers were seen to remonstrate and to threaten, and even to prick and strike the men, to urge them on. But it was in vain. The British were compelled again[4] to give way,

---

[1] Mass. Com. Safety. [2] Prescott's Memoir.

[3] Stedman, vol. I., p. 127. General Howe was three times in the field left by himself, so numerous were the killed and wounded about him. — British officer, June 25. " They once ran and filled some of their boats, the fire was so hot." — Rivington's Gazette, Aug. 3, 1775.

[4] The British accounts acknowledge that their troops were twice driven back: " Twice were they stopped, and twice returned to the charge." — Stedman, vol. I., p. 128. Again, p.127: " It required the utmost exertion in all the officers, from the generals down to the subalterns, to repair the disorder which this hot and unexpected fire produced." A British officer, June 23, says: " The king's troops gave way several times, and it required the utmost efforts of the generals to rally them." Burgoyne says: " A moment of the day was critical; Howe's left was staggered."

Judge Prescott writes of the American fire, on the second assault, as follows: " The discharge was simultaneous the whole length of the line, and though more destructive, as Col. Prescott thought, than on the former assault, the enemy stood the first shock, and continued to advance and fire with great spirit ; but before reaching the redoubt, the continuous, well directed fire of the Americans compelled them to give way, and they retreated a second time, in greater disorder than before. Their officers were seen remonstrating, threatening, and even pricking and striking the soldiers, to urge them on, but in vain. Colonel Prescott spoke of it as a continued stream of fire from his whole line, from the first discharge until the retreat. The ground in front of the works was covered with the dead and wounded, — some lying within a few yards."

and they retreated even in greater disorder than before,—
many running towards the boats. The ground in front of
the American works was covered with the killed and the
wounded.

So long a time elapsed before the British came up again,
that some of the officers thought they would not renew the
attack.[1] General Putnam was on Bunker Hill and in the
rear of it, urging forward the reinforcements. Much delay
occurred in marching these to the field. Indeed, great confusion existed at Cambridge. General Ward was not sufficiently supplied with staff officers to bear his orders; and some
were neglected, and others were given incorrectly. Henry
Knox, afterwards General Knox, aided as a volunteer during
the day, and was engaged in reconnoitre service. Late in the
day General Ward despatched his own regiment, Patterson's
and Gardner's, to the battle-field. Col. Gardner arrived on
Bunker Hill, when Putnam detained a part of his regiment to
labor on the works commenced there, while one company,
under Captain Josiah Harris, took post at the rail fence.
Part of a regiment, under Lieut.-col. Ward, arrived at a critical
time of the battle. Other regiments, from various causes,
failed to reach the lines. Major Gridley, of the artillery,
inadequate to his position, with part of the battalion, marched
a short distance on Cambridge road, then halted, and resolved
to cover the retreat, which he thought to be inevitable. Col.
Frye, fresh from the battle, urged him forward; but Gridley,
appalled by the horrors of the scene, ordered his men to fire
at the Glasgow, and batteries from Cobble Hill. He also
ordered Colonel Mansfield to support him with his regiment,
who, violating his orders, obeyed. Captain Trevett, however,
disobeyed his superior, led his company, with two field-pieces,
to Bunker Hill, where he lost one of them, but drew the other
to the rail fence. Colonel Scammans was ordered to go where
the fighting was, and went to Lechmere's Point. Here he was
ordered to march to the hill, which he understood to mean
Cobble Hill, whence he sent a messenger to General Putnam
to inquire whether his regiment was wanted. This delay
prevented it from reaching the field in season to do any good.

[1] Joseph Pearce and others.

A part of Gerrish's regiment, under Mighil, marched from Cambridge to Ploughed Hill, where Adjutant Christian Febiger, a gallant Danish soldier who had seen service, took the command, called upon the men to follow him, and reached the heights in season to render valuable service.[1] Three additional Connecticut companies, at least, under Captains Chester, Clark, and Coit, arrived in time to take part in the battle; as did also Major Durkee, an old comrade of General Putnam.[2] Captain Chester marched on near the close of the engagement, while the British were coming up the third time. Three regiments were near him when he left Cambridge, which hastened forward in advance of his company; but when Chester overtook them, at Bunker Hill, there was hardly a company in any kind of order. The men had scattered behind rocks, hay-cocks, and apple-trees. Parties, also, were continually retreating from the field; some alleging they had left the fort with leave because they had been all night and day on fatigue without sleep or refreshment; some that they had no officers to lead them; frequently, twenty were about a wounded man, when not a quarter part could touch him to advantage; while others were going off without any excuse. Chester obliged one company, rank and file, to return to the lines.[3] The orders were: " Press on — press on; our brethren are suffering, and will be cut off." [4]

While such was the confusion on Bunker Hill, good order prevailed at the redoubt. Colonel Prescott remained at his post, determined in his purpose, undaunted in his bearing, inspiring his command with hope and confidence, and yet chagrined, that, in this hour of peril and glory, adequate support had not reached him. He passed round the lines to encourage his men, and assured them that if the British were once more driven back they could not be rallied again. His men cheered him as they replied, "We are ready for the red coats again!" But his worst apprehensions, as to ammunition, were realized, as the report was made to him that a few artillery cartridges constituted the whole stock of powder on

---

[1] Scammans' Trial, in Essex Gazette, January, 1776; S. R. Trevett's Letter; William Mardin's Letter; various Ms. depositions. See, also Swett's History, pp. 40, 41. [2] Article in Newspaper; Clark's Letter. [3] Chester's Letter supplies these details. [4] Chester and Webb's Letter, June 19

hand.   He ordered them to be opened, and the powder to be
distributed.   He charged his soldiers "not to waste a kernel
of it, but to make it certain that every shot should tell." [1]   He
directed the few who had bayonets to be stationed at the
points most likely to be scaled.   These were the only preparations it was in his power to make to meet his powerful antagonist.

General Howe, exasperated at the repeated repulses of his
troops, resolved to make another assault.   Some of his officers
remonstrated against this decision, and averred that it would
be downright butchery to lead the men on again; but British
honor was at stake, and other officers preferred any sacrifice
rather than suffer defeat from a collection of armed rustics.[2]
The boats were at Boston; there was no retreat; — "Fight,
conquer, or die!" was their repeated exclamation.[3]   A second
reinforcement, of four hundred marines, under Major Small,
had landed; and General Clinton, who had witnessed from
Copp's Hill the discomfiture of the British veterans, and saw
two regiments on the beach in confusion, threw himself into a
boat, crossed the river, joined General Howe as a volunteer,
and rendered essential aid in rallying the troops.[4]   The latter
had lost their confident air, appeared disheartened, and
manifested great reluctance to marching up a third time.[5]
The officers, at length, formed them for the last desperate
assault.   The British general had learned to respect his
enemy, and adopted a wiser mode of attack.   He ordered the
men to lay aside their knapsacks, to move forward in column,
to reserve their fire, to rely on the bayonet, to direct their
main attack on the redoubt, and to push the artillery forward
to a position that would enable it to rake the breastwork.
The gallant execution of these orders reversed the fortunes of
the day.[6]

---

[1] Judge Prescott's Memoir.   [2] Gordon, vol. I., p. 365.   [3] Webb's Letter.

[4] We should have been forced to retire if General Clinton had not come
up with a reinforcement of five or six hundred men. — Conduct of War, p.
14.   Clinton, from Copp's Hill, saw on the beach two regiments in seeming
embarrassment which way to march. — Burgoyne's Letter.

[5] Committee of Safety Account; Prescott's Memoir.

[6] Stedman; Winslow; Swett; Prescott.   A letter dated June 20, **1775**

General Howe, whose fine figure and gallant bearing were observed at the American lines,[1] led the grenadiers and light-infantry in front of the breastwork, while Generals Clinton and Pigot led the extreme left of the troops to scale the redoubt.[2] A demonstration only was made against the rail fence. A party of Americans occupied a few houses and barns that had escaped the conflagration on the acclivity of Breed's Hill, and feebly annoyed the advancing columns.[3] They, in return, only discharged a few scattering guns as they marched forward.[4] On their right the artillery soon gained its appointed station, enfiladed the line of the breastwork, drove its defenders into the redoubt for protection, and did much execution within it by sending its balls through the passage-way.[5] All this did not escape the keen and anxious eye of Prescott. When he saw the new dispositions of his antagonist, the artillery wheeling into its murderous position, and the columns withholding their fire, he well understood his intention to concentrate his whole force on the redoubt, and believed that it must inevitably be carried. He thought, however, that duty, honor, and the interest of the country, required that it should be defended to the last extremity, although at a certain sacrifice of many lives. In this trying moment, he continued to give his orders coolly. Most of his men had remaining only one round of ammunition, and few more than three rounds, and he directed them to reserve their fire until the British were within twenty yards. At this distance a deadly volley was poured upon the advancing columns, which made them waver for an instant, but they sprang forward without returning it.[6] The American fire soon slackened for want of means, while the columns of Clinton and Pigot reached a position on the southern and eastern sides of the redoubt, where they were protected by its walls. It was now attacked on three sides at once. Prescott ordered those who

says : " In one of the attacks one of our people imprudently spoke aloud that their powder was all gone, which being heard by some of the regular officers, they encouraged their men to march up to the intrenchments with fixed bayonets."

[1] Prescott's Memoir. [2] Page's Plan. [3] Bernier's Plan, and Swett
[4] Prescott's Memoir. [5] Committee of Safety Account. [6] Prescott's Memoir

had no bayonets to retire to the back part of it, and fire on the enemy as they showed themselves on the parapet. A soldier of noble bearing mounted the southern side, and had barely shouted, "The day is ours!" when he was shot down, and the whole front rank shared his fate.[1] But the defenders had spent their ammunition, — another cannon cartridge furnishing the powder for the last muskets that were fired; and its substitute, stones, revealed their weakness, and filled the enemy with hope. The redoubt was soon successfully scaled. General Pigot, by the aid of a tree, mounted a corner of it, and was closely followed by his men, when one side of it literally bristled with bayonets. The conflict was now carried on hand to hand. Many stood and received wounds with swords and bayonets. But the British continued to enter, and were advancing towards the Americans, when Colonel Prescott gave the order to retreat.[2]

When the Americans left the redoubt, the dust arising from the dry, loose dirt was so great that the outlet was hardly visible.[3] Some ran over the top, and others hewed their way through the enemy's ranks. Prescott, among the last to leave, was surrounded by the British, who made passes at him with the bayonet, which he skilfully parried with his sword. " He did not run, but stepped long, with his sword up,"[4] escaping unharmed, though his banyan and waistcoat were pierced in several places.[5] The retiring troops passed between two

---

[1] Letter, June 22, 1775. A newspaper of 1775 states that young Richardson, of the Royal Irish, was the first to mount the parapet. In Clark's Narrative it is stated that the remains of a company of the 63d regiment of grenadiers were the first that succeeded in entering the redoubt. After Captain Horsford had been wounded, and Lieutenant Dalrymple had been killed, a sergeant took the command, made a speech to the few men left, saying, "We must either conquer or die," and entered the works. General Gage recommended the brave sergeant for promotion. — 2d Edition, p. 33.

[2] Mass. Committee of Safety; Judge Prescott's Memoir.   [3] Rivington's Gazette.   [4] Joseph Pearce.

[5] Judge Prescott writes: "The British had entered the redoubt, and were advancing, when Colonel Prescott ordered a retreat. He was among the last; and before leaving it, was surrounded by the enemy, who had entered, and had several passes with the bayonet made at his body, which he parried with his sword, — of the use of which he had some knowledge." He wore a banyan during the battle. In a note, Judge Prescott writes: "My late

divisions of the British, one of which had turned the north-eastern end of the breastwork, and the other had come round the angle of the redoubt; but they were too much exhausted to use the bayonet effectually, and the combatants, for fifteen or twenty rods from the redoubt, were so mingled together that firing would have destroyed friend and foe.[1] The British, with cheers, took possession of the works, but immediately formed, and delivered a destructive fire upon the retreating troops. Warren, at this period, was killed, and left on the field; Gridley was wounded; Bridge was again wounded; and the loss of the Americans was greater than at any previous period of the action.[2] Colonel Gardner, leading on a part of his regiment, was descending Bunker Hill, when he received his death wound. Still his men, under Major Jackson, pressed forward, and with Cushing's, Smith's, and Washburn's companies, of Ward's regiment, and Febiger's party, of Gerrish's regiment, poured between Breed's and Bunker Hill a well-directed fire upon the enemy, and gallantly covered the retreat.[3]

In the mean time the Americans at the rail fence, under Stark, Reed, and Knowlton, reinforced by Clark's, Coit's, and Chester's[4] Connecticut companies, Captain Harris' company, of Gardner's regiment, Lieutenant-colonel Ward, and a few troops, maintained their ground with great firmness and intrepidity, and successfully resisted every attempt to turn their flank. This line, indeed, was nobly defended. The force here did a great service, for it saved the main body, who were retreating in disorder from the redoubt, from being cut off by

friend, Doctor O. Prescott, states the fact. He says that soon after the battle he was at his uncle, Colonel Prescott's house, in Pepperell, and that he shew him his banyan and waistcoat, that had several holes pierced through, and rents made in several places in them, which he told him had been made by British bayonets on Bunker Hill. I also recollect the same thing. Holes were perforated in several places in both banyan and waistcoat."

[1] Gov. Brooks. [2] Brooks; E. Bancroft; Rivington's Gazette. [3] E. Bancroft; Swett; and Mss.

[4] "We joined our army on the right of the centre, just by a poor stone fence, two or three feet high and very thin, so that the bullets came through. —Chester's Letter.

the enemy.[1]   When it was perceived at the rail fence that the force under Colonel Prescott had left the hill, these brave men "gave ground, but with more regularity than could have been expected of troops who had been no longer under discipline, and many of whom never before saw an engagement."[2]   The whole body of Americans were now in full retreat, the greater part over the top of Bunker Hill.

The brow of Bunker Hill was a place of great slaughter.[3] General Putnam here rode to the rear of the retreating troops, and regardless of the balls flying about him, with his sword drawn, and still undaunted in his bearing, urged them to renew the fight in the unfinished works. "Make a stand here," he exclaimed ; "we can stop them yet!" "In God's name, form, and give them one shot more!"[4]   It was here that he stood by an artillery piece until the enemy's bayonets were almost upon him.   The veteran Pomeroy, too, with his shattered musket in his hand, and his face to the foe, endeavored to rally the men.   It was not possible, however, to check the retreat.   Captain Trevett and a few of his men, with great difficulty and great gallantry, drew off the only field-piece that was saved of the six that were in the action. Colonel Scammans, with part of his regiment, and Captain Foster's artillery company, on their way to the field of battle, reached the top of Bunker Hill, but immediately retreated. The whole body retired over the Neck, amidst the shot from the enemy's ships and batteries, and were met by additional troops on their way to the heights.   Among them Major Brooks, with two remaining companies of Bridge's regiment. One piece of cannon at the Neck opened on the enemy, and covered the retreat.[5]

The British troops, about five o'clock, with a parade of triumph, took possession of the same hill that had served them for a retreat on the memorable nineteenth of April.   General Howe was here advised by General Clinton to follow up his

---

[1] The Committee of Safety Account.   Gordon, vol. i., p. 366.   Heath says this line "was nobly defended."

[2] Committee of Safety Account.   [3] Gov. Brooks says "the principal place of slaughter."   [4] Among those who state this are Elihu Wyman, Anderson Minor, and Colonel Wade.   [5] Swett, pp. 47, 48.

success by an immediate attack on Cambridge.[1] But the reception he had met made the British commander cautious, if not timid; and he only fired two field-pieces upon the Americans,[2] who retreated to Winter Hill, Prospect Hill, and Cambridge. Similar apprehensions were entertained on both sides respecting a renewal of the attack : the Americans at Winter and Prospect Hills lay on their arms, while the British, reinforced by additional troops from Boston, threw up during the night a line of breastwork on the northern side of Bunker Hill. Both sides, however, felt indisposed to renew the action. The loss of the peninsula damped the ardor of the Americans, and the loss of men depressed the spirit of the British.[3]

Colonel Prescott, indignant at the absence of support when victory was within his grasp,[4] repaired to head quarters, reported the issue of the battle, already too well known, and received the thanks of the commander-in-chief. He found General Ward under great apprehensions lest the enemy, encouraged by success, should advance on Cambridge, where he had neither disciplined troops nor an adequate supply of ammunition to receive him. Colonel Prescott, however, assured him that the confidence of the British would not be increased by the result of the battle ; and he offered to retake the hill that night, or perish in the attempt, if three regiments of fifteen hundred men, well equipped with ammunition and bayonets, were put under his command. General Ward wisely decided that the condition of his army would not justify so bold a measure.[5] Nor was it needed to fill the measure of Prescott's fame. " He had not yet done enough to satisfy himself, though he had done enough to satisfy his country. He had not, indeed, secured final victory, but he had secured a glorious immortality." [6]

[1] Conduct of the War. [2] Brooks. [3] Gordon.

[4] Judge Prescott writes : " Colonel Prescott always thought he could have maintained his post with the handful of men under his command, exhausted as they were by fatigue and hunger, if they had been supplied with sufficient ammunition, and with bayonets. In their last attack the British wavered under the first fire of the Americans, and if it could have been continued, he felt confident they would have been repulsed, and would never have rallied again." [5] Prescott's Memoir. [6] Colonel Swett's History, p. 49.

CHAPTER VI.

Character of the Bunker Hill Battle. The Question of Command. **Prescott**
Putnam. Warren. Pomeroy.

No engagement of the Revolution possesses an interest so
deep and peculiar, or produced consequences so important,
as the battle of Bunker Hill; and no other engagement is
involved in so much obscurity, perplexity, and controversy.
It is remarkable on many accounts;—in being the first great
battle of the contest; in the astonishing resistance made by
inexperienced militia against veteran troops; in the affecting
character of its prominent incidents; in the sublimity of its
spectacle; and in its influence on the politics of the day, and
the fortunes of the war. It proved the quality of the American soldier, drew definitely the lines of party, and established
the fact of open war between the colonies and the mother
country. It was a victory, with all the moral effect of victory,
under the name of a defeat. And yet, at first, it was regarded
with disappointment, and even with indignation; and contemporary accounts of it, whether private or official, are
rather in the tone of apology, or of censure, than of exultation. The enterprise, on the whole, was pronounced rash in
the conception and discreditable in the execution; and a
severe scrutiny was instituted into the conduct of those who
were charged with having contributed by their backwardness
to the result. No one, for years, came forward to claim the
honor of having directed it; no notice was taken of its returning anniversary; and no narrative did justice to the regiments
that were engaged, or to the officers who were in command.
Passing events are seldom accurately estimated. The bravery,
however, of those who fought it was so resolute, and their
self-devotion was so lofty, as at once to elicit, from all quarters, the most glowing commendation, and to become the

theme of the poet and the orator;[1] and as time rolled on, its connection with the great movement of the age appeared in its true light. Hence the battle of Bunker Hill now stands out as the grand opening scene in the drama of the American Revolution.

It has been remarked, that in a military point of view it would be difficult to assign a just motive to either party for this conflict. It was not very important for the American army to hem in the British army in Boston, by a force posted so near as Bunker Hill, when that object could be accomplished by a force a little further in the rear. While, on the other hand, if the British officers had nothing else in view but to dislodge the occupants of Breed's Hill, it was perfectly competent for them, as they commanded the Mystic and the Charles Rivers, to cut off all communication, and to reduce Prescott and his men to famine. The truth is, both parties were ready and anxious and determined to try the strength of their arms.[2] The Americans were elated — perhaps too much elated — by their success on the nineteenth of April, and at Noddle's Island, and in the skirmishes in the harbor. They felt confident in their ability at least to prevent another excursion into the country, and would be satisfied with nothing short of an expulsion of the British troops from Boston.[3] So bold had they become in bidding defiance to Great Britain! On the other hand, British pride was touched by this exultation and daring, and by the reflection that predictions as to the courage of the Americans and the invincibility of the

[1] Governor Johnstone, in a speech in the House of Commons, October 30, 1775, said : " To a mind who loves to contemplate the glorious spirit of freedom, no spectacle can be more affecting than the action at Bunker's Hill. To see an irregular peasantry, commanded by a physician, inferior in number, opposed by every circumstance of cannon and bombs that could terrify timid minds, calmly wait the attack of the gallant Howe, leading on the best troops in the world, with an excellent train of artillery, and twice repulsing those very troops, who had often chased the chosen battalions of France, and at last retiring for want of ammunition, but in so respectable a manner that they were not even pursued, — who can reflect on such scenes, and not adore the constitution of government which could breed such men ! "

[2] Address of Hon. Daniel Webster, 1843. [3] See Letter of the Committee of Safety, p. 104.

regulars had been so completely falsified. Two regiments, — it had been written, — were sufficient to beat the whole strength of the province;[1] and a force of five thousand was sufficient to overrun the whole of the colonies. Never had high-sounding manifesto been followed by such mortifying results. The veterans of this triumphal march were so closely blockaded, by the force that was pronounced so impotent and was so despised, that their luxurious fare was suddenly changed into salt provision. Thus their daily food stimulated their desire for retaliation. Besides, the army was sent over to bring the Americans to a sense of their duty, and it longed to give them one good drubbing as a necessary step towards it.[2] When, therefore, the British officers saw the redoubt, and saw it filled with its daring band, they could not permit that it should "stand in their very face, and defy them to their teeth." Without calculating the cost, or without caring for it, their object was to destroy the works at once, by the power of the royal army, and to take vengeance, as well as to attain security.[3]

The reason for issuing the order to fortify Bunker Hill has been stated. The council of war had decided not to occupy so exposed a post until the army was better prepared to defend it. But when it was certainly known that the enemy had determined to move into the country, the committee of safety, with that disregard of consequences which characterizes so remarkably the early stage of the revolutionary struggle, advised that this movement should be anticipated. The decision has been pronounced rash. It was followed by desolation and carnage. Much precious blood was shed. Even the "beauty of Israel fell upon his high places." This daring decision, however, was productive of consequences of the highest importance, which a less terrible ordeal would scarcely have produced. They extended throughout the

---

[1] Letter on page 44.   [2] Harris writes, June 12, 1775, — "Affairs at present wear a serious aspect. I wish the Americans may be brought to a sense of their duty. One good drubbing, which I long to give them by way of retaliation, might have a good effect towards it. * * At present, we are completely blockaded, and subsisting almost on salt provision," &c. — Life of Lord Harris, p. 52   [3] Webster's Address, 1843.

war.[1] This is not, however, the place to dwell on them. One of the more immediate of its results — the great political service of the battle — was to establish a state of general hostility. This already existed in Massachusetts, where war, and nothing short of war, had been fully resolved upon ; but it did not exist in some of the other colonies, where the spirit raised by the Lexington alarm had softened into a desire of reconciliation. How different, for instance, was the state of things in New York, where the same military companies were directed by the Provincial Congress to escort, on the same day, General Washington to the seat of war, and Governor Tryon to the seat of power ! But after it had been demonstrated that the New England militia had stood the attack of the British regulars, and had twice repulsed them,[2] after War-

[1] General Wilkinson's Review of the Battle, though clouded by prejudice, and incorrect in some of its details, contains the following discriminating and just remarks on its influence : — " The resolution displayed by the provincials on this memorable day produced effects auspicious to the American cause, and coëxtensive with the war ; for, although compelled by superior numbers to yield the ground, the obstinacy of their resistance put an end to that confidence with which they had been first attacked, and produced measures of caution, bordering on timidity. There can be no doubt that we were indebted to these causes for the unmolested occupancy of our position before Boston." * * " To the cool courage and obstinacy displayed on the occasion, and the moral influence of the bloody lesson which Sir William Howe received on that day, we must ascribe the military phenomenon of a motley band of undisciplined American yeomanry, scarcely superior in number, holding an army of British veterans in close siege for nine months ; and hence it might fairly be inferred that our independence was essentially promoted by the consequence of this single battle."

General Lee, also a soldier of the revolution, regards the severe admonition Sir William Howe received on this day as the most probable explanation of his subsequent timid line of policy. He says : " The sad and impressive experience of this murderous day sunk deep into the mind of Sir William Howe ; and it seems to have had its influence on all its subsequent operations, with decisive control."

[2] Hon. Daniel Webster, in his address of 1843, states, that it rested on indisputable authority, that, when Washington heard of the battle of Bunker's Hill, and was told that for want of ammunition and other causes the militia yielded the ground to the British troops, he asked if the militia of New England stood the fire of the British regular troops ; and being told they did, and reserved their own until the enemy were within eight rods, and then

ren had fallen, and Charlestown had been destroyed, affairs changed their aspect. New confidence was felt in the American arms. There were new justifying causes for open war. The other colonies became arrayed in hostility, side by side, with Massachusetts. And it was certain that peace could never be established between the two countries, except on the basis of an acknowledgment of American independence ! [1]

The commanding officers felt that the army was not prepared for such a conflict. The want of subordination and discipline rendered efficient military command impossible, and hence the proceedings throughout the day were characterized by great confusion. The evidence on this point, early and late, is uniform and decisive, and it relates both to transactions at Cambridge and at Charlestown. During the battle the influence of Colonel Prescott over his men [2] preserved order at his position, but in other parts of the field the troops fought rather in platoons, or individually, — companies entirely losing their order, — than under regular commands; and in some instances, where superior officers attempted to exercise authority, their orders were openly disregarded. Even the orders of General Ward were but feebly carried into effect. Much of this delinquency must be placed at the door of inefficiency on the part of some of the officers; but much of it also

discharged it with fearful effect, he then exclaimed, " The liberties of the country are safe ! " Washington, on the 10th of February, 1776, wrote to Joseph Reed : " With respect to myself, I have never entertained an idea of an accommodation, since I heard of the measures which were adopted in consequence of the Bunker's Hill fight. The king's speech has confirmed the sentiments I entertained upon the news of that affair ; and if every man was of my mind, the ministers of Great Britain should know, in a few words, upon what issue the cause should be put." This issue was a determination to shake off all connection with Great Britain. " This I would tell them, not under cover, but in words as clear as the sun in its meridian brightness."

[1] Hon. Daniel Webster's Address, 1843.

[2] Perfectly understanding his countrymen, remarks Colonel Swett, they were entirely under his control. — p. 22. The depositions often describe his efficiency. Captain Bancroft, who was in the redoubt, thus speaks of Colonel Prescott : "He continued through the hottest of the fight to display admirable coolness, and a self-possession that would do honor to the greatest hero of any age. He gave his orders deliberately, and how effectually they were obeyed I need not tell." — Ms.

must be ascribed to an absence of the principle of subordination, from the generals to the lower officers. The prompt
action of Connecticut, relative to a commander-in-chief, shows
that the evil was felt in its full force.

It is from this cause — the want of subordination, and the
confusion — that it is a question whether there was a general
authorized commander in the battle. Had the army been
fully organized, and had the rank of the officers been established, such a question could not have arisen. It is not one
of recent origin, for there was the same perplexity on this
point, immediately after the battle, that exists now; and
inquiries in relation to it elicited equally unsatisfactory
answers. The orderly book of General Ward not only is
silent on it, but contains no orders for the conduct of the
enterprise. Nor is this deficiency entirely supplied by any
contemporary document. Yet it is from authorities of this
character that a correct conclusion must be drawn. In the
place of a labored argument on this delicate subject, I prefer
to state, as fairly as I am able to do it, the evidence in relation to it that has fallen in my way, state the conclusion it
seems to warrant, and leave the subject to the candid reader.

The Massachusetts committee of safety appointed Reverend
Messrs. Cooper, Gardner, and Thatcher, to prepare an account
of the battle, in which it is stated that the "commander of
the party" gave the order to retreat from the redoubt. This
is dated July 25, 1775. It was written by Rev. Peter
Thatcher, who subsequently stated : "What facts he did not
see himself were communicated to him by Colonel Prescott,
(who commanded the provincials,) and by other persons who
were personally conversant in the scenes which the narrative
describes."

Gen. Ward, in a letter addressed to John Adams, dated Oct.
30, 1775, says : "There has been no one action with the enemy
which has not been conducted by an officer of this colony,
except that at Chelsea, which was conducted by Gen. Putnam."

Rev. John Martin, who was in the battle, related its incidents to President Stiles, who recorded them in his diary,
June 30, 1775. He states that the Americans took possession
of the hill, "under the command of Colonel Prescott," and

that application to General Ward for aid "brought Colonel Putnam and a large reinforcement about noon."

Dr. James Thatcher's military journal contains a narrative of the battle, under the date of July, 1775, which purports to have been recorded at the time. He says: "On the American side, Generals Putnam, Warren, Pomeroy, and Colonel Prescott, were emphatically the heroes of the day, and their unexampled efforts were crowned with glory. The incomparable Colonel Prescott marched at the head of the detachment; and though several general officers were present, he retained the command during the action."

John Pitts, Esq., in a letter dated Watertown, July 20, 1775, addressed to Samuel Adams, then in Congress, says: "I find the letters, in general, from you, and the rest of our friends, complain of not having particular information relative to the late battle of Charlestown. I do assure you, the particulars, any further than what I have already wrote you, I have not been able to obtain from any one. To be plain, it appears to me there never was more confusion and less command. No one appeared to have any but Colonel Prescott, whose bravery can never be enough acknowledged and applauded. General Putnam was employed in collecting the men, but there were not officers enough to lead them on." [1]

Colonel James Scammans printed in the New England Chronicle, February 29, 1776, a report of the court-martial that tried him for alleged misconduct on the day of the battle, with a sketch of the evidence. This report was interspersed with notes. In one of them it is remarked, that "there was no general officer who commanded on Bunker Hill." The notes were undoubtedly by Scammans.

General Charles Lee, in his vindication, in 1778, has a casual allusion to the battle, in adducing proofs of the courage and good qualities of the American soldier. He says: "The Americans were composed in part of raw lads and old men, half armed, with no practice or discipline, commanded without order, and God knows by whom."

Rev. William Gordon, 1788, says: "Orders were issued on

---

[1] This extract was first printed in the oration on the battle delivered by Rev. George E. Ellis.

the 16th of June, that a detachment of a thousand men, under Colonel Prescott, do march at evening, and intrench upon the hill." "General Warren joins the Massachusetts forces in one place, and General Pomeroy in another. General Putnam is busily engaged in aiding and encouraging here and there, as the case requires."

General Heath (1798) says in his memoirs : "Perhaps there never was a better fought battle than this, all things consid· ered ; and too much praise can never be bestowed on the conduct of Colonel William Prescott, who, notwithstanding anything that may have been said, *was the proper commanding officer*, at the redoubt, and nobly acted his part as such, during the whole action." The italics are by General Heath.

General Lee, in his memoirs, (1812,) after stating that General Howe found his enemy posted on Breed's Hill, "commanded by Colonel Prescott," says : "The military annals of the world rarely furnish an achievement which equals the firmness and courage displayed on that proud day by the gallant band of Americans ; and it certainly stands first in the brilliant events of our war. When future generations shall inquire where are the men who gained the highest prize of glory in the arduous contest which ushered in our nation's birth, upon Prescott and his companions will the eye of history beam."

Hon. William Tudor, judge advocate in the trials of the delinquent officers, in a communication printed in the Columbian Sentinel and N. A. Review, 1818, states as follows : "Soon after the arrival of General Washington, as commander-in-chief of the American forces, at Cambridge, in July, 1775, court-martials were ordered to be holden for the trials of different officers, who were supposed to have misbehaved in the important action on Breed's Hill, on the seventeenth of June ; at all of which I acted as judge advocate. In the inquiry which these trials occasioned, I never heard any insinuation against the conduct of General Putnam, who appeared to have been there without any command ; for there was no authorized commander. Colonel Prescott appeared to have been the chief; and according to my best recollections, after forty-three years, the whole business appeared to have been conducted without order or regular command. Each man fought for himself, loaded and fired as he could, and took care to waste no powder, which was a scarce article at the time."

These statements were made by contemporaries, who, out of professional curiosity, or out of fidelity to history, endeavored to ascertain the facts in the case. They were made mostly before controversy had arisen on the subject, and therefore are not warped by known prejudice or partiality. They are also chiefly independent testimonies, — some of them never having been printed before. Rev. Peter Thatcher, whose account is remarkably accurate, and Rev. John Martin, who was in the battle, are equally clear and positive.[1] Gordon, a historian of established reputation for fidelity, was the first to state in print the positions of the commanding officers. He was in the neighborhood at the time, and wrote, probably, with the order before him ; and he uses careful and discriminating language. General Heath was one of the council of war that issued the order, and must have known to whom the command was intrusted. His language agrees with the others. General Ward's remark is decisive that a Massachusetts officer conducted the battle. Dr. James Thatcher, who acted as surgeon in Cambridge, and purports to write at the time, uses unequivocal language, and disposes of the difficulty as to general officers being present. The characteristic allusion of General Charles Lee, and the letter of John Pitts, indicate the early uncertainty on the subject. The statement made by Scammans, that no general officer commanded, elicited no contradiction at the time, and is confirmed by the words of Judge Advocate Tudor.

To these authorities must be added another, of such high character as to be, of itself, almost conclusive, — that of Judge William Prescott, the son of Colonel Prescott. He states in his memoir : " I have always understood and believe that the detachment was originally placed under the command

---

[1] The statement of Thatcher I found at the Antiquarian Hall, Worcester, in his own hand-writing. The relation of Martin is in Stiles' Journal, — copies of which were loaned to me by Hon. Geo. Bancroft and President Sparks.

ot Colonel Prescott, with orders, in writing, from the commander-in-chief; that they marched to Breed's Hill under his command, and there threw up the works; and that neither General Putnam, nor any other officer, ever exercised or claimed any authority or command over him, or the detachment, before or in the battle; that General Putnam was not in the redoubt during the action. All this I have often heard stated by my father, as well as other officers of the detachment."

The conclusion warranted by this evidence is, that the original detachment was placed under the orders of Colonel Prescott, and that no general officer was authorized to command over him during the battle.

Nor, previous to the year 1790, is there in any document, written or printed, that is known to me, an assertion to the contrary, except where the command is assigned to General Warren.[1] It was announced then that a general officer commanded during the whole affair, from beginning to the end. This announcement was made under the following circumstances. General David Humphries published an essay on the life of General Putnam, who was then alive, dated Mount Vernon, July 4, 1788, in which, in a brief account of the battle, he says : "In this battle the presence and example of General Putnam, who arrived with the reinforcement, were not less conspicuous than useful." This language, it will be noticed, agrees remarkably with that of some of the earlier authorities, — especially with Martin, Dr. Thatcher, Pitts, and Gordon, — already quoted. General Putnam died May 29, 1790. Rev. Josiah Whitney preached his funeral sermon, which was published. In a note to this sermon, after remark-

---

[1] Immediately after the battle it was reported in Boston that General Warren had the command. Hence in all the early British accounts this honor is given to him. It is singular, also, that the same statement is made in some of the American accounts. A brief narrative of the battle appeared in " George's Cambridge Almanack, or the Essex Callender," for 1776, in which it is stated that he was " commander-in-chief on this occasion." And as late as 1818, in the Analectic Magazine, he is regarded as the commander ; and it is said General Putnam " directed the whole, on the fall of General Warren." Some of the soldiers also say that, though he went on as a volunteer, yet he was persuaded to take the command. It is, however, **now** generally admitted, that he served only as a volunteer.

ing that the language of Humphries' essay on the battle was not satisfactory to the friends of General Putnam, Mr. Whitney says : " The detachment was first put under the command of General Putnam. With it he took possession of the hill, and ordered the battle from beginning to end. These facts General Putnam gave me soon after the battle, and also repeated them to me after his life was printed." Colonel Swett also states that the general made the same declarations to his son.

I have met few contemporary allusions to General Putnam's agency in the battle, besides those which have been quoted. William Williams, in a letter dated Lebanon, Conn., June 20, 1775, 10 o'clock at night, and addressed to the Connecticut delegates in Congress, says : "I receive it that General Putnam commanded our troops, perhaps not in chief." Captain Chester's letter gives the fact that he ordered the Connecticut troops to Charlestown after the British landed. In the report (1775) made to the Massachusetts Provincial Congress, it is stated that on Bunker Hill he ordered Captain Callender, who was going down the hill, " to stop and go back ; " and in the court-martial held on Colonel Scammans (1775) one of the witnesses stated that Colonel Scammans sent to General Putnam to see whether his regiment was wanted, and, on Bunker Hill, that the general ordered this regiment forward. Major Jackson, in his journal, writes, (June 16, 1775,) "General Putnam, with the army, went to intrench on Bunker Hill." The same fact is stated in some of the newspapers. President Stiles, under the date of June 20, 1775, recorded in his diary various rumors from camp, and, among others, that General Putnam, with 300 men, took possession of Bunker Hill on the night of the 16th. On the 23d, however, he derived additional details from several who had visited the camp, been " with General Putnam in his tent on Prospect Hill," and heard him describe the battle. He then writes : "Putnam was not at Bunker's Hill at the beginning, but soon repaired hither, and was in the heat of the action till towards night, when he went away to fetch across this reinforcement which ought to have come before. Soon after, and before he could return, our men began to retreat." I have not seen any disparaging comments on General Putnam's services on this day, previous to those in Wilkinson's Memoirs, printed in 1816; nor any statement that the first detachment was put under his command previous to that of Whitney's sermon, delivered in 1790.

General Putnam, in a letter dated New York, May 22, 1776, makes an allusion to his services on this day, which has a bearing on the case. This letter was addressed to the Cambridge committee of safety, and remonstrated against the treatment that Mrs. Putnam had received from an agent of this committee. He says: "Pray did not I labor and toil night and day, through wet, and cold, and venture my life in the high places of the field, for the safety of my country, and the town of Cambridge in particular? For it was thought we could never hold Cambridge, and that we had better quit it, and go back and fortify on the heights of Brookline. I always told them we must hold Cambridge; and pray did not I take possession of Prospect Hill the very night after the fight on Bunker Hill, without having any orders from any person? And was not I the only general officer that tarried there? The taking of said hill I never could obtain leave for before, which is allowed by the best judges was the salvation of Cambridge, if not of the country." [1]

It is worthy of remark, that, though the general evidently considered it to be important to make out a strong case for himself, he does not state that the original detachment was put under his command, or that he ordered the battle. The authority for this statement, if the depositions of the soldiers

---

[1] The committee, in reply, dated June 18, 1776, state that General Putnam's conduct "while in Cambridge, in every respect, and more especially as a general, (without having it set forth,) we hold in the highest veneration, and ever shall."

Again, the committee state : "Nothing was ever aimed at treating you or yours unbecoming the many obligations that we are under for the extraordinary services you have done to this town, which must always be acknowledged with the highest gratitude, not only by us, but by rising generations." These extracts, and the one in the text, are taken from original letters, for which I am indebted to J. Harlow, Esq.

How widely different is this language of gratitude and justice from the disparaging language of later date! Rising generations have not always acknowledged the patriotism of this brave and noble-hearted man.

be excepted, appears to rest mainly, if not entirely, on con-
versations held with General Putnam. Without intending to
question the honor or the veracity of any one, it is more reasonable to conclude that the facts communicated by the general
have not been stated exactly and with the proper discrimina-
tions, than it is to conclude that so many independent contemporary authorities are incorrect in stating that the first
detachment was placed under the orders of Colonel Prescott.

Colonel Prescott, therefore, was the only regular commander
of the party who fortified Breed's Hill. He was detached
on a special service, and he faithfully executed his orders.
He filled at the redoubt, the most important post, the duty
of a commanding officer, from the hour that ground was
broken until it was abandoned. He detached guards to
the shores, directed the labor of the works, called councils
of war, made applications to General Ward for reinforcements, posted his men for action, fought with them until
resistance was unavailing, and gave the order to retreat.
General officers came to this position, but they did not give
him an order, nor interfere with his dispositions. When General Warren, for instance, entered the redoubt, Colonel Prescott tendered to him the command; but Warren replied that he
had not received his commission, and should serve as a volunteer. "I shall be happy," he said, "to learn from a soldier
of your experience." Colonel Prescott, therefore, was left in
uncontrolled possession of his post. Nor is there any proof
that he gave an order at the rail fence, or on Bunker Hill.
But he remained at the redoubt, and there fought the battle
with such coolness, bravery,[1] and discretion, as to win the
unbounded applause of his contemporaries, and to deserve,

The bravery of Colonel Prescott has been universally acknowledged.
Thus, Samuel Adams, September 26, 1775, writes to Elbridge Gerry:
"Until I visited head quarters, at Cambridge, I never heard of the valor of
Prescott at Bunker's Hill." Hon. Daniel Webster, in the North American
Review, 1818, says: "In truth, if there was any commander-in-chief in the
field, it was Prescott. From the first breaking of the ground to the retreat,
he acted the most important part; and if it were proper to give the battle a
name, from any distinguished agent in it, it should be called Prescott's
battle." See also Colonel Swett's history, and Rev. Geo. E. Ellis' oration.

we hope the Post

about one hour and twenty minutes after the Attack was
small Arms, this nearly the State of Facts tho' imperfect &
too general we think if anyways satisfactory to you will
afford pleasure to your most obedient humble Servt.

William Prescott

To the hon'ble John Adams Esq.)

through all time, the admiration and gratitude of his countrymen.

Colonel Prescott, the son of Hon. Benjamin Prescott, of
Groton, was born in 1726. He served with distinction as
lieutenant of a company of foot, under General Winslow, at
the capture of Cape Breton. He was invited to accept a commission in the regular army, which he declined. He became
a warm patriot, and was chosen to command the regiment of
minute-men. On the Lexington alarm, he promptly marched
to the scene of action at their head. He continued in the
service through the year 1776, at New York; and when the
Americans retreated from the city, he brought off his men in
such good order as to be publicly commended by Washington.
He served as a volunteer under General Gates, at the capture
of Burgoyne. He retired to Pepperell, set off from Groton in
1753, where he lived on his farm, dispensing a generous hospitality, until his death. His last military service was in the
Shays insurrection of 1786, when he repaired to Concord
with his side-arms to protect the court. He was an acting
magistrate during the remainder of his life. He died in Pepperell, October 13, 1795. A simple tablet over his grave bears
an inscription stating his name, the date of his death, and his
age.

Colonel Prescott was over six feet in height, of strong and
intelligent features, with blue eyes and brown hair. He was
bald on the top of his head, and wore a tie wig. He was
large and muscular, but not corpulent. He was kind in his
disposition, plain but courteous in his manners; of a limited
education, but fond of reading; never in a hurry, and cool and
self-possessed in danger.[1]

[1] Colonel Prescott married Abigail Hale, of Sutton, who died October 21,
1821, aged 88. They had one son, Hon. William Prescott, of Boston, representative, senator, and judge, who died in 1844, — sustaining through life
a character which, for modest talent, substantial learning, and absolute fidelity in every relation of life, was such as rarely adorns the walks of professional excellence. Judge Prescott's memoir of the battle has been used with
a reliance warranted by the clear intellect and high probity of its author.

Judge Prescott married Catherine G. Hickling, daughter of Thomas Hickling, Esq., of the Island of St. Michael's. Of their seven children four died
in infancy. Edward G., an Episcopalian clergyman, died in 1844 ; Elizabeth

General Putnam exhibited throughout the bravery and generous devotion that formed a part of his nature. Though of limited education, fiery and rough in speech, he was a true patriot, and a fine executive officer. He was in command of the Connecticut troops stationed in Cambridge, and shared with them the peril and glory of this remarkable day. In a regularly organized army his appearance on the field, by virtue of his rank, would have given him the command. But it was an army of allies, whose jealousies had not yielded to the vital principle of subordination; and he was present rather as the patriotic volunteer than as the authorized general commander. He exercised an important agency in the battle. He was received as a welcome counsellor, both at the laying out of the works and during the morning of the engagement. Besides being in the hottest of the action at the rail fence and on Bunker Hill, — fighting, beyond a question, with daring intrepidity, — he was applied to for orders by the reinforcements that reached the field, and he gave orders without being applied to. Some of the officers not under his immediate command respected his authority, while others refused to obey him.[1] But no service was more brilliant than that of the Connecticut troops. They said: " He acts nobly in every thing."[2] That he was not as successful in leading the Massachusetts troops into action ought, in justice, to be ascribed neither to his lack of energy nor of conduct, but to the hesitancy of inexperienced troops, to the want of spirit in their officers and to the absence of subordination and discipline in the army.

married Hon. Franklin Dexter; and William Hickling is the historian of Ferdinand and Isabella, who is adding so much reputation to the name. He married the grand-daughter of Captain Linzee, who commanded the sloop-of-war Falcon, that cannonaded the works on Breed's Hill The swords used by Colonel Prescott and by Captain Linzee on the 17th July are now crossed on the walls of the fine library of the historian. Colonel Prescott's is quite a neat-looking rapier. — Butler's Groton. Ms. Letter.

[1] Col. Sargent, Dec. 20, 1825, states, that he applied three times to Ward for permission to march to Charlestown, but it was not until about 4, P. M., when it was too late, that he could get it; and also states that Putnam, then on Prospect Hill, " sent an officer to order me on to the hill; but finding I did not attend to his order, he sent a second, who I took no notice of. A third came open-mouthed, saying," &c. [2] Chester and Webb, June 19.

He did not give an order to Colonel Prescott, nor was he in
the redoubt during the action.[1]

[1] The mass of matter relative to General Putnam's movements on this day
presents the following account of them as the most probable:—On the evening
of June 16, he joined the detachment at Charlestown Neck ; took part in the
consultation as to the place to be fortified ; returned in the night to Cambridge
went to the heights, on the firing of the Lively, but immediately returned to
Cambridge ; went again to the heights about ten o'clock ; was in Cambridge
after the British landed ; ordered on the Connecticut troops, and then went to
the heights ; was at the rail fence at the time the action commenced ; was in
the heat of the battle, and during its continuance made great efforts to induce
the reinforcements to advance to the lines ; urged labor on works at Bunker
Hill ; was on the brow of this hill when the retreat took place ; retreated
with that part of the army that went to Prospect Hill, and remained here
through the night. He was on horseback, and in a few minutes' space of
time could be not only at any part of the heights, but even at Cambridge. It
is not, therefore, at all strange, that statements made by the soldiers as to the
time when, and the place where, they saw the general, amid the confusion
of so terrific a scene, cannot be reconciled ; and more especially as these
statements were made after an expiration of forty or fifty years.

The extracts on page 165 will show how General Putnam stood with his
contemporaries at Cambridge. The following extract from an article on the
battle, printed in the Connecticut Courant in 1775, shows the popular feeling : " In this list of heroes, it is needless to expatiate on the character and
bravery of Major-general Putnam, whose capacity to form and execute great
designs is known through Europe, and whose undaunted courage and martial
abilities strike terror through all the hosts of Midianites, and have raised him
to an incredible height in the esteem and friendship of his American brethren :
it is sufficient to say, that he seems to be inspired by God Almighty with a
military genius, and formed to work wonders in the sight of those uncircum-
cised Philistines, at Boston and Bunker Hill, who attempt to ravage this
country and defy the armies of the living God."

The officers of the army bear testimony to General Putnam's value and
bravery. He was not a great general, but he was a useful officer. Thus
Washington, January 30, 1776, writes : " General Putnam is a valuable
man and a fine executive officer ;" and in March, 1776, he was selected to
lead four thousand men in the contemplated attack on Boston. On hearing
of this proposed attack, Joseph Reed, Washington's private secretary for
some time, wrote to Washington, March 15, as follows : " I suppose Old
Put was to command the detachment intended for Boston on the 5th instant,
as I do not know any officer but himself who could have been depended on
for so hazardous a service." — Reed's Life, vol. I., p. 172. So true was the
saying of him, that " He dared to lead where any dared to follow." Again :
when the British landed at Long Island, Reed writes to his wife : " General
Putnam was made happy by obtaining leave to go over ——, the brave old

General Warren exerted great influence in the battle. Having served zealously and honorably in the incipient councils that put in motion the machinery of the Revolution, he had decided to devote his energies to promote it in its future battle-fields. He was accordingly elected major-general on the 14th of June, but had not received his commission on the day of the battle. Though he is understood to have opposed the measure of occupying so exposed a post as Bunker Hill, yet he avowed the intention, if it should be resolved upon, to share the peril of it; and to the affectionate remonstrance of Elbridge Gerry he replied: Dulce et decorum est pro patria mori. On the 16th of June he officiated as president of the Provincial Congress, passed the night at Watertown, and though indisposed, repaired on the morning of the 17th to Cambridge, where he threw himself on a bed. When he learned that the British would attack the works on Breed's Hill, he declared his headache to be gone; and, after meeting with the committee of safety, armed himself and went to Charlestown. A short time before the action commenced, he was seen in conversation with General Putnam, at the rail fence, who offered to receive his orders. General Warren declined to give any, but asked "Where he could be most useful?" Putnam directed him to the redoubt, remarking, that "There he would be covered." "Don't think," said Warren, "I come to seek a place of safety; but tell me where the onset will be most furious." Putnam still pointed to the redoubt. "That is the enemy's object, and if that can be defended the day is ours." General Warren passed to the redoubt, where the men received him with enthusiastic cheers. Here, again, he was tendered the command, by Colonel Prescott. But Warren declined it, — said that he came to encourage a good cause, and gave the cheering assurance that a reinforcement of two thousand was on its way to aid them. He mingled in the fight, behaved with great bravery, and was among the last to leave the redoubt. He was lingering, even to rashness, in his retreat. He had proceeded but a few rods, when a ball struck him in

man was quite miserable at being kept here." — p. 220. No higher military testimony than this can be adduced, for Reed was a soldier, and as capable of judging as any person in the army.

the forehead, and he fell to the ground. On the next day visitors to the battle-field — among them Dr. Jeffries and young Winslow, afterwards General Winslow, of Boston — recognized his body, and it was buried on the spot where he fell. After the British had left Boston, the sacred remains were sought after, and again identified. In April they were re-interred, with appropriate ceremonies, when Perez Morton delivered a eulogy. They were first deposited in the Tremont Cemetery, and subsequently in the family vault under St. Paul's Church, in Boston.

The intelligence of his death spread a gloom over the country. The many allusions to him, in contemporary letters and in the journals, indicate how strong a hold he had on the affections of his countrymen. "The ardor of dear Dr. Warren," says one, "could not be restrained by the entreaty of his brethren of the Congress, and he is, alas, among the slain! May eternal happiness be his eternal portion." Mrs. Adams, July 5, writes: "Not all the havoc and devastation they have made has wounded me like the death of Warren. We want him in the senate; we want him in his profession; we want him in the field. We mourn for the citizen, the senator, the physician, and the warrior." General Howe could hardly credit the report that the president of Congress was among the killed; and when assured of it by Dr. Jeffries, he is said to have declared that this victim was worth five hundred of their men. Nor was his death known for a certainty at Cambridge, until a few days after the battle. On the 19th of June, the vote of the Provincial Congress, in assigning a time to choose his successor, says he was "supposed to be killed."

Eloquence and song, the good and the great, have united in eulogy on this illustrious patriot and early martyr to the cause of the freedom of America. No one personified more completely the fine enthusiasm and the self-sacrificing patriotism that first rallied to its support. No one was more widely beloved, or was more highly valued. The language of the committee of safety, who knew his character, and appreciated his service, though brief, is full, touching and prophetic. "Among the dead was Major-general Joseph Warren; a man whose memory will be endeared to his countrymen, and to

the worthy in every part and age of the world, so long as
virtue and valor shall be esteemed among mankind." [1]

[1] The contemporary accounts of the death of General Warren differ much
from each other; so, also, do the subsequent statements of the soldiers who
aver that they saw him fall. Among the relations is that of the connection
of Major Small with his death. Colonel Trumbull states, March 30, 1818,
that when in London, in 1786, Colonel Small gave him two anecdotes of the
battle of Bunker Hill. One — that on the second attack, General Putnam
saved his (Small's) life, by rushing forward and striking up the muzzles of
guns aimed at him : and the other — that on the capture of the redoubt, Small
endeavored to save the life of Warren. Seeing him fall, Small ran to him,
spoke to him; but he only looked up, smiled, and died. Major Alexander
Garden, also, heard Small's story, and in a letter dated June 2, 1818, says,
" I myself heard the British General Small, in the year 1791, when I passed
the summer in England, declare, that to the friendship of Putnam he owed
his life at the battle of Bunker's Hill, for that when left almost alone, he prevented his men from firing on him, repeatedly saying, " Kill any but him, but
spare Small." Major Garden further states, that he met Small at Major
Pinckney's, where he was sitting to Colonel Trumbull for his portrait. " He
has paid me the compliment of endeavoring to save the life of Warren, (said
the general,) but the fact is, that life had fled before I saw his remains."
These incidents, however, wear too much the air of romance to be implicitly
relied upon. That Major Small felt grateful for an interference at some time
in his behalf is undoubtedly true. It might have been the incident given on
page 79.

The concluding portion of Captain Chester's excellent letter on the battle
is lost. I regret that endeavors to recover it have proved unsuccessful.
It is not improbable that it contains something about Warren. In the
" Eulogium," printed in 1781, the following passage, coinciding with other
accounts of his gallantry, indicates that Warren's last words were addressed
to Captain Chester : —

> " Ah, fatal ball! Great Warren feels the wound,
> Spouts the black gore! the shades his eyes surround;
> Then instant calls, and thus bespeaks with pain
> The mightiest captain of his warring train : —
> Chester,* 't is past! All earthly prospects fly,
> Death smiles! and points me to yon radiant sky.
> My friends, my country, force a tender tear, —
> Rush to my thoughts, and claim my parting care.
> When countries groan by rising woes oppressed,
> Their sons by bold exploits attempt relief.

* Col. John Chester, of Wethersfield, in the State of Connecticut, then a captain
wno behaved with the greatest intrepidity in the battle of Bunker Hill.

General Seth Pomeroy behaved so well in the battle, that in some of the accounts he is assigned a separate command. Thus President John Adams, in a letter,[1] (June 19, 1818,) says: " Who was the first officer of Massachusetts, on Bunker Hill or Breed's Hill? I have always understood, he was Colonel Pomeroy, or General Pomeroy. Colonel Prescott might be the most determined, persevering, and efficacious officer of Massachusetts; but Pomeroy was certainly his superior in command." General Pomeroy was a veteran of the French wars, as brave as he was patriotic. It is admitted that he also served as a volunteer. He requested of General Ward a horse to take him to the field, and one was supplied. On his arrival at Charlestown Neck, he declined to expose the horse to the severe fire that raked it, and coolly walked across. He joined

> Already, long, unaided we 've withstood
> Albion's whole force, and bathed the fields with blood.
> No more, my friend, our country asks no more ;
> Wisdom forbids to urge the unequal war.
> No longer trust your unavailing might,
> Haste, — lead our troops from the unequal fight ! —
>   Farewell ! —
> Senates shall hail you with their glad acclaim,
> And nations learn to dread Columbia's name.
> He could no more ! — thick mists obscure his eyes,
> And from his cheeks the rosy color flies.
> His active soul, disburdened of its clay,
> To distant regions wings its rapid way."

[1] President Adams, in this letter, makes the following remarks in relation to the army : " The army at Cambridge was not a national army, for there was no nation. It was not an United States army, for there were no United States. It was not an army of united colonies, for it could not be said in any sense that the colonies were united. The centre of their union, the Congress of Philadelphia, had not adopted nor acknowledged the army at Cambridge. It was not a New England army, for New England had not associated. New England had no legal legislature, nor any common executive authority, even upon the principles of original authority, or even of original power in the people. Massachusetts had her army, Connecticut her army, New Hampshire her army, and Rhode Island her army. These four armies met at Cambridge, and imprisoned the British army in Boston. But who was the sovereign of this united, or rather congregated, army, and who its commander-in-chief? It had none. Putnam, Poor, and Greene were as independent of Ward as Ward was of them."

the force at the rail fence, and was received with cheers.   He
fought with great spirit, and kept with the troops until the
retreat.   His musket was shattered by a ball, but he retained
it, and with it continued to animate the men.   He thought it
strange that Warren, "the young and chivalrous soldier,"
says Colonel Swett, "the eloquent and enlightened legislator,
should fall, and he escape, old and useless, unhurt."   Soon
after the battle, he declined, on account of age, the appointment as first brigadier-general of the army, but as colonel
commanded a regiment in the Jerseys.   His exposure brought
on pleurisy, and he died at Peekskill, New York.

James Otis, an invalid, was at Watertown living with
James Warren, who married his sister Mercy.   He, who
had so nobly served his country with his pen and in
the council, could not resist an impulse to aid it in the
field.   " Your brother," Warren, on the 18th of June,
wrote to his wife, " borrowed a gun, &c., and went
among the flying bullets at Charlestown, and returned last
evening at ten o'clock." [1]

[1] Proceedings of the Mass. Hist. Society, April, 1871, p. 68.

CHAPTER VII.

Services of the Regiments. Notices of the Officers. Numbers engaged.
British Criticism. Destruction of Charlestown.

It is difficult to assign with precision the credit due to the
American regiments engaged in the Bunker Hill battle. None
of the early accounts mention them in detail. No official
report specifies the service they performed. And the only
guide, in the printed material of 1775, is a list of the killed
and wounded of each regiment, that appeared in a Providence
newspaper. The official returns of the army, previous to
June 17, are very imperfect, while those of a later date contain names of soldiers not in the action. I propose to devote
a few pages to such notices of the regiments and their officers, and such incidents connected with the battle, as appear
authentic.[1]

William Prescott's regiment, from Middlesex, was commissioned May 26, and a return of this date is the latest, before
the battle, I have seen. Its lieutenant-colonel, John Robinson, and its major, Henry Wood, behaved with great coolness
and bravery. Its adjutant, William Green, was wounded.
Captains Maxwell and Farwell were badly wounded; and
Lieutenants Faucett and Brown were wounded, — the former
mortally, and was left in the hands of the enemy. Lieut. Prescott, a nephew of the colonel, and probably of this regiment,
received a ball in the arm, but continued to load his musket,
and was passing by the sally-port to discharge it, when a
cannon shot cut him in pieces.

James Frye's regiment, from Essex, was commissioned
May 20. The latest return is dated May 26. James Bricket
was lieutenant-colonel; Thomas Poor, major; Daniel Hardy,
adjutant; Thomas Kittredge, surgeon. Colonel Frye did not

---

[1] See the Appendix for a table of the companies of the several regiments,
and the number of the men.

go to Breed's Hill with his regiment on the evening of June
16, on account of indisposition; but was in the battle, behaved
with spirit, and was active in urging on reinforcements.
Lieutenant-colonel Bricket, a physician, was wounded early
in the action, and, with other surgeons, repaired to the north
side of Bunker Hill, and remained in attendance on the
wounded.

Ebenezer Bridge's regiment was commissioned May 27.
Moses Parker was lieutenant-colonel; John Brooks, major;
Joseph Fox, adjutant; John Bridge, quartermaster. A return,
dated June 23, gives but nine companies belonging to it.
Though the whole regiment was ordered to parade on the
16th of June, yet, it is stated that three of its companies did
not go on under Colonel Prescott.   Ford's company reached
the field just before the action began; and a portion of this
regiment, — two companies, — under Major Brooks, were on
the way to the hill when the Americans were retreating.
Colonel Bridge, though wounded on the head and in the neck
by a sword cut, and though he was one of the last to retreat,
did not escape the scrutiny that took place in relation to the
battle.   It was charged against him that he kept too cau-
tiously covered in the redoubt.   He was tried, and acquitted
on the ground of indisposition of body.

Lieutenant-colonel Parker was a skilful and brave veteran
of the French wars, and behaved with great gallantry in the
action.   A ball fractured his knee, and he was left in the
redoubt.   The British carried him a prisoner to Boston, lodged
him in the jail, where, after the amputation of his leg, he
died on the 4th of July, aged forty-three.   He was a good
officer, much beloved by his regiment, and his loss was
severely felt.   An obituary notice of him, — in the New England Chronicle, July 21, 1775, — says: "In him fortitude,
prudence, humanity, and compassion, all conspired to heighten
the lustre of his military virtues;" and it states, that " through
the several commissions to which his merit entitled him, he
had always the pleasure to find that he possessed the esteem
and respect of his soldiers, and the applause of his countrymen."   The notice concludes in the following strain : "God
grant each individual that now is, or may be, engaged in the

American army, an equal magnitude of soul; so shall their names, unsullied, be transmitted in the latest catalogue of fame; and if any vestiges of liberty shall remain, their praises shall be rehearsed through the earth 'till the sickle of time shall crop the creation.' "

Major Brooks — afterwards Governor Brooks — was not on the hill in the afternoon. His duties on this day have been stated. Captain Walker, whose daring reconnoitre service has been described, was carried to Boston, severely wounded. His leg was amputated, but he did not receive proper attention, and died during the following August. Captain Coburn's clothes were riddled with balls. Captain Bancroft fought nobly in the redoubt, and was wounded. Captain Ford behaved with much spirit.

Moses Little's regiment was not commissioned until June 26. A return, dated June 15, of nine companies, reports Captain Collins' company in Gloucester, and Captain Parker's as ready to march from Ipswich. Depositions state that, on the evening of June 16, Captains Gerrish and Perkins were at West Cambridge, and that Captain Lunt was detached to Lechmere's Point, as a guard. Captain Perkins', Wade's, and Warner's companies were led on by Colonel Little, before the action commenced; Captain Lunt went on near its close. Colonel Swett states that Captain Warner, who narrowly escaped, led on but twenty-three men, and that seventeen of these were either killed or wounded. Only forty are returned as killed and wounded of this regiment. Colonel Little is mentioned as behaving with spirit. Depositions state that Isaac Smith was lieutenant-colonel, —— Collins, major, and Stephen Jenkins, adjutant. The accounts of this regiment are very confused.

Ephraim Doolittle's [1] regiment was commissioned June 12,

[1] Doolittle's orderly book contains the following. June 16. — Parole, Lebanon. Countersign, Coventry. Field-officer of the day, Colonel Nixon; of the picket guard to-night, Major Brooks. Field-officer of the main guard to-morrow morning, Lt.-col. Hutchinson. Adjutant of the day, Holden.

June 17. — Parole, Deerfield. Countersign, Conway. Field-officer of the day, Col. Gerrish. Field-officer of the picket guard to-night, Majo Wood. Field-officer of the main guard to-morrow morning, Lt.-col. Baldwin. Adjutant of the day, Febiger.

when a return names only seven companies. The colonel and lieutenant-colonel were absent on the day of the battle, and Major Willard Moore led on, it is stated, three hundred of its men. Few details are preserved of the service of this regiment, or of the conduct of its officers. The depositions speak in glowing terms of the good qualities of Major Moore. He was a firm patriot, and a generous and chivalrous soldier. On the second attack he received a ball in the thigh, and while his men were carrying him to the rear another ball went through his body. He called for water, but none could be obtained nearer than the Neck. He lingered until the time of the retreat, when, feeling his wounds to be mortal, he requested his attendants to lay him down, leave him, and take care of themselves. He met with a soldier's death. He was from Paxton. He took a prominent part in the Worcester Convention in September, 1774; was chosen captain of the minutemen January 17, 1775; and, on the Lexington alarm immediately marched for Cambridge. Few notices appear of individuals of this regiment. Robert Steele, a drummer, stated in 1825, that he "beat to Yankee Doodle when he mustered for Bunker Hill on the morning of the 17th of June, 1775."

Samuel Gerrish's regiment, about which so much has been written, was neither full nor commissioned. On the 19th of May it was reported to be complete; but there were difficulties in relation to six of the companies, which were investigated June 2. Four companies were in commission June 17, and four more were commissioned June 22. Depositions station, June 16, three companies at Chelsea, three at Cambridge, and two at Sewall's Point. At a meeting of eight captains of this regiment, June 16, at Chelsea, Loammi Baldwin was chosen lieutenant-colonel, Richard Dodge, major. Christian Febiger was adjutant, Michael Farley was quartermaster, and David Jones, surgeon. The conduct of the colonel of this regiment became the occasion of severe comment. A disparaging allusion to him occurs in Dr. Church's traitorous letter, in 1775; Wilkinson stations him on Bunker Hill, and with him all the reinforcements that came on after Stark passed to the rail fence; the revolutionary depositions are equally severe. In some of the statements the whole regiment is also included. This, however, does gross injustice to a part of it, if not to the whole of it. Part of it went on, under its gallant adjutant, Febiger, and did good service. Of Colonel Gerrish's conduct, Colonel Swett says: "A complaint was lodged against him, with Ward, immediately after the battle, who refused to notice it, on account of the unorganized state of the army. He was stationed at Sewall's Point, which was fortified; in a few weeks, a floating battery made an attack on the place, which he did not attempt to repel, observing, ' The rascals can do us no harm, and it would be a mere waste of powder to fire at them with our four-pounders.' It was evening, the lights were extinguished, and all the British balls flew wide of the fort. For his conduct on this occasion, and at Bunker Hill, he was arrested immediately, tried, found guilty of 'conduct unworthy an officer,' and cashiered." This was August 19, 1775. It was thought by the judge advocate of the court that he was treated far too severely.

Adjutant Christian Febiger behaved with great gallantry in leading on a portion of this regiment in time to do efficient service. He was a Danish lieutenant, and enlisted April 28. He afterwards went with Arnold to Quebec, where he behaved with the resolution and intrepidity of a veteran, and gave many proofs of great military abilities. He was taken prisoner in the attack. He subsequently rose to the rank of colonel, and distinguished himself at the memorable storming of Stony Point, in 1779, where he led a column by the side of General Wayne.

Thomas Gardner's regiment, of Middlesex, was commissioned on the 2d of June. William Bond was lieutenant-colonel, and Michael Jackson was major. After the British landed, this regiment was stationed in the road leading to Lechmere's Point, and late in the day was ordered to Charlestown. On arriving at Bunker Hill, General Putnam ordered part of it to assist in throwing up defences commenced at this place. One company went to the rail fence. The greater part, under the lead of their colonel, on the third attack, advanced towards the redoubt. On the way, Colonel Gardner was struck by a ball, which inflicted a mortal wound

While a party was carrying him off, he had an affecting interview with his son, a youth of nineteen, who was anxious to aid in bearing him from the field. His heroic father prohibited him, and he was borne on a litter of rails over Winter Hill. Here he was overtaken by the retreating troops. He raised himself on his rude couch, and addressed to them cheering words. He lingered until July 3, when he died. On the 5th he was buried with the honors of war.[1] He was in his fifty-second year, and had been a member of the General Court, and of the Provincial Congress. He was a true patriot, a brave soldier, and an upright man. An obituary notice of him in the Essex Gazette, July 13, 1775, says: "From the era of our public difficulties he distinguished himself as an ardent friend to the expiring liberties of America; and by the unanimous suffrages of his townsmen was for some years elected a member of the General Assembly; but when the daring encroachments of intruding despotism deprived us of a constitutional convention, and the first law of nature demanded a substitute, he was chosen one of the Provincial Congress; in which departments he was vigilant and indefatigable in defeating every effort of tyranny. To promote the interest of his country was the delight of his soul. An inflexible zeal for freedom caused him to behold every engine of oppression with contempt, horror, and aversion." He devoted to military affairs not only a large share of his time, but of his fortune. His private character is highly eulogized. He was, "to his family kind, tender, and indulgent; to his friends, unreserved and sincere; to the whole circle of his acquaintance, affable, condescending, and obliging; while veneration for religion augmented the splendor of his sister virtues." [2]

[1] Extract from Washington's orders, July 4, 1775. "Colonel Gardner is to be buried to-morrow, at three o'clock, P. M., with the military honors due to so brave and gallant an officer, who fought, bled, and died in the cause of his country and mankind. His own regiment, except the company at Malden, to attend on this mournful occasion. The place of these companies, in the lines, on Prospect Hill, to be supplied by Colonel Glover's regiment, till the funeral is over."

[2] In 1776, a tract was published in Philadelphia, entitled "The Battle of Bunker's Hill. A Dramatic Piece, of five acts, in Heroic Measure. By a

Major Jackson had a personal encounter with a British officer, whom he killed, while he received a ball through his side. His life was preserved by his sword belt. He was recognized by his antagonist, with whom he had served in former wars.

One of the companies of this regiment — Captain Josiah Harris' — was raised in Charlestown. Colonel Swett pays this company — the last to retreat — the following compliment: "They were fighting at their own doors, on their own natal soil. They were on the extreme left, covered by some loose stones thrown up on the shore of the Mystic, during the day, by order of Colonel Stark. At this most important pass into the country, against which the enemy made the most desperate efforts, like Leonidas' band, they had taken post, and like them they defended it till the enemy had discovered another."

General Ward's regiment, of Worcester, was commissioned May 23. Jonathan Ward was lieutenant-colonel; Edward Barnes, major; Timothy Bigelow, second major; James Hart, adjutant; William Boyd, quartermaster. This regiment was not ordered to Charlestown until late in the afternoon, and halted on its way; but a detachment from it pushed on, and arrived in season to take part in the action. Lieutenant-colonel Ward, with a few men, reached the rail fence; and Captains Cushing and Washburn, and another company, fired upon the British after the retreat commenced from the

Gentleman of Maryland." In the dedication, the author says, "It was at first drawn up for an exercise in oratory." The three American officers named are Warren, Putnam, and Gardner. Several speeches are put into the mouth of Gardner. One, after he had been desperately wounded, will give a sufficient idea of the matter and style of the piece: —

> " A musket ball, death-winged, has pierced my groin,
> And widely op'd the swift curr'nt of my veins.
> Bear me, then, soldiers, to that hollow space,
> A little hence, just in the hill's decline.
> A surgeon there may stop the gushing wound,
> And gain a short respite to life, that yet
> I may return, and fight one half hour more.
> Then shall I die in peace, and to my God
> Surrender up the spirit which he gave."

redoubt. The remainder of the regiment, under Major Barnes, retreated before it got near enough to engage the enemy.

Jonathan Brewer's regiment, of Worcester and Middlesex, consisted, June 15, of 397 men. William Buckminster was lieutenant-colonel, and Nathaniel Cudworth major,—all of whom did excellent duty in the battle. On the same day, the committee of safety recommended the officers of this regiment to be commissioned, with the exception of Captain Stebbins, who did not have the requisite number of men. Colonel Swett states that this regiment went on about three hundred strong; revolutionary depositions state one hundred and fifty. It was stationed mostly on the diagonal line between the breastwork and rail fence. Few details are given respecting Colonel Brewer, other than that he was consulted often by Prescott, behaved with spirit, and was wounded; or of Major Cudworth,—the same who led the Sudbury minute-men to attack the British troops on the 19th of April. Lieutenant-colonel Buckminster acquired much reputation for bravery and prudence in the battle. Just before the retreat, he received a dangerous wound from a musket ball entering his right shoulder, and coming out in the middle of his back. This made him a cripple during life. He was much respected for his sterling integrity, patriotism, and goodness of heart. He was born in Framingham in 1736, removed in 1757 to Barre, was elected in 1774 to command the minute-men, and after his arrival in camp was chosen lieutenant-colonel. He died in 1786.[1]

John Nixon's regiment, from Middlesex and Worcester, was neither full nor commissioned, and both the returns and the details of it are very meagre. Only three companies appear in a list dated June 16, and the officers of them are all that appear to have been in commission at this date. Colonel Swett states that three hundred were led on to the field

---

[1] The inscription on his monument is said to faithfully describe his character: — "Sacred to the memory of Colonel William Buckminster. An industrious farmer, a useful citizen, an honest man, a sincere Christian, a brave officer, and a friend to his country; in whose cause he courageously fought, and was dangerously wounded at the battle of Bunker's Hill. He was born Dec. 15, A. D. 1736. Died June 22, A. D. 1786."

by Colonel Nixon, who behaved with great gallantry. He was badly wounded, and carried off the hill.

Benjamin R. Woodbridge's regiment, of Hampshire, also, was not commissioned, and there are few details of it, or of its officers, in the accounts of the battle. A return dated June 16 names eight captains, four lieutenants, four ensigns, and three hundred and sixty-three men. Abijah Brown was lieutenant-colonel, and William Stacy major. Colonel Swett names this regiment, also, as going on three hundred strong. But in this case, and in the case of Nixon's, it is probably too high an estimate.

Asa Whitcomb's regiment, of Worcester, had but few companies in the battle. One account, by a soldier, states that Captain Benjamin Hastings, belonging to it, led on a company of thirty-four, and took post at the rail fence. This name does not occur in a return dated June 3. Two companies, Captains Burt's and Wilder's, were probably in the battle.

James Scammans' regiment, from Maine, did not advance nearer the battle than Bunker Hill; and its colonel was tried for disobedience of orders, but acquitted. This trial was printed at length, in the N. E. Journal of February 1776. In a petition, dated November 14, 1776, he requested a commission to raise a regiment, " being willing to show his country that he was ready at all times to risk his fortune and life in defence of it." It commenced as follows: " Whereas his conduct has been called in question respecting the battle of Charlestown, in June, 1775, wherein the dispositions made were such as could render but little prospect of success."

John Mansfield's regiment was ordered to Charlestown, but marched to Cobble Hill, to protect the detachment of artillery, under Major Scarborough Gridley. Colonel Mansfield was tried for " remissness and backwardness in the execution of his duty," sentenced " to be cashiered, and rendered unfit to serve in the continental army." Colonel Swett remarks, that he " was obviously guilty of an error only, arising from inexperience."

Richard Gridley's battalion of artillery, notwithstanding the great exertions that had been made to complete it, was not settled at the time of the battle. It consisted of ten com-

panies, — four hundred and seventeen men. In a return
dated June 16, Scarborough Gridley, son of the colonel, is
titled lieutenant-colonel, and William Burbeck major; but
the committee of safety of this date recommended Congress
to commission the captains and subalterns of the train, and
William Burbeck as lieutenant-colonel, Scarborough Gridley
as first major and David Mason as second major. But these
officers were not commissioned until June 21, when Gridley
was made second major. Three companies were in battle:
Captain Gridley's, Trevett's, and Callender's. One other —
Capt. Foster's — advanced as far as Bunker Hill, when it was
obliged to retreat. Details of the conduct of these companies
have been given. All accounts agree that the artillery, in
general, was badly served.

Colonel Richard Gridley, the chief engineer of the army,
who planned the works on Breed's Hill, was a veteran of the
French wars, and distinguished himself at the siege of Louisburg. He was taken ill on the morning of the 17th, after the
fatigue of the night, and left the hill; but returned before the
action commenced, and fought until the retreat, aiding in discharging one of the field-pieces. He was struck, near the
close of the battle, by a ball, and entered his sulky to be
carried off; but meeting with some obstruction, had but just
left it, when the horse was killed and the sulky was riddled
by the enemy's shot. The veteran engineer was active in
planning the fortifications that were thrown up immediately
after the battle. He received from the Provincial Congress
the rank of major-general; and commissioned September 20,
1775, to take the command of the artillery in the continental
army. In November, he was superseded by Colonel Knox.
Washington, December 31, stated to Congress that no one in
the army was better qualified to be chief engineer; and his
services were again called for, on the memorable night when
Dorchester Heights were fortified.   After the British had
left Boston, he was intrusted with the duty of again throwing up works in Charlestown, and other points about the
harbor. He died at Stoughton, June 21, 1796, aged eighty-
four.

Major Scarborough Gridley, who was ordered with additional artillery companies to Charlestown, but took post at Cobble Hill to fire at the Glasgow frigate, was tried by a court-martial, of which General Greene was president. The following was the sentence, September 24, 1775 : "Major Scarborough Gridley, tried at a late court-martial, whereof Brigadier-general Greene was president, for 'being deficient in his duty upon the 17th of June last, the day of the action upon Bunker's Hill,' the court find Major Scarborough Gridley guilty of a breach of orders. They do, therefore, dismiss him from the Massachusetts service ; but, on account of his inexperience and youth, and the great confusion that attended that day's transactions in general, they do not consider him incapable of a continental commission, should the general officers recommend him to his excellency." He was a son of Colonel Gridley ; and parental partiality procured his appointment in preference to that of Benjamin Thompson, afterwards the celebrated Count Rumford. The latter accompanied Major Brooks the last time he was ordered on, and met the Americans in their retreat.

Captain Callender, for disobedience of orders and alleged cowardice, was tried June 27, — the first of the trials on account of this battle. The court sentenced him to be cashiered ; and Washington, in an order, July 7, declared him to be "dismissed from all further service in the continental service as an officer." But Capt. Callender despised the charge of cowardice ; and, determining to wipe out the unjust stigma, continued in the army as a volunteer. At the battle of Long Island he fought with such signal bravery that Washington ordered the sentence to be erased from the orderly book, and his commission to be restored to him. He was taken prisoner by the enemy, August 27, 1776. He remained over a year in the hands of the British. A touching petition, dated September 15, 1777, was addressed to the government of Massachusetts by his wife, in his behalf. "Your petitioner," it says, "with four helpless infants, is now, through the distress of a kind and loving husband, a tender and affectionate parent, reduced to a state of misery and wretchedness and want, truly pitiable." Her devotion had found a way of relief, by an exchange, and it was successful. Colonel Swett

states that this brave soldier left the service at the peace with
the highest honor and reputation.

Captain S. R. Trevett's gallantry and perseverance rescued
the only field-piece saved of the six taken to the field. He lived
to an advanced age.

The New Hampshire troops consisted of the regiments of
Colonels Stark and Reed, and one company, Reuben Dow's,
in Prescott's regiment. They fought with great bravery.

Colonel John Stark's regiment was large and full. There
is no return, however, specifying the number of men, in the
office of the secretary of state of New Hampshire. In the roll
Isaac Wyman is named lieutenant-colonel; Andrew McClary,
major, (though the records of the Congress state that he was
appointed major of the third or Poor's regiment;) Abiel Chandler, adjutant; John Caldwell, quartermaster; David Osgood,
chaplain; Obadiah Williams, surgeon; Samuel McClintock,
chaplain.

Colonel Stark — afterwards the hero of Bennington — be
haved with his characteristic bravery. After he had detached,
early in the morning, a third of his men, it is said he visited
the redoubt in company with his major, when he found his
men in the hollow between Winter and Ploughed Hills. On
leading the troops into action, he made a spirited address, and
ordered three cheers to be given. By his order, also, the
stones on the beach of Mystic River were thrown up in the
form of a breastwork. These are nearly all the particulars
relating to his conduct that have been stated. But all
accounts speak of his coolness and intrepidity.

When the order was received for the remainder of this regiment to march to Bunker Hill, it was paraded in front of a
house used as an arsenal, where each man received a gill cup
full of powder, fifteen balls, and one flint. After this the cartridges were to be made up, and this occasioned much delay.
Hence the regiment did not get to the hill until about two
o'clock.

The major of this regiment, Andrew McClary, was a
favorite officer. He was nearly six feet and a half in height,
and of an athletic frame. During the action he fought with
great bravery; and amidst the roar of the artillery his sten·

torian voice was heard animating the men, and inspiring them with his own energy. After the action was over, he rode to Medford to procure bandages for the wounded; and, on his return, went with a few of his comrades to reconnoitre the British, then on Bunker Hill. As he was on his way to rejoin his men, a shot from a frigate lying where Cragie's Bridge is, passed through his body. He leaped a few feet from the ground, pitched forward, and fell dead on his face. He was carried to Medford, and interred with the honors of war. He was, General Dearborn writes, a brave, great, and good man. A spirited notice of him appeared in the New Hampshire Gazette, dated Epsom, July, 1775. It says: "The major discovered great intrepidity and presence of mind in the action, and his noble soul glowed with ardor and the love of his country; and, like the Roman Camillus, who left his plough, commanded the army, and conquered his opponents, so the major, upon the first intelligence of hostilities at Concord, left his farm and went a volunteer to assist his suffering brethren, where he was soon called to a command, which he executed to his eternal honor, and has thereby acquired the reputation of a brave officer and a disinterested patriot; and may his name be held in respect by all the lovers of liberty to the end of time, while the names of the sons of tyranny are despised and disgraced, and nothing left to them but the badges of their perfidy and infamy! May the widow of the deceased be respected for his sake; and may his children inherit his spirit and bravery, but not meet with his fate!"

Captain Henry Dearborn, who afterwards became so distinguished in the history of the country, both in civil and military capacities, commanded one of the companies of this regiment, and has supplied an account of the action full of interesting details.

The chaplain of the regiment, Dr. McClintock, was in the battle, animating the men by his exhortations, prayers, and intrepidity.

James Reed's regiment, consisting, June 14, of 486 rank and file, was stationed at Charlestown Neck. Israel Gilman was lieutenant-colonel; Nathan Hale, major; Stephen Peabody, adjutant; Isaac Frye, quartermaster; Ezra Green, surgeon. Few details have been preserved of the service of this regiment. Colonel Reed was, Colonel Swett remarks, "a highly respectable officer, and served at Ticonderoga in 1776. His letters to the New Hampshire Congress bear evidence of a patriotic spirit, while his orders to his regiment evince a good disciplinarian. No special mention appears of him in the accounts of the battle. General Folsom, however, in writing of the gallantry of the New Hampshire troops, makes no discrimination. Adjutant Peabody behaved, General Sullivan writes, with great courage and intrepidity. William Lee, first orderly sergeant of Spaulding's company, "not only fought well himself," — say the officers and men of this company, in a petition to Washington, August 10, 1775, — " but gave good advice to the men to place themselves in right order, and to stand their ground well."

The Connecticut forces at Cambridge were under the command of General Putnam. His regiment (see page 100) was full, containing ten companies. Experience Storrs was his lieutenant-colonel, John Durkee his first major, and Obadiah Johnson his second major. A letter dated June 20, 1775, states that the whole of this regiment, excepting Captain Mosely's company, was in the action. Two companies that appear in the returns as belonging to General Spencer's regiment were certainly in the battle, — Chester's and Coit's. The number given — one hundred and twenty — as constituting the fatigue party that went on under Knowlton on the night of the 16th, rests on Grosvenor's letters. Chester states, that "by orders from head quarters, one subaltern, one sergeant, and thirty privates, were draughted out over night to intrench, from his company." Captain Clark, in a letter, June 17, 1818, says, he received orders from General Putnam "to detach one ensign, with twenty-eight men," to march early in the evening of the 16th of June. Draughts were made from Putnam's and Knowlton's company, and probably from one other.[1] No order for more of the Connecticut forces to go on appears to

[1] It is certain that the two hundred Connecticut men went on which Chester states were called for. Thus, Sylvester Conant, of Storrs' company, was on the hill during the night ; Josiah Cleaveland states that thirty of his company went on.

have been given, until General Putnam gave it, after the British landed, about noon, on the 17th.

The conduct of the Connecticut troops is mentioned in terms of high commendation in the private letters and the journals of the time. Major Durkee; Captains Knowlton, Chester, Coit; Lieutenants Dana, Hide, Grosvenor, Webb, Bingham, and Keyes, are specially named as deserving of credit. One letter states that the officers and soldiers under the command of Major Durkee, Captains Knowlton, Coit, Clark, and Chester, and all the Connecticut troops ordered up, and some from this province, did honor to themselves and the cause of their country. An article printed directly after the battle in the Connecticut Courant says: "Captain Chester and Lieutenant Webb, who marched up to the lines and reinforced the troops, by their undaunted behavior, timely and vigorous assistance, it is universally agreed, are justly entitled to the grateful acknowledgments of their country." They went on near the close of the battle. In a letter dated July 11, 1775, and addressed to Silas Dean, Lieutenant Webb gives a vivid idea both of the hotness of the fire, and of the desperate nature of the hand-to-hand contests of the day. "For my part, I confess," he writes, "when I was descending into the valley, from off Bunker Hill, side by side of Captain Chester, at the head of our company, I had no more thought of ever rising the hill again than I had of ascending to heaven, as Elijah did, soul and body together. But after we got engaged, to see the dead and wounded around me, I had no other feeling but that of revenge. Four men were shot dead within five feet of me, but, thank Heaven, I escaped, with only the graze of a musket ball on my hat. I think it my duty to tell you of the bravery of one of our company. Edward Brown stood side by side with Gershom Smith, in the intrenchments. Brown saw his danger, — discharged his own and Smith's gun when they came so close as to push over our small breastwork. Brown sprang, seized a regular's gun, took it from him, and killed him on the spot; brought off the gun in triumph, and has it now by him. In this engagement we lost four brave men, and four wounded."

The conduct of Captain Thomas Knowlton elicited high

praise. He was a native of Boxford, Massachusetts, but while a boy removed to Ashford, Connecticut. He served with distinction in the French wars, then became a prosperous farmer; and on his appearing on the Lexington alarm, as a volunteer in the Ashford militia company, to march to the camp, was unanimously elected captain. General Putnam knew his merit, and selected him to command the fatigue party to accompany Colonel Prescott. He commenced the construction of the rail fence protection, and fought here with admirable bravery and conduct, until the retreat. He received from a Bostonian a gold-laced hat, a sash and gold breast-plate, for his behavior in this battle. Soon after, he was promoted; and while major, he made, January 8, 1776, a daring and successful excursion into Charlestown, to burn several houses used by the British; and as lieutenant-colonel, was the confidant of Washington in the enterprise of the memorable Nathan Hale. On the 16th of September, 1776, while exhibiting his usual intrepidity, he was killed at the battle of Harlem Heights. Washington, in the general orders, after alluding to his gallantry and bravery, and his fall while "gloriously fighting," said he "would have been an honor to any country." He was about thirty-six when he was killed.

General Ward expressed his thanks to the troops engaged in this battle, in the following order, of June 24: "The general orders his thanks to be given to those officers and soldiers who behaved so gallantly at the late action in Charlestown. Such bravery gives the general sensible pleasure, as he is thereby fully satisfied that we shall finally come off victorious, and triumph over the enemies of freedom and America."

So conflicting are the authorities, that the number of troops engaged, on either side, cannot be precisely ascertained. "The number of the Americans during the battle," Colonel Swett says, "was fluctuating, but may be fairly estimated at three thousand five hundred, who joined in the battle, and five hundred more, who covered the retreat." General Putnam's estimate was two thousand two hundred. General Washington says the number engaged, at any one time, was one thousand five hundred, and this was adopted by Dr. Gordon. This is as near accuracy as can be arrived at

General Gage, in his official account, states the British force at "something over two thousand," and yet the same account acknowledges one thousand and fifty-four killed and wounded. This certainly indicates a force far larger than two thousand. Neither British accounts, nor the British plans of the battle, mention all the regiments that were in the field. Thus, the movements of the second ʻbattalion of marines are not given; yet the official table of loss states that it had seven killed and thirty wounded; and Clarke, also, states it was not until after the Americans had retreated that General Gage sent over this second battalion, with four regiments of foot, and a company of artillery. Americans, who counted the troops as they left the wharves in Boston, state that five thousand went over to Charlestown; but, probably, not even four thousand were actually engaged.

Statements were made as to the numbers engaged, in a debate in the House of Commons, December 7, 1775. The lord mayor, — Mr. Sawbridge, — said it had been very fashionable, both within and without doors, to stigmatize the Americans as cowards and poltroons, but he believed the truth would be found on the other side; for he was well informed that the king's troops, in the action of Bunker's Hill, consisted of twenty-five hundred men, and the provincials not quite fifteen hundred; and even those fifteen hundred would have completely defeated the king's troops, if their ammunition had not been totally spent. Lord North said, he was but an indifferent judge of military operations; but, by the best accounts he could obtain, the provincials were, at least, three to one, and were, besides, very strongly intrenched. He estimated the number of Americans at eight thousand, at least. Colonel Morris estimated the Americans at five thousand, and the British at twenty-five hundred.

The time the battle lasted is variously stated; some accounts state four hours, but they include the heavy fire of artillery that covered the landing. The committee of safety (Ms.) account says: "The time the engagement lasted, from the first fire of the musketry till the last, was exactly one hour and a half." The losses of individuals in the battle were allowed by the colonies, and there are hundreds of petitions from the soldiers in it. They often state the number of times the petitioner discharged his musket. Thus, one says: "He discharged his piece more than thirty times, within fair gun-shot, and he is confident he did not discharge it in vain." Another says: "He had an opportunity of firing seventeen times at our unnatural enemies, which he cheerfully improved, being a marksman." Several letters unite in stating the time of the action at one hour and a half. The general battle, with small arms, began about half past three, and ended about five.[1]

The following is the record in General Ward's orderly book,—the only reference to the battle it contains,—of the loss of the Americans: "June 17. The battle of Charlestown was fought this day. Killed, one hundred and fifteen; wounded, three hundred and five; captured, thirty.[2] Total,

---

[1] No mention is made of colors being used on either side. At one of the patriotic celebrations of 1825, a flag was borne which was said to have been unfurled at Bunker Hill; and tradition states that one was hoisted at the redoubt, and that Gage and his officers were puzzled to read by their glasses its motto. A Whig told them it was — "Come if you dare!" In the eulogy on Warren is the following, in a description of the astonishment of the British on seeing the redoubt: —

> "Soon as Aurora gave the golden day,
> And drove the sable shades of night away,
> Columbia's troops are seen in dread array,
> And waving streamers in the air display."

In a Ms. plan of the battle, colors are represented in the centre of each British regiment.

[2] The following list of prisoners taken by the British June 17 appeared in the journals of September, 1775: —

Lieutenant-colonel Parker, . .	Chelmsford, ...	Dead.
Captain Benjamin Walker, . .	Chelmsford, ...	"
Lieutenant Amaziah Fausett, .	Groton, ...	"
Lieutenant William Scott, . .	Peterborough, . .	Alive.
Sergeant Robert Phelps, . .	Lancaster, ...	Dead.
Phineas Nevers, ...	Windsor, ...	"
Oliver Stevens, ...	Townsend, ...	"
Daniel McGrath, ...	Unknown, ...	"
John Perkins, ...	New Rutland, . . .	Alive
Jacob Frost, ...	Tewskbury, ...	"

four hundred and fifty." They, also, lost five pieces of cannon out of six, and a large quantity of intrenching tools. The following table shows the loss sustained by each regiment, and presents a somewhat different result:—

	Killed.	Wounded.		Killed.	Wounded
Prescott's,	42	28	Gridley's,	0	4
Bridge's,	15	29	Ward's,	1	6
Frye's,	15	31	Scammans',	0	2
Brewer's,	7	11	Gerrish's,	3	2
Little's,	7	23	Whitcomb's,	5	8
Gardner's,	6	7	Stark's,	15	45
Nixon's,	3	10	Reed's,	5	21
Woodbridge's,	1	5	Putnam & Coit Co.,	11	26
Doolittle's,	0	9	Chester's Co.,	4	4

Killed, 140; wounded, 271;[1] captured, 30.

Some of the dead were buried on the field of battle. One deposit appears to have been a trench near the line of the

Amasa Fisk,	Pepperell,	Dead.
Daniel Sessions,	Andover,	Alive.
Jonathan Norton,	Newburyport,	"
Philip Johnson Beck,	Boston—Mansfield,	"
Benjamin Bigelow,	Peckerfield,	"
Benjamin Wilson,	Billerica,	"
Archibald McIntosh,	Townsend,	Dead.
David Kemp,	Groton,	"
John Deland,	Charlestown,	Alive.
Lawrence Sullivan,	Wethersfield,	"
Timothy Kettell, (a lad,)	Dismissed Charlestown.	
William Robinson,	Unknown,	Dead.
Benjamin Ross,	Ashford, Conn.,	"
John Dillon,	Jersey, Old England,	"
One unknown,		"
William Kench,	Peckerfield,	"
James Dodge,	Edinburgh, Scotland,	"
William Robinson,	Connecticut,	"
John Lord,	Unknown,	"
James Milliken,	Boston,	"
Stephen Foster,	Groton,	"

Total,—20 dead, 10 alive, 1 dismissed.

[1] This list has been made up from letters, official returns, and an article in a Providence newspaper. The latter is not correct. It does not give the loss in Reed's regiment.

almshouse estate, running parallel with Elm-street. Here a
arge number of American buttons have been found attached
to bones. Americans were buried in other places in Charlestown, which are known from similar circumstances. The
wounded were carried to the western side of Bunker Hill, and
then to Cambridge. Doctors Thomas Kittredge, William
Eustis,—afterwards governor,—Walter Hastings, Thomas
Welsh, Isaac Foster, Lieut.-col. Bricket, David Townsend,
and John Hart, were in attendance. The house of Governor Oliver, in Cambridge, known as the Gerry estate, was
occupied as a hospital. Many of the soldiers who died
of their wounds were buried in a field in front of this house.
Rev. Samuel Cook's house, at West Cambridge, was also
used for a hospital. The prisoners were carried to Boston
jail.

The loss of the British was admitted, in the official account,
to have been two hundred and twenty-six killed, eight hundred and twenty-eight wounded: total, one thousand and
fifty-four. But the Americans set it as high as fifteen
hundred. The wounded, during the whole night and the
next day, were conveyed to Boston, where the streets were
filled with groans and lamentation. A letter, June 30, 1775,
says: "I have seen many from Boston who were eye-wit-
nesses to the most melancholy scene ever beheld in this part
of the world. The Saturday night and Sabbath were taken up
in carrying over the dead and wounded; and all the wood-
carts in town, it is said, were employed,—chaises and coaches
for the officers. They have taken the workhouse, almshouse,
and manufactory-house, for the wounded." The physicians,
surgeons, and apothecaries of Boston rendered every assistance in their power. The processions were melancholy
sights. "In the first carriage," writes Clarke, " was Major
Williams, bleeding and dying, and three dead captains of the
fifty-second regiment. In the second, four dead offi:ers; then
another with wounded officers." The privates who died on
the field were immediately buried there,—"in holes,"—
Gage's report states. Collections of bones have been occasionally found on the east side of Breed's Hill, in digging wells or
cellars, having attached to them buttons, with the numbers

of the different regiments. "On Monday morning," a British account says, "all the dead officers were decently buried in Boston, in a private manner, in the different churches and churchyards there."

A large proportion of the killed were officers, and among them some highly distinguished. Lieutenant-colonel Abercrombie, at the head of the grenadiers, was shot while storming the works. He was a brave and noble-hearted soldier; and when the men were bearing him from the field, he begged them to spare his old friend Putnam. "If you take General Putnam alive," he said, "don't hang him; for he's a brave man." He died on the 24th of June.

Major Pitcairn, the commander of the marines, was widely known in the country from his connection with the events of the nineteenth of April, and many of the Americans claim the honor of having killed him in this battle. Dr. John Eliot wrote in his almanac the following account of his fall: "This amiable and gallant officer was slain entering the intrenchments. He had been wounded twice; then putting himself at the head of his forces, he faced danger, calling out, 'Now for the glory of the marines!' He received four balls in his body." [1] He was much beloved by his command. "I have lost my father," his son exclaimed as he fell. "We have all lost a father," was the echo of the regiment. His son bore him to a boat, and then to a house in Prince-street, Boston, where he was attended by a physician, at the special request of General Gage,[2] but soon died. He was a courteous and accomplished officer, and an exemplary man. His son was soon promoted.[3]

Major Spendlove, of the forty-third regiment, another distinguished officer, died of his wounds. He had served with

---

[1] Memorandum in his almanac of 1775. [2] Ms. Letter. [3] A British account states that he was shot from the houses. Gage's official account implies that he did not die on the field. "Major Pitcairn wounded — since dead." The following notice appears in a newspaper of Aug. 15, 1775 : "Lieutenant Pitcairn, of the marines, (who brought his father, Major Pitcairn, when mortally wounded at Boston, off the field of action,) is appointed a captain-lieutenant and captain in the said corps, though not in his turn, as an acknowledgment of the services of his gallant father." — Major Pitcairn had eleven children. A pension of £200 a year was settled on his widow.

unblemished reputation, upwards of forty years, in the same regiment, and been three times wounded, — once when with Wolfe on the Plains of Abraham, again at the reduction of Martinico, and at the capture of Havana. His conduct at the battle was favorably mentioned by the commander. Other officers of merit fell. Captain Addison, related to the author of the Spectator, and Captain Sherwin, Howe's aid-de-camp, were killed. The slaughter of officers occasioned great astonishment in England.

Of the officers who acted as aids to General Howe, all were wounded, and only one of them, Lieutenant Page, of the engineers, lived to reach England.[1] He distinguished himself at the storming of the redoubt, and made the fine plan of the battle that was the first correct one engraved in England, and is now first engraved in this country for this work. Many of the wounded officers returned to England; and for many months the British journals contain notices of their arrival, and presentation at court. One of them, selected as a specimen, reads as follows : " March, 28, 1776. — Yesterday Capt. Cockering, who lost his arm at Bunker's Hill, was introduced to his majesty at St. James', by the Duke of Chandois, and graciously received; at the same time his majesty was pleased to present him with a captain's commission in a company of invalids."

The British journals contain many comments on this battle, and for years they continued to publish incidents in relation to it. For several months after it took place letters from officers engaged in it continued to appear in them. They were astonished at its terrible slaughter. It was compared with other great battles, especially with those of Quebec and of Minden. Officers who had served in all Prince Ferdinand's campaigns remarked, that " so large a proportion of a detach-

---

[1] The London Chronicle, January 11, 1776. —"A few days ago arrived in town, from Boston, Lieutenant Page, of his majesty's corps of engineers, on account of the wounds he received the 17th of June, in the action at Charlestown. This gentleman is the only one now living of those who acted as aids-de-camp to General Howe, so great was the slaughter of officers that day. He particularly distinguished himself in the storming of the redoubt for which he received General Howe's thanks. "

ment was never killed and wounded in Germany." It far exceeded, in this respect, and in the hotness of the fire, the battle of Minden. The manner in which whole regiments and companies were cut up was commented upon. The 5th, 52d, 59th, and the grenadiers of the Welsh Fusileers are specially mentioned. One company of grenadiers, of the 35th, persevered in advancing after their officers fell, and five of their number only left, and they led on by the oldest soldier. This was adduced as a memorable instance of English valor; and it was exultingly asked, "What history can produce its parallel?" Attempts were made to account for the facts that so many of the British, and so few of the Americans, fell. One officer writes of the former, that the American rifles "were peculiarly adapted to take off the officers of a whole line as it marches to an attack." Another writes, "That every rifleman was attended by two men, one on each side of him, to load pieces for him, so that he had nothing to do but fire as fast as a piece was put into his hand; and this is the real cause of so many of our brave officers falling." One reason given why the British troops killed so few of the provincials was, that the over-sized balls used by the artillery would not permit of a true shot.[1] Mean-time, transports with the wounded, and with the remains of the regiments which had been so cut up, as they arrived in England, continued to afford living evidence of the terrible realities of this conflict.[2]

The British officers described the redoubt as having been so strong that it must have been the work of several days. One says: "The fortification on Bunker Hill must have been the work of some days; it was very regular, and exceeding

[1] A British paper says: "The reason why the royal army killed so few of the rebels was entirely owing to the mistake of those who had the care of the artillery, — taking with them a prodigious number of twelve pound shot for six pound pieces. Hence," the article gravely says, "it naturally required a great while to ram down such disproportioned shot; nor did they, when discharged, fly with that velocity and true direction they would have done, had they been better suited to the size of the cannon."

[2] March 5, 1776. — "A few days ago the shattered remains of the 18th regiment of foot, which was engaged in the action at Bunker's Hill, and reduced to only twenty-five men, arrived at Maidstone."— British newspaper

strong." [1]   A plan of it appeared in the Gentleman's Magazine, which is here presented as a curious memorial of the battle. It is called "Plan of the Redoubt and Intrenchment on the Heights of Charlestown, (commonly called Bunker's Hill,) opposite Boston, in New England, attacked and carried by his majesty's troops, June 17, 1775."

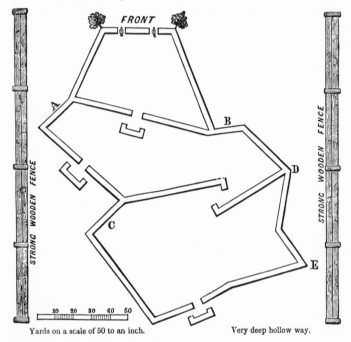

Yards on a scale of 50 to an inch.   Very deep hollow way.

The Gentleman's Magazine says: "This redoubt was well executed. In the only side on which it could be attacked were two pieces of cannon. In the two salient angles were two trees, with their branches projecting off the parapet, to prevent an entry being made on the angles. The two flanks

[1] This letter, Boston, June 22, says: "The fortification on Bunker Hill must have been the work of some days; it was very regular, and exceeding strong, insomuch that here the rebels thought themselves secure from danger, and sure of success in destroying the town of Boston, which they had determined to do. Here they reserved their fire till our noble troops were almost under their ramparts, and stubbornly opposed them. Had the rebels gained the day, the town of Boston could not have stood long."

(A and B) of the intrenchment were well contrived, as the fire from them crossed within twenty yards of the face of the redoubt. The flank C sufficiently secures its face; and the bastion D, with its flanks E and B, is the best defence against such troops as might endeavor to pass or cut down the fence."

General Dearborn says: "It was a square redoubt, the curtains of which were about sixty or seventy feet in extent, with an intrenchment or breastwork extending fifty or sixty feet from the northern angle, towards Mystic River. In the course of the night the ramparts had been raised to the height of six or seven feet, with a small ditch at their base; but it was yet in a rude, imperfect state."

General Howe, it was conceded even by his enemies, behaved with great bravery through the whole battle. Of the notices of him in the British journals, I select the following: "General Howe, during the whole engagement on the 17th of June last, was in the most imminent danger; and Mr. Evans, an English servant, who went over with him, could not be prevailed on to quit him till the whole of the action was over. Evans attended the whole time with wine and other necessaries for the refreshment of the general and those about him; during which, Evans had one of the bottles in his hand dashed to pieces, and got a contusion on one of his arms at the same time, by a ball from some of the provincials."

General Clinton's services were highly commended, and great influence was ascribed to his advice. Few details, however, are mentioned of his conduct, besides his rally of the troops for the third attack, and his advice to follow up the victory by a close pursuit. Few particulars, also, are named of General Pigot. General Gage attributed "the success of the day, in a great measure, to his firmness and gallantry."

General Gage was severely criticised. It was said: though he was urged to take possession of the Heights of Charlestown, he did not even reconnoitre the ground, and this neglect was a great error: "another error certainly was that instead of confining our attack to the enemy's left wing only, the assault was made on the whole front:[1] the army should have landed in their rear and cut off their retreat: the troops should have marched up in column on

[1] Stedman's History of the American War, vol. 1, 129.

the first attack, and carried the works by the bayonet : the unnecessary load they bore exhausted them before they got into action : Mystic River was neglected, for the Symmetry transport might have taken a position at high water in the rear of the Americans, and played on their flank at the rail fence; or one of the covered boats, musket-proof, and carrying a heavy piece of cannon, might have been towed close in to the shore. And when the field was won, the success was less brilliant than it might have been, and ought to have been, for no pursuit was ordered after the Americans retreated. These criticisms, for the most part, were as just as they were severe. The issue of this battle destroyed the military reputation of General Gage, and occasioned his recall.

Nor did the British troops, gallantly as they behaved, escape the denunciations of party. Many allusions to their conduct on this day were made in the debates of Parliament. Thus Colonel Barre, February 20, 1776, said the troops, out of aversion to the service, misbehaved on this day. General Burgoyne arose with warmth, and contradicted Colonel Barre in the flattest manner. He allowed that the troops gave way a little at one time, because they were flanked by the fire out of the houses, &c., at Charlestown, but they soon rallied and advanced; and no men on earth ever behaved with more spirit, firmness, and perseverance, till they forced the enemy out of their intrenchments. This charge, in general, was certainly undeserved. At no time was British valor more needed to insure success, and at no time, General Gage remarked, was it "more conspicuous than in this action." In the general orders of June 19 was the following tribute : "The commander-in-chief returns his most grateful thanks to Major-general Howe, for the extraordinary exertion of his military abilities on the 17th inst. He returns his thanks also to Major-general Clinton and Brigadier-general Pigot, for the share they took in the success of the day ; as well as to Lieutenant-colonels Nesbit, Abercrombie, Gunning, and Clarke; Majors Butler, Williams, Bruce, Tupper, Spendlove, Small, and Mitchell; and the rest of the officers and soldiers, who, by remarkable efforts of courage and gallantry, overcame every disadvantage, and drove the rebels from their redoubt and strong-holds on the heights of Charlestown, and gained a complete victory." [1]

The wanton destruction of Charlestown excited indignation at home, and sympathy abroad. It had been repeatedly threatened previous to the battle. Its importance, in a military point of view, added to the bold and decided part it bore in the previous ten years' controversy, seemed to mark it for sacrifice. The threat of the nineteenth of April has been stated. The British general, on the 21st of April, sent to the selectmen a message to this effect, — that if American troops were allowed to occupy the town, or throw up works on the heights, the ships would be ordered to fire on it; and subsequently, probably when a part of the army marched into the town, General Gage sent word to the citizens that if the troops were not removed he would burn it. Consequently, a committee waited upon General Ward, informed him of the threat, and stated that if the good of the cause required that the troops should remain they would not object. Comment is unnecessary on so interesting a fact, and one so honorable to the patriotism of the inhabitants of Charlestown. [2]

In consequence of these threats, the belief in town was very general that its destruction would follow any military operations within the peninsula. Hence the inhabitants, with the

---

[1] On the 6th of September the acknowledgments of the crown were expressed in nearly similar terms.

[2] Among the Mss. of Richard Devens, of Charlestown, is the following : "This town was given up. Upon the appearance of some American troops on B. Hill, Gen. G. (Gage) sent over from B. (Boston) and threatened the town that if (the) men were not removed from the hill he would burn the town. A committee from the T. (town) waited on the C. in chief, G. W., (commander-in-chief, General Ward,) informed him of the threat they had received from G. G., (General Gage,) and at the same time informed him that if it was for (the) good of the whole they would not object."

An article in the London Chronicle, 1777, by one conversant with the ground and the battle, says : "So long before (the 17th) as the 21st of April, a message had been sent to the selectmen of Charlestown, that if they suffered the rebels to take possession of their town, or to throw up any works to annoy the ships, the ships would fire upon them."

Gordon says : "General Gage had for some time resolved upon burning the town, when once any works were raised by the Americans upon the hills belonging to it."

exception of about two hundred, had removed into the country, — some residing with friends, the poor supported by the
towns. Many carried with them their most valuable effects.
Others had secreted their goods in various places, as in dried
wells, in cellars, and holes dug in the ground. Committees
were appointed to superintend the supply of provisions to
those who remained. None could pass the Neck, however,
without a permit from a person stationed at the "Sun Tavern," at this place. The owners of the pastures went in to mow
the fields, and on the day previous to the battle the grass was
cut in the neighborhood of the rail fence. The town, therefore, on the day of the battle, was nearly deserted.

A few of the citizens, however, remained up to the hour of
the engagement. While the British were embarking, Rev.
John Martin, who fought bravely in the action,[1] and was with
the troops all night, left Breed's Hill, went to Charlestown
Ferry, and with a spy-glass — Dr. Stiles writes — "viewed
the shipping, and observed their preparations of floating batteries, and boats filling with soldiers. There were now in
Charlestown a considerable number of people — one hundred or
two hundred, or more, men and women — not yet removed,
though the body of the people and effects were gone. While
he called in at a house for a drink of water, a cannon ball
from the shipping passed through the house. He persuaded
the inhabitants to depart, but they seemed reluctant. He
assured them that it would be warm work that day." He
returned to the hill, but soon, about noon, went down again.
" Mr. Cary and son," he says, — "still at their own house, —
urged him to take some refreshment and rest, as he had been
fatigued all night. He lay down at Mr. Cary's about ten
minutes, when a ball came through the house. He rose and

---

[1] The following paragraph, dated New-Port, July 3, 1775, appeared in a
newspaper:

" Last Friday evening the Rev. Mr. John Martin, who fought gallantly at
Bunker's Hill, and is since appointed to a post in the Rhode Island regiment,
preached an animating sermon in this town, from Nehemiah iv., and part of
the 14th verse: ' Be not afraid of them : Remember the Lord which is great
and terrible, and fight for your brethren, your sons and daughters, your wives
and your daughters.' The next morning he preached another sermon, at
five o'clock, and then set out for the camp."

returned, and then the town evacuated with all haste." Advertisements in the journals indicate that furniture was carried out on this day.

General Burgoyne's letter supplies the most authentic description of the burning of the town. He writes of the British columns as they were moving to the attack: "They were also exceedingly hurt by musketry from Charlestown, though Clinton and I did not perceive it till Howe sent us word by a boat, and desired us to set fire to the town, which was immediately done; we threw a parcel of shells, and the whole was immediately in flames." The town was burning on the second attack. The smoke was seen a great distance. "Terrible indeed was that scene," — a letter from Salem reads, — "even at our distance. The western horizon in the day-time was one huge body of smoke, and in the evening a continued blaze; and the perpetual sound of cannon and volleys of musketry worked up our imaginations to a high degree of fright." The houses within the peninsula, with the exception of a few in the neighborhood of Mill-street, were entirely consumed. The number of buildings was estimated at about four hundred; and the loss of property at £117,982 5s. 2d.[1] Some of the property secreted was found by the British, while much of it was recovered by the owners on the evacuation of the town. Many from Boston had deposited goods in this town for safe keeping, and these were consumed. Dr. Mather lost his library. The inhabitants made several applications to the General Court and to Congress for indemnification for their loss, but without effect.

The destruction naturally excited great indignation in the colonies. John Langdon, in a letter dated Philadelphia, July 3, 1775, writes: "The low, mean revenge and wanton cruelty of the ministerial sons of tyranny, in burning the pleasant town of Charlestown, beggars all description; this does not look like the fight of those who have so long been friends, and would hope to be friends again, but rather of a most cruel enemy, — though we shall not wonder when we reflect, that it is the infernal hand of tyranny which always has, and ever

[1] This estimate was made by a large committee, chosen by the town for this purpose in March, 1776.

will, deluge that part of the world (which it lays hold of) in blood."

The British Annual Register of 1775 said : "The fate of Charlestown was also a matter of melancholy contemplation to the serious and unprejudiced of all parties. It was the first settlement made in the colony, and was considered as the mother of Boston, — that town owing its birth and nurture to emigrants of the former. Charlestown was large, handsome, and well built, both in respect to its public and private edifices ; it contained about four hundred houses, and had the greatest trade of any port in the province, except Boston. It is said that the two ports cleared out a thousand vessels annually for a foreign trade, exclusive of an infinite number of coasters. It is now buried in ruins. Such is the termination of human labor, industry, and wisdom, and such are the fatal fruits of civil dissensions."

I thus have attempted to present the chief incidents of this memorable battle. It is its connection with the cause of American liberty that gives such an importance to this occasion, and such an interest to its minute details. In conclusion, I cannot forbear to extract the following reflections contained in an article of the October number of the North American Review of 1818, which is understood to be from the pen of Hon. Daniel Webster : —

"No national drama was ever developed in a more interesting and splendid first scene. The incidents and the result of the battle itself were most important, and indeed most wonderful. As a mere battle, few surpass it in whatever engages and interests the attention. It was fought on a conspicuous eminence, in the immediate neighborhood of a populous city ; and consequently in the view of thousands of spectators. The attacking army moved over a sheet of water to the assault. The operations and movements were of course all visible and all distinct. Those who looked on from the houses and heights of Boston had a fuller view of every important operation and event than can ordinarily be had of any battle, or than can possibly be had of such as are fought on a more extended ground, or by detachments of troops acting in different places, and at different times, and in some measure independently of each other. When the British columns were advancing to the attack, the flames of Charlestown (fired, as is generally supposed, by a shell) began to ascend. The spectators, far outnumbering both armies, thronged and crowded on every height and every point which afforded a view of the scene, themselves constituted a very important part of it.

"The troops of the two armies seemed like so many combatants in an amphitheatre. The manner in which they should acquit themselves was to be judged of, not, as in other cases of military engagements, by reports and future history, but by a vast and anxious assembly already on the spot, and waiting with unspeakable concern and emotion the progress of the day.

"In other battles the *recollection* of wives and children has been used as an excitement to animate the warrior's breast and nerve his arm. Here was not a mere recollection, but an actual *presence* of them, and other dear connections, hanging on the skirts of the battle, anxious and agitated, feeling almost as if wounded themselves by every blow of the enemy, and putting forth, as it were, their own strength, and all the energy of their own throbbing bosoms, into every gallant effort of their warring friends.

"But there was a more comprehensive and vastly more important view of that day's contest than has been mentioned, — a view, indeed, which ordinary eyes, bent intently on what was immediately before them, did not embrace, but which was perceived in its full extent and expansion by minds of a higher order. Those men who were at the head of the colonial councils, who had been engaged for years in the previous stages of the quarrel with England, and who had been accustomed to look forward to the future, were well apprised of the magnitude of the events likely to hang on the business of that day. They saw in it not only a battle, but the beginning of a civil war of unmeasured extent and uncertain issue. All America and all England were likely to be deeply concerned in the consequences. The individuals themselves, who knew full well what agency they had had in bringing affairs to this crisis, had need of all their courage ; — not that disregard of personal safety, in which the vulgar suppose true courage to consist, but that high and fixed moral sentiment, that steady and decided purpose, which enables men to pursue a distant end, with a full view of the difficulties and dangers before them, and with a conviction, that, before they arrive at the proposed end, should they ever reach it, they must pass through evil report as well as good report, and be liable to obloquy as well as to defeat.

"Spirits that fear nothing else, fear disgrace; and this danger is necessarily encountered by those who engage in civil war. Unsuccessful resistance is not only ruin to its authors, but is esteemed, and necessarily so, by the laws of all countries, treasonable. This is the case at least till resistance becomes so general and formidable as to assume the form of regular war. But who can tell, when resistance commences, whether it will attain even to that degree of success? Some of those persons who signed the Declaration of Independence in 1776 described themselves as signing it 'as with halters about their necks.' If there were grounds for this remark in 1776, when the cause had become so much more general, how much greater was the hazard when the battle of Bunker Hill was fought!"

"These considerations constituted, to enlarged and liberal minds, the moral sublimity of the occasion; while to the outward senses, the movement of armies, the roar of artillery, the brilliancy of the reflection of a summer's sun from the burnished armor of the British columns, and the flames of a burning town, made up a scene of extraordinary grandeur."

CHAPTER VIII.

The Environs of Boston fortified.   The Continental Army established
Description of the American Camp.

THE extraordinary news of the battle of Bunker Hill naturally created astonishment and alarm ; and the day following
— Sunday, June 18 — was characterized around Boston by
exciting rumor, intense anxiety, and painful suspense.   A circular of the committee of safety, stating that the British troops
were moving into the country, and calling upon the militia to
march forthwith to Cambridge, though soon countermanded,
served to increase the excitement.   The militia promptly
repaired to the camp.   Thousands accompanied them, to ver-
ify the great reports, or to learn the fate of friends, or to aid
in preventing further inroads of the enemy.   The roar of the
British cannon had not ceased.   Mrs. Adams writes : "It
began on Saturday morning about three o'clock, and has not
ceased yet, and it is now three o'clock Sabbath afternoon."
A shower came up during the afternoon, when there was a
cessation of the cannonade.   It was believed, however, that
the British would move out of Boston.   Mrs. Adams continues : "It is expected they will come out over the Neck to-night,
and a dreadful battle must ensue.   Almighty God ! cover the
heads of our countrymen, and be a shield to our dear friends."
   In Boston, there was hardly less distress or less alarm.   The
remains of the gallant officers, the hundreds of as gallant
privates, that were borne through the streets, together with
the lamentations of the mourners, made up heart-rending
scenes.   They had a depressing effect upon all.   It was in
vain the soldiers called to mind their victory, if victory it
could be called.   The officers felt that it was purchased at too
dear a price, and there was an air of dejection in their looks.
This dejection was seen also in the men.   Bitter were the
reflections that were cast on the policy that had cut down the

flower of the troops. "A disagreeable murmur now (June 25) runs through the army, which ever most disagreeably invades the general's ears." Again the officers and the royalists dreaded the vengeance of the exasperated people, and felt apprehensive that the town would be attacked, and be burnt over their heads. The Tories again established a night patrol, forty-nine each night, to relieve the troops of this duty. Two hundred volunteered in this work. General Gage issued (June 19) an ill-natured proclamation. He stated that the selectmen and others had repeatedly assured him that all the inhabitants had delivered up their fire-arms, though he had at the same time advices to the contrary; and that he had since full proof that many had been perfidious in this respect, and had secreted great numbers. He required those who had any "immediately to surrender them at the court-house," and he declared "that all persons in whose possession any fire-arms might hereafter be found should be deemed enemies to his majesty's government." The British general had no intention of marching out of Boston. His main object was self-preservation, — to prevent a surprise, and to strengthen his defences.

Charlestown presented (June 18) melancholy evidence of the complicated horrors of the battle-field. A few persons were allowed to visit it from Boston. The smoke of its dwelling-places still rose on the air; the dying and the dead still lay upon its hills. Among the details of the scene is the statement that ninety-two bodies were counted on the line of the rail fence protection.[1] General Howe spent the preceding night on the heights, and his troops lay on their arms. He was placed in the command of this post, which he continued to hold until General Gage was recalled. He was immediately supplied with additional troops. On the night of the 17th he commenced a breastwork on the north-western declivity of Bunker Hill, and stationed two regiments, the 47th and 52d, in the main street from the burying-ground to the Neck. Subsequently regular working parties, relieved every four hours, labored night and day in throwing up defences. Gen-

---

[1] The description of the scenes in Boston, Charlestown, and the neighborhood, is derived from diaries and letters of 1775.

eral Howe personally inspected these works, and made himself exceedingly popular with his men by sharing their
fatigue. His first general order expressed the hope that the
troops, in their new encampment, would show an attention to
discipline and regularity equal to the bravery they had so
remarkably displayed. They were forbidden to cut down
trees; to pilfer in the deserted houses, on pain of death; to
fire upon individuals from the advanced guard, unless they
were fired upon. A picket guard of two hundred was posted
at the Neck, another at the "rebel redoubt," a third at the
hill at Moulton's Point, and one at the old ferry. Subsequently, a guard was stationed in the old burying-ground.
All the posts and rails were ordered to be gathered and piled
in the redoubt; the boards were used for the floors of tents;
the loose wood—the remains of the devoted town—was
collected for fuel. Every fair day the tents were struck, and
when the tide permitted, sea bathing was enjoined both morning and evening.[1]

The British commander might well feel insecure without
strong defences, as he witnessed the alacrity with which the
militia poured into the American camp, and the expedition
with which smiling gardens and fruitful fields were turned into
formidable fortifications. Besides the militia, General Ward
was reinforced by regularly enlisted troops. New Hampshire supplied another regiment, excepting one company,
under Colonel Poor; Connecticut ordered on the remainder of
Colonel Parsons' regiment, and voted (June 20) to place the
whole of its troops under General Ward; Rhode Island
ordered on the remainder of its troops, and voted (June 28) to
place its forces under the general commander. The Massachusetts regiments were soon filled up and commissioned.
There were now an authorized commander and a united
army. War now was to be carried on in earnest, and the
British general saw, not merely how little the Americans
were intimidated, but how much they were encouraged, by
the issue of the Bunker Hill battle. "Our troops are in high
spirits," one writes, "and their resolution increases; they

---

[1] Waller's Orderly Book; Carter's Letters.

long to speak with them (the British) again. "This battle has been of infinite service to us," another writes; it has "made us more vigilant, watchful, and cautious." "I wish we could sell them another hill at the same price," writes General Greene. "The enterprising genius and intrepidity of these people," writes a Virginian of the New Englanders, "are amazing. They are now intent on burning Boston, in order to oust the regulars; and none are more eager for it than those who have escaped out and who have left their whole property in it."

Notwithstanding the high spirits of the army, strong apprehensions were felt of a visit from the enemy. The Provincial Congress (June 24) made an earnest appeal to the colony of Connecticut for "an immediate augmentation" of its troops. It represented that it "had the best grounds to suppose, that as soon as the enemy had recovered a little breath from their amazing fatigues of the 17th of June," and their losses should be made up by arrivals of new troops, they would make "the utmost efforts" to force the American lines, destroy the magazines, and thereby "strike general terror and amazement into the hearts of the inhabitants of the whole continent." Similar appeals were made to Rhode Island and New Hampshire. It also made a representation to the General Congress, which closed with the suggestion, that if a commander-in-chief should be appointed, no part of the continent so much required his immediate presence as Massachusetts.

Up to this time there appears to have been hesitancy in commencing intrenchments on the hills around Boston, but works were now prosecuted with great vigor and success.

General Putnam, on the night of the battle, took post on Prospect Hill, and commenced throwing up intrenchments. "I found him," his son says, "on the morning of the 18th of June, about ten o'clock, on Prospect Hill, dashing about among the workmen throwing up intrenchments, and often placing a rod with his own hands.[1] He wore the same clothes he had on when I left him on the 16th, and said he had neither put them off nor washed himself since, and we might

---

[1] Ms. Memoirs by Daniel Putnam, for the use of which I am indebted to Col. Swett.

well believe him, for the aspect of all here bore evidence that he spoke the truth." One half of eight of the Massachusetts regiments were ordered (June 20) to be drafted daily, to relieve the troops at work here. The regiments of Colonels Brewer, Nixon, Mansfield, Gerrish, Woodbridge, Scammans, Little, and Gardner, were ordered (23d) to encamp on, or near this hill; and the officers were directed not to leave their posts without the permission of the general.[1] Nearly four thousand troops were here on the 30th of June. It has two eminences, both of which were strongly fortified and connected by a rampart and fosse. The works were soon considered (letter, July 3) almost impregnable. The regiments above named, for the most part, continued here until the new arrangement (July 22) of the army was made. This fine hill commanded an extensive prospect, and both the British and American lines were in full view from it. It is called on some of the maps Mount Pisgah.

Winter Hill was also occupied on the night of the battle. Here the New Hampshire troops stopped and began to throw up defences. Until this time, the only force posted here was a guard consisting of a subaltern, two sergeants, and twenty men. The New Hampshire forces, reinforced by Colonel Poor's regiment, continued here. The latter regiment, owing to a want of tents, was obliged to quarter in Medford. General Folsom arrived June 20, and took the command of them. The works were vigorously carried on. The fort on this hill is said to have been larger, and the intrenchments to have been more numerous, than those of any of the other positions of the army. The New Hampshire troops, joined, perhaps, by a regiment from Rhode Island, continued to defend this hill, until after the arrival of Washington.

At Cambridge the works commenced near the colleges, and ran towards Charles River. Here, however, as has been stated, works were thrown up before the battle of Bunker Hill. It continued to be the head quarters of the army during the siege.

On the Roxbury side works were also vigorously carried on

---

[1] Fenno's and Ward's Orderly Books.

under the direction of General Thomas. Samuel Gray, July 12, thus describes them: "On this side, we have a fort upon the hill, westward of the meeting-house; an intrenchment at Dudley House, including the garden, and extended to the hill east of the meeting-house. A small breastwork across the main street, and another on Dorchester road, near the bury-ing-ground. One on each side of the road through the lands and meadows, a little south of the George tavern Across the road are trees, the top toward the town of Boston, sharpened, and well pointed, to prevent the progress of the light horse. A redoubt near Pierpont's, or Williams' Mill, and another at Brookline, the lower end of Sewall's Farm, to obstruct their landing; and another breastwork at Dorchester." On the 24th of June heavy cannon were planted at the works on the hill above Roxbury Workhouse, and on the 1st of July shot were thrown from them into Boston.

In preparing these works, there was a great call for engi-neers. The veteran Colonel Gridley acted as chief, and was aided by his son. Lieutenant-colonel Rufus Putnam, Captain Josiah Waters, Captain Baldwin of Brookfield, Captain Henry Knox, afterward General Knox, were actively and efficiently employed.[1]

An irregular warfare was kept up from the 17th of June until the 3d of July, when Washington took the command. Shot and shells were at intervals discharged from Boston, and the American camp was several times alarmed with the report that the British were making a sally. A company of minute-men, before the 19th of April, had been embodied among the Stockbridge tribe of Indians, and this company[2]

---

[1] Heath's Memoirs.

[2] The Provincial Congress authorized this enlistment of minute-men. A letter of July 9, says: "Yesterday afternoon some barges were sounding the river of Cambridge, (Charles,) near its mouth, but were soon obliged to row off, by our Indians, (fifty in number,) who are encamped near that place."

The British complained, and with reason, of this mode of warfare. Lieut. Carter writes, July 2, 1775: "Never had the British army so ungenerous an enemy to oppose; they send their riflemen, (five or six at a time,) who conceal themselves behind trees, &c., till an opportunity presents itself of taking a shot at our advanced sentries; which done, they immediately retreat."

repaired to the camp. On the 21st of June, two of the Indians, probably of this company, killed four of the regulars with their bows and arrows, and plundered them.[1] On the next day the British fired from Boston.

The camp, on the 24th, was in alarm at the prospect of the regulars coming out. At noon the enemy commenced a heavy cannonade from Boston Neck, and threw shells into Roxbury. But through the alertness of the men, the town was saved, and no damage was done. "Such was the courage of our soldiers," a letter states, "that they would go and take up a burning carcass or bomb, and take out the fuse."[2] Two Americans, attempting to set Brown's barn on fire, were killed. The next day, also, an attempt was made, without success, to burn the buildings on Boston Neck, when a firing took place between the parties. This day the Indians killed more of the British guard.

On the 26th there was a skirmish at Boston Neck. A party of the British, about day-break, advanced and fired on the American sentinels, near the George tavern. The picket guard turned out, and after sharp firing the British retreated Two Indians went down near Bunker Hill, and killed a sentry. On the 30th a fire was opened from Roxbury into Boston, which was returned. A twenty-four pound ball from the same place, (July 1,) struck on the British parade-ground, and occasioned some confusion.

On the 2d of July, (Sunday,) in the morning, the British commenced a brisk cannonade from the lines on Boston Neck, and threw shells into Roxbury. A carcass set fire to the house of Mr. Williams, which was consumed. But the daring activity of the troops, working in the face of a constant and heavy fire from the enemy, prevented the flames from spreading.

In the mean time, the second General Congress, which assembled at Philadelphia on the 10th of May, had unani-

---

[1] John Kettell's Diary. This commences May 17, and continues to Sept. 31, 1775. He was subsequently an influential citizen of Charlestown — its postmaster and town clerk.

[2] Ms. Letters of Col. Miller, of Rhode Island, for which, and other favors I am indebted to S. G. Drake, Esq.

mously resolved to put the country into a state of defence, had adopted, on the motion of John Adams, the army besieging Boston, and had voted to raise ten companies of riflemen in Pennsylvania, Maryland, and Virginia. This was the origin of the far-famed continental army. Four major-generals were appointed; namely, Artemas Ward, Charles Lee, Phillip Schuyler, and Israel Putnam; and eight brigadier-generals; namely, Seth Pomeroy, Richard Montgomery, David Wooster, William Heath, Joseph Spencer, John Thomas, John Sullivan, and Nathaniel Greene. An adjutant-general — Horatio Gates — was also appointed, with the rank of brigadier. On the 15th of June, Colonel George Washington was chosen commander-in-chief. A long controversy arose in relation to some of these appointments, and especially because Putnam was advanced over Spencer, and Pomeroy over Thomas. General Spencer left the army without visiting Washington, or making known his intention, and General Thomas consented to remain only after the urgent solicitations of his friends. At length these difficulties were, in a great measure, removed, by Spencer's consenting to return, and to take rank after Putnam, and Pomeroy's declining to serve.

On the 21st of June General Washington set out from Philadelphia to join the army. He was everywhere received on his route with the respect due to his station. At New York he heard of the battle of Bunker Hill, and this increased his anxiety to reach the camp. A committee of the Massachusetts Provincial Congress met him at Springfield. He reached Cambridge on the 2d of July, about two o'clock, escorted by a cavalcade of citizens and a troop of light horse. On the 3d he assumed the command of the army.

When General Washington reached Watertown, the Provincial Congress, in session there, honored him with a congratulatory address. "While we applaud," they said, "that attention to the public good manifested in your appointment, we equally admire that disinterested virtue and distinguished patriotism, which alone could call you from those enjoyments of domestic life, which a sublime and manly taste, joined with a most affluent fortune, can afford, to hazard your life, and to endure the fatigues of war, in defence of the rights of mankind, and the good of your country." After complimenting him on the despatch made in his journey, they remarked on the hurry with which the army was necessarily collected, and the want of discipline in the soldiers : — " The greatest part of them have not before seen service; and though naturally brave and of good understanding, yet, for want of experience in military life, have but little knowledge of divers things most essential to the preservation of health, and even of life. The youth in the army are not impressed with the absolute necessity of cleanliness in their dress and lodging, continual exercise, and strict temperance, to preserve them from diseases frequently prevailing in camps; especially among those who, from their childhood, have been used to a laborious life." In conclusion, Congress assured him that they would contribute all the aid in their power in the discharge of the duties of his exalted office. Washington replied to this address on the 4th of July. " In exchanging" he said, " the enjoyments of domestic life for the duties of my present honorable but arduous station, I only emulate the virtue and public spirit of the whole province of Massachusetts Bay, which, with a firmness and patriotism without example in modern history, has sacrificed all the comforts of social and political life, in support of the rights of mankind, and the welfare of our common country. My highest ambition is, to be the happy instrument of vindicating those rights, and to see this devoted province again restored to peace, liberty, and safety."

A congratulatory address was also made to General Lee. It says — " We admire and respect the character of a man who, disregarding the allurements of profit and distinction his merit might procure, engages in the cause of mankind, in defence of the injured, and relief of the oppressed. From your character, from your great abilities and military experience, united with those of the commander-in-chief, under the smiles of Providence, we flatter ourselves with the prospect of discipline and order, success and victory." The general made a neat reply, in which he remarked. — " Nothing can be so flattering to me as the good opinion and approbation of the delegates of a free and uncorrupt people."

On assuming the command[1] of the army, the commander-in-chief immediately visited its posts and reconnoitred the works of the enemy. In a letter dated July 10, he describes the lines as follows: "I found the latter (British) strongly intrenching on Bunker's Hill, about a mile from Charlestown, and advanced about half a mile from the place of the late action, with their sentries extended about one hundred and fifty yards on this side of the narrowest part of the Neck, leading from this place to Charlestown. Three floating batteries lie in Mystic River, near their camp, and one twenty gun ship below the ferry place, between Boston and Charlestown. They have also a battery on Copp's Hill, on the Boston side, which much annoyed our troops in the late attack. Upon Roxbury Neck, they are also deeply intrenched and strongly fortified. Their advance guards, till last Saturday, occupied Brown's houses, about a mile from Roxbury meeting-house, and twenty rods from their lines; but, at that time, a party from General Thomas' camp surprised the guard, drove them in, and burned the houses. The bulk of their army, commanded by General Howe, lies on Bunker's Hill, and the remainder on Roxbury Neck, except the light horse, and a few men in the town of Boston.

"On our side, we have thrown up intrenchments on Winter and Prospect Hills, — the enemy's camp in full view, at the distance of little more than a mile. Such intermediate points as would admit a landing, I have, since my arrival, taken care to strengthen, down to Sewall's Farm, where a strong intrenchment has been thrown up. At Roxbury, General Thomas has thrown up a strong work on the hill, about

---

[1] From general orders, July 4, 1775: — The Continental Congress having now taken all the troops of the several colonies which have been raised, or which may hereafter be raised, for the support and defence of the liberties of America, into their pay and service, they are now the troops of the United Provinces of North America; and it is to be hoped that all distinctions of colonies will be laid aside, so that one and the same spirit may animate the whole, and the only contest be, who shall render, on this great and trying occasion, the most essential service to the great and common cause in which we are all engaged.

Thomas Mifflin was appointed aid-de-camp to General Washington, and Joseph Reed his secretary. Samuel Osgood was aid-de-camp to General Ward, and Samuel Griffin to General Lee.

two hundred yards above the meeting-house; which, with the brokenness of the ground, and a great number of rocks, has made that pass very secure. The troops raised in New Hampshire, with a regiment from Rhode Island, occupy Winter Hill; a part of those of Connecticut, under General Putnam, are on Prospect Hill. The troops in this town are entirely of the Massachusetts; the remainder of the Rhode Island men are at Sewall's Farm. Two regiments of Connecticut, and nine of the Massachusetts, are at Roxbury. The residue of the army, to the number of about seven hundred, are posted in several small towns along the coast, to prevent the depredations of the enemy."

A private letter, also of July 10, gives a more particular view of the American works : "About two hundred rods below the college we have a redoubt, which begins the line ; then about sixty rods from that another redoubt, and lines continued near an hundred rods ; then at Charlestown road, on the west side of the road, at the foot of Prospect Hill, another redoubt and strong fortification ; then on Prospect Hill is Putnam's Post, a very strong fortification ; then between that and Winter Hill a strong citadel and lines over Charlestown road to Mystic ; then in Mr. Temple's pasture (Ten Hills Farm) a strong redoubt that commands to Mystic River ; so that we have a complete line of circumvallation from Charles River to Mystic River." "On Roxbury side the enemy have dug across the Neck, and let the water through ; and our people in turn have intrenched across the outer end of the Neck, and are strongly fortified there, and on the hill by the meeting-house." [1]

General Washington found himself at the head of a body of armed men,[2] rather than of regular ranks of soldiers, — of

[1] The town of Malden requested, June 23, that measures might be taken for its defence. The Provincial Congress appointed a committee to take the subject into consideration, who directed them to make the best use of artillery they could for their defence, and to apply to the general of the army. No works of importance appear to have been erected in Malden during the siege.

[2] I found a mixed multitude of people here, under very little discipline order, or government. — Washington's letter, July 27, 1775. The orderly books of this period attest the difficulty of reducing the men to the habits of

men grown rugged in the calls of labor, patriotic, true to the American cause, but with high notions of independence, and hence impatient of the necessary restraints of a life of war. Discipline was lax, offences were frequent, there was no general organization, and, worse than all, hardly powder enough in the camp for nine cartridges to a man. Washington felt the difficulty of maintaining, with such material, a line of posts so exposed against an army of well-disciplined and well-supplied veterans. He was obliged to keep every part of his extended works well guarded, while the enemy could concentrate his force on any one point, and without an hour's notice could make a formidable attack. It was under such circumstances that he was obliged to remodel his army, and summon order to arise out of confusion.

General Washington called a council of war, (July 9,) consisting of the major-generals and brigadiers. They estimated the force of the British at 11,500, — too high an estimate, however, — and that at least an army of 22,000 was necessary to act successfully against it; whereas there were only 17,000 enrolled, including the sick and the absent, and only 14,500 fit for duty. The council decided unanimously to maintain the positions that had been taken, and adopt measures to strengthen the army. The commander-in-chief was directed to apply to the Provincial Congress of Massachusetts for a temporary reinforcement, and steps were taken to increase the recruits. It was agreed that, should the army be attacked by the enemy and routed, the place of rendezvous should be Wales Hill, in the rear of the Roxbury lines; and also, that it was neither expedient to take possession of Dorchester Point, nor to oppose the enemy if they should attempt to take possession of it.

The army was arranged in three grand divisions, each consisting of two brigades or twelve regiments, in which the

the soldier's life. Offences were frequent. Intoxication, peculation, false returns, disobedience of orders, disrespect to officers, want of soldier-like conduct, were the most common offences ; and the punishment administered consisted of pecuniary fines, standing in the pillory, riding the wooden horse, drumming out of camp, whipping at the head of the regiment, or in still more public places.

troops from the same colony, as far as practicable, were brought together. The right wing, under Major-general Ward, consisted of two brigades, as follows: —

1. BRIGADIER-GENERAL THOMAS.

Regiments.	Total.		Regiments.	Total.	
General Ward,	453	Mass.	Colonel Cotton,	500	Mass.
" Thomas,	500	"	" Davidson,	493	"
Colonel Fellows,	434	"	" D. Brewer,	374	"
" Learned,	489	"			

2. BRIGADIER-GENERAL SPENCER.

Regiments.	Total.		Regiments.	Total.	
General Spencer,		Conn.	Colonel Walker,	491	Mass.
Colonel Parsons,	2333	"	" J. Reed,	495	"
" Huntington,		"	Independents,	239	"

This division of the army was stationed at Roxbury, and its southern dependencies.

The left wing was placed under the command of Major-general Lee, who had under him Brigadier-general Greene, stationed at Prospect Hill, and General Sullivan,[1] at Winter Hill. These brigades were as follows: —

1. BRIGADIER-GENERAL SULLIVAN.

Regiments.	Total.		Regiments.	Total.	
Colonel Stark,		N. Hamp.	Colonel Nixon,	412	Mass.
" Poor,	1664	"	" Mansfield,	470	"
" Reed,		"	" Doolittle,	333	"

2. BRIGADIER-GENERAL GREENE.

Regiments.	Total.		Regiments.	Total.	
Colonel Varnum,		R. Isl.	Colonel Whitcomb,	523	Mass.
" Hitchcock,	1085	"	" Gardner,	417	"
" Church,		"	" J. Brewer,	301	"
			" Little,	472	"

The centre, stationed at Cambridge, was commanded by Major-general Putnam. These brigades were as follows: —

1. BRIGADIER-GENERAL HEATH.

Regiments.	Total.		Regiments.	Total.	
General Heath,	483	Mass.	Colonel Phinney,	319	Mass.
Colonel Patterson,	409	"	" Gerrish,	498	"
" Scammans,	456	"	" Prescott,	430	"

[1] General Sullivan had succeeded General Folsom in the command of the New Hampshire forces.

2. SENIOR OFFICER

Regiments.	Total.		Regiments.	Total.	
General Putnam,		Conn.	Colonel Bridge,	470	**Mass.**
Colonel Glover,	454	Mass.	" Woodbridge,	366	"
" Frye,	406	"	" Sargent,		"

Of these regiments, General Heath's was ordered to take post at No. 2, Colonel Patterson's at No. 3, Colonel Scammans' at No. 1 and the redoubt between that and No. 2, Colonel Prescott's at Sewall's Point, and Colonel Gerrish's to furnish the companies for Chelsea, Malden, and Medford.

The total of the above, as returned, without including Colonel Sargent's regiment, which had not been completed, was 16,770. To this must be added the regiment of artillery, under Colonel Richard Gridley, of 489 men; and Major Train's company of Rhode Island artillery, of 96 men.[1]

The environs of Boston presented at this period an animating sight. Time had wrought out wonderful changes in their political condition. Hardly a century had elapsed since the two principal passes into the country — Boston Neck and Charlestown Neck — were fortified to save the infant American civilization from the inroads of the savage; now the beautiful hills that surrounded them and commanded them were covered with all the pomp and pride of war, to protect the same civilization from being destroyed from without by the hand that should have protected it. The unrivalled natural scenery could not pass unobserved by a lover of nature. "The country," writes an officer in Boston, "is most

[1] The following is the return of the army made pursuant to a general order of July 3, 1775: —

Colonies.	No. of regiments.	Commissioned officers and staff.	Non-comm'sd officers.	Rank and file.					
				Present fit for duty.	Sick present.	Sick absent.	On furlough.	On command	Total.
Massachusetts, . . .	26	789	1326	9396	757	450	311	774	11688
Connecticut, ...	3	125	174	2105	212	2	14		2333
New Hampshire, . .	3	98	160	1201	115	20	49	279	1664
Rhode Island, . . .	3	107	108	1041	24	18	2		1085
	35	1119	1768	13743	1108	490	376	1053	16770

beautifully tumbled about in hills and valleys, rocks and woods, interspersed with straggling villages, with here and there a spire peeping over the trees, and the country of the most charming green that delighted eye ever gazed on." [1] The beauty of nature was now intermingled, on the land, with white tents, glittering bayonets, and frowning cannon, while no small portion of the navy of England rode proudly in the harbor. Occasionally the scene was enlivened by a peaceful parade or a hostile skirmish. These sights were no less novel than interesting; and thousands flocked to the neighborhood, either to greet their friends, or to witness the exciting scenes.

Among others, Rev. William Emerson has furnished a graphic description of the camp, after the arrival of Washington. "There is great overturning in the camp, as to order and regularity. New lords, new laws. The Generals Washington and Lee are upon the lines every day. New orders from his excellency are read to the respective regiments every morning after prayers. The strictest government is taking place, and great distinction is made between officers and soldiers. Every one is made to know his place, and keep in it, or be tied up and receive thirty or forty lashes, according to his crime. Thousands are at work every day from four till eleven o'clock in the morning. It is surprising how much work has been done. The lines are extended almost from Cambridge to Mystic River, so that very soon it will be morally impossible for the enemy to get between the works, except in one place, which is supposed to be left purposely unfortified, to entice the enemy out of their fortresses. Who would have thought, twelve months past, that all Cambridge and Charlestown would be covered over with American camps, and cut up into forts and intrenchments, and all the lands, fields, orchards, laid common, — horses and cattle feeding in the choicest mowing land, whole fields of corn eaten down to the ground, and large parks of well-regulated locusts cut down for firewood and other public uses? This, I must say, looks a little melancholy. My quarters are at the foot of the famous Prospect Hill, where such great preparations are made

[1] Capt. Harris, afterwards Lord Harris.

for the reception of the enemy. It is very diverting to walk among the camps. They are as different in their form as the owners are in their dress; and every tent is a portraiture of the temper and taste of the persons who encamp in it. Some are made of boards, and some of sail-cloth. Some partly of one and partly of the other. Again, others are made of stone and turf, brick or brush. Some are thrown up in a hurry; others curiously wrought with doors and windows, done with wreaths and withes, in the manner of a basket. Some are your proper tents and marquees, looking like the regular camp of the enemy. In these are the Rhode Islanders, who are furnished with tent-equipage, and everything in the most exact English style. However, I think this great variety is rather a beauty than a blemish in the army." [1]

The commander-in-chief was received with warmth by the army, and everything about him inspired confidence and hope. The house occupied by him is still standing in Cambridge, and is known as Washington's head quarters. The contemporary accounts name him with enthusiasm. "I have been much gratified this day" — Thatcher writes, July 20 — "with a view of General Washington. His excellency was on horseback, in company with several military gentlemen. It was not difficult to distinguish him from all others; his personal appearance is truly noble and majestic, being tall and well-proportioned. His dress is a blue coat with buff-colored facings, a rich epaulette on each shoulder, buff under dress, and an elegant small-sword; a black cockade in his hat." Mrs. Adams writes to her husband, July 16: "I was struck with General Washington. You had prepared me to entertain a favorable opinion of him, but I thought the half was not told me. Dignity, with ease and complacency, the gentleman and soldier, look agreeably blended in him. Modesty marks every line and feature of his face. Those lines of Dryden instantly occurred to me :

> Mark his majestic fabric ! he 's a temple
> Sacred by birth, and built by hands divine ;
> His soul 's the deity that lodges there ;
> Nor is the pile unworthy of the god."

[1] Sparks' Washington, vol. iii., p. 491.

CHAPTER IX.

Fortification of Ploughed Hill.   Skirmishes.   Distress in Boston.

GENERAL WASHINGTON, while introducing subordination into
the army, made great efforts to strengthen his position, to
confine the enemy closely to their quarters, and to cut off their
supplies of provisions.   The belief was long entertained that
the British were preparing for an attack, and the camp was
occasionally alarmed with reports that they were coming
out.   Every precaution was taken to prevent surprise, and
parties in whale-boats were soon on the watch every night,
to give early notice of any movements by water.   On the day
Washington took the command (July 3) it was supposed the
British were about to attack the lines on Winter Hill, where
General Folsom was in command.   Colonel Glover's regiment
was ordered to be ready at a moment's warning to support
General Folsom.   Colonel Prescott was ordered to take
possession of the woods leading to Lechmere's Point, and if
an attack was made in this quarter, Colonel Glover was
directed to support him.[1]

Early in July a correspondence between Generals Lee and
Burgoyne attracted much attention.   General Lee had served
with General Burgoyne in Portugal, and an intimate friendship
had long existed between them.   On the arrival of the latter
in Boston, General Lee, then in Philadelphia, wrote to his friend
a letter full of invectives against the British ministry, and containing an elaborate statement of his views of the merits of
the contest.   Though written with a warmth approaching to
violence, General Burgoyne replied to it courteously, and
proposed an interview with General Lee at Brown's house,
on Boston Neck.   This letter was sent out (July 8) by a
trumpeter.   The letter and the expediency of the proposed
interview were laid before the Provincial Congress.   Though

[1] Washington's Orderly Book, in Force's American Archives.

Congress, to prevent jealousy, appointed Elbridge **Gerry to** attend General Lee, they suggested whether it "might not have a tendency to lessen the influence which the Congress would wish to extend to the utmost of their power, to facilitate and succeed the operations of the war." In consequence of this hint, General Lee, in a note to General Burgoyne, declined to meet him. The correspondence between the two generals was published, and was commented on in the journals.

On the 8th of July, about two in the morning, a party of volunteers, under Majors Tupper and Crane, attacked the advanced guard of the British at Brown's house, on Boston Neck, within three hundred yards of their main works. A party of six, detached about ten o'clock the preceding evening, gained the rear of the guard-house; and the remainder of the volunteers secreted themselves in the marsh on each side of the Neck. Two brass field-pieces were drawn quietly across the marsh to within three hundred yards of the house. On a signal from the advance party, two rounds of shot were fired into the house, when the guard retreated with precipitation to the lines. The six men immediately set fire to the house and another building. The party took several muskets and retreated without loss. A scattering fire from the outposts continued some time. The British moored a floating battery up in the bay so as to cover the right flank of their works on Boston Neck.[1]

On the 11th a party of Americans drove in the British guard on Boston Neck, and burnt Brown's store. A visiter in the camp at Roxbury this day says, — "We were amused with a heavy fire of cannon and mortars from the lines of the regulars on the Neck, and from one of their floating batteries, against two hundred of our men, who were throwing up a breastwork in front of the George tavern, on the same Neck, and within a few rods of the regulars' advanced guard ; our people kept on their work, and never returned a shot. Three bombs burst near our men, without injuring one of them ; most of the cannon shot were taken up and brought to the general. It is divert-

---

[1] Heath's Memoirs, p. 23.   Penn. Packet, 1775.

ng to see our people contending for the balls as they roll along." On this day a liberty-pole was raised on Winter Hill; and at night a party went from Roxbury camp to Long Island, and brought off fifteen prisoners, 200 sheep, 19 cattle, 13 horses, and 3 hogs. The prisoners were carried to Concord.[1]

On the 12th, in the forenoon, Colonel Greaton, with a party of 136 men, went in whale-boats to Long Island, burnt the house on it, and the barns, with a large lot of hay done up in bundles and intended for the British horses. An armed schooner, and several barges, made for the Americans, and some of the ships near the island cannonaded them; but, though they narrowly escaped being taken', Colonel Greaton and his daring band gained the shore. One American was killed in this affair. A letter dated on this day says: " We have just got over land from Cape Cod a large fleet of whale-boats; in a day or two, we shall man them in Cambridge and Mystic Rivers, and try to keep our enemy's boats from insulting us. The regulars do not seem willing to come out, but our people are perpetually provoking them." This day six transports full of men arrived in the harbor.

A party of Americans were at work on the rocky hill, then Colonel Williams', south-west of the works above Roxbury workhouse. The British opened (July 13) a heavy cannonade upon them, but did no damage. This work, Heath says, was one of the strongest that were erected. General Washington visited the Roxbury camp this day. On the day following there was also firing from Boston, and a Connecticut soldier was killed.

The declaration of the Continental Congress, setting forth the causes and necessity of their taking up arms, was read on

---

[1] Kettell's Diary; Heath; Force's Archives, II., 1650.

On the 13th of July the Provincial Congress revised the commission of the committee of safety, and continued in it full executive power until the 30th of July, or until their commission should be abrogated by the representatives. The committee consisted, at this time, of John Hancock, Benjamin Church, Benjamin White, Joseph Palmer, Richard Devens, Abraham Watson, Azor Orne, Benjamin Greenleaf, Nathan Cushing, Samuel Holten, and Enoch Freeman.

the 15th, before the army at Cambridge, by President Langdon. General Washington, other general officers, and a large number of people, were present. It was received with great enthusiasm, and was immediately responded to by three huzzas. On the 18th, it was read to the troops on Prospect Hill, under the immediate command of General Putnam "After which," the Essex Gazette states, "an animated and pathetic address to the army was made by the Rev. Mr. Leonard, chaplain to General Putnam's regiment, and succeeded by a pertinent prayer; when General Putnam gave the signal, and the whole army shouted their loud amen by three cheers; immediately upon which, a cannon was fired from the fort, and the standard lately sent to General Putnam was exhibited flourishing in the air, bearing on one side this motto, — 'An Appeal to Heaven!' and on the other side, — ' *Qui Transtulit Sustinet!*' The whole was conducted with the utmost decency, good order, and regularity, and to the universal acceptance of all present. And the Philistines on Bunker's Hill heard the shout of the Israelites, and being very fearful, paraded themselves in battle array."

In the evening (18th) a strong party took possession of an advanced post in Roxbury, and the next day there was an incessant cannonade kept up on the works. There was an appearance of a sally by the British during this cannonade. "But," a letter states, "they disappointed General Thomas, who commands there, and made an excellent disposition to receive them. Roxbury is amazingly strong. I believe it would puzzle ten thousand troops to go through it, — I mean of the best in the world."

Thursday, the 20th, was a day of general fasting and prayer. In general orders it was directed to be religiously observed in the camp. The troops, in attending worship, were ordered to take their arms, ammunition, and accoutrements, and be prepared for immediate action. The labor on the works was ordered to be suspended, if, in the judgment of the officers, their condition would permit.

A party under Major Vose, of Heath's regiment, in whaleboats, landed on Nantasket Point, before day, and set fire to the light-house. At daylight the men-of-war discovered them, and fired upon them. An eye-witness says: — "I ascended an eminence at a distance, and saw the flames of the light-house ascending up to heaven like grateful incense, and the ships wasting their powder. Our men proceeded from thence to Point Shirley, in order to drive off some young colts which were there. A party of regulars attacked them, but were repulsed and drove into their boats." Major Vose returned the next day. He burnt the wooden portions of the light-house, brought off its furniture, lamps, &c., and the boats. He also brought from Nantasket a thousand bushels of barley, and a quantity of hay. An armed schooner and several barges engaged the detachment, and wounded two Americans. Major Vose gained much credit for his success in this enterprise.

An occasional cannonade, the coming in of deserters from the enemy, the arrangement of the army into brigades, and the arrival of the riflemen from the south, constituted the chief incidents of the siege for eight days. The general orders indicate a strict attention to discipline. They prohibited all conversation, both by officers and soldiers, with the enemy's sentries, and declared that any guilty of it should be tried by a court-martial, and punished with the utmost severity. They prohibited the injury of trees; enjoined the faithful reading of the orders; discouraged the application for furloughs, and required the prompt delivery of returns. One order (July 17) says: "If, after what has happened, the enemy, in revenge of their late loss, should dare to attempt forcing our lines, the army may be assured, that nothing but their own indolence and remissness can give the least success to so rash an enterprise." The southern riflemen attracted much attention. They had enlisted with great promptness, and had marched from four to seven hundred miles. In a short time, large bodies of them arrived in camp. They were remarkably stout, hardy men, dressed in white frocks or rifle-shirts, and round hats, and were skilful marksmen. At a review, a company of them, while on a quick advance, fired their balls into objects of seven inches diameter, at the distance of two hundred and fifty yards. They were stationed on the lines, and became terrible to the British. The accounts of their prowess were circulated over England.   One of them, taken prisoner, was carried there, and the papers describe him minutely, as a remarkable curiosity.[1]

The British officers, about this time, were much annoyed at the success of the American sentinels in dispersing hand-bills among their rank and file.   One was framed, entitled "An address to the soldiers;" and another contained the following comparison : —

PROSPECT HILL.	BUNKER'S HILL.
I. Seven dollars a month.	I. Three pence a day.
II. Fresh provisions and in plenty.	II. Rotten salt pork.
III. Health.	III. The scurvy.
IV. Freedom, ease, affluence, and a good farm.	IV. Slavery, beggary, and want.

"These bills," says a letter, July 24, "are blown into their camp, and get into the hands of their soldiers, without the officers being able to prevent it.   Major Bruce complained, at an interview the other day, of such usage.   We retorted his decoying our sentries from their posts, two rascals having left us a day or two before, by his or some other officer's means." Colonel Reed, also, sent to General Gage a copy of the decla-ration of the united colonies, who pronounced its contents to be "as replete with deceit and falsehood as most of their (the Americans) publications." [2]

The works on Winter Hill were prosecuted with vigor at this time.   General Lee sent, July 24, the following note to General Sullivan : — "General Lee begs General Sullivan will get as much work as possible out of the men this day.   If they cannot all work on the face of the citadel, let them deepen and widen the ditch of the flank and rear faces, and heighten the parapet all round.   P. S.   For God's sake, finish and strengthen the abatis."

On the 29th of July the British planted a bomb battery on

---

[1] A letter, July 19, says : — "The general uniforms are made of brown Holland and Osnaburghs, something like a shirt, double caped over the shoul-der, in imitation of the Indians ; and on the breast, in capital letters, is their motto, ' Liberty or Death ! ' "

[2] Gage's Letter, July 24.

Bunker Hill, advanced their guard on Charlestown Neck further into the country, and began to throw up an abatis to protect it, cutting down large trees for this purpose.[1] Washington, in the evening, ordered the York county rifle company to cut off these outposts, and bring off a prisoner. The company attempted this service in the following manner. Captain Dowdle and thirty-nine men filed off to the right, and crept on their hands and knees to the rear of the enemy's works; Lieutenant Miller, with a party, in like manner, got behind the sentries on the left. But just as the two divisions were about to join, a party of the British came down from Bunker Hill to relieve the guard, and discovered the riflemen. Both sides fired. The riflemen killed five and took two pris-

---

[1] Col. William T. Miller, of the Rhode Island forces, was at Prospect Hill, and in a letter dated "Camp Prospect Hill, July 29, 1775," gives an incident relating to cutting down trees, and the camp rumors, as follows : —
"I had the honor to be field officer of the day here yesterday ; and as I was visiting the out sentries, which stand within half musket shot of the enemy's sentries, the regulars came out with a party, and began to cut some trees and remove some fencing stuff which was between the sentries. I beckoned to two officers who commanded there, one of whom I took to be Major Bruce of the regulars, who came out and met me between the sentries, when I told him that his conduct in felling the timber so near our sentries created a jealousy, and desired him to desist from any further encroachments ; when he told me he thought the trees, &c., which they were getting, were as near their lines as they were to ours, and that they had not interrupted our men in cutting hay close to the lines; and he promised me he would advance no further. I immediately returned, and reported what had happened to Major-general Lee, who thanked me for my conduct.
"I also saw a gentleman that came out of Boston yesterday, who says the people of Boston and the soldiers are very sickly and much dejected ; that General Gage had given orders for all the inhabitants of Boston that have a mind to depart by water to return their names, and they should have liberty to depart. We have three deserters from the regulars come into this camp since we came here, one of whom found his own brother here in the camp Their meeting was very affecting. One hath deserted by way of Roxbury, who it is thought will prove a very serviceable man to our army, as he is able to give a plan of all the works and fortifications in Boston, and knows all their plans. He says he can direct the army to storm Boston, with the loss of very few men ; that it has been in contemplation among the Gageites to set Boston on fire, and withdraw all the troops and ships. But we ought not to catch at such shadows as that. We have nothing under God to depend upon, but our own strength."

oners, and retreated, having one man captured.   General
Howe, in general orders the following day, stated that had his
directions relative to reliefs been complied with, "the soldiers
could not have failed to destroy a number of the rebels last
night."

On the 30th, Sunday, at eleven o'clock, about five hundred British troops marched over the Neck, and built a
slight breastwork to cover their guard.   The American camp
was in alarm through the day, and at night the troops lay on
their arms.   The British, mortified at the success of the riflemen, resolved to retaliate on the American sentries, and hence
the night proved an eventful one.   About one o'clock a British floating battery went up Charles River, within three hundred yards of Sewall's Point, and discharged a number of
shot into the American works on both sides of the river.   At
the same time a party sallied out towards Roxbury, drove in
the American sentinels, set fire to the George tavern, and
returned to the works.   The picket guard at Charlestown
Neck attacked and drove in the American advanced guard of
sixty men, who, being reinforced by orders of General Lee,
beat off the enemy, recovered their ground, killed several,
and took seven muskets, without the loss of a man.   This
simultaneous firing kept the army in a state of alarm
through the night, as the design of the British general was
not known.[1]

The enemy had commenced rebuilding the light-house, and
this day, July 31, Major Tupper, with three hundred men,
was detached with orders to disperse the working party.   The
enemy prepared to receive the Americans in a hostile manner
Major Tupper landed in good order on the island, marched up

---

[1] A royalist lady in Boston, in a letter dated August 10, 1775, gives a
vivid picture of the alarm felt by the residents during this night : — "We
were roused about one o'clock on the morning of the 31st ult. by the most
dreadful cannonading I ever heard.   It seemed to be a general attack on all
sides around us.   It is impossible to convey an idea how terrible it was in the
dead of night, with the apprehensions that naturally seize every one, either
of the enemy breaking in, or the town being set on fire.   It appears that
they attempted again to cut off our outposts, upon which General Howe
attacked their intrenchments with cannon and bombs on that side ; and we
attacked them in several places besides, at the same time, all in the dark."

to the works, killed ten or twelve on the spot, and took the remainder prisoners. Having demolished the works, the party were ready to embark, but the tide leaving them, they were obliged to remain until its return. Meantime, a number of boats came up from the men-of-war to reinforce those at the island, and a smart firing from both parties took place. A field-piece, under Major Crane, planted on Nantasket Point to cover a retreat, sunk one of the boats, and killed several of the crew. Major Tupper brought his party off with the loss of only one man killed, and two or three wounded. He killed and captured fifty-three of the enemy. Washington, the next day, in general orders, thanked Major Tupper, and the officers and soldiers under his command, " for their gallant and soldier-like behavior," and remarked that he doubted not " but the continental army would be as famous for their mercy as their valor."

No movements were made, nor were there any skirmishes of importance, in the early part of August. General Washington felt more anxious than ever at the shortness of his supply of powder. A council of war (August 3) was held on this important subject, when the whole stock was represented to be only 9,937 pounds. Measures were taken to procure a supply from the neighboring colonies. "Our situation," Washington wrote to Congress, "in the article of powder, is much more alarming than I had the most distant idea of." He felt the more anxious, as he was expecting an attack. Things looked like it in Boston. Detachments of the enemy practised embarking in boats daily, and rowing about the harbor; and they paraded in large detachments of seven or eight hundred, with their light horse, on Charlestown common, where their brilliant appearance contrasted strangely with the homely garb of the continentals. They kept up, too, a continual cannonade. Colonel Reed writes, (August 7,) " The enemy, having more ammunition to sport than we have, divert themselves every day with cannonading our lines; but with very little effect, except where the imprudence of some of our own people exposes them to danger. Two were killed at the lines last week, by running after cannon shot. We scarcely lie down or rise up, but with the expectation that the night or

the day must produce some important event."[1]   He writes
August 24: "The word 'powder' in a letter sets us all on
tiptoe.   We have been in a terrible situation, occasioned by a
mistake in a return; we reckoned upon three hundred quar-
ter-casks, and had but thirty-two barrels."   He remarked that
this damped their spirits, and obliged them " to bear with the
rascals on Bunker Hill, when a few shot, now and then, in
return, would keep the men attentive to their business, and
give the enemy alarms."

A few incidents may be worthy of notice.   Kettell, Aug. 1,
writes: "They continue quarrelling on the common.   The
riflemen keep round, picking them (the British) off.   They
fire in from their hill and their batteries, and our men pick up
the balls; fired eight or ten guns from the ship, but did no
mischief.   We raised a high liberty-pole upon Rand's Hill
(at) five o'clock this afternoon, and gave three cheers all
round, and then fired a twenty-four pounder at the ship."
The next day, in the skirmish, the Americans burnt a barn
near the Charlestown Neck, in which hay was stored, and
wounded a British officer, who was carried within the lines.
On the 6th, Sunday, a party landed from two barges, covered
by a floating battery, on the Malden side of Penny Ferry,
(where Malden Bridge is,) and set the ferry-house on fire.[2]
On the 13th two barges and two sail-boats, on their way to
the floating battery in Mystic River, bearing near Malden
Point, Captain Lindsey's company opened a smart fire upon
them, which obliged them to return; when they commenced
a fire on a party of Americans, under Lieut.-colonel Baldwin,
stationed in Chelsea, which was briskly returned.   "Our
brave Yankees, so called," Kettell writes, "played the man,
and beat them."   On the 20th, the British, it was thought,

---

[1] Reed's life of President Reed, vol. i., p. 117.

[2] Kettell writes, August 10 :"Thursday, cloudy.   Much firing among the
sentries.   A flag of truce was sent out this afternoon, with three letters.   He
was a drum-major of the grenadiers.   I heard that he brought an account of
the men killed since yesterday morning, — amounts to forty odd.   A man in
Boston sent a letter to his brother in the army, and says that they are taking
all the interest out of Boston, and everything that is good for anything.
Some thunder.   Considerable of rain this evening."

were about to sally out of Charlestown, when the camp was alarmed, and the men ordered to lie on their arms. On the 25th there was a smart firing at the relief of guard, and the British exercised their cavalry on Charlestown common.[1]

The next enterprise was an important one. In front of Winter Hill, and within point-blank shot of Bunker Hill, is Ploughed Hill, now Mount Benedict. Washington determined to take possession of it. For weeks it had been rumored that the British intended to come out of Boston, and storm the American intrenchments;[2] and hence it was expected that taking possession of a post so exposed would bring on a general action. This made the occasion one of uncommon inter-

---

[1] It was customary, for several years, to celebrate the anniversary of the 14th of August, 1765, the day of the first forcible resistance to the acts of the British Parliament, when the stamp office in Boston was demolished. The following account appeared in the newspapers : —

Cambridge, Aug. 14, 1775.

This day the field-officers of the 6th brigade, under the command of Col. James Frye, met at the house of Jonathan Hastings, Esq., to celebrate the 14th of August, where the following toasts were drunk, viz : —

1. The Continental Congress.
2. Success to our undertaking.
3. The memorable 14th of August, 1765.
4. May American valor ever prove invincible to the attempts of ministerial tyranny to oppress them.
5. The twelve United States.
6. All our friends in Great Britain.
7. Liberty without licentiousness.
8. A speedy and happy conclusion to the present unhappy disputes.
9. The 19th of April.
10. A speedy entrance, possession, and opening, of the town of Boston.
11. The president of the Continenta Congress.
12. General Washington, and the other general officers of the American army.
13. A speedy export of all the enemies of America, without any drawback.
14. Immortal honor to that patriot and hero, Doctor Warren, and the brave American troops who fought the battle on the 17th of June, 1775.

[2] Col. Jedediah Huntington, August 26, writes : " We have been told that our enemies have for some time past been boasting the 25th August, intending then to make a visit to us, and that General Gage has given Earl Percy the command of the lines on the Neck, who is to exhibit such proofs of his military abilities as will retrieve the honor he lost at the Lexingtor affray ; but matters remain this morning *in statu quo.*"

est in the camp.   On the night of August 26 a fatigue party
of a thousand, with a guard of twenty-four hundred, under
General Sullivan, marched on to this hill, and worked so dili-
gently, during the night, that in the morning the works were
strong enough to form a good protection against the enemy's
cannon.   About nine o'clock, on the 27th, Sunday, the British
began a heavy cannonade from Bunker Hill, and from one of
the ships hauled into Mystic River, and from two floating batteries stationed in this river, which continued throughout the
day.   Adjutant Mumford, of Colonel Varnum's Rhode Island
regiment, and a soldier, had their heads shot off, and a rifleman was mortally wounded.   On account of the scarcity of
powder in the camp, this cannonade was not returned.   A nine-
pounder, however, was planted on a point at the Ten Hills
Farm to play against the two floating batteries, and so effectual was the shot that one of them was sunk and the other
was silenced.   At night the firing ceased.   On Monday morning the enemy, were observed from Chelsea, to be drawn up
and in motion on Bunker Hill.   The camp was alarmed ; five
thousand troops were marched to Ploughed Hill and to the
Charlestown road ; and Washington expected, and even hoped,
that at high water the British intended to attack him.   Until
three o'clock in the afternoon "the most awful silence was
observed on both sides."   The enemy declined the challenge.
They continued for several days to bombard the works.   On
the 10th of September the firing had ceased.[1]

In the mean time, so successful a blockade had made an impression on the British commander, and was seriously felt by
the troops and the people of Boston.   General Gage, although
he had received reinforcements since the battle of Bunker Hill,
began to despair of reducing Massachusetts to submission
He informed Lord Dartmouth (July 24) that the rebellion was
general.   "This province began it," he said, "I might say
this town, for here the arch-rebels formed their scheme long
ago.   This circumstance brought the troops first here, which
is the most disadvantageous place for all operations."   He

---

[1] Newspapers of 1775 ; Sparks' Washington ; General Sullivan's letter,
in Force's Archives, ii., 1755 ; the date should be August 29, 1775, instead
of July.

suggested that the province of New York might be more easily reduced, and that the friends of government there might be able to raise forces to join the troops. His general orders of this period rather indicate apprehensions of an attack from the Americans than any idea of moving into the country. Thus an order of August 28 enjoined the utmost alertness from the troops, as well in the day as in the night; and it predicted, that in case "the rebels presumed to make an attack" they would meet with a fate similar to that of the 17th of June.

In the last week in July the number of inhabitants was stated at 6753; the number of troops, with their dependents, women and children, at 13,600. The town became sickly, both among the people and the troops, for neither had been accustomed to live on salt provision. "We are in the strangest state in the world," a lady writes, August 10, "surrounded on all sides. The whole country is in arms, and intrenched. We are deprived of fresh provisions, subject to continual alarms and cannonadings, the provincials being very audacious, and advancing near to our lines, since the arrivals of Generals Washington and Lee to command them."

The troops had an abundance of salt provision, and of fish, but this exclusive diet rendered many unfit for service. The weather was extremely hot. They were encamped on the common, and in other places, without proper shade to screen them from the sun, or without sufficient straw to lie on in their tents. "It is not to be wondered," a letter, August 2, says, "that the fatigue of duty, bad accommodation, and the use of too much spirits," should produce fevers in the camp. "The soldiers cannot be kept from rum; sixpence will buy a quart of West India rum, and fourpence is the price of a quart of this country rum." "Even the sick and wounded have often had nothing to eat but salt pork and fish." The sailors were better off. The ships had a wider range, and got supplies of fresh meat along the coasts. "Even in those that lie in Boston harbor," a letter states, "though the men have a great deal of fatiguing duty in boats, yet they are coolly and cleanly lodged on board; the decks are shaded with awnings, the lower ports are open, the hammocks are up, and the ships washed inside and out twice a day, and there is always a little air of wind on the water that is not upon the shore." The sailors were more accustomed to salt diet, and had besides a full supply of wine and spruce beer, and they enjoyed good health. General Gage made exertions to obtain supplies of fresh meat from the neighboring colonies; and a fleet that returned from a plundering excursion [1] from the neighborhood of New London, and the capture of an American vessel with stores, gave him a temporary supply. "With these trophies of victory," — the Essex Gazette states, August 17, — "on their arrival in Boston, the bells, we hear, were set to music, to the no small joy and comfort of the poor, half-starved Tories."

The patriotic portion of the inhabitants were annoyed by the stringent regulations of martial law, and often insulted by the conduct of individual soldiers. Sometimes these insults were minutely related in the journals. The citizens [2] were charged with taking plans of the works, with making signals from the church steeples, with holding correspondence with

[1] General Gage, Aug. 20, 1775, informed Lord Dartmouth of the arrival of this fleet, " with about 1800 sheep, and above 100 head of oxen, which will be some relief to the troops in general, and of great benefit to the hospitals." This letter was published, when there appeared in the London Chronicle the following impromptu, written on hearing that a detachment of regulars had returned safe to Boston with the sheep : —

> In days of yore the British troops
>   Have taken warlike kings in battle ;
> But now, alas ! their valor droops,
>   For Gage takes naught but — harmless cattle.

> Britons, with grief, your bosoms strike !
>   Your faded laurels loudly weep !
> Behold your heroes, Quixote-like,
>   Driving a timid flock of — sheep.

[2] Prisoners, inhabitants of Boston, Sept. 2, 1775 : —

Master Lovell, imprisoned sixty-five days, charged with being a spy, and giving intelligence to the rebels.

Mr. Leach, sixty-five days, charged with being a spy, and suspected of taking plans.

Mr. Peter Edes, son of Mr. Benjamin Edes, printer, and Mr. William Starr, seventy-five days each, for having fire-arms concealed in their houses.

Mr. John Gill, printer, twenty-nine days, for printing treason, sedition, and rebellion. — Newspaper, 1775.

their friends. Dr. Eliot writes, "We are offenders for a word." Some were thrown into prison, — among others, Master Lovell and Mr. Edes. At the commencement of the siege passes to go out might be bought, and some paid as high as forty dollars for them, but they were generally refused. At length the scarcity of provisions made so many inhabitants a burden to General Gage, and he endeavored to make an arrangement for their removal from Boston. A notification[1] was posted up in town, requesting such as wished to go into the country to leave their names with James Urquhart, town major, and in two days upwards of two thousand applied. Many hesitated as to the course to take, being unwilling to leave their effects subject to the plunder of the soldiery, and as unwilling to remain and suffer the hazards of the siege. No plate of any kind was allowed to be carried away, nor more than five pounds in cash. But much silver found its way out, and many are the stories told as to the way the men concealed it among their goods, and the women quilted it in their garments. Some were refused permission to leave. Many who obtained it landed at Chelsea, and scattered through the country. There is much matter relating to the poor at this period. They were provided for by the Provincial Congress, and donations also continued to be made for their relief. Congress (July 5) authorized the town clerk to summon the citizens of Boston to meet at Concord, July 18, to choose representatives to the General Court. The patriots who continued in town were much annoyed. Among other vexations, they saw their celebrated liberty-tree cut down by the troops and the Tories. Armed with axes, the Essex Gazette (August 31) says, "they made a furious attack upon it. After a long spell of laughing and grinning, sweating, swearing, and foaming, with malice diabolical, they cut down a tree because it bore the name of liberty." A soldier was killed during the operation. Be it known, says the Gazette,

---

[1] Notification. — All persons who are desirous of leaving the town of Boston are hereby called upon to give in their names to the town major forth with. By order of his excellency the general,

JAMES URQUHART, Town Major

Boston, 24th July, 1775.

"that the grand American tree of liberty, planted in the centre of the united colonies of North America, now flourishes with unrivalled, increasing beauty, and bids fair, in a short time, to afford under its wide-spreading branches a safe and happy retreat for all the sons of liberty, however numerous and dispersed." [1]

The Tories were willing to put up with the inconveniences of the siege, in consideration of the boon of security. One writing to a friend (August 10) says: "Although we are deprived of the comforts and luxuries, and some of the conveniences of life, yet, our being in a place of safety lessens the want of those conveniences; and I heartily wish you and your good family were as safe as we are here, out of the reach of the Tory hunters." This letter names "a Mr. Hitchborn, a young lawyer," taken prisoner, as on board of the Preston, and as standing fair "for the gallows." They felt confident that the rebellion would be put down. They had

---

[1] A tract was printed in 1775, entitled, "Voyage to Boston." The traveller was supplied by "the native genius of North America" with a mantle which had the virtue of rendering the wearer invisible. After being in the midst of Gage's council of war, he visited the liberty-tree while the Tories were cutting it down, and describes the scene as follows : —

> "Now shined the gay-faced sun with morning light,
> All nature joyed exulting at the sight,
> When swift as wind, to vent their base-born rage,
> The Tory Williams and the Butcher Gage
> Rushed to the tree, a nameless number near,
> Tories and negroes following in the rear —
> Each, axe in hand, attacked the honored tree,
> Swearing eternal war with Liberty ;
> Nor ceased their strokes, 'till each repeating wound
> Tumbled its honors headlong to the ground ;
> But e'er it fell, not mindless of its wrong,
> Avenged, it took one destined head along.
> A Tory soldier on its topmost limb —
> The genius of the shade looked stern at him,
> And marked him out that same hour to dine
> Where unsnuffed lamps burn low at Pluto's shrine,
> Then tripped his feet from off their cautious stand;
> Pale turned the wretch — he spread each helpless hand
> But spread in vain — with headlong force he fell,
> Nor stopped descending 'till he stopped in hell."

manifested their loyalty by volunteering to act as patrol, and now enrolled themselves into regiments.[1] "We learn from Boston" — Col. Reed writes, Aug. 24 — "that they have been employed in cutting off all the limbs of the trees in the town for fascines, — that the Tories and refugees are regimented, have a green uniform, and are called the king's volunteers." The Essex Gazette, the same day, says: "We are informed that the negroes in Boston were lately summoned to meet in

[1] The following extracts from Draper's Gazette will give some idea of things in Boston : —

Sept. 21, 1775. —"Last week the Rev. Doctor Morrison received a call to the elegant new church in Brattle-street, vacated by the flight of Dr. Cooper ; and on Sunday he delivered an excellent discourse to a genteel audience. His discourse tended to show the fatal consequences of sowing sedition and conspiracy among parishioners, which this pulpit has been most wickedly practising ever since the corner-stone was laid.

We are desired to acquaint the public that service will begin every Sunday at 11 o'clock, at Dr. Morrison's church, in Brattle-street.

Tuesday a Snow arrived from Cork, laden with claret, pork, and butter ; she brings advice of great armaments fitting out in England, which may be expected here in the course of next month ; and that a certain popular magistrate had been sent to the tower, from whence ('t is imagined) he will be drawn on a sledge to Tyburn, there to meet the reward due to treason and rebellion.

A brigade of Irish Roman Catholics is forming in Munster and Connaught, in order to be sent to Boston, to act against the rebels.

Col. Gorham, lately arrived from England, has almost completed his battalion here, which is called the Royal Fencible Americans.

Several other corps are actually raising in the northern provinces, with great success, and many deluded people have left the rebels to enter therein

We hear a certain person of weight among the rebels hath offered to return to his allegiance, on condition of being pardoned and provided for ; what encouragement he has received remains a secret."

Sept. 28, 1775. —"Such is the abundance of fuel, and provision for man and beast, daily arriving here, that instead of being a starved, deserted town, Boston will be, this winter, the emporium of America for plenty and pleasure.

The Hivernal concert will be open on Thursday next, and the play-house (Faneuil Hall) will shew away with the tragedy of Zara on Tuesday, the 17th of October, and continue to perform on those days weekly.

Six hundred pounds sterling (donation money) are received from Canada, 'or the sick and wounded soldiers of his majesty's army.

The Cerberus man-of-war arrived on Tuesday "

Faneuil Hall, for the purpose of choosing out of their body a certain number to be employed in cleaning the streets, — in which meeting Joshua Loring, Esq., presided as moderator. The well-known Cæsar Merriam opposed the measure, for which he was committed to prison, and confined until the streets are all cleaned." The journals contain a minute description of a street-fight that took place in August, between Commissioner Hallowell and Admiral Graves. In September the arrival of supplies of provisions made things look a little more cheerful in Boston. Madam Draper's Gazette predicted (Sept. 28) that Boston, instead of being a starved, deserted town, would be, this winter, the emporium of America for plenty and pleasure.

The treatment of the prisoners taken at Bunker Hill, and at other places, occasioned an interesting correspondence between the commanding generals of the two armies. They were thrown into a common jail. No distinction was made between officers and soldiers; and though, in July, a message from them stated that they were treated kindly, yet it was reported in August that they were treated with severity. This called for action on the part of Washington. "The occasion," Sparks writes, "awakened recollections of more than common interest. Just twenty years had elapsed since he and Gage fought side by side on the bloody battle-field of the Monongahela. An intimacy then subsisted between them, which was cherished afterwards by a friendly correspondence. Far different was the relation in which they now stood to each other, at the head of contending armies : the one obeying the commands of his sovereign, the other upholding the cause of an oppressed people." Their letters were significant of the change. Washington's was severe in the mere relation of the facts already stated. In addition, he stated that some, languishing with wounds and sickness, had been amputated in the unworthy situation of a jail; and he informed Gage (August 11) that he should be obliged to resort to the necessity of retaliation. General Gage's reply (13th) was arrogant and insulting : " Britons, ever preëminent in mercy, have outgone common examples, and overlooked the criminal in the captive. Upon these principles, your prisoners, whose lives,

by the laws of the land, are destined to the cord, have hitherto been treated with care and kindness, and more comfortably lodged than the king's troops in the hospitals; indis-
criminately, it is true, for I acknowledge no rank that is not
derived from the king." He then stated, that he had intelligence that the Americans were guilty of inhumanity in the
treatment of British prisoners. General Washington replied
to this letter on the 20th, in which he denied the correctness
of this intelligence, and read him a wholesome political lesson:
"You affect, sir, to despise all rank not derived from the same
source with your own. I cannot conceive one more honorable than that which flows from the uncorrupted choice of a
brave and free people, — the purest source and original fountain of all power. Far from making it a plea for cruelty, a
mind of true magnanimity and enlarged ideas would compre-
hend and respect it." On receiving Gage's first letter, Washington resolved to treat the British prisoners the same way
the Americans were treated, and ordered Colonel Reed, his
secretary, to direct those at Watertown and Cape Ann to be
confined in Northampton jail. Accordingly, Captain Knight
and others were immediately sent to Northampton. Washington, however, soon changed his mind with regard to their
imprisonment, and the order was countermanded. The three
letters on this subject were published together in October, by
order of Congress.

The following notes passed between General Washington
and Sir William Howe, this month : —

"*Charlestown Camp, 22d August*, 1775.

"SIR : — The men under your command having repeatedly
fired upon the officers of his majesty's troops, before they
were returned to the outworks of this camp from parleys that
have been brought on by your desire, I am to request all further intercourse between the two camps may be at an end,
your own letters excepted, which will be received, if you are
pleased to send them by a drummer.

"I am, sir, your most obedient servant,

"W. HOWE.

"GEORGE WASHINGTON, Esq., Cambridge."

" To Sir William Howe.

" *Camp at Cambridge, 23d August,* **1775.**

" Sir : — I flatter myself you have been misinformed as to the conduct of the men under my command, complained of in yours of yesterday. It is what I should highly disapprove and condemn.

" I have not the least objection to put a stop to the intercourse between the two camps, either totally or partially. It obtained through the pressing solicitations of persons cruelly separated from their friends and connections, and I understood was mutually convenient.

" I am, sir, your most obedient humble servant,

" George Washington."

The month of September passed without any important military enterprise about Boston, though some incident daily occurred that served to give life and animation to the camp. Skirmishes continued between the American riflemen and the British regulars; while, at intervals, shot and shells were discharged, both by day and night, from the lines of the enemy. The British paid special attention to the new works at Ploughed Hill. On the 2d two shells fell inside of them, but did no damage; on the 20th and 21st, after a furious cannonade of shot and shells at the works, and at a fatigue party near them, they killed an ox and wounded two men; on the 25th nine shells were discharged at them, without success. On the side of Roxbury, the month opened with a severe cannonade, which killed two and wounded several Americans. On the 2d the British threw up a slight work on Boston Neck, in advance of their lines, to cover their guard. This was followed, on the 6th, by a similar movement, without molestation, by the Americans, though within musket-shot of the enemy. This work was below the George tavern. On the 10th a strong work at Lamb's Dam was completed, and mounted with four eighteen-pounders. On the 23d the British discharged one hundred and eight cannon and mortars on the works at Roxbury, without doing any damage. On the 27th Major Tupper, with two hundred men, embarked in whaleboats at Dorchester, landed on Governor's Island, brought off twelve head of cattle, two fine horses, burnt a pleasure-boat just ready to be launched, and returned without loss to the camp.[1] It was on the 13th of this month that Washington detached Colonel Arnold, with one thousand men, to Quebec.

[1] The following song shows the spirit of the times. It is taken from the New Hampshire Gazette of September 12, 1775 : —

LIBERTY TREE, — A NEW SONG.

TUNE — *The Gods of the Greeks.*

In a chariot of light, from the regions of day,
　The Goddess of Liberty came ;
Ten thousand celestials directed the way,
　And hither conducted the Dame.
A fair budding branch from the gardens above,
　Where millions with millions agree,
She brought in her hand, as a pledge of her love,
　And the plant she named LIBERTY TREE.

The celestial exotic struck deep in the ground,
　Like a native it flourished and bore :
The fame of its fruit drew the nations around,
　To seek out this peaceable shore.
Unmindful of names or distinctions they came,
　For freemen like brothers agree ;
With one spirit endued, they one friendship pursued,
　And their temple was LIBERTY TREE.

Beneath this fair tree, like the patriarchs of old,
　Their bread in contentment they ate ;
Unvexed with the troubles of silver and gold,
　The cares of the grand and the great.
With timber and tar they Old England supplied,
　And supported her power on the sea ;
Her battles they fought, without getting a groat,
　For the honor of LIBERTY TREE.

But hear, O ye swains, ('t is a tale most profane,)
　How all the tyrannical powers,
King, Commons, and Lords, are uniting amain,
　To cut down this guardian of ours :
From the east to the west blow the trumpet to arms ;
　Through the land let the sound of it flee,
Let the far and the near — all unite with a cheer,
　In defence of our LIBERTY TREE.

The fitting out this memorable expedition occupied a large share of his time. The details of it, however, do not come within the limits of this work.

Washington was compelled by circumstances around him to pursue an inactive defensive policy. This, together with the condition of his army, more especially as to enlistments, weighed heavily on his mind. The Connecticut and Rhode Island troops were engaged only until the first of December, and those of Massachusetts only until the first of January; and he was desirous, before this time, by "some decisive stroke," to drive the enemy from Boston, and thus to relieve the country from the expense of an army. On the 8th of September, he addressed a circular to his major and brigadier-generals, calling a council of war on the following Monday; and he requested them to consider, preparatory to the meeting, whether it was expedient to make a simultaneous attack, by land and water, on Boston. This council was held on the 11th, consisting of the commander-in-chief, Major-generals Ward, Lee, and Putnam; and Brigadier-generals Thomas, Heath, Sullivan, Spencer, and Greene. It was unanimously agreed, "That it was not expedient to make the attempt at present, at least." On the 21st of September, Washington communicated this result to Congress, and stated that he had not wholly laid aside the project of an attack. He remarked, "Of this I hope the honorable Congress can need no assurance, that there is not a man in America who more earnestly wishes such a termination of the campaign as to make the army no longer necessary." His secretary, Joseph Reed, in a letter, September 29, expressed the views entertained on this point in the camp: — " Boston must, I fear, be given up for the common safety. The army and navy here must, at all events, be destroyed this winter. Should it be reinforced, the consequences to America will be dreadful. I preach this doctrine with all my might, and hope the committee of Congress, who are expected here this week, will confirm it. The general is anxious to strike some decisive stroke, and would have done it before this, if matters had not been misrepresented to him." In an elaborate letter (September 21) Washington forcibly describes his situation : — " My situation is inexpressibly distressing—to see the winter fast approaching upon a naked army, the time of their service within a few weeks of expiring, and no provision yet made for such important events. Added to these, the military chest is totally exhausted; the paymaster has not a single dollar in hand. The commissary-general assures me he has strained his credit for the subsistence of the army to the utmost. The quartermaster-general is precisely in the same situation; and the greater part of the troops are in a state not far from mutiny, upon the deduction from their stated allowance."

Washington, at this period, received many applications for detachments from the main army, to defend the towns along the coast from the pillage parties of the enemy; and among them, formal requests from the legislature of Massachusetts, and the governor of Connecticut. It was a delicate task to refuse them, for it might create serious disaffection among the people; it was a dangerous policy to grant them, for it would have so seriously weakened the army as to have exposed it to a successful attack. Washington, taking council of the sternest dictates of public duty, declined to comply with these requisitions. In reply to a letter of the patriotic Governor Trumbull, September 21, he said: "I wish I could extend protection to all; but the numerous detachments, necessary to remedy the evil, would amount to a dissolution of the army, or make the most important operations of the campaign depend upon the piratical expeditions of two or three men-of-war and transports." The policy of leaving isolated points to the protection of the local militia was acted upon through the war.

CHAPTER X.

Recall of General Gage. Proclamations of General Howe. New Organization of the American Army. Armed Vessels.

GENERAL GAGE saw reason to alter his opinion of the colonists after a short experience, and in a despatch of June 25, 1775, told Lord Dartmouth much wholesome though unwelcome truth. After regretting his loss of the 17th, he wrote: "The trials we have had show the rebels are not the despicable rabble too many have supposed them to be; and I find it owing to a military spirit, encouraged among them for a few years past, joined with an uncommon degree of zeal and enthusiasm, that they are otherwise." He informed his superior that the conquest of the country was not an easy work. It could only be effected by time and perseverance, and by strong armies attacking it in various quarters. He remarked of the colonists, that "In all their wars against the French, they never showed so much conduct, attention, and perseverance, as they do now." The general here was in error. The colonists manifested the same spirit in conquering Louisburg, and in saving the remnant of Braddock's army. His perceptive powers had been blinded by contempt. When he represented that, in conquering a square mile of territory, a detachment made up of the flower of his army had one half of its number killed and wounded, and that after a complete victory, the whole of his army was closely besieged, it became necessary, in accounting for such facts, to admit the presence of something besides cowardice.

General Gage, though in favor of occupying New York, regarded the evacuation of Boston as a measure of too much danger, and difficulty, and importance, to be taken without having the sanction of government. He accordingly determined to winter his army in its present position, and the last of September he commenced preparations to quarter it in the houses of the inhabitants. In consequence of this determination, it was necessary to remove the furniture from the buildings that would be required; and on the 1st of October, Crean Brush received a commission authorizing him to receive for safe keeping such goods as the people might voluntarily intrust to him. On the 2d General Gage issued a proclamation requiring a return of the names of all inhabitants, the army and navy excepted, and their places of abode, unto the town major, at his office, in Long-lane, on or before the 5th of October. On the 7th he issued a proclamation appointing "Joshua Loring, Jr., Esq., to be sole vendue master and auctioneer, in and for the town of Boston," and strictly prohibiting any other person from doing such business.

This was one of the last official acts of General Gage in Boston. Just before the reception, in England, of intelligence of the battle of Bunker Hill, a despatch had been made out for him, in which a sketch of future operations was drawn, and important questions were proposed for his consideration. But when this intelligence arrived, a separate letter was written, bearing the same date with the other,—August 2,—and closing in the following terms: "From the tenor of your letters, and from the state of affairs after the action of the 17th, the king is led to conclude that you have little expectation of effecting anything further this campaign, and has therefore commanded me to signify to you his majesty's pleasure, that you do, as soon as conveniently may be after you receive this letter, return to England, in order to give his majesty exact information of everything that it may be necessary to prepare, as early as possible, for the operations of next year, and to suggest to his majesty such matters in relation thereto as your knowledge and experience of the service enable you to furnish." He was directed to leave the other despatch, when he came away, with General Howe, who would succeed him in the command. These letters were received in Boston, by the Cerberus, on the 26th of September. General Gage replied in full to the letter of Lord Dartmouth, in a communication dated October 1, which certainly bears the marks of ability, good sense, and sound judgment. Subsequent events show, that if the ministry rejected the

general, they accepted his advice.   He recommended **the**
occupancy of New York, and stated the difficulty of making
New England the seat of the war.   "I am of opinion," he
wrote, "that no offensive operations can be carried on to
advantage from Boston.   On the supposition of a certainty
of driving the rebels from their intrenchments, no advantage
would be gained but reputation; victory could not be improved, through the want of every necessary to march into
the country.   The loss of men would probably be great, and
the rebels be as numerous in a few days as before their defeat;
besides, the country is remarkably strong, and adapted to their
way of fighting."

General Gage immediately prepared for his departure.   On
this occasion he received several testimonials from his friends.
On the 6th his council, and the leading loyalists, presented
separate addresses to him, drawn up in a similar loyal tone,
and expressing gratitude for his civil and military services.
Both of them are highly eulogistic of his personal character.
That of the inhabitants is reserved in its endorsement of his
proceedings; that of the council is fulsome in its flattery.   It
not only expressed "profound respect" for his "prudence,
benevolence, and candor," in civil affairs, but for the "steadi-
ness, vigilance, and humanity," of his military career.   They
presented their "loyalty to the best of kings" as their title
"to the care and protection" of Gage's successors; and they
requested him to assure their "gracious sovereign" that they
were "unalienably attached to his sacred person and government." [1]   Gage, in one of his replies, lamented the miseries
brought upon this once happy country, through the deep
designs and dark contrivances of ambitious men, to raise
themselves from obscurity to power and emoluments.   He
could not reflect "without pain upon the infatuation of the

---

[1] The council, in their address, said : "We have seen with pleasure the
many efforts you have made to avert this unhappy rebellion.   We lament
that the success has not been equal to your endeavors.   But the undisturbed
constancy and firmness with which you have pursued this principle, opposed
to every abuse which wickedness, delusion, or enthusiasm could devise, has
been as much the object of admiration to the loyal, as the subject of disappointment to the disaffected, people of this province."

multitude " " who enjoyed perfect liberty, who felt no oppression, but, deceived and betrayed, had flown to arms to avert evils that existed only in imagination;" and "in lieu of liberty had madly erected a tyranny upon the most free, happy, and lenient government." The country loyalists in Boston presented (the 7th) another address to Gage, which vied with that of the council in its fulsome flattery. Their regrets at his departure were relieved by the hopes of his speedy return; their lamentations at the few who dared to stem the torrent of rebellion and sedition were softened by the anticipation of the establishment of the rightful supremacy of Parliament over America. Gage, in his reply, gave them the welcome assurance that, during his absence, his successors in civil and military command would afford them every favor and protection. This language indicated that he expected to resume his command in America, after he had given the "exact information" which the British cabinet demanded and needed. He sailed October 10 for England, and soon found that his services would be dispensed with. He did not return to America. On this day General Howe took the command.[1]

General Howe was superior in ability to his predecessor, inferior to him in education, and no better informed of the temper of the people he was ordered to conquer. He had learned, however, to respect their courage, and was as averse as his predecessor had been to offensive operations about Boston. His reasoning, of the inductive cast, was conclusive. If the works of a single night, unfinished as they were, ill-supplied with ammunition and cannon as they were, cost so much blood to carry, what would be the sacrifice in storming lines made formidable by the labor of months, and frowning with heavy artillery? And if successful, no other end would be gained than to drive the Americans from one stronghold to

[1] Boston, Oct. 10, 1775. —"The king having ordered the commander-in-chief to repair to Britain, and that, during his absence, Major-general Carleton should command his majesty's forces in Canada, and upon the frontiers, with the full powers of commander-in-chief; and that Major-general Howe should have the like command within the colonies on the Atlantic Ocean, from Nova Scotia to West Florida inclusive, — orders are hereby given to the troops to obey the said major-general accordingly."— Howe's Orderly Book.

another. In his letter in reply to the important despatch of August 2, which was dated October 9, he frankly stated to Lord Dartmouth, "That the opening of the campaign from this quarter would be attended with great hazard, as well from the strength of the country, as from the intrenched position the rebels had taken." He recommended an entire evacuation of Boston. Further south the army might possibly penetrate into the country, but here it could only defend this post, and send out plundering expeditions, without having the power of reducing the inhabitants. In the beginning of the letter he assured Lord Dartmouth that Boston, "without the most unforeseen accident, would be in no danger from the enemy during the winter;" at the close of the letter he earnestly solicited the arrival of the destined reinforcement early in the spring. In the mean time he proposed to keep quiet, and to attempt nothing material. The British veterans in Boston would "shortly have full employment in preparing quarters for the winter;" while the reinforcement of five battalions of two thousand, expected from Ireland, would enable him "to distress the rebels by incursions along the coast." He "hoped Portsmouth, in New Hampshire, would feel the weight of his majesty's arms." Such was the policy prescribed by the ministry[1] to bring the freemen of America to the feet of the British throne. It was carried out to the letter by the king's generals, in their wanton sacrifice of life and property. Its mission was to widen the breach between England and her colonies, to break the charm of loyalty that so long had bound them together, and thus to pave the way for political independence and national unity.

The change of commanders was popular with the army. They thought General Gage lacked enterprise and nerve. They thought he had been too lenient to the people of Boston,

[1] This savage policy was expressly authorized by the British government although it affected to be displeased at the destruction of Falmouth. It ought to have the full odium of it. Thus Lord Dartmouth, in a despatch dated October 22, 1775, authorized Howe to employ the troops in " attacking and doing their utmost to destroy any towns in which the people should assemble in arms, hold meetings of committees or congresses, or prevent the king's courts of justice from assembling."

and too favorably disposed, out of family connections, towards the body of the colonists. They fancied General Howe to possess opposite qualities. One letter says, "he is in the highest estimation and honor among his brave countrymen;" another account says, "even the blunders of Bunker Hill were forgotten, so happy were most people at the change." He had proved himself brave and energetic in battle, and generous and humane in sharing the fatigues and in ministering to the necessities of the troops. Measures more decisive and uncompromising were expected.[1]

General Howe first improved his defences, and provided quarters for his troops. The main works in progress at this time were, a fort on Bunker Hill, and additional fortifications at Boston Neck. The former was so far completed, October 26th, that a general order designated the manner in which the several regiments were to line it in case of an attack. This was a very strong work. In describing it, an account says: "I do not recollect whether you saw Charlestown-side in that forwardness to give you any idea of its present strength; nor can I, with words, well describe the plan; — suffice it to say, that we thought six hundred men, commanded by two field-officers, so fully sufficient to protect it against the whole rebel army, that the flushes are levelled, and the Neck left open for their approach." General Clinton took the command of this post September 29, on the promotion of General Howe.

---

[1] In England the British commander was much blamed for his inactivity. A British journal, Sept. 23, says : " With a degree of apathy scarce reconcilable to the honor of a great nation, we see our whole force penned up in America by a rabble of half-armed militia-men. Even on the element of our nation, the sea, we have been strangely inactive, if not negligent. Both by sea and by land our commanders have been, with reason, complained of ; and while we complain like women, we have not the spirit of men to remove them from places which they fill so awkwardly."

The British officers wrote various apologies to their friends in England for this inaction. A letter, dated August 19, says, that the Bunker's Hill business of the 17th of June has convinced the provincials so entirely of the irresistible intrepidity of our troops, that they have attempted nothing of any moment since. They have formed a line of contravallation from Mystic River, which runs by Bunker's Hill round to Dorchester, about eight miles in extent, and carry on the *petit guerre* of popping at sentries

Adjutant Waller's orderly book, kept on the heights, gives glimpses of camp scenes. The troops were enjoined to maintain a high state of discipline. They were occasionally assembled for divine service, when they were directed to appear "clean," to be arrayed in order, and to be "as much as possible sheltered by a grove of trees." Sometimes rogues were barbarously flogged, and deserters were hung on Charlestown Neck. Views of the heights sent to England represent two clusters of tents, — one on Bunker Hill, and the other on Breed's Hill. These beautiful hills, at this time unincumbered with scarcely a building, and in full view of the surrounding country, presented a fine appearance, as the British troops, in their brilliant uniforms, paraded on their summits.

The British general was uncommonly busy in Boston. Many buildings near the hay-market, at the south end, were pulled down, and an opening was made from water to water. Here the troops were engaged in raising works. Six hundred men were employed on Boston Neck. The lines here also were made very strong. Other defences also were thrown up. "Our works," Carter writes, October 19, "are daily increasing; we are now erecting redoubts on the eminences on Boston common; and a meeting-house, where sedition has been often preached, is clearing out, to be made a riding-house for the light dragoons."

General Howe, on the 28th of October, issued three proclamations, which created much indignation. In one he stated that several inhabitants had "lately absconded," to join, as he apprehended, "his majesty's enemies, assembled in open rebellion;" and he threatened any who were detected in an attempt to leave the town, "without his order or permission given in writing," with "military execution." Any who escaped he should treat as traitors, "by seizure of their goods and effects." A second proclamation prohibited any person who had thus obtained permission to go out from taking more than five pounds in specie, and threatened offenders with the forfeit of the whole sum discovered, and with such fine and imprisonment as might be adjudged proper for the offence. To insure sharpness, he promised that one half of the moneys thus detected should go to the informer. A third proclamation recommended the inhabitants to associate themselves into companies, which were to be employed solely within the precincts of the town, to preserve order and good government. They were to be armed, such as were able, and to be allowed fuel and provisions equal to the allowance of the troops. This proclamation was equivalent to a threat; for it said, in order "that no one might plead ignorance," the association, under the direction of Hon. Peter Oliver, Foster Hutchinson, and William Brown, Esquires, would continue in session four days in the Council Chamber. Up to this time the Tories in the country, and even the officers of the crown, if neutral, were generally unmolested. It could not, however, be expected, that there could be burning of towns and seizure of private property on the one side, and forbearance on the other side. Washington (Nov. 12) recapitulated the substance of these harsh proclamations, and ordered Gen. Sullivan, about to repair to Portsmouth, N. H., to seize all officers of government there who had given proofs of their unfriendly disposition to the patriot cause. On the same day he gave similar orders to Governor Trumbull, of Connecticut. He wrote (Nov. 15) also to Governor Cooke, of Rhode Island, as follows: "Would it not be prudent to seize on those Tories who have been, are, and that we know will be, active against us? Why should persons, who are preying on the vitals of the country, be suffered to stalk at large, whilst we know they will do us every mischief in their power?"

No skirmish of importance occurred in October in the neighborhood of Boston, nor was a new position taken. Early in the month there was a sharp cannonade on Roxbury, but after this, things for some days continued remarkably quiet. On the 19th, the Essex Gazette states that scarcely a gun had been fired for a fortnight. On the 4th, a small fleet, under Capt. Mowatt, sailed out of Boston. It consisted of a sixty-four, a twenty gun ship, two sloops of eighteen guns, two transports, and six hundred men. They took two mortars, four howitzers, and other artillery. This was the fleet that burnt Falmouth. About the 12th a naval skirmish took place at Beverly. One of the privateers fitted out at this place was driven in by the Nautilus man-of-war, and getting aground in a cove just out of the harbor, the people collected, stripped her, and carried her guns ashore. The ship also got aground, but was able to bring her broadside to bear on the privateer, when she began to fire upon it. The Salem and Beverly people soon returned the compliment from the shore, and the firing lasted for two or three hours. When the tide rose the ship got off. The privateer was but little damaged. On the night of the 17th the Americans saluted the British camp on Boston common. Carter writes: "They brought three floats (with a piece of cannon in each) out of Cambridge River, and fired a number of shot, — some of which went over, several fell short; in fine, we had not even a tent-cord broke." The assailants did not fare so well. One of their cannon burst, damaging the battery, and wounding some of the men. Colonel Huntington writes, Oct. 19: "We had three fine floating batteries, — two in Cambridge, and one in Mystic River. Two of them remain good yet; and about twenty flat-bottom boats, that will carry near an hundred men each, besides a number of whale-boats."

Dr. Belknap (Oct. 20) visited the lines at Roxbury, and writes: "Nothing struck me with more horror than the present condition of Roxbury; that once busy, crowded street is now occupied only by a picquet-guard. The houses are deserted, the windows taken out, and many shot-holes visible; some have been burnt, and others pulled down, to make room for the fortifications. A wall of earth is carried across the street to Williams' old house, where there is a formidable fort mounted with cannon. The lower line is just below where the George tavern stood; a row of trees, root and branch, lies across the road there, and the breastwork extends to Lamb's Dam, which makes a part thereof. I went round the whole, and was so near the enemy as to see them (though it was foggy and rainy) relieve their sentries, which they do every hour. Their outmost sentries are posted at the chimneys of Brown's house." [1]

Washington, during October, was occupied with making preparations for the winter, and in a new organization of the army. He was not in a condition to act offensively. This

[1] Life of Dr. Belknap, p. 92

inactivity, however, grew more and more irksome to the commander, and more unsatisfactory to the country; and it occasioned audible murmurs. It was believed that an assault on Boston was delayed out of a desire to spare its inhabitants, and to save their property. Congress, either sharing this feeling or willing to hazard an engagement, suggested to the commander-in-chief, that if he thought a successful attempt against the British troops practicable, it would be advisable to make the "attack upon the first favorable occasion, and before the arrival of reinforcements." But Washington hardly needed this hint, for at no period of his command was he more solicitous to act on the offensive than during the siege of Boston. He stated his position, and the necessity of his continuing to act on the defensive, in a letter dated October 5, 1775: " The enemy in Boston and on the heights of Charlestown are so strongly fortified, as to render it almost impossible to force their lines, thrown up at the head of each neck. Without great slaughter on our side, or cowardice on theirs, it is absolutely so. We therefore can do no more than keep them besieged, which they are to all intents and purposes, as closely as any troops upon earth can be, that have an opening to the sea. Our advanced works and theirs are within musket-shot. We daily undergo a cannonade, which has done no injury to our works, and very little hurt to our men. These insults we are compelled to submit to for want of powder, being obliged, except now and then giving them a shot, to reserve what we have for closer work than cannon distance." [1]

[1] A paper dated October 28, 1775, gives the names, rates, and situation of the navy in Boston harbor: —

The Boyne — mounts 64 guns, and lies near the western end of Spectacle Island.

The Preston — 50 guns — is now moored for the winter between Long Wharf and Hancock's Wharf, at the eastern end of the town.

The Scarborough, and another sloop, — one of twenty and the other of sixteen guns, — are moored at a small distance to the southward of the Preston.

There are at present no other ships of force in the harbor, except the Mercury, stationed at the north-west side of the town, upon Charles River.

A plan was proposed to capture the Preston by surprise.

Washington was much relieved by the arrival (October 15) of a committee from Congress, appointed to consult with other committees, in relation to a new organization of the army. It consisted of Dr. Franklin, Hon. Thomas Lynch, of Carolina, and Colonel Harrison, of Virginia.[1] Deputy Governor Griswold and Judge Nathaniel Wales were present from Connecticut; Deputy Governor Cooke from Rhode Island ; Hon. James Bowdoin, Colonel Otis, Hon. William Sever, and Hon. Walter Spooner, of the Massachusetts council. The president of the Provincial Congress appeared for New Hampshire. The labors of this "committee of conference" continued several days, — from the 18th to 22d, — and embraced all the points of the proposed new army. Joseph Reed acted as secretary. His records have been preserved. On the last day the delegates from the several colonies stated the number of men each colony could supply before the 10th of March, and the terms on which they could be enlisted. Massachusetts could furnish twenty thousand men, on the terms on which the present army were raised; viz., a coat, forty shillings a month, — one month's pay being advanced ; and a greater number on any emergency. Connecticut could supply eight thousand men, at forty shillings a month, and forty shillings bounty. New Hampshire could furnish three thousand at forty shillings, without a bounty. Rhode Island could not go any further than to continue its force of fifteen hundred men. The conference decided that the General Court of Massachusetts ought properly to take cognizance of all armed vessels fitted out by its citizens, and that commissions should be granted, and captures made, at least under some authority; and that captures made by armed vessels in the pay of the continent should be disposed of by the general for the public use. The result of this conference was extremely satisfactory to Washington. A plan was agreed upon for a new organization of the army, which provided for the enlistment of twenty-six regiments, of eight companies each, besides riflemen and artillery. This

---

[1] General Greene writes, October 16, 1775 : " The committee of Congress arrived last evening, and I had the honor to be introduced to that very great man Doctor Franklin, whom I viewed with silent admiration during the whole evening. Attention watched his lips, and conviction closed his periods."

plan, and the details of it, were substantially adopted by Congress.

On the 23d and 24th, the delegates from Congress held a formal conference with Washington on sundry matters upon which no order had been made by Congress. The most prominent of them was the important measure of an attack on Boston. A council of war,[1] convened in consequence of an intimation from Congress, had decided that at present it was not practicable. Washington desired the delegates to state how far it might be deemed advisable to destroy the troops in Boston by bombardment; in other words — whether the town and the property were to be so considered that an attack on the troops should be avoided when it evidently appeared that the town must, in consequence, be destroyed? The delegates considered the subject of too much importance to be decided by them, and referred it to Congress.[2] Dr. Belknap was in the camp during this conference, and dined with a party consisting of the delegates and the generals. He writes of the conversation: " Lynch, Harrison, and Wales wished to see

---

[1] At a council of war, held at head-quarters October 18, 1775, present his excellency General Washington ; Major-generals Ward, Lee, Putnam ; Brigadier-generals Thomas, Heath, Sullivan, Greene, Gates.

The general acquainted the members of the council, that he had called them together in consequence of an intimation from the Congress that an attack upon Boston, if practicable, was much desired. That he therefore desired their opinions on the subject.

General Gates. — That under present circumstances it is improper to attempt it.

General Greene. — That it is not practicable under all circumstances ; but if ten thousand men could be landed at Boston, thinks it is.

General Sullivan. — That at this time it is improper. The winter gives a more favorable opportunity.

General Heath. — Impracticable at present.

General Thomas. — Of the same opinion.

General Putnam. — Disapproves of it at present.

General Lee. — Is not sufficiently acquainted with the men to judge ; therefore thinks it too great a risk.

General Ward. — Against it.

General Washington.

[2] The documents in relation to this committee of conference may be found in American Archives, vol. III.

Boston in flames.   Lee told them it was impossible to burn it
unless they sent men in with bundles of straw on their backs
to do it.   He said it could not be done with carcass and hot
shot; and instanced the Isle Royal, in St. Lawrence River,
which was fired at in 1760 a long time, with a fine train of
artillery, hot shot, and carcasses, without effect." [1]

In October much excitement was occasioned in the camp,
and in the colonies, by the discovery of a correspondence of
Dr. Church, who had been a prominent patriot, with the
enemy.   In the month of July, he gave a letter to a woman
who was going to Newport, with directions to go on board
a British man-of-war stationed there, and give it to its commander, Captain Wallace.   She applied to Mr. Wainwood,
a patriot, to assist her in getting access to the vessel, who
artfully drew from her the fact of her errand.   It occurring to
him that the letter might be from a traitor in the army, he
prevailed on her to intrust the delivery of it to him.   He
then imparted the secret to Mr. Maxwell, another patriot,
who opened the letter, and found it written in characters
which he did not understand.   The matter here rested until
Mr. Wainwood received a letter from the woman, manifesting
uneasiness as to the missing letter.   This led them to conclude that such correspondence might be still continued.
They then advised with Mr. Henry Ward, of Providence, who
sent the letter, with an account of the matter, to General
Greene.   He immediately conferred with Washington.   The
woman was examined, and after some hesitation, she said
Dr. Church gave her the letter.   He was then arrested.   The
letter was deciphered by Rev. Samuel West.   It was mostly
made up of a description of the force of the Americans, but
contained no disclosure of consequence, and no expressions
prejudicial to the cause of the country.   Dr. Church, as soon
as the contents were found out, wrote an incoherent account of
the matter to Washington, in which he attempted to vindicate
himself from any design unfriendly to his country.   A council of war assembled, (October 3,) before which Dr. Church
confessed that he wrote the letter, stated that his object was

[1] Life of Dr. Belknap, 96.

to effect a speedy accommodation of the dispute, but protested
his innocence of any traitorous design. The council were
not satisfied, but were unanimously of opinion that he had
carried on a criminal correspondence. They decided to refer
the case to Congress; and in the mean time to confine the
prisoner closely, and allow no person to visit him but by
special direction.

Washington immediately laid the matter before Congress.
It also came before the committee of conference in the camp.
This body, after discussion, resolved to refer Dr. Church for
trial and punishment to the Massachusetts General Court, with
the understanding that no procedure should be had until the
pleasure of Congress was known.

Dr. Church underwent next the ordeal of the General Court.
He was examined by this body October 27. His letter was
read, and he made a long and curious speech in his own justification. It failed to convince his associates of his innocence,
and he was, November 2, expelled from his seat. His fate
was decided by the Continental Congress. It resolved,
November 6, that he should be confined in a jail in Connecticut, " without the use of pen, ink, or paper, and that no person be allowed to converse with him, except in the presence
and hearing of a magistrate of the town, or the sheriff of the
county, where he should be confined, and in the English language," until the further order of Congress. He was imprisoned at Norwich. In the following May he petitioned
Congress for his release from confinement, on the ground of
declining health. This was granted, on the condition that he
should be removed to Massachusetts, and be put in the charge
of the council of this colony; and that he should give his
parole, with sureties in the penalty of one thousand pounds,
not to hold correspondence with the enemy, or to leave the
colony without license.[1] He accordingly returned to Boston,

[1] The documents relative to this affair are voluminous. They are collected
in the American Archives. See Sparks' Washington, vol. III. Dr.
Church, during his confinement, wrote two long and earnest letters to Washington's secretary, Joseph Reed, in relation to his case. — Reed's Life of
President Reed, vol. I., p. 123.

and during the year 1776 obtained permission to visit the West Indies. The vessel in which he sailed was never heard of.

Efficient measures were taken this month to fit out armed vessels. The necessity of them to cut off the enemy's supplies prompted the efforts made (see pages 110, 111) in the Massachusetts Provincial Congress to authorize them, before the battle of Bunker Hill. A report in relation to them was considered in this body, (June 19,) and after debate, "the matter was ordered to subside." Meantime, the Rhode Island Assembly (June 12) authorized two vessels to be fitted out,— one of eighty men, under Abraham Whipple; the other of thirty men, under Christopher Whipple. They were cruising in July. Connecticut authorized (July 1) two armed vessels to be fitted out. So important was it to distress the British, that Washington, under his general authority, authorized vessels to be equipped. The first captain he commissioned was Nicholas Broughton, of Marblehead, whose instructions are dated September 2, 1775. He was addressed as "captain in the army of the united colonies of North America," and was directed "to take the command of a detachment of said army, and proceed on board the schooner Hannah, at Beverly." Captain Broughton immediately sailed, and captured the ship Unity. His vessel, or the name of it, seems the next month to have been changed.

Washington soon made contracts for other vessels. He received instructions from Congress, October 5, to commission vessels to capture the enemy's transports, and was especially directed to capture "two north-country built ships, of no force," but loaded with military stores. Every effort was then made to fit out a small fleet of six schooners, but they were not all ready for sea until the last of October. On the 29th the Lynch, commanded by Captain Broughton, and Franklin, by Captain Selman, had sailed for the St. Lawrence; the Lee, by Captain Manly, sailed this day on a cruise; the Warren, by Captain Adams, and the Washington, by Captain Martindale, were to sail the 30th; the Harrison. Captain Coit, was on a cruise. It would require too much space to relate the fortunes of this little fleet. Some of the vessels were unfortunate. Captain Martindale was captured, and, with his crew, was carried to England. Others, how-ever, were highly successful.

Meantime, public opinion and individual daring compelled the Massachusetts Assembly to act on this subject. Persons petitioned to be permitted to fit out privateers, and Newbury-port and Salem memorialized in favor of public armed ves-sels being authorized. And more than this, — vessels were captured by enterprising seamen, without acting under any authority. At length, September 28, the Assembly appointed a committee to consider the subject. This committee not reporting, the Assembly, October 6th, "enjoined it to sit," and appointed Elbridge Gerry a member. A law was drawn up, during this month, by Messrs. Gerry and Sullivan, author-izing armed vessels, and establishing a court for the trial and condemnation of prizes; and finally, November 13, it was passed. This is said to be the first law establishing American naval warfare.[1]

The vessels commissioned by Washington — the first com-missioned by the authority of the united colonies — sailed under the pine-tree flag. This was the flag of the floating-batteries. Colonel Reed, October 20, 1775, writes to Colonels Glover and Moylan: — "Please to fix upon some particular color for a flag, and a signal by which our vessels may know one another. What do you think of a flag with a white ground, a tree in the middle, the motto 'Appeal to Heaven'? This is the flag of our floating batteries." Moylan and Glover replied, (October 21,) that as Broughton and Selman, who sailed that morning, had none but their old colors, they had appointed the signal by which they could be known by their friends to be "the ensign up to the main toppinglift." That the pine-tree flag, however, was carried by the colonial

[1] The Continental Congress, Oct. 13, authorized a vessel of ten guns and eighty men to be fitted out, and voted to equip another vessel, — both to cruise to the eastward, and intercept the enemy's transports. On the 30th it authorized two other vessels, of twenty and thirty-six guns, and determined that the second vessel, authorized 13th, should have fourteen guns. It appointed a committee to carry this vote into execution. On the 28th of November it agreed to a code of regulations for "the navy of the united colonies." — Journals of Congress.

cruisers is certain, because one was captured, and the British papers (January, 1776) describe its colors as follows:
" The flag taken from a provincial privateer is now deposited in the admiralty; the field is white bunting, with a
spreading green tree; the motto, ' Appeal to Heaven.' " A
map of Boston and vicinity was published in Paris in 1776,
which has the following representation of this flag:

CHAPTER XI.

The new Organization of the Army. Fortification of Cobble Hill and Lechmere's Point. State of the American Camp. Distresses of the British
Army. Boston in December.

SIX months had elapsed since the breaking out of hostilities
between the colonies and Great Britain. During this period
things had been gradually tending to a state of open, regular
war, by sea as well as by land. Not only had the people
become accustomed to the idea of settled hostility, but they
were entertaining the idea of political independence. This
had been broached in various quarters by sagacious patriots,
and had been favorably received. The American camp
was alive with it. "I found," Dr. Belknap writes, October
19, "that the plan of independence was become a favorite
point in the army, and that it was offensive to pray for the
king." General Greene advocated the policy of a declaration,
in a letter, Oct. 23, evincing great foresight, and filled with
admirable reasoning. After stating that "people began heartily to wish it," he said : "The alternative is a separation from
Great Britain, or subjugation to her." "We had as well be in
earnest first as last ; for we have no alternative but to fight it
out, or be slaves." This, also, was the policy that would be
the most likely to secure foreign aid. France was the real
enemy of Great Britain, and desired to see its power dimin-
ished ; but she would refuse to intermeddle in the dispute until
she saw there was no hope of an accommodation. Should she,
without such a declaration, supply warlike stores, and should
the breach between the colonies and Great Britain be afterwards made up, "she would incur the hostility of her rival,
without reaping any solid advantage." Such was the reasoning of this clear-headed general. Such was, undoubtedly, the
political sentiment of the camp, held alike by the commander-
in-chief and the rank and file. Such was the growing pub-

lic opinion, not only of Massachusetts, but of other colonies.
Abroad the contest was watched with intense interest. England felt that its arms had been humiliated. France was
deliberating whether to take sides in the contest. Europe was
astonished to see so fine a British army rendered so entirely
useless. Thus numerous were the eyes that were fixed on the
dawning of American independence !

The success thus far was gratifying to those who knew the
difficulties that had been overcome. The general officers, in
a long address to the soldiers,[1] Nov. 24, remarked : "The
ministerial army, with three of their most esteemed generals
at their head, have been able to effect nothing. Instead of
overrunning and ravaging the continent, from north to south,
as they boasted they would do, they find themselves ignominiously cooped up within the walls of a single town." Instead
of the disaffection of some of the colonies, which the ministry
pledged themselves to the people of England would be the
case, the union became stronger every day. Georgia, it was
just announced, had acceded to it, which made up the Thirteen United Colonies. Although the success of the American
arms might not have altogether come up to the expectations
of the people, or even of the Congress, it satisfied the general
officers.

Nor was it overlooked that this success had been mainly
achieved by four only of the colonies, — by the forces of Massachusetts, Connecticut, Rhode Island, and New Hampshire.
One regiment from the south had joined the army; but a por
tion of it — Morgan's celebrated rifle-corps — had been detached to Quebec. This left New England mostly to its own
resources. It is true there were reasons why it should have
made these large exertions. It was the chief object of ministerial vengeance. It was the immediate object of hostile
attack ; and the duty of repelling this attack fell more properly to its hands. In this day of trial New England did not
disappoint the expectations entertained of it by the friends of
freedom.

And of New England it is but sheer justice to keep in view
the efforts of Massachusetts. It was as much the great sup-

---

[1] This address is in the American Archives, vol. III., p. 1666.

porter of the colonies, in this day of action, as Boston had been the great leader of the towns, in the day of preparation. Its service, perhaps, is best told in contemporary language, elicited by contemporary jealousy. "Let it be remembered," — Elbridge Gerry wrote, Oct. 9, 1775, — "that the first attack was made on this colony; that we had to keep a regular force, without the advantage of regular government; that we had to support in the field from twelve to fourteen thousand men, when the whole forces voted by the other New England governments amounted to eight thousand five hundred only. That New Hampshire found it impracticable to support its own troops at so short a notice, and was for a considerable time actually supplied with provisions from this province. That after we had ransacked the seaports, and obtained all that was not wanted for their support, and had stopped two cargoes of flour owned in Boston, it was found that all the pork and grain in the government would not more than supply the inhabitants and the army until the new crops came in; and that there was no way left, unassisted as we were by the continent, or any other colony, — for we never had a barrel of continental flour to supply the army, — but to write a circular letter to every town in the counties of Worcester, Hampshire, and Berkshire, desiring them, in the most pressing terms, to send in provisions, and engaging that the inhabitants should be allowed the customary price in their respective towns, and the teamsters the usual rate for carting. But for this measure the forces of this colony and New Hampshire must have been dispersed." [1] This presents a striking view of some of the difficulties which the indomitable men who had thrown down the gauntlet to Great Britain were obliged to encounter. The general histories of this time abound with others. It required as stout hearts to struggle through them as it did to meet the enemy in the shock of battle.

It is not surprising that merit so great excited envy in other colonies. Even the pressure of external danger could not repress it. "The eyes of friends and foes," Gerry wrote, "are fixed on this colony; and if jealousy or envy can sully its reputation, they will not miss the opportunity." A jeal

[1] Life of Elbridge Gerry, vol. I., p. 115.

ousy of New England is often seen in contemporary documents. It seems strange, at this day, that, at a time when the
pressure of external danger demanded close union, such an
assurance as the following was considered necessary: "I
assure the gentlemen from the southward," — wrote General
Greene, October 16, — "that there could not be anything more
abhorrent to * * * than a union of these colonies for the purpose of conquering those of the south." Hence the strong
desire of Washington to supplant this local jealousy by a
union spirit. And in the new organization of the army, one
point was to make it as much as possible a continental, rather
than a colonial, army. In considering the difficulties which
the commander-in-chief had to surmount, this jealousy should
not be overlooked.

In carrying out the plan of the committee of conference for
the organization of the army, adopted by the Continental Congress, a new arrangement of officers was necessary. The old
army contained thirty-eight regiments; the plan for the new
army contemplated only twenty-six regiments. Much judgment was required in the delicate duty of reduction, to avoid
the imputation of prejudice or of partiality. The officers
selected were such as appeared best qualified to perform all
the duties, and to undergo all the fatigues, of a military life.
This whole business gave Washington and his generals great
perplexity. There is much matter about it in the letters of
the day. The men would not enlist unless they were allowed
their favorite commanders; many of the officers would not
serve unless their rank was adjusted to meet their expectations. "The trouble I have in the arrangement of the army,"
— Washington writes, November 11th, — "is really inconceivable." At length this obstacle was overcome, and (Nov.
12) recruiting orders were given out. It was expected that
most of the old army would reënlist, and that the difficulties
had been surmounted. Washington was doomed to severe
disappointment. A month's exertions only procured five
thousand recruits. Washington's patience and patriotism
were put to a severe test. His correspondence presents a
vivid picture of his trials. "Such a dearth of public (spirit)
and want of virtue," he wrote, "such stock-jobbing and fer-

tility in all the low arts, to obtain advantages of one kind and another, I never saw before, and pray God I never may be witness to again." [1]

During November a skirmish occurred at Lechmere's Point, and ground was broken at Cobble Hill. On the 9th Lieutenant-colonel Clark, at the head of six companies of light infantry and a hundred grenadiers, — about four hundred men, — embarked in boats from Boston, and landed at Lechmere's Point, to carry off the stock there. It was at high water, when the place was an island. The Cerberus and several floating batteries covered the party. The alarm was given. Colonel Thompson, with his regiment of riflemen, joined by Colonel Woodbridge, with a part of his regiment and part of Patterson's regiment, marched down to meet the enemy. To get on to the point, the troops were obliged to ford the causeway, in the face of the British, when the water was several feet deep. This they did with much spirit. The enemy, however, were about to embark under cover of the fire of the British man-of-war, of a floating battery, and the fire of a battery on Charlestown Neck. They lost two men, and carried off ten cows. The Americans had two men dangerously wounded by grape shot from the ship. Some of the troops behaved with great spirit. Major Mifflin, a favorite officer, Mrs. Adams writes, " flew about as though he would have raised the whole army." In a few instances, the men were backward. " The alacrity of the riflemen and officers upon the occasion,"

---

[1] The following order shows that it was intended the new army should be in uniform : — " October 28. It is recommended to the non-commissioned officers and soldiers, whose pay will be drawn in consequence of last Thursday's orders, (especially to those whose attachment to the glorious cause in which they are engaged, and which will induce them to continue in the service another year,) to lay out their money in shirts, shoes, stockings, and a good pair of leather breeches, and not in coats and waistcoats, as it is intended that the new army shall be clothed in uniform. To effect which, the Congress will lay in goods upon the best terms they can be bought anywhere for ready money, and will sell them to the soldiers without any profit ; by which means, a uniform coat and waistcoat will come cheaper to them than any other clothing of the like kind can be bought. A number of tailors will be immediately set to work to make regimentals for those brave men who are willing at all hazards to defend their invaluable rights and privileges."

writes Washington, "did them honor, to which Colonel Patterson's regiment, and some others, were equally entitled."
He praised them in the general orders the next day. He
noticed, in the order, the conduct of some,—names unknown,
—who manifested backwardness in crossing, and reprimanded
the officers for the manner in which the arms of several of the
regiments appeared. Colonel Clark, British, acted under the
immediate eye of General Clinton, who was so well satisfied
with his conduct that he praised it in the general orders.
The affair, somewhat highly colored for the press, was viewed
with exultation in the colonies. Washington regarded this
manœuvre of the enemy only as the prelude to a general
attack on his lines.[1]

On the night of the 22d of November, a strong detachment
of the army, under General Putnam, broke ground at Cobble
Hill, (McLean Asylum,) without the least annoyance from
the enemy. The fatigue men worked until the break of day,
when the whole party retired. On the following night
another detachment, under General Heath, was ordered to
complete the works. It was expected that the British would
sally out of Boston and attack the intrenching party, and
Colonel Bridge, with his regiment, was ordered to the foot of
the hill, and to patrol towards the bay and neck during the
night. Colonel Bond's regiment, and the picket guard on
Prospect Hill, were ordered to be ready to support General
Heath. But the enemy continued inactive. Two British
sentinels came off in the night to the detachment. The fortification was finished without receiving a single shot. "It is

---

[1] Lieutenant Carter, in a letter dated "Charlestown Heights, November
13, 1775," gave the following account of this affair : "On the 9th instant, six
companies of light infantry, and a hundred grenadiers, embarked in flat-boats,
and landed on Phipps' Farm, (the Cerberus frigate covering the descent,) a
piece of land which, at high tide, is an island ; it lies directly under Mount
Pisgah, where the enemy have a very strong redoubt ; they threw several shot
at our people, who brought off some cattle, and returned to camp without
having a man hurt. Immediately on the embarkation of our troops, the
enemy came on to the farm in great numbers, and boldly fired with small
arms after the boats ; the Cerberus threw some shot amongst them, which,
by the information of deserters since come in, killed seven and wounded
eleven "

allowed," the Essex Gazette states, "to be the most perfect piece of fortification that the American army has constructed during the present campaign, and on the day of its completion was named Putnam's impregnable fortress." Washington could account for the inactivity of the enemy only by supposing that he was meditating some important enterprise.[1]

The commander-in-chief regarded his position, at this time, as extremely critical. "Our situation," he writes, November 28, "is truly alarming; and of this General Howe is well apprized, it being the common topic of conversation when the people left Boston last Friday. No doubt, when he is reinforced, he will avail himself of the information." Washington made the best disposition he was able for a defence. He described the additional works thrown up this month as follows: "I have caused two half-moon batteries to be thrown up for occasional use, between Lechmere's Point and the mouth of Cambridge River, and another work at the causey going to Lechmere's Point, to command that pass, and rake the little rivulet that runs by it to Patterson's Fort. Besides these, I have been and marked out three places between Sewall's Point and our lines on Roxbury Neck, for works to be thrown up, and occasionally manned, in case of a sortie when the bay gets froze."

In November, the American armed vessels, which had caused Washington much perplexity, met with various success. The Fowey man-of-war captured the Washington, Captain Martindale. On the other hand, several British vessels were brought into Salem and Beverly, and the month closed amid great exultations at the capture of the British ordnance brig Nancy, by Captain Manly, commander of the Lee. She was carried into Cape Ann. So complete was the assortment of military stores on board of her, that Washington, on receiving the intelligence, (November 30,) was apprehensive that the British general would make a bold movement to recover the ship. "I instantly," he wrote, "upon

---

[1] Essex Gazette; Heath's Memoirs; Sparks' Washington; Reed's Life vol. i., p 129.

receiving the account, ordered four companies down to **protect** the stores, teams to be impressed to remove them without delay, and Colonel Glover to assemble the minute-men in the neighborhood of Cape Ann, to secure the removal to places of safety." Among the articles of this truly fortunate capture, were two thousand muskets; one hundred thousand flints; thirty thousand round shot, for one, six, and twelve pounders; over thirty tons of musket shot; eleven mortar beds. Among the trophies was a thirteen inch brass mortar, weighing 2700 pounds. A letter of Colonel Moylan describes the joy of the camp when the stores arrived. He says: "Such universal joy ran through the whole camp as if each grasped victory in his hand; to crown the glorious scene, there intervened one truly ludicrous, which was Old Put (General Putnam) mounted on the large mortar, which was fixed in its bed for the occasion, with a bottle of rum in his hand, standing parson to christen, while god-father Mifflin gave it the name of Congress. The huzzas on the occasion, I dare say, were heard through all the territories of our most gracious sovereign in this province." [1]

Washington, in December, in spite of a severe spell of cold weather, and a heavy fall of snow, built strong works at Lechmere's Point. He commenced planting a bomb-battery here on the night of Nov. 29th, and the next day the party came off without being interrupted. This work was prosecuted several days, without a gun being fired by the enemy. Washington says, Dec. 15, that he was "unable, upon any principle whatever, to account for their silence, unless it be to lull us into a fatal security, to favor some attempt they may have in view about the time the great change they expect will take place the last of this month. If this be their drift, they deceive themselves, for, if possible, it has increased my vigilance, and induced me to fortify all the avenues to our camps, to guard against any approaches upon the ice." At no time during

---

[1] A British account, after mentioning the capture of the Nancy, says: " Several other vessels have been surprised by their insignificant bomb-boats. I trust it will not last, and that they will pay dear for all in the spring. Indeed, I make no doubt of it, if the force intended arrives early enough to act "

the siege, perhaps, was the expectation more generally entertained in the army of an assault from the enemy than during
the progress of this work. "Not an officer in the army,"
wrote Washington, "but looks for an attack." On the 12th
he commenced a causeway over the marsh leading to Lechmere's Point, and carried a covered way (16th) nearly to the
top of the hill. Then a detachment of three hundred men,
under General Putnam, (17th,) broke ground near the water
side, within half a mile of a British man-of-war. The morning was foggy, and the party at work was not discovered
until about noon, when the ship began to cannonade with
round and grape shot, and a battery at Barton's Point, with
twenty-four-pounders and mortars. A soldier was wounded,
and the party was driven from the works. On the next morning Captain Smith, of the artillery, played an eighteen-pounder
from Cobble Hill upon the vessel with such effect that she
weighed anchor and dropped down below the ferry ; and General Heath, being ordered to prosecute the work begun by
General Putnam, went on to the hill with another detachment.
Notwithstanding a renewed cannonade from the enemy's
batteries, he continued to labor with efficiency and success.
Shells fell, burst, and covered the party with dirt, and one
broke in the air about seventy feet above it. The men in
the works were ordered, when sentinels cried "A shot," to
settle down, and not leave their places. The British could
see this manœuvre from their batteries. One of the commanders of the artillery is said to have told the general that the fire
did no good, and advised its discontinuance, as it only inured
the Americans to danger. The fire ceased in the afternoon,
when Washington, and other officers, visited the hill. The
works, during several successive days, continued to be prosecuted, though under a severe discharge of shot and shells
from the enemy, — some of which were fired from Bunker
Hill. Two redoubts were thrown up, one of them intended
for a mortar ; and a covered line of communication was built
along the causeway, quite up to the redoubts.[1] This position

---

[1] Heath's Memoirs ; Letters of 1775. This battery much annoyed the
British. Their letters have much to say about it. One, Dec. 31, says :
"If the rebels can complete the new battery which they are raising, this

was regarded as highly important in case of an attack on the British. "It will be possible," wrote Colonel Moylan, "to bombard Boston from Lechmere's Point. Give us powder and authority, (for that, you know, we want, as well as the other,) I say give us these, and Boston can be set in flames."

An unsuccessful attempt was made on the 28th, at night, to surprise the British outposts on Charlestown Neck. The party attempted to cross on the ice from Cobble Hill, but, on reaching the channel of the river, one of the men slipped down, and his piece went off. This alarmed the British, and the detachment returned.[1]

During this month Capt. Manly made more captures, and his praise was in every mouth. One vessel was from Glasgow, loaded with coals and dry goods. Colonel Moylan writes: "There were a vast number of letters, and what is really extraordinary, not one that does not breathe enmity, death, and destruction, to this fair land." Had all the captains appointed by Washington been as successful as Manly in cruising near Boston, the consequences to the British must have been far more serious. Broughton and Selman, this month, returned from the St. Lawrence. They were unfortunate in their supply of provisions, and in the character of their warfare. Other captains were unfit for their duties. In consequence, the Americans, in the latter part of December and former part of January, heard of vessels constantly arriv-

town will be on fire about our ears a few hours after, — all our buildings being of wood, or a mixture of brick and woodwork. Had the rebels erected their battery on the other side of the town, at Dorchester, the admiral and all his booms would have made the first blaze, and the burning of the town would have followed. If we cannot destroy the rebel battery by our guns, we must march out and take it sword in hand."

[1] Dec. 25. — "Some persons have been so curious as to note the number of men killed by the firings of the enemy on Cambridge side of the American lines, and on the Roxbury, as also the number and nature of their firings. The account stands thus : From the burning of Charlestown to this day, the enemy have fired upwards of 2000 shot and shells, — an equal number of twenty-four-pounders with any other sort. They threw more than 300 bombs at Ploughed Hill, and 100 at Lechmere's Point. By the whole firing on Cambridge side they killed only seven, and on Roxbury side just a dozen." — Gordon's History, vol. I., p. 429.

ing at Boston, — some of which might have been intercepted. However, in a short time, the sea swarmed with public vessels and privateers from several of the colonies. They often made successful cruises, and British commerce suffered severely from their enterprise.

Washington suffered intense anxiety, during this month, on account of the threatened desertion of a large part of his command. The Connecticut troops demanded a bounty, and because it was refused, they became mutinous; and, deaf to the entreaties of their officers, regardless of the contempt with which their own government threatened to treat them on their return, they resolved to quit the lines on the 6th of December. A convention, composed of a committee of the General Court and of officers of the army, assembled at head-quarters to devise measures to meet the crisis. It was determined to call in three thousand of the minute-men of Massachusetts, and two thousand from New Hampshire, to be in camp December 10th, when the time of most of the Connecticut troops would be out. This was communicated to these troops, and they were ordered to remain until this date. "Notwithstanding this," Washington wrote (Dec. 2) to Governor Trumbull, "yesterday morning most of them resolved to leave the camp; many went off, and the utmost vigilance and industry were used to apprehend them; several got away with their arms and ammunition." This conduct called forth the severest condemnation in the army, and met with a prompt rebuke from the patriotic people of Connecticut.

Massachusetts met the call made upon it with its accustomed patriotism, and with uncommon promptness. General Sullivan, in a letter dated November 30, in urging upon the New Hampshire committee of safety an early compliance with the requisition of Washington, said: "I hope the eager speed with which the New Hampshire forces will march to take possession of and defend our lines will evince to the world their love of liberty and regard to their country. As you find the business requires much infinite haste, I must entreat you not to give sleep to your eyes nor slumber to your eyelids till the troops are on their march." The alacrity with which both of these colonies responded to this call, and the good conduct of the militia after their arrival in the camp, proved extremely gratifying to Washington. The number called for was nearly all at the lines at the appointed time. On the 18th of December General Greene wrote: "The Connecticut troops are gone home; the militia from this province and New Hampshire are come in to take their places. Upon this occasion they have discovered a zeal that does them the highest honor. New Hampshire behaves nobly."

In consequence of this ardor in the cause, Washington began to feel, so far as men were concerned, under no apprehensions of an attack. The letters from camp are in a more cheerful vein. One, Dec. 13, says: "I have the satisfaction to tell you things wear a better complexion here than they have done for some time past. The army is filling up. The barracks go on well. Firewood comes in. The soldiers are made comfortable and easy. Our privateers meet with success in bringing in vessels that were going to the relief of Boston." General Greene writes, (18th,) "The army is filling up. I think the prospect is better than it has been. Recruits come in out of the country plentifully, and the soldiers in the army begin to show a better disposition, and to recruit cheerfully." The army was much elated and encouraged also by news of the success of the Americans in Canada.

A visiter (Dec. 20) gave the following sketch of the American camp: — "About two months ago I viewed the camps at Roxbury and Cambridge. The lines of both are impregnable; with forts (many of which are bomb-proof) and redoubts, supposing them to be all in a direction, are about twenty miles; the breastworks of a proper height, and in many places seventeen feet in thickness; the trenches wide and deep in proportion, before which lay forked impediments; and many of the forts, in every respect, are perfectly ready for battle. The whole, in a word, the admiration of every spectator; for verily their fortifications appear to be the works of seven years, instead of about as many months. At these camps are about twenty thousand men. The generals and other officers, in all their military undertakings, solid, discreet, and courageous; the men daily raving for action, and seemingly void of fear. There are many floating batteries, and bateaux in abundance; besides this strength, ten thousand militia are ordered in that government, to appear on the first summons. Provisions and money there are very plenty, and the soldiers faithfully paid. The army in great order, and very healthy, and about six weeks ago lodged in comfortable barracks. Chaplains constantly attend the camps, morning and night; prayers are often offered up for peace and reconciliation, and the soldiers very attentive. The roads at the time I viewed the camps were almost lined with spectators, and thousands with me can declare the above, respecting the camps, to be a just description."

The army was well supplied with provisions. A general order, December 24, 1775, directed the rations to be delivered in the following manner : —

Corned beef and pork, four days in a week.

Salt fish one day, and fresh beef two days.

As milk cannot be procured during the winter season, the men are to have one pound and a half of beef, or eighteen ounces of pork, per day.

Half pint of rice, or a pint of Indian meal, per week.

One quart of spruce beer per day, or nine gallons of molasses to one hundred men per week.

Six pounds of candles to one hundred men per week, for guards.

Six ounces of butter, or nine ounces of hog's lard, per week.

Three pints of peas or beans per man per week, or vegetables equivalent, — allowing six shillings per bushel for beans or peas, two and eight-pence a bushel for onions, one and four-pence per bushel for potatoes and turnips.

One pound of flour per man each day; hard bread to be dealt out one day in the week, in lieu of flour.

The army, however, had suffered much for want of firewood and hay. The Massachusetts Assembly endeavored to relieve this suffering, by calling on the towns within twenty miles of Boston to furnish specific quantities at stated times, according to the population of each town, and its distance from camp. A committee was authorized also to procure wood from such woodlands as it thought proper, even without the consent of the owner, a reasonable price being paid for it. This energetic procedure, after a time, procured a sufficient supply. General Greene, December 31, wrote as follows : — " We have suffered prodigiously for want of wood. Many regiments have been obliged to eat their provision raw, for want of fuel to cook it ; and notwithstanding we have burnt up all the fences, and cut down all the trees, for a mile round the camp, our sufferings have been inconceivable. The barracks have been greatly delayed for want of stuff. Many of the troops are yet in their tents, and will be for some time, especially the officers. The fatigues. of the campaign, the suffering for want of food and clothing, have made a multitude of soldiers heartily sick of service." [1]

In England, in the mean time, the intelligence from Boston, official and private, occasioned severe animadversions on the inactivity of the troops, and on the conduct of the ministry. The debates in Parliament, in October and November, abound with allusions to the army. "They" — (the Americans) exclaimed Burke, Nov. 1 — coop· it up, besiege it, destroy it, crush it. Your officers are swept off by their rifles, if they show their noses." " They burn even the light-house" — said Colonel Barre — "under the nose of the fleet, and carry off the men sent to repair it." Its alarming sickness, its want of fresh provisions, the insults heaped upon it by the daring enterprise of the Americans, were dwelt upon with no little effect. The ministers quailed under such heavy blows. To relieve themselves of the grave charge of neglect, they resolved to send immense quantities of stores to Boston, and purchased, among other articles, five thousand oxen, fourteen thousand sheep, a vast number of hogs, ten thousand butts of beer, five thousand chaldrons of coal, and even fagots, for fuel. A few items show the enormous expense that was

---

[1] Accounts of the weak state of the American army were frequently published in the British papers. One of them says : " The provincial troops before Boston are in want of clothing and firing to a degree scarcely to be credited, and must break up their camp before winter, but will probably attempt a *coup de main*. They have burnt all the fruit-trees and those planted for ornament in the environs of Cambridge, and are mutinous beyond measure."

incurred to support, at such a distance, an unnatural war in a
land of plenty. Twenty-two thousand pounds were paid for
vegetables, casks and vinegar; nearly as much for hay,
oats, and beans; half a million was paid for corn, flour,
and salted provisions. So great was the demand for transports that it raised the price of tonnage, which served to swell
the cost. From various causes, the vessels chartered to freight
these supplies delayed their day of sailing until late in the
season. Then contrary winds detained them, tempests tossed
them about, many foundered at sea, the British Channel was
strewed with the floating carcasses of the dead animals, and
a great portion of the vegetables fermented and perished. Of
the transports that got clear of the coasts, some were driven to
the West Indies, and others were taken by the American privateers; so that, after all the vast labor and expense, but an
inconsiderable portion of the supplies reached the place of
destination.[1]

The representations made to the British ministry elicited
instructions to General Howe to move to New York or to the
south, unless an alteration for the better took place. There
he might supply his troops with provisions, and by a sudden
enterprise, if not subdue, at least strike terror to the rebellious
colonies. "The situation of the troops," — Lord Dartmouth
wrote, September 5th, in a letter received November 9th, —
"cooped up in a town, exposed to insult and annoyance, if not
to surprise, from more places than one, deprived of the comforts

---

[1] Annual Register, 1775–6; Register of Debates; London Chronicle
General Gage, on his return, had given the ministry information as to things
in Boston more flattering than "exact." Thus the London Chronicle of
Nov. 18, 1775, says: "The accounts given by General Gage of the army
in Boston are much more favorable than were expected; the utmost harmony
subsists among all ranks of it. The numbers in the hospitals have been daily
decreasing for these two months; from which time fresh provisions have been
very plenty there. On the other hand, the provincials become every day
more dissatisfied, being much distressed for want of proper clothing to defend
them from the inclemency of the season." It was stated that three hundred
of the soldiers wounded at Bunker Hill had recovered and resumed their places
in their respective regiments. There is much matter about Gage in the journals. One says: "We hear that General Gage, on his arrival in England,
is to be created Lord Lexington, Baron of Bunker Hill."

and necessaries of life, wasting away by disease and desertion
faster than we can recruit, and no longer either the objects of
terror or cause of distress to the rebels, is truly alarming."
The removal before winter, therefore, was regarded not only
as advisable but as necessary. The British general, however,
could not remove without hazard, nor remain without suffering; and he was obliged to write, in reply, (November 26,)
that his majesty's intentions could not be carried into execution. He had not tonnage enough, were all the vessels in the
port, by eleven thousand tons, to go at one embarkation, and
he dared not weaken his army by division. Nor would his
force allow him to undertake any enterprise of consequence to
the service. On the 27th General Howe wrote another long
letter describing the state of the army, and accompanied it
with tables of statistics of the quantity of stores on hand, and
the quantity that would be wanted for the spring campaign.[1]
At this time he began to entertain apprehensions of a serious
deficiency of provisions; and after the capture of the Nancy,
and of other store-ships, his advices betray his alarm. He
apprized Lord Dartmouth (December 2d) of the state of his
supplies, of some of the captures, and of the uncertainty of
the arrival of the transports ordered to Boston. On the 13th,
he sent by the Tartar intelligence of the capture of other vessels, loaded with every kind of woollen goods and articles
necessary for clothing, and expressed " very alarming apprehensions" respecting the supply of provision; "especially,"
he remarked, "as demands for this article are increased from
the transports, provisions for seamen being expended from the
pressing wants of useful persons, who must be supported for
their services; and of many others, who have ever been

---

[1] General Howe, November 27, 1775, states the number of horses, cattle
and sheep, as follows : Light dragoons, 234 horses ; generals and officers,
160 horses; royal artillery, 200 horses; deputy quartermaster-general, 80
horses ; 100 cattle ; 400 sheep. Total — 674 horses, 100 cattle, 400 sheep.

An account, Dec. 2d, says : — " Ships, &c., at Boston, — Boyne, 70 guns ;
Preston, 50 ; Phœnix, 40 ; Lively, 20.; Scarborough, 20 ; Empress of Rus-
sia, 20, — for the lighthouse ; Raven, 16 ; Scimetar, 14 ; Viper, 10 ; George,
10 ; Spitfire, 8 ; Cruizer, 8 ; Hope, (schooner,) 6 ; three small tenders, 4 guns
each ; Custom-house schooner, 4 ; Job Williams, (a Tory,) master."

attached to government." In consequence of "rebel privateers infesting the bay," he suggested that in future supplies should be sent out "in ships-of-war, without their lower deck guns, or in sufficient force to defend themselves against these pirates."

At this period General Howe endeavored to enlist the loyalists in the service of the army. In this he was successful. A general order (November 17) alludes to three companies, as follows: "Many of his majesty's loyal American subjects residing in Boston, with their adherents, having offered their service for the defence of the place, the commander-in-chief has ordered them to be armed, and formed into three companies, under the command of the Honorable Brigadier-general Timothy Ruggles, to be called the Loyal American Associators. They will be distinguished by a white sash round the left arm. Honorable Timothy Ruggles commandant." Another order (December 7th) states, that "Some Irish merchants residing in town, with their adherents, having offered their service for the defence of the place," they were armed, and formed into a company called "Loyal Irish Volunteers," and distinguished by a white cockade. James Forrest was appointed the captain, and their duty was to mount guard every evening. Another order (December 9th) names the Royal Fencible Americans,—Colonel Gorham's corps. A letter from him states, that "he had already got three hundred, most of whom were Europeans, who have deserted from the corps of riflemen." Many deserters from the Americans were riflemen, but this must have been an exaggerated statement. I have met with no account as to the number of the loyalists of Boston who joined the British ranks.

In consequence of the scarcity of provisions, things began to wear a sombre aspect in Boston. A proclamation issued by General Howe (November 6th) indicates his apprehensions, and the distress of the citizens even in November. It commenced as follows: "Whereas the present and approaching distresses of many of the inhabitants in the town of Boston, from the scarcity and high prices of provisions, fuel, and other necessary articles of life, can only be avoided by permitting them to go where they may hope to procure easier means of subsistence." Inhabitants who wished to leave town were requested to leave their names with the town major before twelve o'clock, on the ninth instant. During this month several regiments in Boston struck their tents, and went into the houses allotted to them. Some of the meeting-houses were converted into barracks.

The army in December[1] suffered much for want of the necessaries of life, food, clothing, and fuel. A few store-ships from England got in, but furnished but a small portion of the supplies that were needed and were expected. To add to the distress, winter set in with uncommon severity. Before the barracks were ready on Bunker Hill, for the winter garrison, the troops encountered cutting winds and driving snows. These troops, at length, (11th and 12th,) struck their tents. Lieutenant-col. Agnew, with seven hundred men, was left in "the three redoubts erected on the heights." General Clinton, with the remainder, moved into Boston. There are long descriptions of the sufferings of the troops and inhabitants at this period. One account (December 14) says: "The distress of the troops and inhabitants in Boston is great beyond all possible description. Neither vegetables, flour, nor pulse for the inhabitants; and the king's stores so very short, none can be spared from them; no fuel, and the winter set in remarkably severe. The troops and inhabitants absolutely and literally starving for want of provisions and fire. Even salt provision is fifteen pence sterling per pound." The small-pox broke out, and spread alarm through the troops, who were generally inoculated. The British commanders considered this disease alone as a sufficient protection against an assault from their antagonists.[2]

[1] On the 5th the Boyne sailed for England, with General Burgoyne on board. A London paper, Dec. 30, says: "Yesterday morning the Generals Gage and Burgoyne, the Earl Dartmouth, and Lord George Germaine, went to the queen's house, and had a conference with his majesty for upwards of two hours, on which account his majesty did not ride out to take the air."

[2] The following is from the newspaper printed in Boston: — "Boston, December 14, 1775. Last Thursday a piratical brig, with ten carriage-guns and seventy-five men, fitted out at Plymouth, and commanded by one Martingale, was taken by the Foway man-of-war and brought in here. The prisoners we have are to be sent to England in the Tartar, which sails this

Plundering, also, — if the numerous cases of discipline of this period be a fair criterion to judge from, — kept pace with the increase of suffering, and seemed almost to bid defiance to the efforts made to stop it. General Howe had every motive to check licentiousness, to respect private property, and to preserve order; and he dealt with merciless severity with cases of robbery by house-breaking. Some of the offenders were hung; some were sentenced to receive four hundred, some six hundred, some one thousand, lashes on the bare back with a cat-o'-nine-tails. This discipline was extended to receivers of stolen goods. In one case, the wife of one of the privates, convicted of this offence, was sentenced " to receive one hundred lashes on her bare back, with a cat-o'-nine-tails, at the cart's tail, in different portions of the most conspicuous parts of the town, and to be imprisoned three months." The instances of discipline, while they confirm the contemporary relations of robbery and licentiousness, prove that they are unjust in ascribing them to the disposition or to the policy of the British commander.

The want most easily supplied was that of fuel, and this was obtained by demolishing the poorest of the buildings. The " useless houses" in Charlestown — so an order terms the few that escaped the general conflagration — were the first that were directed to be pulled down. They were divided into lots, and portions were assigned to each regiment. In Boston,

day. Several other ships, likewise, sail this day for England, two of which carry the officers of the 18th and 59th regiments.

" It is currently reported that the Continental Congress have declared the colonies in a state of independency.

" We are informed that there is now getting up at the theatre, and will be performed in the course of a fortnight, a new farce, called the Blockade of Boston."

In copying this, an American editor remarks : " It is more probable, before that time, the poor wretches will be presented with a tragedy called the Bombardment of Boston."

In the London Chronicle of Dec. 2 is the following : " General Burgoyne has opened a theatrical campaign, of which himself is sole manager, being determined to act with the provincials on the defensive only. Tom Thumb has been already represented, while, on the other hand, the provincials are preparing to exhibit early in the spring Measure for Measure "

so scanty was the supply dealt out, that the soldiers, notwith-standing severe prohibitions, demolished houses and fences, without waiting for orders. The evil became so great, that General Howe (December 5th) directed "the provost to go his rounds, attended by the executioner, with orders to hang up on the spot the first man he should detect in the fact, without waiting for further proof for trial." No supply hav-ing arrived, an order was issued (14th) authorizing working parties to take down the Old North Church and one hundred old wooden houses.

Boston, at this period, presented its most deplorable aspect. Hostile cannon were planted on its hills and lawns, and an insolent soldiery sat around its hearth-stones, or used its buildings for fuel, or wantoned in its temples of worship. Faneuil Hall was a play-house, where the efforts of the sons of liberty were turned into ridicule. Its patriot popula-tion, exposed to the ill-treatment of the army and to the espionage of its adherents, in want of the necessaries of life, and cut off from relief which friends would gladly have extended, were obliged to endure the severest trials. The pursuits of commerce and of the mechanic arts, the freedom of the press, of speech and of public meetings, the courts, the churches and the schools, were all interrupted. Even the air was filled with unwelcome noise, as the morning and evening guns sounded from Beacon Hill, or as the relief guards marched with their music to perform their stated duties. In a word, Boston under rigid martial law was like a prison, and it is not strange that the inhabitants who sided with the patriots longed to leave a place so filled with hated sights and sounds, and to breathe. although in poverty and exile, the free air of the surrounding hills. Necessity obliged General Howe to promote their departure. and hundreds were permitted to go in boats to Point Shirly, whence they dis-persed into the country.[1]

[1] Watertown, Nov. 27. "On Friday last General Howe sent three hundred men, women, and children, poor of the town of Boston, over to Chelsea, without anything to subsist on, at this inclement season of the year, having, it is reported, only six cattle left in the town for Shubael Hewes, butcher-master-general, to kill."—Newspaper.

CHAPTER XII.

The American Army. Knowlton's Expedition. The British receive Supplies Dorchester Heights occupied. Boston evacuated.

THE first day of the memorable year of seventeen hundred and seventy-six was the day which gave being to the new continental army. On this occasion the UNION FLAG OF THE THIRTEEN STRIPES was hoisted in compliment to the THIRTEEN UNITED COLONIES.[1] On this day the king's speech at the open-

---

[1] It has been stated (p. 103) that the New England troops marched to the field under their colony flags, and that (p. 262) the pine-tree flag of Massachusetts was on the floating batteries, and was carried by the colonial vessels. Another flag is alluded to in 1775, called "The Union Flag." The notice in the text is the first time I have met with it in the camp. British observers in Boston occasionally mention the colors of the flags in the American camp; sometimes they describe them to be "wholly red," sometimes to be "blue streamers," sometimes as having on them the motto "An appeal to Heaven." Washington (Jan. 4) states the fact in the text, and that it was raised in compliment to the United Colonies. Also, that without knowing or intending it, it gave great joy to the enemy, as it was regarded as a response to the king's speech. The Annual Register (1776) says the Americans, so great was their rage and indignation, burnt the speech, and "changed their colors from a plain red ground, which they had hitherto used, to a flag with thirteen stripes, as a symbol of the number and union of the colonies." Lieut. Carter, however, is a still better authority for the device on the union flag. He was on Charlestown Heights, and says, January 26 : "The king's speech was sent by a flag to them on the 1st instant. In a short time after they received it, they hoisted an union flag (above the continental with the thirteen stripes) at Mount Pisgah; their citadel fired thirteen guns, and gave the like number of cheers" This union flag also was hoisted at Philadelphia in February, when the American fleet sailed under Admiral Hopkins. A letter says it sailed "amidst the acclamations of thousands assembled on the joyful occasion, under the display of a union flag, with thirteen stripes in the field, emblematical of the thirteen united colonies."

There was, in 1775, another flag, at the south, the device of which is described as being "a snake with thirteen rattles, the fourteenth budding, described in the attitude of going to strike, with the motto 'Don't tread on me.'" This is said to have been the flag raised by the Alfred, and to have

ing of Parliament was received in the camp. It declared
that the "rebellious war" was "manifestly carried on for the
purpose of establishing an independent empire." It announced
that the spirit of the British nation was too high, and its
resources were too numerous, to give up so many colonies,
which it had planted with great industry, nursed with great
tenderness, and protected with "much expense of blood and
treasure."   It had become the part of wisdom and clemency
to put a speedy end to the disorders in America by the most
decisive exertions. Hence the navy had been increased, the
land forces had been augmented, and negotiations had been
commenced for foreign aid.

The king's language was rather calculated to nurture the
idea of independence than to crush it.   " He breathes revenge,
and threatens us with destruction," wrote General Greene.
" America must raise an empire of permanent duration, supported upon the grand pillars of truth, freedom, and religion,
based upon justice, and defended by her own patriotic sons."
" Permit me," he says to a member of Congress, (January 4,)
" to recommend, from the sincerity of my heart, ready at all
times to bleed in my country's cause, a declaration of independence ; and call upon the world, and the great God who
governs it, to witness the necessity, propriety, and rectitude
thereof."   Such were the sentiments, and such was the spirit,
that continued to pervade the American camp.   Such was
American resolution, when it was proclaimed that the Cossack
and the Hessian were to be hired to crush American liberty.

The army, on this day, was weaker than at any other
time during the siege. The changes that took place in it
necessarily caused great confusion. Thousands of the old
regiments were hurrying home, and many with open feelings

been carried by the Alliance, under Paul Jones, when she dashed through a
British fleet of twenty-one sail, and made her escape. Some accounts represent this to have been the flag of the American fleet in 1776. Probably this
device was confined to a colony.

The legislature of Massachusetts, April 29, 1776, ordered the naval flag
of the colony to be a white flag, with a green pine-tree, and an inscription,
" Appeal to Heaven."

The present national colors were adopted by Congress in 1777.

of discontent. A large number had brought into the field their own fire-arms. Owing to the scarcity of this article, they were ordered to be prized by inspectors, paid for accordingly, and retained for service. Some of the soldiers, dissatisfied with the value affixed to their property, regarded this measure as unjust and tyrannical, and hence, though necessary, it occasioned great difficulty. From these circumstances, and from others, this season was one of keen anxiety to the commander-in-chief. He alluded with great force to his position, in a long and eloquent general order of this date, and urged on the troops a strict attention to discipline. " When everything dear to freemen was at stake," he enjoined them to acquire the knowledge and conduct necessary in war. "An army without order, regularity, or discipline," he remarked, "is no better than a commissioned mob." At length this critical period was successfully passed. "Search the volumes of history through," — he wrote, January 4th, — "and I much question whether a case similar to ours is to be found; namely, to maintain a post against the flower of the British troops for six months together, without powder, and then to have one army disbanded, and another to be raised, within the same distance of a reinforced army. It is too much to attempt." General Greene, the same day, wrote : " We have just experienced the inconveniences of disbanding an army within cannon-shot of the enemy, and forming a new one in its stead. An instance never before known. Had the enemy been fully acquainted with our condition. I cannot pretend to say what might have been the consequence."

And yet, weak as the army was, scantily supplied as it was with arms, with powder, and even with the necessary comforts of life, the country was looking to see it expel the British forces from Boston. It was in the midst of the confusion of the new year that Washington received a resolution of Congress, passed December 22, after long and serious debate, authorizing him to make an assault upon the troops "in any manner he might think expedient, notwithstanding the town, and property in it, might be destroyed." It was in communicating this resolve that President Hancock, who had a large property in Boston, wrote : " May God crown your attempt

with success. 1 most heartily wish it, though I may be the
greatest sufferer." Anxious to meet the expectations of Congress, and of the country,[1] Washington, January 16, again
submitted the question of an attack to a council of war, with
the declaration, that, in his judgment, it was "indispensably
necessary to make a bold attempt to conquer the ministerial
troops in Boston before they could be reinforced in the spring,
if the means should be provided, and a favorable opportunity
should offer." Hon. John Adams and Hon. James Warren
took part in this council, and it was unanimously agreed that
a vigorous attempt ought to be made on Boston as soon as it
was practicable. The present force, however, was inadequate
to such an enterprise; and the council advised Washington to
make a requisition on Massachusetts, New Hampshire, and
Connecticut, for thirteen regiments of militia, to be at Cambridge by the first of February, and to remain until the last
of March. Congress approved of this measure of calling out
the militia, and resolved that Washington, in doing it, exhibited "a further manifestation of his commendable zeal for the
good of his country." In writing to that body on the 24th,
he remarked: "No man upon earth wishes more ardently
to destroy the nest in Boston than I do; no person would be
willing to go greater lengths than I shall to accomplish it, if
it shall be thought advisable. But if we have neither powder
to bombard with, nor ice to pass on, we shall be in no better
situation than we have been in all the year; we shall be
worse, because their works are stronger."

---

[1] Washington, Jan. 14, wrote: "The reflection upon my situation, and
that of this army, produces many an uneasy hour, when all around me are
wrapped in sleep. Few people know the predicament we are in, on a thousand accounts; fewer still will believe, if any disaster happens to these lines,
from what cause it flows. I have often thought how much happier I should
have been, if, instead of accepting of a command under such circumstances, I
had taken my musket upon my shoulder and entered the ranks; or, if I could
have justified the measure to posterity and my own conscience, had retired
to the back country, and lived in a wigwam. If I shall be able to rise superior to these, and many other difficulties which might be enumerated, I shall
most religiously believe that the finger of Providence is in it, to blind the
eyes of our enemies; for surely, if we get well through this month, it must
be for want of their knowing the disadvantages we labor under."

Washington, at this time, received intelligence of the reverses in Canada, in the repulse and death of General Montgomery. A council (Jan. 16) considered the critical affairs in that quarter, and resolved that in the feeble state of the army before Boston it was not expedient to detach any force from these lines to Canada, but that three regiments of the thirteen called for should be directed to march with all possible expedition to reinforce General Schuyler. Of this requisition of thirteen regiments, seven were apportioned to Massachusetts, four to Connecticut, and two to New Hampshire, to serve until April 1, if required. In writing to these governments, (Jan. 16,) Washington urgently solicited their attention as to arms, ammunition, blankets, kettles, clothing, as "from his amazing deficiency" in the camp, it was not in his power to supply them.

No enterprise of importance took place this month, except a daring attempt on Charlestown. A few houses (fourteen) along the Main-street, in the neighborhood of the Bunker Hill tavern, or Mill-street, had escaped the general conflagration and the demolition for fuel, and were now used by the British. General Putnam detached (Jan. 8th) a party of about two hundred men, under the command of Major Knowlton, aided by Brigade-majors Henly and Cary, to destroy these houses, and bring off the guard stationed in them. About nine o'clock in the evening the party crossed the mill-dam from Cobble Hill. Major Cary was directed to proceed to the houses furthest from the dam, and set fire to them; while another party, under Major Henly, was ordered to wait until this was done, and then set fire to those nearest to it. But some of the party set fire to the latter first. The flames gave the alarm to the enemy on Bunker Hill. Guns were immediately discharged from every quarter of the fort, indicating the confusion of the defenders, and affording no little amusement to General Putnam and his staff, who were spectators of the affair from Cobble Hill. Nor was this the only alarm. The attack was made in the midst of the performance, in Boston, of the British play, entitled "The Blockade of Boston," in which the figure designed to burlesque Washington enters in an uncouth gait, with a large wig, a long rusty sword, attended by a country servant with a rusty gun. A sergeant suddenly appeared, and exclaimed, " The Yankees are attacking our works on Bunker Hill!" At first this was supposed by the audience to be a part of the diversion; but when General Howe called out "Officers to your alarm posts!" the people dispersed, amidst fainting and shrieking among the females. Major Knowlton burnt eight of the houses, killed one man, who made resistance, and brought off five prisoners, without sustaining any damage. Majors Knowlton, Cary, and Henly, were much praised for their good conduct on this occasion, and were thanked in the general orders of the next day.[1]

This month several captures were made by the armed ves-

---

[1] January 9. — Parol, Knowlton ; Countersign, Charlestown. The general thanks Major Knowlton, and the officers and soldiers who were under his command last night, for the spirit, conduct, and secrecy, with which they burnt the houses near the enemy's works upon Bunker's Hill. The general was in a more particular manner pleased with the resolution the party discovered, in not firing a shot, as nothing betrays greater signs of fear, and less of the soldier, than to begin a loose, undirected, and unmeaning fire, from whence no good can result, nor any valuable purposes answered.

A British letter gives the following account of this affair : — " Boston, Jan. 29. — The rebels have been very quiet ever since I arrived. They gave a small alarm about a fortnight ago, which occasioned a little confusion, but was soon over. The officers have fitted up a play-house, and some of them had wrote a farce, called the Blockade of Boston. The first night it was to be acted the house was very full. The play being over, the curtain was hauled up for the entertainment to begin, when a sergeant came in and told the officers the alarm-guns were fired at Charlestown, which made no small stir in the house, every one endeavoring to get out as fast as possible ; and immediately we heard a pretty smart firing of small arms. It being dark, and the rascals making a great huzzaing, I did not know what to make of it at first ; but it was soon over, so that I went quietly to sleep about eleven o'clock, and next morning found all the mischief had been done was three or four men taken, who had been among the old ruins of Charlestown, a mill burnt down, and the company disappointed of their entertainment."

Another letter states that " The Busy Body " had been performed, and the play of the Blockade was about to be commenced, when a sergeant represented the "burning of two or three old houses " as a general attack on Boston. " But it is very evident the rebels possess a sufficiency of what Falstaff terms the better part of valor, to prevent their making an attempt that must inevitably end in their own destruction." This play was again announced, " with the tragedy of Tamerlane." Sometimes play-bills were sent out directed to Washington and the other general officers.

sels. Washington (January 31) writes: "Our commodore, Manly, has just taken two ships, from Whitehaven to Boston, with coal and potatoes, and sent them into Plymouth, and fought a tender close by the light-house, where the vessels were taken, long enough to give his prizes time to get off; in short, till she thought best to quit the combat, and he to move off from the men-of-war, which were spectators of this scene."

Through the month of February, also, no enterprise of importance was undertaken. A few British soldiers (1st) began to pull down the old tide-mills in Charlestown, but a few shot from Cobble Hill dispersed them; and a party of Americans (8th) went from Winter Hill and burnt them. Several cows were near the British outposts at Charlestown Neck, when a party (5th) drove them in. This brought on a brisk fire of cannon and musketry. A party of the British from the castle, and another from Boston, several hundred grenadiers and light-infantry, crossed over (14th) to Dorchester Neck, to surprise the American guard there, seventy in number, and nearly succeeded. The guard barely escaped. The houses were burned, and two persons were captured. Three British sentinels were captured on Boston Neck (23d) without a gun being fired. The works at Lechmere's Point were strengthened, and heavy cannon and a mortar were planted. Another mortar was placed at Lamb's Dam. Discipline was rigidly enforced. "Our life in camp," Lieutenant Shaw writes, (Feb. 14,) "is confined. The officers are not allowed to visit Cambridge, without leave from the commanding officer, and we are kept pretty closely to our duty. The drum beats at daybreak, when all hands turn out to man the lines. Here we stay till sunrise, and then all are marched off to prayers. We exercise twice a day, and every fourth day take our turns on guard. Opinions are various whether Boston is to be attacked or not. I think it a difficult question to answer. However, if it should be judged expedient to do it, I hope our troops will act with sufficient resolution to command success."[1]

Though Washington was heartily tired of his forced inac-

[1] Shaw's Journal, p. 8.

tivity, yet such was his weakness that he was obliged, for a season, to continue it.   On the 9th of February he stated that two thousand of his men were without firelocks, and that he was obliged to conceal the state of his army even from his own officers.   And yet the public continued impatient for the long-expected attack on Boston.   On the 10th he wrote : "I know that much is expected of me.   I know that without men, without arms, without ammunition, without anything fit for the accommodation of a soldier, little is to be done." [1]   A feeling of conscious integrity sustained the American commander on this trying occasion.   In a few days things wore a more favorable aspect.   Ten regiments of the neighboring militia arrived in camp, large supplies of ammunition were received, and Washington once more felt like pressing offensive measures.   At a council of general officers, held February 16, 1776, Washington represented that when the new regiments were all in from Massachusetts, New Hampshire, and Connecticut, if complete, they would amount to 7280 men ; that the regiments in camp amounted to 8797 men fit for duty, besides officers, and 1405 men on command which might be ordered to join their respective regiments immediately ; while, from the best intelligence that could be obtained from Boston, the strength of the British army did not much exceed 5000 men fit for duty.   He asked their opinion in relation to a general assault, while the bays were partly frozen,

---

[1] Washington, in one of his familiar letters to Joseph .Reed, dated February 10, 1776, writes as follows of an assault : " I observe what you say in respect to the ardor of chimney-corner heroes.   I am glad their zeal is in some measure abated, because, if circumstances will not permit us to make an attempt upon B., or if it should be made and fail, we shall not appear altogether so culpable.   I entertain the same opinion of the attempt now which I have ever done.   I believe an assault will be attended with considerable loss ; and I believe it would succeed, if the men should behave well ; without it, unless there is equal bad behavior on the other side, we cannot. As to an attack upon B. Hill, (unless it could be carried by surprise,) the loss, I conceive, would be greater in proportion than at Boston ; and if a defeat should follow would be discouraging to the men, but highly animating if crowned with success.   Great good or great evil would result from it, — it is quite a different thing to what you left, being by odds the strongest fortress they possess, both in rear and front."

and before the British should receive their expected reinforcement. The council were of opinion that an assault was improper, on account of the inadequate state of the army as it respected men, arms, and powder. They estimated the British troops, including new-raised corps and armed Tories, at a much larger number than 5000. They were furnished with artillery, were doubly officered, were protected by a fleet, and possessed of every advantage the situation of the place afforded. They resolved, however, that a cannonade and bombardment of Boston would be advisable, as soon as a sufficient supply of powder was received, and not before;[1] and that in the mean time preparations should be made to take possession of Dorchester Hill, with a view of drawing out the

[1] January 24, 1776. — The general ordered the regiments to be brigaded in the following manner : —

Brigadier-general Thomas' brigade, — Learned's, Joseph Reed's, Whitcomb's, Ward's, and Bailey's regiments.

Brigadier-general Spencer's brigade, — Parsons', Huntington's, Webb's, and Wyllys' regiments.

Brigadier-general Greene's brigade, — Varnum's, Hitchcock's, Little's, and Bond's regiments.

Brigadier-general Heath's brigade, — Prescott's, Sergeant's, Phinney's, Greaton's, and Baldwin's regiments.

Brigadier-general Sullivan's brigade, — James Reed's, Nixon's, Stark's, and Poor's regiments.

Brigadier-general ————— brigade, — Glover's, Patterson's, Arnold's, and Hutchinson's regiments.

The troops were accommodated in barracks this winter, as follows : —

At Prospect Hill,	3464
At different places, — Number One, Inman's House, &c.,	3460
At Roxbury,	3795
At Dorchester,	814
At Sewall's Point,	400
At Cambridge Barracks,	640
At Winter Hill,	3380
In the College,	640
In the New College,	640
In the Old College,	240
North Chapel,	160
	17633

Exclusive of the private houses in Cambridge.

enemy; and also of Noddle's Island, if the situation of the water, and other circumstances, would admit of it.

This decision of the council of war did not change Washington's belief in the feasibility of a successful assault. The ice was strong enough to bear the troops, the works were sufficiently advanced to cover them, and the army were eager for action. He at no time felt more keenly his position. "To have the eyes of a whole continent," he wrote to Congress, February 18, 1776, " fixed with anxious expectation of hearing some great event, and to be restrained in every military operation, for want of the necessary means to carry it on, is not very pleasing, especially as the means used to conceal my weakness from the enemy conceal it also from our friends, and add to their wonder."

The British general continued inactive during the winter. Admiral Shuldham arrived (Dec. 30th) to succeed Admiral Graves in the command of the fleet, and reinforcements also arrived. There had been serious differences between Howe and Graves. Much of the suffering endured by the army was charged to the want of vigilance and enterprise of the admiral in not protecting the store-ships. In the month of January Sir Henry Clinton, and a small fleet, sailed from Boston on a secret expedition. Washington supposed the object of it was to take possession of New York, and he ordered General Lee (Jan. 8th) to proceed there and put the city in the best posture of defence that circumstances would permit. But Clinton's object was North Carolina. It was an expedition planned by the ministry at the solicitation of Governor Martin. The orders for the conduct of it were of a savage character.[1] But it proved a signal failure; as did most of the expeditions,

---

[1] Lord Dartmouth gave General Howe minute instructions relative to this expedition, in a letter dated October 22. He had been assured that the inhabitants of the southern colonies would join the king's army. If deceived in this, Clinton was directed to gain possession " of some respectable post to the southward," from which " the rebels might be annoyed by sudden and unexpected attacks of their towns upon the sea-coast during open winter." These attacks Dartmouth thought " might be made very distressing" to the Americans, and would be no inconsiderable advantage to the British. Clinton was positively ordered to " destroy any towns" that refused submission

Sparks writes, " undertaken at the suggestion of the colonial governors and zealous partisans of the crown, whose wishes and hopes betrayed them into a deplorable ignorance of the state of the country and character of the people." [1]

General Howe, in a long despatch, (January 16,) gave his views of the present and future operations of the army. He intimated a doubt of the success of the southern expedition, and of the policy of making drains from his main army. With an army of twenty thousand men, having twelve thousand at New York, six thousand at Rhode Island, and two thousand at Halifax, exclusive of the force destined for Quebec, a different aspect might be put upon affairs at the end of the ensuing campaign. "With fewer troops," he says, " the success of any offensive operations will be very doubtful." Nor was the American army " in any ways to be despised;" for it had in it " many European soldiers, and all, or most of the young men of spirit in the country, who were exceedingly diligent and attentive in their military profession." At the conclusion of this despatch he informed Lord Dartmouth, that " the leaders of the rebels seemed determined, since the receipt of the king's speech among them, to make the most diligent preparations for an active war;" and that it was his firm opinion they would not retract until they had tried their fortune in battle and were defeated.

In the mean time things in Boston assumed a more cheerful aspect. General Howe, to relieve the necessities of his army and its dependents, sent vessels to Nova Scotia, the Southern Colonies, and the West Indies, for supplies. The arrival of some of them, laden with rice and coal, together with store-ships from England, in spite of the daring activity of the American privateers, relieved for a season the wants of the troops and the people. On the 19th of January, by a general order, the demolition of houses and wharves ceased; the tools in possession of the regular working parties were called in, and the men engaged in this business were directed " to be made as clean and decent as possible immediately." [2] The orderly books throughout the whole of the siege bear evidence

[1] Sparks' Washington, vol. III., 223.   [2] British Orderly Book.

of the attention paid to the looks of the soldiers, as well as to their discipline, comfort, and health. When on duty the men were " to appear decently dressed and accoutred ;" none were to be sent to parade " without having the hair properly and smoothly clubbed," and none were to appear under arms with tobacco in their mouths. The officers were ordered to wear sashes on duty; to be uniformly dressed in quarter leggins or boots. The marines wore short gaiters, and the roses were to be in front of their hats. Even the shape of the coats was prescribed in the general orders. Directions of this sort ar frequent. An order dated January 13, 1776, presents a curious picture of the habits and appearance of the soldiers. " The commanding officer is surprised to find the necessity of repeating orders, that long since ought to have been complied with, as the men on all duties appear in the following manner ; viz., — hair not smooth and badly powdered, several without slings to their firelocks, hats not bound, pouches in a shameful and dirty condition, no frills to their shirts, and their linen very dirty, leggins hanging in a slovenly manner about their knees, some men without uniform stocks, and their arms and accoutrements by no means so clean as they ought to be. These unsoldier-like neglects must be immediately remedied."

General Howe felt secure in his strong-holds. He wrote to Lord Dartmouth, — " We are not under the least apprehension of an attack upon this place from the rebels, by surprise or otherwise;" on the contrary, he professed to wish " that they would attempt so rash a step, and quit those strong intrenchments to which they may attribute their present safety." He had no disposition, however, to make a sally out of Boston. The loyalists around him felt unbounded confidence in the ultimate triumph of the power of Great Britain. A single illustration will show the strength of this feeling. On the 10th of January, Crean Brush, in a memorial, offered to raise a body of volunteers, of not less than three hundred, on the same pay and gratuity as were received by the new raised Royal Fencible Americans; and after " the subduction of the main body of the rebel force" should have been accomplished, he requested to be allowed an independent command of three hundred men, " to occupy the main posts on Connecticut River, and open a line of communication westward toward Lake Champlain," — with such a force promising to put down symptoms of rebellion in that quarter ![1] The officers endeavored to relieve the tedium of the blockade by social amusements. " We had a theatre," one of them writes, " we had balls, and there is actually on foot a subscription for a masquerade. England seems to have forgot us, and we endeavored to forget ourselves." The winter, though severe at first, proved to be a mild one. " The bay is open," Col. Moylan wrote from the American camp in January ; — " everything thaws here except Old Put. He is still as hard as ever, crying out for powder — powder, — ye gods, give us powder ! " The absence of ice and want of powder checked military enterprise, prevented the effusion of blood, and left the British to enjoy in tranquillity their sports. Though General Howe had resolved to evacuate Boston, yet he determined to wait until he had additional transports and sufficient provisions for a long voyage; and, also, until a favorable season should arrive. Then he might withdraw without loss, and with safety and honor. His policy, therefore, was to remain quiet.

But Washington's operations suddenly and sadly deranged the plans of the British commander. In the latter part of February the American army was sufficiently strong to warrant even the cautious council of war in adopting offensive measures. Colonel Knox, with an enterprise and perseverance that elicited the warmest commendations, had brought from Crown Point and Ticonderoga, over frozen lakes and almost impassable snows, more than fifty cannon, mortars, and howitzers;[2] a supply of shells had been procured from the king's store at New York and an ordnance brig; and even powder became comparatively plenty in the camp. The

---

[1] Mss. in Massachusetts Secretary of State Office.

[2] Colonel Knox brought from Fort George, on forty-two sleds, 8 brass mortars, 6 iron mortars, 2 iron howitzers, 13 brass cannon, 26 iron cannon, 2300 lbs. lead, and 1 barrel of flints. On the 17th of December, at Fort George, he wrote to Washington, — " I hope in sixteen or seventeen days to present to your excellency a noble train of artillery, the inventory of which I have enclosed."

works nearest Boston had been very strong. "We have," Washington wrote, February 26, "under many difficulties, on account of hard frozen ground, completed our work on Lechmere's Point. We have got some heavy pieces of ordnance placed there, two platforms fixed for mortars, and everything for any offensive operation. Strong guards are now mounted there, and at Cobble Hill." Ten regiments had come in to strengthen the lines. A day was therefore fixed upon to take possession of Dorchester Heights. This, it was rightly judged, would bring on a general action, or would force the British army from the metropolis. Washington, on the 26th, apprized the Council of Massachusetts of his intention, and requested them to order the militia of the towns contiguous to Dorchester and Roxbury " to repair to the lines at these places, with their arms, ammunition, and accoutrements, instantly upon a signal being given." The Council promptly complied with this requisition. "I am preparing," he wrote the same day, "to take post on Dorchester Heights, to try if the enemy will be so kind as to come out to us." "I should think," he wrote to Congress the same day, "if anything will induce them to hazard an engagement, it will be our attempting to fortify these heights, as, on that event's taking place, we shall be able to command a great part of the town, and almost the whole harbor, and to make them rather disagreeable than otherwise, provided we can get a sufficient supply of what we greatly want." [1]

---

[1] Extract from general orders, February 26, 1776. "All officers, non commissioned officers, and soldiers, are positively forbid playing at cards, and other games of chance. At this time of public distress, men may find enough to do in the service of their God and their country, without abandoning themselves to vice and immorality.

" As the season is now fast approaching when every man must expect to be drawn into the field of action, it is highly important that he should prepare his mind, as well as everything necessary for it. It is a noble cause we are engaged in; it is the cause of virtue and mankind; every temporal advantage and comfort to us, and our posterity, depends upon the vigor of our exertions; in short, freedom or slavery must be the result of our conduct; there can, therefore, be no greater inducement to men to behave well. But it may not be amiss for the troops to know, that, if any man in action shall presume to skulk, hide himself, or retreat from the enemy without the

The American camp, in the beginning of March, presented indications of an approaching conflict. Chandeliers, fascines, screwed hay, in large quantities, were collected for intrenching purposes; two thousand bandages were prepared to dress broken limbs; forty-five bateaux, each capable of carrying eighty men, and two floating batteries, were assembled in Charles River; and the militia from the neighboring towns, applied for by Washington, February 26, were pouring into the camp with patriotic alacrity. Washington had determined not only to take possession of Dorchester Heights, but, should subsequent circumstances warrant the enterprise, to make the long purposed attack on Boston.

This design was kept a profound secret, and to divert the attention of the enemy, a severe cannonade and bombardment, on the night of the second of March, were commenced against Boston from Cobble Hill, Lechmere's Point, and Lamb's Dam, Roxbury. It shattered many houses, and one shot wounded six men in a regimental guard-house. The British returned the fire with spirit, and threw a thirteen-inch shell as far as Prospect Hill, but did no essential damage. The Americans, in firing, burst two thirteen-inch mortars, — one of them the "Congress," — and three ten-inch mortars. They had not been properly bedded. A similar cannonade was continued on the night of Sunday, the third of March.

On the night of Monday, March 4th, the attention of the British was again occupied by a severe cannonade. In return they fired shot and shells. But while the occupants of Boston were employed in their personal safety, and with the damage done to buildings, the American camp was full of activity. About seven o'clock, General Thomas, with two thousand men, marched to take possession of Dorchester Heights. A covering party of eight hundred led the way; the carts with the intrenching tools followed; then twelve hundred troops, under the immediate command of General Thomas; and a train of three hundred carts, loaded with fascines and hay, brought up the rear. The detachment, mov-

orders of his commanding officer, he will be instantly shot down as an example of cowardice ; cowards having too frequently disconcerted the best formed troops by their dastardly behavior."

ing with the greatest silence, reached its place of destination about eight o'clock. The covering party then divided, — one half proceeding to the point nearest Boston, and the other half to the point nearest to the castle, — while the working party commenced labor. Bundles of hay were placed along Dorchester Neck, on the side next to the enemy, by which the carts passed, some of them several times, during the night. The occasion was one of intense interest and excitement. The moon shone brightly, cannon and mortars sounded a continuous roar, and shells occasionally burst high in the air.[1] At about four in the morning, a relief party went on. The labors of the night, under the direction of the veteran Gridley and Colonel Rufus Putnam, were such that, ere morning dawned, two forts were in sufficient forwardness to constitute a good defence against small arms and grape shot. "Perhaps," Heath writes, "there never was so much work done in so short a space of time."

The day following, March 5, was memorable as the anniversary of the "Boston Massacre." The British were again astonished to see the redoubts that had been so quickly thrown up by the Americans, and that loomed with so threatening an aspect in the haze of early dawn. "The rebels have done more in one night than my whole army would have done in a month," is said to have been General Howe's remark. "It must have been the employment of at least twelve thousand men," he wrote to Lord Dartmouth. One of his officers wrote: "They were raised with an expedition equal to that of the Genii belonging to Aladdin's Wonderful Lamp." But astonishment soon gave way to reflection. These works commanded both the harbor and the town. Admiral Shuld-

---

[1] Report of the number of shot and shells fired into Boston on the night of the 4th of March, 1776 : —

Lamb's Dam. — Five 13 inch shells, six 10 inch shells — 11 ; forty-two 24 pound shot, thirty-eight 18 pound shot — 80.

Lechmere's Point. — Thirty-two 24 pound shot, fourteen 18 pound shot — 46. Two 10 inch shells.

Cobble Hill. — Eighteen 1⌐ pound shot.

Total, — 144 shot, 13 shells.

HENRY KNOX, Colonel Regiment Artillery.

ham was decided in the opinion that the fleet could not ride in safety unless the Americans were dislodged; and the army was as insecure as the fleet. There were but two alternatives — either to evacuate the town, or to drive the Americans from their works. General Howe promptly made his decision. He entertained a high sense of British honor, as well as of his own honor. He commanded a force, which, by loyalists here, and by the government at home, was considered sufficient to look down all opposition; and which, in the character of its officers, in the disposition and ardor of the men, and in its powerful train of artillery, would be considered respectable in any country, and dangerous by any enemy. With such means at command, to give up the town that had been the original cause of the war, and the constant object of contention since its commencement, to a raw and despised militia, seemed, exclusive of other ill consequences, a disgrace too great to be borne.[1] He therefore resolved to hazard much, rather than to submit to such an indignity; and so critical was his situation, that he determined to attack the new works with all the force he could bring to bear on them.

Accordingly, twenty-four hundred men were ordered to embark in transports, rendezvous at Castle William, and at night make an attack on the works. The command was assigned to the brave, generous, chivalric Earl Percy. These preparations were observed in the American camp.

It was now a time of intense interest with Washington and his whole army; and the surrounding heights were again filled with spectators, in the expectation of seeing the scenes of Bunker Hill acted over again. The command of General Thomas, reinforced by two thousand men, was in high spirits, and ready and anxious to receive the enemy. No labor had been spared to make the works strong. The hills on which they were built being steep, rows of barrels, filled with loose earth, were placed in front, to be rolled down, and thus to break the attacking columns. Washington came upon the ground; "Remember it is the 5th of March, and avenge the death of your brethren," he said, as he animated the troops.

[1] Annual Register, 1776.

He fully expected an engagement, and was highly gratified with the temper and resolution of his army.

Meantime a fine detachment of four thousand chosen troops was under parade at Cambridge, near fort number two, ready to make an assault on the British lines in Boston. This detachment was arranged in two divisions, — one under General Sullivan, and the other under General Greene, and the whole was commanded by General Putnam. On signals being given, they were to have embarked in the boats near the mouth of Charles River, and, under the cover of three floating batteries, to attack Boston. The first division was to land at the powder-house, and gain possession of Beacon Hill and Mount Horam; the second division was to land at Barton's Point, or a little south of it, and, after securing that post, join the other division, force the gates and works at the neck, and let in the troops from Roxbury.

But the two armies, thus ready and anxious for a conflict that could not have failed to have been bloody and destructive, were not yet permitted to meet. In the afternoon the wind blew furiously, and prevented the ships from reaching their destination; and so great was the surf on the shore where the boats were to have landed, that they could not live in it. The attempt, therefore, became impracticable. The following day the wind was boisterous, and the rain was excessive. The attack was still further delayed, while the Americans continued to strengthen their works. General Howe, at length, was forced to abandon his plan, and the troops returned to Boston. Washington had made arrangements so satisfactory to himself, — so completely was everything working according to his wishes, — that he could not forbear lamenting his disappointment at not meeting the enemy.[1]

---

[1] Gordon (vol. II., p. 39) states, that, at the council of war called to fix upon the time for taking possession of Dorchester Heights, the Quartermaster-general, Colonel Mifflin, was summoned for the first time. He was in favor of the night of the 4th, as it would have a great effect, in case of a battle the next day, to remind the troops of the "massacre." General Gates thought it an improper time, and it was carried for that night by one majority.

General Howe's situation, on the 7th of March, was perplexing and critical. The fleet was unable to ride in safety
in the harbor. The army, exposed to the mercy of the American batteries, not strong enough to force the lines, was humiliated and discontented. The loyalists were expecting and
claiming the protection that had been so often guaranteed to
them. In addition, the belief was general that no despatches
had been received from the government since October.
"This," a British letter states, "could not fail of making
everybody feel uneasy; it looked as if we were left destitute,
to get out of a bad scrape as we liked best." "The fleet and
army complain of each other, and both of the people at
home." To remain in Boston was to expose the troops to the
greatest danger; to withdraw from Boston would occasion a
severe loss of property. General Howe convened his officers
in council, and made a speech so able as to carry conviction.
It was determined, at whatever cost, to save the army; and
on this eventful day of anxiety and alarm General Howe
resolved to evacuate the town. The conclusion was a mortifying one. He had, in letters to the ministry, scorned the
idea that he was in danger from his antagonist, and wished
the "rebels" would "attempt so rash a step" as to attack
him; the "rebels" had no sooner placed themselves in a position that was equivalent to an attack, than he felt obliged to
quit, without an effort, the strong-holds that had so long sheltered him. Nor was this all. He had given to the ministry
strong reasons why the army should not move from Boston
until reinforced: as he was sailing out of the harbor he
received the reply of the ministry, who supposed him still at
his post, approving of his resolution to remain, as an evacuation, under such circumstances, would be an unadvisable
measure !

This resolution came unexpected to the Tories. "Not the

Notwithstanding the intense anxiety of this day, Rev. Peter Thatcher, of
Malden, delivered at Watertown the customary oration in commemoration of
the massacre, before a meeting of the citizens of Boston legally warned. It
was received with universal approbation. A committee was appointed to
thank the orator in the name of the town, and to request a copy for the press.
Dr. Cooper made the prayer on this occasion.

last trump," Washington wrote, "could have struck them with greater consternation." They were unprepared to see a power they regarded as invincible baffled by an army they affected to despise; and rather than meet their offended countrymen, they preferred to brave the dangers of a tempestuous voyage, to endure the annoyance of insufficient accommodation, and, with whatever property they might save, to follow the fortunes of the disgraced army. "The people of the town," a letter states, "who were friends of the government, took care of nothing but their merchandise, and found means to employ the men belonging to the transports in embarking their goods; by which means several of the vessels were entirely filled with private property, instead of the king's stores." Thus, in the scramble and confusion, the public good shrunk into insignificance, compared with private interests; and hence it was that such large quantities of military stores were left behind. The British commander, however, immediately commenced preparations for departure. Ammunition, warlike magazines of all kinds, were put on board the ships; heavy artillery were dismounted, spiked, or thrown into the sea; and some of the works were demolished. "The necessary care of the women, children, sick, and wounded," a letter states, "required every assistance that could be given. It was not like the breaking up of a camp, where every man knows his duty; it was like departing your country, with your wives, your servants, your household furniture, and all your encumbrances. The officers, who felt the disgrace of a retreat, kept up appearances. The men, who thought they were changing for the better, strove to take advantage of the present times, and were kept from plunder and drink with difficulty." General Howe, in his official account to the Earl of Dartmouth, says: "A thousand difficulties arose on account of the disproportion of transports for the conveyance of the troops, the well-affected inhabitants,[1] their most valuable

---

[1] Lord Dartmouth, as early as August 2, 1775, wrote to General Gage: "If we are driven to the difficulty of relinquishing Boston, care must be taken that the officers and friends of the government be not left exposed to the rage and insult of rebels, who set no bounds to their barbarity."

property, and the quantity of military stores to be carried away."

The keenest anxiety was now felt for the fate of Boston. The idea of its destruction had been entertained, at various times, in both of the hostile camps. Heretofore the danger had been from without. Its friends, moved by the stern dictates of patriotism, had resolved to offer it, if necessary, as a sacrifice on the altar of American freedom. Now, however, the danger came from within. General Howe threatened to destroy it in case his army was assaulted. The admiral moved his ships in fearful array round the town; while the melancholy ruins of Charlestown made the inhabitants sensibly feel that the threat might not prove an idle one. They took measures to avert, if possible, so great a calamity. A delegation of influential citizens communicated with the British commander, through General Robertson. The following formal statement of the result of that conference, having no special address, but intended for General Washington, was sent by Messrs. Amory and Johonnot to the American lines by a flag of truce : —

Boston, 8th March, 1776.

As his excellency General Howe is determined to leave the town, with the troops under his command, a number of the respectable inhabitants, being very anxious for its preservation and safety, have applied to General Robertson for this purpose, who, at their request, has communicated the same to his excellency General Howe, who has assured him that he has no intention of destroying the town, unless the troops under his command are molested during their embarkation, or at their departure, by the armed force without; which declaration he gave General Robertson leave to communicate to the inhabitants. If such an opposition should take place, we have the greatest reason to expect the town will be exposed to entire destruction. Our fears are quieted with regard to General Howe's intentions. We beg we may have some assurance that so dreadful a calamity may not be brought on by any measures without. As a testimony of the truth of the above, we have signed our names to this paper, carried out by Messrs.

Thomas and Jonathan Amory and Peter Johonnot, who **have,** at the earnest entreaties of the inhabitants, through the lieutenant-governor, solicited a flag of truce for this purpose.

JOHN SCOLLAY,
TIMOTHY NEWELL,
THOMAS MARSHALL,
SAMUEL AUSTIN.

This paper was received at the lines at Roxbury by Colonel Learned, who carried it to head-quarters; and in return, the next day, wrote to the messengers as follows : —

Roxbury, March 9, 1776.

Gentlemen, — Agreeably to a promise made to you at the lines yesterday, I waited upon his excellency General Washington, and presented to him the paper handed to me by you, from the selectmen of Boston. The answer I received from him was to this effect : 'That, as it was an unauthenticated paper, without an address, and not obligatory upon General Howe, he would take no notice of it.' I am, with esteem and respect, gentlemen, your most obedient servant,

EBENEZER LEARNED.

To Messrs. AMORY and JOHONNOT.[1]

This answer was, apparently, uncompromising. Neither party, however, desired a general action. Washington's object was to gain possession of the town, and it was in accordance with his principles and feelings to accomplish it, if possible, without bloodshed. Humanity and policy united to save it from the ravage and destruction that would inevitably accompany an assault. Howe's object was to save his army. He did not feel strong enough to meet his antagonists in the neighborhood of Boston. He could not act to advantage in this quarter. And it was his policy to avoid risk, and try his fortune, with all the force he could command, on a new field. Hence this informal negotiation, without placing either party under obligations, produced a tacit understanding between both parties that saved much bloodshed. General Howe left the town without doing material injury to it, and General

---

[1] Sparks' Writings of Washington, vol. III., Appendix

Washington allowed the troops to embark without molestation. The American army was held in readiness to make an
assault at any moment, in case indications appeared that
injury was intended to the town.

Washington, however, went on with his preparations. On
the 9th he planted a battery at the north-east of Bird's Hill,
near the water at Dorchester Neck, with the intention of
annoying the British shipping. Nook's Hill, situated also in
Dorchester, which was still nearer Boston, and which completely commanded it, was especially dreaded by the British
commander. Its possession by the Americans would place him
entirely at their mercy. At night a strong detachment was
sent to plant a battery there, and act as circumstances might
require. Some of the men imprudently kindled a fire behind
the hill, which revealed their purpose to the British, who
commenced a severe cannonade upon them. This proved
another dreadful night to the terror-stricken people of Boston.
During the whole of it there was a roar of cannon and mortars, — on the part of the Americans, from Cobble Hill, Lechmere's Point, Cambridge, and Roxbury, — on the British side,
from the lines on the Neck and the castle. More than eight
hundred shot were fired during the night. Five Americans
were killed, and the works at Nook's Hill were suspended.[1]

[1] Mrs. Adams, in a letter commenced March 2, and closed Sunday evening, March 10, gives a vivid description of the cannonade during this period.
The following are extracts from this letter : —

March 2.

I have been in a continual state of anxiety since you left me. It has been
said " to-morrow," and " to-morrow," for this month, but when the dreadful
to-morrow will be I know not. But hark ! The house this instant shakes
with the roar of cannon. I have been to the door, and find it is a cannonade
from our army. Orders, I find, are come, for all the remaining militia to
repair to the lines Monday night, by twelve o'clock. No sleep for me
to-night.

Sunday Evening, 3d March.

I went to bed after twelve, but got no rest ; the cannon continued firing,
and my heart beat pace with them all night. We have had a pretty quiet
day, but what to-morrow will bring forth, God only knows.

Monday Evening.

I have just returned from Penn's Hill, where I have been sitting to hear
the amazing roar of cannon, and from whence I could see every shell which

This movement, however, hastened the preparations of General Howe. He issued (10th) a printed proclamation, ordering the inhabitants to deliver all linen and woollen goods to Crean Brush. In concluding, this document stated that, "If, after this notice, any person secretes or keeps in his possession such articles, he will be treated as a favorer of the rebels." But a written commission given this day, under General Howe's signature, to this officer, went much further. It stated that there were in town large quantities of goods, which, "in the possession of the rebels, would enable them to carry on war;" and authorized him to "take possession of all such goods as answered this description," and put them on board the Minerva ship, and brigantine Elizabeth.[1]

was thrown. The sound, I think, is one of the grandest in nature, and is of the true species of the sublime. 'T is now an incessant roar ; but O, the fatal ideas which are connected with the sound ! How many of our dear countrymen must fall !

Tuesday Morning.

I went to bed about twelve, and rose again a little after one. I could no more sleep than if I had been in the engagement ; the rattling of the windows, the jar of the house, the continual roar of twenty-four-pounders, and the bursting of shells, give us such ideas, and realize a scene to us of which we could scarcely form any conception. * * I hope to give you joy of Boston, even if it is in ruins, before I send this away.

Sunday Evening, March 10.

A most terrible and incessant cannonade from half-after eight till six this morning. I hear we lost four men killed, and some wounded, in attempting to take the hill nearest to the town, called Nook's Hill. We did some work, but the fire from the ships beat off our men, so that they did not secure it, but retired to the fort upon the other hill. — Mrs. Adams' Letters, pp. 68—71.

[1] Most, if not all, the printed proclamations of Howe, during the siege, are among the rich collections of the Massachusetts Historical Society. They were circulated in hand-bills. The following is copied from the original, with General Howe's autograph, in the office of the Secretary of State :

Sir, — I am informed there are large quantities of goods in the town of Boston, which, if in possession of the rebels, would enable them to carry on war. And whereas I have given notice to all loyal inhabitants to remove such goods from hence, and that all who do not remove them, or deliver them to your care, will be considered as abettors of rebels. You are hereby authorized and required to take into your possession all such goods as answer this description, and to give certificates to the owners that you have received them for their use, and will deliver them to the owners' order, unavoidable accidents

This day (10th) the horse transports were ordered to fall down to Castle William. A large body of the grenadiers and light-infantry, and the fifth and tenth regiments, were selected to cover the retreat by land, and the Chatham and Fowey ships, by water. Many cannon were spiked, many gun-carriages were broken, and much ammunition was thrown over the wharves. The army was much embarrassed between the necessity of being continually on duty, and the immediate attention required to save property. Many of the officers had laid out money in furniture and conveniences to make their situation comfortable. No purchasers of these articles could now be found. The crisis left no choice of measures, and regrets were useless. The embarkation of stores and people went on. Some, ascertaining they could not carry their furniture with them, began to destroy it.

The day following (11th) was signalized by the operations of Crean Brush. He was a conceited New York Tory, as ignorant of the American character as he was insolent in the discharge of his official duties. At the head of parties of Tories, under cover of his commission, he broke open stores, stripped them of their goods, and carried them on board the ships. It is not strange that this authorized plunder was imitated by lawless bands of men from the fleet and the army. They broke open shops and dwelling-houses, "carrying destruction," says Gordon, "wherever they went; what they could not carry away they destroyed." The next day (12th) the same scenes were renewed, though expressly forbidden in orders. Those found guilty of plundering, or in firing a house, were threatened with death.[1]

excepted. And you are to make inquiry if any such goods be secreted or left in stores ; and you are to seize all such, and put them on board the Minerva ship, or the brigantine Elizabeth. Given under my hand, at headquarters, Boston, this tenth day of March, 1776.

W. Howe, Com. Chief

To Crean Brush, Esquire.

[1] The details of the last days of the British in Boston are given in British letters, and in Mss. in the State House. The brigantine Elizabeth was captured, with Crean Brush on board, and among the Mss. are depositions respecting his conduct, his commission, lists of goods &c. Gordon writes, March 6th, from a journal kept in Boston, and gives many interesting facts — History, vol. ii., p. 42.

On the 14th the streets in different parts of the town were
barricaded, and dispositions were made for a departure.
Stores were plundered by sailors, acting under their officers,
and under the pretext of orders from the admiral.[1] On the
15th proclamation was made by the crier for the inhabitants
to keep in their houses from eleven o'clock in the morning
until night, to prevent them from annoying the troops during
their embarkation. But an easterly breeze sprung up, and
the army was ordered to its barracks. On the 16th the troops
did much mischief by defacing furniture, damaging goods, and
breaking open stores. They were only waiting a fair wind to
go on board the ships.

During this exciting period the journals continued to chronicle the success of the Americans on the sea. On the 6th it
was announced that the Yankee Hero had sent into Newbury-
port a fine brig of 200 tons burden; and, on the 14th, that
Captain Manly had sent into Portsmouth an armed ship of
240 tons, loaded with provisions for Boston; and had also
sent into Cape Ann a ship of 300 tons, filled with stores for
the army. A transport brig of fourteen guns, laden with
naval stores and provisions, ran ashore at the back of the
cape. The people boarded her, and unloaded her cargo. She
had on board five barrels of powder, and five hundred pounds
of specie.

In the mean time Washington, who had but partial information of the proceedings in Boston, became more and more
impatient to see the British evacuate it. He wrote to Congress on the 13th, that he "fully expected, before this, that
the town would have been entirely evacuated." He felt that

---

[1] On this day General Howe issued the following order: —

March 14. — The commander-in-chief finding, notwithstanding former
orders that have been given to forbid plundering, houses have been forced
open and robbed, he is therefore under a necessity of declaring to the troops
that the first soldier who is caught plundering will be hanged on the spot.

The commander-in-chief, having been informed that depredations have been
committed in the town-house, offers the following rewards to any person or
persons who shall convict any person or persons of cutting and defacing the
king's and queen's picture, and destroying the records and other public
papers, viz: For the king's picture £50, for the queen's picture £50, for
other pictures, records, and public papers, £20.

Howe might be deceiving him, and that the arrival of additional troops and vessels, hourly expected, might change the aspect of affairs. On this day a council of war was held at General Ward's quarters, in Roxbury, — Washington, Ward and Putnam, Thomas, Sullivan, Heath, Greene and Gates, were present. It was determined that if Boston were not evacuated the next day it would be advisable, "at all events," to fortify Nook's Hill the next night. It was also determined to detach the rifle battalion and five regiments the next day to New York. It was also concluded, that, should Boston be evacuated, it would be unnecessary to employ any part of the army for the defence of Massachusetts, as its militia were adequate for this work. Orders were immediately issued for the rifle battalion to be in readiness to march the next day by ten o'clock; and for Stark's, Webb's, Patterson's, Greaton's, and Bond's regiments, to march on Friday. These regiments, however, did not march for New York until the 18th. The orders of the day threaten any who, on the retreat of the enemy, should be detected in pillaging in Boston, with the severest punishment. "The inhabitants of that distressed town," they say, "have already suffered too heavily from the iron hand of oppression. Their countrymen surely will not be base enough to add to their misfortunes."

On Saturday, March 16, Washington brought matters to a crisis. A strong detachment was sent to Nook's Hill to fortify it. The British discovered it, and cannonaded it during the night. The Americans did not return the fire, but maintained their ground. General Howe then resolved to evacuate the town without further delay. He commenced very early in the morning of Sunday, March 17th, the embarkation of his army. About nine o'clock the garrison left Bunker Hill, and a large number of boats, filled with troops and inhabitants, put off from the wharves of Boston.[1]

[1] A British officer writes as follows, of the embarkation: "Nantasket Road, March 17. — According to my promise, 1 proceed to give a brief account of our retreat, which was made this morning between the hours of two and eight. Our troops did not receive the smallest molestation, though the rebels were all night at work on the near hill which I mentioned to you in my last letter, and we kept a constant fire upon them from a battery o.

When these movements were observed in the American camp, the troops stationed at Cambridge and Roxbury paraded. General Putnam, at the head of several regiments, embarked in boats in Charles River, and landed at Sewall's Point. Though a large body of the enemy was seen to leave Bunker Hill, yet the sentries appeared to be faithfully performing their duties. Two men, however, sent forward to reconnoitre, found that the fortress was left in charge of wooden sentinels, and immediately gave the joyous signal that it was evacuated. A detachment soon took possession of it. General Putnam ordered another detachment to march forward and take possession of Boston, while the remainder of the troops returned to Cambridge. Meantime, General Ward, with about five hundred troops from Roxbury, under the immediate command of Colonel Ebenezer Learned, who unbarred and opened the gates, entered Boston in that direction, Ensign Richards bearing the standard. They picked their way through great numbers of crow's-feet, which had been scattered over the Neck by the enemy, to retard the advance of an attacking force. The command of the whole was assumed by General Putnam, who proceeded to occupy the important posts, and thereby become possessed, the New England Journal says, "in the name of the thirteen United Colonies of North America, of all the fortresses of that large and once flourishing metropolis, which the flower of the British army, headed by an experienced general, and supported by a formidable fleet of men-of-war, had but an hour before evacuated in the most precipitous and cowardly manner."

The small-pox prevailed in some parts of the town, and Washington was obliged to adopt stringent measures to preserve the health of the troops. He positively forbade, on the

---

twenty-four-pounders. They did not return a single shot. It was lucky for the inhabitants now left in Boston they did not ; for I am informed everything was prepared to set the town in a blaze, had they fired one cannon. The dragoons are under orders to sail to-morrow for Halifax, — a cursed cold, wintry place, even yet ; nothing to eat, less to drink. Bad times, my dear friend. The displeasure I feel from the very small share I have in our present insignificancy is so great, that I do not know the thing so desperate I would not undertake, in order to change our situation."

19th, all officers, soldiers, and others, from entering Boston without a pass, or without being sent on duty. The orders of this day say : "As soon as the selectmen report the town to be cleansed from infection, liberty will be given to those who have business there to go in. The inhabitants belonging to the town will be permitted to return to their habitations, proper persons being appointed at the Neck, and at Charlestown Ferry, to grant them passes."

On the next day (20th) the main body of the army marched into Boston. "While marching through the streets," Thatcher writes, "the inhabitants appeared at their doors and windows; though they manifested a lively joy at being liberated from their long confinement, they were not altogether free from a melancholy gloom which ten tedious months' siege has spread over their countenances."

On the 21st Washington issued a proclamation calculated to maintain amity between the troops and the citizens. It called upon the inhabitants to make known to the quartermaster-general "all stores belonging to the ministerial army" that might be secreted in the town ; and it enjoined on the officers of the army "to assist the civil magistrates in the execution of their duty, and to promote peace and good order."

On the 22d a concourse of people, full of friendly solicitude, crowded into town. "It is truly interesting," writes Thatcher, "to witness the tender interviews and fond embraces of those who have been long separated, under circumstances so peculiarly distressing."

General Howe's effective force, including seamen, was about eleven thousand men. More than a thousand refugees left Boston with the army, as follows : — members of the council, commissioners, custom-house officers, and other persons who had been in some official station, one hundred and two; clergy, eighteen; persons from the country, one hundred and five; merchants and other inhabitants of Boston, two hundred and thirteen; farmers, traders and mechanics, three hundred and eighty-two; total, nine hundred and twenty-four. All these returned their names on their arrival at Halifax. About two hundred others did not return their names. The fleet dropped down to Nantasket Road, where it lingered ten days. During this period the enemy burnt the block-house and barracks, and demolished the fortifications on Castle William.   On the 27th of March the greater part of the fleet sailed for Halifax.[1]

Washington, on the 18th, ordered five regiments, and a portion of artillery, under General Heath, to march for New York.   He felt much embarrassed by the stay of the fleet at Nantasket.   On learning its departure, he ordered the whole army to the south, with the exception of five regiments left for the protection of Boston, under General Ward.   On the 27th, a brigade, under General Sullivan, marched; on the 1st of April, another division; and on the 4th, General Spencer, with the last brigade.   On this day Washington also left Cambridge for New York.

The British left a few vessels at Nantasket, where they continued to lie for over two months, to the great annoyance of the people.   The fleet consisted of a fifty-gun ship, Commodore Banks, the Milford, the Yankee Hero, (captured by the Milford,) an armed brig, and two schooners.   They were subsequently joined by seven transports filled with Highlanders.

The five regiments left under the command of General Ward were stationed by Washington as follows : two in Boston, one at Dorchester Heights, one at Charlestown, and one at Beverly.   Such (April 16) continued to be their position.

[1] While lying in the harbor the officers wrote many letters descriptive of their feelings.   One writes, March 26 : "Expect no more letters from Boston.   We have quitted that place.   Washington played on the town for several days.   A shell, which burst while we were preparing to embark, did very great damage.   Our men have suffered.   We have one consolation left. You know the proverbial expression, 'neither Hell, Hull, nor Halifax,' can afford worse shelter than Boston.   To fresh provision I have, for many months, been an utter stranger.   An egg was a rarity.   Yet I submit.   A soldier may mention grievances, though he should scorn to repine when he suffers them.   The next letter from Halifax."

Another writes, March 25 : "We were cannonaded fourteen days by the provincial army, and at last, after many losses, embarked on board several vessels, and are got thus far.   The provincials fired eighteen-pounders, and threw an innumerable quantity of shells, into the town.   We do not know when we are going, but are in great distress.   The spectacle is truly terrible. I wish I was with you.   The provincials, after we left Boston, marched into it, with drums beating and colors flying."

Great apprehensions were entertained of a return of the British fleet, and complaints were made at the delay in completing fortifications for the defence of the harbor. The inhabitants volunteered to build a fort at Noddle's Island. A large number, among them several of the clergy, worked on it in the beginning of May until it was completed.

General Ward employed the troops left under his command also in throwing up works. He wrote to Washington (May 4) that the forts on Fort Hill, Boston, at Charlestown Point, and Castle Point, were almost completed, with a number of heavy cannon mounted in each; that a work was in good forwardness on Noddle's Island; and that a detachment of the army was at work at Castle Island, repairing the batteries there. These works were carried on under the immediate superintendence of Colonel Gridley.

In May there was a valuable prize taken within sight of the British fleet, which led to a sharp naval combat in the harbor. Captain James Mugford, of the schooner Franklin, one of the continental cruisers, (May 17,) fell in with the transport ship Hope, bound for Boston. He captured her without opposition. Captain Mugford determined on bringing his prize into Boston, but she ran ashore at Pulling Point. Her cargo was brought to town in a large number of boats. It contained a fine assortment of military stores; and as there were fifteen hundred whole barrels of powder, it was pronounced the most valuable prize that had been taken. On the 19th (Sunday) Captain Mugford, in the Franklin, fell down the harbor to sail on a cruise, but, in the evening, got aground at Point Shirley. A small privateer, the Lady Washington, also anchored near the Franklin. About midnight thirteen boats from the men-of-war at Nantasket attacked the two armed schooners. The crews of both fought their assailants with the greatest intrepidity. Captain Mugford sunk two of the boats. But while fighting bravely, he received a mortal wound. He still continued to animate his men, exclaiming, "Do not give up the ship, — you will beat them off!" In a few minutes he died. His men beat off the enemy's boats. No other American was killed. The remains of Captain Mugford were carried to Marblehead for interment.

Much impatience was felt by the people to have the British fleet driven from the harbor. It consisted (June) of eight ships, two snows, two brigs, and one schooner. They had several hundred Highlanders on board. General Benjamin Lincoln planned an expedition to drive the fleet to sea. The Council of Massachusetts ordered him to carry it into execution, and authorized him (June 11) to call out the militia for this purpose. On the 13th the people of Boston were notified, by beat of drum, that an enterprise was to be undertaken against the British at Nantasket, and to build fortifications in the lower harbor. General Ward ordered a part of the continental troops to aid in this work. Detachments from Colonels Marshall's and Whitney's regiments, and a battalion of the train under Lieut.-colonel Crafts, embarked at Long Wharf, and sailed for Pettick's Island and Hull. Here they were joined by additional troops and companies from the sea-coast. About six hundred men were gathered at each place. About the same number of militia from the towns about the harbor, and a detachment of artillery, took post on Moon Island, at Hoff's Neck, and at Point Alderton. A detachment of the army, under Colonel Whitcomb, with two eighteen-pounders and a thirteen-inch mortar, took post at Long Island. The whole were under Colonel Whitcomb.[1] Owing to a calm, the troops did not gain their stations until the morning of the

[1] General Ward's Letter, June 16, 1775 ; Gordon's History, II., p. 88 ; American Archives, vol. VI., p. 915 ; Life of General Lincoln.

In an account of this expedition a journal remarks : " It is worthy of special notice that the 14th of June, 1774, was the last day allowed for trading vessels to leave or enter the port of Boston, through the cruelty of a British act of Parliament ; and that the 14th of June, 1776, through the blessing of God upon the operations of a much injured and oppressed people, was the last day allowed for British men-of-war or ministerial vessels to remain, or enter within the said port but as American prizes. Thus has Providence retaliated."

This work was done at a fortunate time. In three days two British transports, the George and the Annabella, were captured after a short and sharp action. Among the trophies were Colorel Archibald Campbell, and about three hundred Highlanders. Major Menzies, of this corps, was killed in the action, and was interred in Boston the next day, with military honors. Two other transports, with Highlanders on board, were captured about this time, — the Ann and the Lord Howe.

14th. Shot were first discharged at the fleet from Long Island. Commodore Banks returned the fire with spirit until a shot pierced the upper works of his ship, when he made signals for the fleet to get under way, and after blowing up the light-house, went to sea. Thus was Boston harbor cleared of an enemy.

27

View of the lines on Boston Neck, from the Post near Brown's House.

CHAPTER XIII.

American Congratulations. British Comments. Condition of Boston.
Conclusion.

THE intelligence of the evacuation of Boston occasioned
great joy in the colonies. It was regarded as reflecting the
highest honor on Washington and his army, and, indeed, as a
glorious triumph. The result of this long siege was as
encouraging to the friends of American liberty as it was dis-
heartening to its enemies. Washington received congratulations from every quarter on his success.

The selectmen of Boston waited on the general, and presented to him the following address : —

May it please your Excellency, —

The selectmen of Boston, in behalf of themselves and fel-
low-citizens, with all grateful respect, congratulate your
excellency on the success of your military operations, in the
recovery of this town from an enemy, collected from the once
respected Britons, who, in this instance, are characterized by
malice and fraud, rapine and plunder, in every trace left
behind them.

Happy are we that this acquisition has been made with so
little effusion of human blood, which, next to the Divine
favor, permit us to ascribe to your excellency's wisdom, evidenced in every part of the long besiegement.

If it be possible to enhance the noble feelings of that person, who, from the most affluent enjoyments, could throw
himself into the hardships of a camp to save his country,
uncertain of success, 't is then possible this victory will height-
en your excellency's happiness, when you consider you have
not only saved a large, elegant, and once populous city from
total destruction, but relieved the few wretched inhabitants
from all the horrors of a besieged town, from the insults and
abuses of a disgraced and chagrined army, and restored many

inhabitants to their quiet habitations, who had fled or safety to the bosom of their country.

May your excellency live to see the just rights of America settled on a firm basis, which felicity we sincerely wish you; and, at a late period, may that felicity be changed into happiness eternal!

JOHN SCOLLAY,
TIMO. NEWELL,
THOS. MARSHALL,
SAMUEL AUSTIN,
OLIVER WENDELL,
JOHN PITTS,

Selectmen
of
Boston.

To His Excellency GEORGE WASHINGTON, Esq.,
General of the United Forces in America.

General Washington made the following reply to this address: —

To the Selectmen and Citizens of Boston, —

Gentlemen, — Your congratulations on the success of the American arms give me the greatest pleasure.

I most sincerely rejoice with you on being once more in possession of your former habitations; and, what greatly adds to my happiness, that this desirable event has been effected with so little effusion of human blood.

I am exceedingly obliged by the good opinion you are pleased to entertain of my conduct. Your virtuous efforts in the cause of freedom, and the unparalleled fortitude with which you have sustained the greatest of all human calamities, justly entitle you to the grateful remembrance of your American brethren; and I heartily pray that the hand of tyranny may never more disturb your repose, and that every blessing of a kind Providence may give happiness and prosperity to the town of Boston.

GEO. WASHINGTON.

On the 29th of March a joint committee from the Council and House of Representatives of Massachusetts waited upon Washington with a long and flattering testimonial. It alluded to the early resistance of this colony to the tyrannical policy, "impelled by self-preservation and the love of freedom;" to the satisfaction at the appointment of Washington to be the commander-in-chief; to the wisdom and prudence and success of his measures; and it concluded as follows: "May you still go on, approved by Heaven, revered by all good men, and dreaded by those tyrants who claim their fellow-men as their property. May the United Colonies be defended from slavery by your victorious arms. May they still see their enemies flying before you; and (the deliverance of your country being effected) may you, in retirement, enjoy that peace and satisfaction of mind which always attend the good and great; and may future generations, in the peaceable enjoyment of that freedom the exercise of which your sword shall have established, raise the richest and most lasting monuments to the name of Washington." To this address the general returned a feeling reply. At this time the current was setting strong in favor of a declaration of independence, and hence the allusion with which this reply closes: "May this distressed colony and its capital, and every part of this wide extended continent, through His Divine favor, be restored to more than their former lustre and happy state, and have peace, liberty, and safety, secured upon a solid, permanent, and lasting foundation."

Congress received the intelligence of the evacuation on the 25th of March, and immediately, on the motion of John Adams, passed a vote of thanks to Washington, and the officers and soldiers under his command, for their wise and spirited conduct, and ordered a gold medal to be struck and presented to the general. Also it raised a committee, consisting of John Adams, John Jay, and Stephen Hopkins, to prepare a letter of thanks. This letter was reported to Congress and adopted April 2.

Philadelphia, April 2, 1776.

Sir, — It gives me the most sensible pleasure to convey to you, by order of Congress, the only tribute which a free people will ever consent to pay, — the tribute of thanks and gratitude to their friends and benefactors.

The disinterested and patriotic principles which led you to the field have also led you to glory; and it affords no little consolation to your countrymen to reflect, that, as a peculiar greatness of mind induced you to decline any compensation

Copy of a Gold Medal presented to General Washington
by Congress on the Evacuation of Boston.

Arms of the Washington Family, obtained from the Heralds College London.
2. Copy of General Washington's Seal.

for serving them, except the pleasure of promoting their happiness, they may, without your permission, bestow upon you the largest share of their affection and esteem.

Those pages in the annals of America will record your title to a conspicuous place in the temple of fame, which shall inform posterity that, under your directions, an undisciplined band of husbandmen, in the course of a few months, became soldiers; and that the desolation meditated against the country by a brave army of veterans, commanded by the most experienced generals, but employed by bad men, in the worst of causes, was, by the fortitude of your troops, and the address of their officers, next to the kind interposition of Providence, confined for near a year within such narrow limits as scarcely to admit more room than was necessary for the encampments and fortifications they lately abandoned.

Accept, therefore, sir, the thanks of the United Colonies, unanimously declared by their delegates to be due to you, and the brave officers and troops under your command; and be pleased to communicate to them this distinguished mark of the approbation of their country.

The Congress have ordered a gold medal, adapted to the occasion, to be struck, and, when finished, to be presented to you.

I have the honor to be, with every sentiment of esteem, sir, your most obedient and very humble servant,

JOHN HANCOCK, President.

To His Excellency GENERAL WASHINGTON.

The medal, which was struck in Paris, from a die cut by Duvivier, contains on the obverse a head of Washington in profile, exhibiting an excellent likeness, and around it the inscription:

GEORGIO WASHINGTON SVPREMO DVCI EXERCITVVM ADSERTORI LIBERTATIS COMITIA AMERICANA.[1]

On the reverse is the town of Boston in the distance, with a fleet in view, under sail. Washington and his officers are on horseback in the foreground, and he is pointing to the ships as they depart from the harbor. The inscription is:

---

[1] Sparks' Washington. The description in the text is by Mr. Sparks

Hostibus primo fugatis Bostonium recuperatum, xvii. Mar-
tii, mdcclxxvi.

The congratulations of individuals were more spirited than
those of public bodies. An extract from one of the letters of
this period will show their tone. "What an occurrence is
this to be known in Europe!" writes Elbridge Gerry, March
26. "How are Parliamentary pretensions to be reconciled?
Eight or ten thousand British troops, it has been said, are sufficient to overrun America; and yet that number of their veterans, posted in Boston, (a peninsula fortified by nature,
defended by works the product of two years' industry, surrounded by navigable waters, supported by ships of war, and
commanded by their best generals,) are driven off by about
one-thirtieth of the power of America. Surely the invincible
veterans labored under some great disadvantage from want of
provisions or military stores, which the Americans were amply
provided with! Directly the reverse. They had provisions
enough; ammunition, muskets and accoutrements, for every
man, and a piece of ordnance for every fifteen; while the
Americans were almost destitute of all these, and after twelve
months' collection had only a sufficiency of powder to tune
their cannon for six or eight days. I am at a loss to know
how Great Britain will reconcile all this to her military
glory."

The intelligence was received with astonishment in England. The ministry were again deeply mortified. A brief
official announcement of the evacuation appeared in the London Gazette. It stated that General Howe, on the 7th of
March, determined to remove from Boston, and that the
"embarkation was effected the 17th of the same month, with
the greatest order and regularity, and without the least interruption."[1] Again, they kept back full intelligence of the

---

[1] The whole announcement was as follows: "White-Hall, May 3. — General Howe, commander-in-chief of his majesty's forces in North America,
having taken a resolution on the seventh of March to remove from Boston to
Halifax with the troops under his command, and such of the inhabitants,
with their effects, as were desirous to continue under the protection of his
majesty's forces; the embarkation was effected the 17th of the same month,
with the greatest order and regularity, and without the least irterruption

transaction, and affected to be not the least disconcerted by
the loss of Boston. Parliament was then in session, and the
subject was called up on the 6th of May by Colonel Barre,
who moved for an address to his majesty praying that copies
of the despatches of General Howe and Admiral Shuldham
might be laid before the House. His remarks were severe
against the ministry. He had been informed there was a
capitulation between Howe and Washington, through the
intervention of the selectmen, by which General Howe was to
leave his stores and not burn the town. But the Gazette did
not mention it, nor did it give the public any reasons for
Howe's quitting Boston. He trusted that the government
would present more satisfactory information than that of the
flimsy scrap of paper — the official account — which he held
in his hand. Lord North, in reply, stated that the army was
not compelled to abandon Boston; that the general did not
come in to any compromise whatever; that the troops embarked with all possible coolness and regularity, and even
perfectly at their ease; that the evacuation of Boston was no
loss of glory, no disgrace, it was only a change of place.
Great Britain had the same men and the same ships, but only
in another place. Lord John Cavendish said that the House
had proceeded from the beginning on actual misinformation;
that it was owned that the information was false, that the
whole British empire had been lost at the national expense of
twenty millions, in precisely eleven months from the date of
the defeat at Lexington to the evacuation of Boston. Mr.
Hartley insisted that General Howe was driven from Boston,
and that nothing but a dread of having his whole army cut
to pieces, or made prisoners, induced him to make so precipitate and unexpected a retreat; and that "the great chain
which held both countries was now broken," and that he
"feared America was forever lost." Mr. Burke declared that
every measure which had been adopted or pursued was

from the rebels. When the packet came away the first division of transports
was under sail, and the remainder were preparing to follow in a few days;
the admiral leaving behind as many men-of-war as could be spared from the
convoy, for the security and protection of such vessels as might be bound to
Boston."

direc;ed to impoverish England, and to emancipate America; and though in twelve months nearly two hundred pounds a man had been spent for salt beef and sour-kroute, that the troops could not have remained ten days longer if the heavens had not rained down manna and quails. Mr. Ellis regarded the evacuation of Boston as a diminution of credit, and a great calamity, and as a measure that would give éclat to the American cause; and that it was a reflection on General Howe to say it was anything else but a harsh necessity. General Conway affirmed that the British arms in this evacuation had been dishonored; that British councils had fallen into contempt, and the honor of the nation deeply wounded. Lord George Germaine's (the minister's) explanation was feeble. He understood that General Howe never intended to begin operations from Boston, and asserted there was no agreement between the two commanders: General Washington had changed his position, which, no doubt, obliged General Howe to change his position.

Another debate took place in the House of Lords. On the 10th of May the Duke of Manchester, — who made a call for the despatches, — in a remarkable speech reviewing the general policy of the ministry and the military operations, used severe language on the loss of Boston. He alluded to the martial spirit displayed by the Americans at Bunker Hill, where "an apothecary's late 'prentice (Warren) led forth armies, displayed the warrior's skill and intrepidity, and met a death a Roman might have envied;" in Arnold's expedition to Quebec — a march a Hannibal would have admired; in the siege of the British army and in forcing it from Boston. Here, he said, "We are informed of this extraordinary event by a gazette, published by authority from government, in which it is related that General Howe had quitted Boston; no circumstances mentioned to palliate the event, no veil but that of silence to cast over the disgrace. But, my lords, though government account is short and uncircumstantial, yet private intelligence, public report, on which, till it is with authenticity denied, I must rely, informs us that General Howe quitted not Boston of his own free will, but that a superior enemy, by repeated efforts, by extraordinary works, by fire of their batteries, rendered the place untenable. I mean not the least most distant censure on him; his reputation stands fixed on too firm a basis to be easily shaken; I do believe all that in that situation could by the best officers be attempted, was tried to the utmost. But, my lords, circumstances obliged him to quit that post he could not possibly maintain. The mode of the retreat may, to the general, do infinite honor, but it does dishonor to the British nation. Let this transaction be dressed in what garb you please, the fact remains, that the army which was sent to reduce the province of Massachusetts Bay has been driven from the capital, and that the standard of the provincial army now waves in triumph over the walls of Boston."

The Earl of Suffolk, in defence of the ministry, announced that Howe had instructions, as early as October, to quit Boston whenever he thought proper; that it was not intended to carry on military operations in Massachusetts; that it was only a shifting of position to carry into execution measures already agreed on, the first object of which was "to secure Halifax against any attack of the rebels;" that he could not perceive their superior courage, for they permitted the troops to embark without molestation; that there was no convention, stipulation, concession or compromise, whatever, made; that, after securing Halifax, the design was to penetrate by that way into the interior country, and pursue his future intended operations.

The Marquis of Rockingham was severe in his reply, because he was so exact in his facts. His information was derived from letters written on the spot. He contended that the troops were compelled to quit the town, and were permitted to quit it by agreement. He then alluded to the instructions given by the ministry to destroy the American towns, and asked, "Why not destroy the town in pursuance of the general instructions, when they thought proper to shift their position? or, if compelled to abandon it, why not raze it to the foundations, by way of retaliation? If there was no convention, no treaty or agreement, how will they answer to government of this disobedience of orders?" He then reca pitulated the events of the last days of the siege, and said

"If those accounts are true, of which I have very little doubt, your lordships will perceive, though possibly there might have been no formal convention or capitulation signed, which I understood was avoided by the generals on both sides, for particular reasons, that in whatever manner the business might have been negotiated, it had every substantial requisite of a treaty or compromise, as much as if it had been ever so solemnly authenticated or subscribed. The troops were permitted to evacuate the town without interruption, because they engaged, on the other hand, not to burn or destroy it, either previous to their departure, or after they got on board their ships."

The Earl of Effingham stated substantially the same facts. He affirmed, that after the prevention of the purposed attack on Dorchester Heights by a storm, the only alternative that remained for Howe, in order to save his army, was to enter into a convention.

The Earl of Sherburne went over the same ground, and made the same points. He then said : " 'The noble earl (Suffolk) who has this day entertained your lordships so ably tells you that General Howe has only shifted his position, — that he is gone to the relief of Halifax, which is in a defenceless state. Why was that place, from which such wonders are to be achieved, left in a defenceless state ? " He never understood an actual abandonment of an enterprise to be a shifting a position.

The ministry, immediately on receiving the official despatches, approved of the evacuation of Boston. Lord George Germaine (May 3, 1776) wrote to General Howe as follows : " The miscarriage of the despatches [1] has been very unfortunate, and your not having received supplies would have been fatal, but for the step you very prudently took of withdrawing from the town of Boston, which, under the circumstances you have stated, is a measure very much approved by the king, and, in the execution of which, you have given the fullest proof of his majesty's wisdom and discernment in the choice

[1] General Howe had received no letters from the government, when he wrote, since October 22, 1775. He sent his despatches by Major Thompson. afterwards the celebrated Count Rumford.

of so able and brave an officer to command his troops in America."

General Howe's conduct, during the siege, continued for years to be criticised in Parliament and out of it. He might complain with reason, after receiving the approval of ministers, that they should have kept silent when he was calumniated. In the newspapers and in pamphlets the comments were frequent and sharp. An extract from an article will indicate the nature of this criticism. After reviewing some of the incidents of the siege, the writer remarks : " Now, I beg leave to ask Sir William Howe, whether Boston was tenable or not ? He had, indeed, staked his reputation as a general on the affirmative. If it was not, how could he, or his favorite engineer, overlook this (Dorchester) post ? Could they suppose that the rebels, who, before winter, had made regular approaches to the foot of this hill, would fail, as soon as the season opened, to occupy the top of it ? Why were no precautions taken to prevent it ? Why was not a post established there, as at Bunker's Hill ? Or if Boston was tenable, as the general had pledged himself, and I confess I have not the least doubt of, why, in God's name, was it so shamefully abandoned ? Why were the army and the loyalists obliged to combat war, pestilence and famine, through the winter, at Boston, only to be hurried from it in the spring ? Or why was the town finally evacuated with circumstances so dispiriting to the troops, and so encouraging to the rebels ? All the cannon at Charlestown, the greatest part of those at the lines on the Neck, two thirteen-inch mortars, and other ordnance, amounting in the whole to (serviceable and unserviceable) one hundred pieces, great quantities of military stores, and even provisions, fell into the hands of the rebels. And as though something was still wanting to swell their triumph and make it complete, a convention was entered into with the rebels, with General Howe's knowledge and approbation, that the town should not be injured in case they would suffer the troops to embark without interruption. The agreement was religiously kept. As the last division of troops embarked at the Long Wharf, a flag was hoisted on the steeple of a church, and Washington entered the town with drums beat-

ing, music playing, colors flying, and in all the pride and
exultation of victory." [1]

However just, in a military point of view, the criticism
might have been, relative to the long neglect of Dorchester
Heights, no other course but an evacuation remained to General Howe after Washington had got possession of them.
Nor could he have prosecuted operations against the American
lines with any chance of success. They were numerous and
strong.   "Nothing," it has been remarked, "but the enthusiasm of liberty could have enabled the men of America to have
constructed such works. In history they are equalled only
by the lines and forts raised by Julius Cæsar to surround the
army of Pompey." [2]   Hence the British army accomplished
all that could be expected of an army placed in such a condition.

Washington's conduct met with universal approval.   The
people had been impatient to see the British driven out of Boston.   Congress shared this feeling, and hence the repeated
expression of its wish that Washington should venture an
assault.   It was doubted whether it was possible to keep the
army together during so long and wearisome a siege.   It was
supposed that the stimulus of a triumph was necessary to
sustain the American cause.   Washington felt all this, and
was not, also, indifferent to the wishes of Congress.   Hence

[1] This extract is taken from a pamphlet, entitled " A View of the Evidence
relative to the Conduct of the American War," &c., 1779. It was one of the
publications that caused General Howe to demand an inquiry into his operations in America. In the evidence given during this investigation, the
events of the siege occupy a conspicuous place.

The following extract from a speech of Mr. Wilkes, Nov. 18, 1777, will
show what language continued to be used in Parliament : — " Let us recollect, sir, what passed after Boston was taken by the British forces. Our
general was soon besieged in that capital of New England, ignominiously
cooped up there many months with twenty regiments, and at last driven from
thence. I know the coloring given to this retreat by the court party among
us, and have been nauseated with the cant terms of our generals' changing
their quarters, and shifting their positions ; but I know, likewise, that their
artillery and stores were left behind. All the military men of this country
now confess that the retreat of General Howe from Boston was an absolute
flight, — as much so, sir, as that of Mahomet from Mecca."

[2] Article in Silliman's Journal.

his repeated proposals to his general officers to make an attack
on Boston. However strong might have been his belief of
the feasibility of a successful assault, it can now be scarcely
doubted but that the adverse decisions of the councils of war
were correct.[1] Such enterprises are counted hazardous, even
when made by veterans in war. How much greater is the
hazard when raw levies are to be led against disciplined
troops, protected by intrenchments as strong as science and
labor can make them. When all the advantage that could
have been reasonably calculated on by an attack, had been
attained without the effusion of blood or the destruction of
property, when the British troops had been driven ingloriously
out of Boston, the censure that had been cast upon the Fabian
policy of Washington was changed into a general approval
of the wisdom of his councils. It was seen that the British,
in abandoning the town that had been proclaimed the cause
of the struggle, in reality suffered a defeat; and that the
Americans, in getting possession of it, in reality achieved a
triumph.

Boston was not injured so much, either by the bombardment or by the troops, as it had been reported. Dr. Warren
went in two hours after the British left. He writes in his
diary : " The houses I found to be considerably abused inside,
where they had been inhabited by the common soldiery, but
the external parts of the houses made a tolerable appearance.
The streets were clean, and, upon the whole, the town looks
much better than I expected. Several hundred houses were
pulled down, but these were very old ones." Washington
wrote to President Hancock that his house had received no
damage worth mentioning; that his family pictures were
untouched, and his furniture was in tolerable order; and that
the damage done to the houses and furniture generally was
not equal to the report; but that the inhabitants suffered
much from being plundered by the soldiery at their departure. Other contemporary letters contain similar statements
as to the general appearance of the town. The interior of
many of the houses had been badly used.[2]

[1] Reed's Life of President Reed, vol. i., p. 121.
[2] A report was prepared by the selectmen, agreeable to an order of the

Many of the public buildings were in a shameful condition. The Old South Church, obnoxious to the British on account of the town-meetings held in it, had been made a riding-school. Deacon Newell (October 27) writes in his diary as follows: "The spacious Old South meeting-house taken possession of for this purpose. The pulpit, pews and seats, all cut to pieces, and carried off in the most savage manner as can be expressed, and destined for a riding-school. The beau tiful carved pew, with the silk furniture, of Deacon Hubbard's, was taken down and carried to ——'s house by an officer, and made a hog-stye. The above was effected by the solicitation of General Burgoyne." Dirt and gravel were spread over the floor; the south door was closed; a bar was fixed, over which the cavalry leaped their horses at full speed; the east galleries were allotted to spectators; the first gallery was fitted up as a refreshment room. A stove was put up in the winter, and here were burnt for kindling many of the books and manuscripts of Prince's fine library. The parsonage house belonging to this society was pulled down for fuel.

The Old North Chapel, built in 1677, which was in good repair, and might have stood many years, was pulled down for fuel. The steeple of the West Church, built of large timber, was also taken down, and afforded no small supply. Many trees were cut down on the common, and in other places. The celebrated Liberty Tree furnished fourteen cords of wood. The common was much disfigured. Much of it was turned up into fortifications. Faneuil Hall was fitted up, by subscription, into a very neat theatre, under the countenance of General Howe. The Brattle-street Church[1] and the Hollis-street Church were occupied by the troops for barracks.

The most important of the fortifications were found entire, and exceedingly strong. Several persons, who went into

legislature, of the amount of damage suffered by Boston during the operation of the Port Bill and the siege. The total was estimated at £323,074 14s. 6d.

[1] A shot from the American lines struck the tower of this church, which was picked up by Mr. Turell, preserved in his family, and was subsequently fastened into the tower where it struck.

Boston soon after the British troops left it, have given partial descriptions of their appearance. "We found," one says, "the works upon the Neck entire, the cannon spiked up, the shells chiefly split, and many of the cannon carriages cut to pieces; these lines upon the Neck were handsomely built, and so amazingly strong that it would have been impracticable for us to have forced them. The other works were not so well constructed as I imagined we should have found them, especially at the bottom of the common, and on Beacon Hill. They appeared to be ill-constructed, and designed for little but to frighten us." [1]

Dr. Warren had an opportunity of seeing the forts as they were left by the enemy, and describes their appearance. Two redoubts, situated in the neighborhood of Beacon Hill, appeared to me, he says, "to be considerably strong. There were two or three half-moons at the hill upon the bottom of the common for small arms, and there were no embrasures at the redoubt above mentioned. Just by the shore, opposite Lechmere's Point, is a bomb battery, lined with plank, and faced with a parapet of horse-dung, being nothing but a simple line; near it lies a thirteen-inch mortar, a little moved from its bed. This is an exceeding fine piece, being, as I am sure, seven and a half inches thick at the muzzle, and near twice that over the chamber, with an iron bed all cast as one piece, the touch-hole spiked up. Just above it, upon the ascent of the hill, was a three-gun battery of thirty-two-pounders. The cannon are left spiked up, and shot drove into the boxes. There was only a simple line, being plank filled with dirt. Upon Beacon Hill were scarcely more than the fortifications of nature, — a very insignificant shallow ditch, with a few short pickets, a platform, and one twenty-four-pounder, which could not be brought to bear upon any part of the hill. This was left spiked up, and the bore crammed. Copp's Hill, at the north, was nothing more than a few barrels filled with dirt, to form parapets, — three twenty-four-pounders upon (a) platform, left spiked and crammed; all these, as well as the others, on carriages. The parapet in this fort, and on Beacon

[1] Edward Bangs' Ms. Diary, — for which, and for other favors, I am indebted to J. Wingate Thornton, Esq.

Hill, did not at all cover the men who should work the cannon. There was a small redoubt behind for small arms, very slender indeed. Fort Hill was only five lines of barrels filled with earth, very trifling indeed. Upon the Neck the works were strong, consisting of redoubts, numbers of lines with embrasures for cannon, a few of which were left as the others. A very strong work at the old fortification, and another near the hay-market. All these were ditched and picketed. Hatch's Wharf was a battery of rafters, with dirt, and two twelve-pounders, left as the others. One of these I saw drilled out and cleared for use, without damage. A great number of other cannon were left at the north and south batteries, with one or both trunnions beat off. Shot and shells in divers parts of the town, some cartridges, great quantities of wheat, hay, oil, medicine, horses, and other articles, to the amount of a great sum." Washington was evidently surprised at the formidable character of the main works. "The town of Boston," he writes, "was almost impregnable — every avenue fortified."

Charlestown presented one unbroken scene of desolation — here and there only a wall or a chimney. Dr. Warren, on the 21st of March, visited it, and described it as follows : — " This day I visit(ed) Charlestown, and a most melancholy heap of ruins it is. Scarcely the vestiges of those beautiful buildings remain to distinguish them from the mean cottages. The hill which was the theatre upon which the bloody tragedy of the 17th of June was acted commands the most affecting view I ever saw in my life. The walls of magnificent buildings tottering to the earth below — above, a great number of rude hillocks, under which are deposited the remains of clusters of those deathless heroes who fell in the field of battle. The scene was inexpressibly solemn. When I considered myself as walking over the bones of many of my worthy fellow-countrymen, who jeoparded and sacrificed their lives in these high places ; when I considered that whilst I (was) musing (on) the objects around me, I might be standing over the remains of a dear brother, whose blood had stained these hallowed walks; with veneration did this inspire me. How many endearing scenes of fraternal friendship

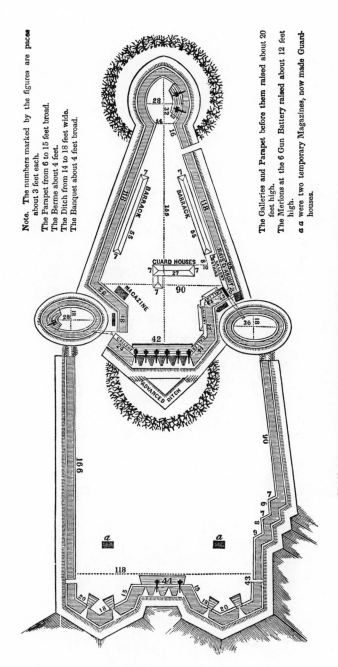

Note. The numbers marked by the figures are paces about 3 feet each.

The Parapet from 6 to 15 feet broad.
The Berme about 4 feet.
The Ditch from 14 to 18 feet wide.
The Banquet about 4 feet broad.

The Galleries and Parapet before them raised about 20 feet high.
The Merlons at the 6 Gun Battery raised about 12 feet high.
a a were two temporary Magazines, now made Guard-houses.

PLAN OF THE FORT ERECTED BY THE BRITISH ON BUNKER HILL

now past and gone forever, presented themselves to my view! But it is enough. The blood of the innocent calls for vengeance on the guilty heads of the vile assassins. O may our arms be strengthened to fight the battles of our God! When I came to Bunker Hill I found it exceeding strong. The front parapet, about thirteen feet high, composed of earth contain(ed) in plank, supported by huge timber, with two lookouts upon the top. In the front of this were two bastions, and a semi-circular line, with very wide trenches, and very long pickets as well as trenches. Within, the causeway was secured with a —— and brush. All that part of the main fort which was not included with(in) (the) high works above mentioned, viz., the rear, was secured by another parapet, with a trench picketed inside as well as out. There was a half-moon which commanded the river at the side." [1] Washington pronounced this work "amazingly strong." "Twenty thousand men," he says, "could not have carried it against one thousand, had that work been well defended." This work was destroyed by the American troops immediately after the British evacuated the town.[2] Dr. Warren describes the other works in Charlestown as follows: "There was a block-house upon School-house Hill, enclosed by a very strong fence spiked, and a dungeon and block-house upon Breed's Hill, enclosed in a redoubt of earth, with trenches and pickets. The works which had been cast up by our forces had been entirely levelled." [3]

[1] Dr. Warren's Diary. Some of this interesting Ms. is hardly legible.

[2] The barracks attached to this fortress were moved into various parts of Charlestown, and improved for dwelling-houses. The low building opposite the City Hall, in Bow-street, on the Austin estate, was one of these barracks. The groundwork of this fortress could be, until recently, very distinctly traced.

[3] I have been often informed that the redoubt and works raised by the Americans were entirely levelled by the British while they were in possession of Charlestown. Contemporary accounts, however, (except the one in the text,) do not indicate this. In Waller's Orderly Book, (Ms.,) kept in Charlestown, there are several allusions to the "Rebel Redoubt." A guard was immediately (June 19) stationed "in the redoubt stormed by the army;" it was ordered (June 20) to be cleared, and a shed built in it, to shelter the guard; the posts and rails were ordered (June 21) to be "carried to the redoubt, and piled up in order." The tools in the camp were ordered

I have attempted to present a faithful narrative of the opening scenes of the war of the American Revolution.   The siege
of Boston must be regarded not only as one of the most interesting incidents connected with this great contest, but as one
of the memorable events of history.   When the people of
Massachusetts saw that the British government was determined to inflict on them the blight of despotic law, — a law
that destroyed their ancient charter, and that undermined
their ancient liberties, — they resolved, at every hazard, to
resist its execution.   When a British army was concentrated
to enforce submission, they resolutely prepared for self-defence.
So thoroughly was this work done, and so strong was the sustaining sentiment of the community, that, on the first invasion
of their soil, it seemed as though the fable of the dragon's
teeth was realized in the armed hosts that started up to repel
the insult.   The expedition sent to Concord was driven back
in disgrace to its quarters; and, within twenty-four hours,
the whole British army was confined to the bounds of a small
peninsula, was cut off from all relief by land, and was
reduced to humiliating expedients for subsistence.

(August 5) to be "carried to the Rebel Redoubt."   Other redoubts in town
are named, as "the Grenadier Redoubt," which were undoubtedly thrown
up by the British troops.

In addition to this, General Wilkinson states in his memoirs, that, on the
evacuation of the town, he accompanied Colonels Stark and Reed over the
battle-field.   While he names "the vestiges" of the rail fence breastwork,
he speaks of "resting on the parapet" where the patriots fought.   He says:
"Arrived on the field of battle, where those officers had performed conspicuous parts, with anxious inquiry I traced the general disposition of our yeomanry on that eventful day, and the particular station of each corps; I
marked the vestiges of the post and rail fence on the left, and the breastwork
thrown up on the beach of Mystic River, which covered our armed citizens.
I paced the distance to the point from whence the British light-infantry, after
three successive gallant charges, were finally repulsed.   I examined the
redoubt, the intrenchment, the landings and approaches of the enemy, and
every point of attack and defence.   Resting on the parapet where, nine
months before, 'valor's self might have stood appalled,' I surveyed the
whole ground at a glance, and eagerly devoured the information imparted by
my brave companions."

The small mound on the north-eastern corner of the Monument-square is
said to be the remains of the original breastwork.

The British generals, after for sixty days denying the fact of being in a state of siege, determined to penetrate into the country. It was announced in England that General Gage would garrison Boston, and that Generals Howe, Clinton, and Burgoyne, would take the field, and disperse the colonial army. To carry out this plan, they fixed upon a time to occupy one of the heights of land that commanded their position. To their astonishment a redoubt suddenly appeared on another height, equally commanding in its position, which was filled with the daring Americans. To dislodge them, a detachment marched out to a conflict as bloody as history had on record. This experience appears to have changed the spirit of the British generals and the British troops. It shook out of them their arrogance and contempt. It made them respectful, if not timid. They afterwards manifested no disposition to measure strength with their antagonists. They attained to the belief that there was something about Massachusetts — either in the nature of the country or in the temper of its people — that made it a most unfit place for military operations. If they entertained offensive plans, they did not attempt to carry them into effect. And thus a well-appointed army, with accomplished officers, with cavalry and a fine train of artillery, supplied with every science of war, of undoubted bravery and backed by a powerful fleet, was satisfied if allowed to remain unmolested in its strongholds until it chose to change its position.

It was not so, however, with the Americans. They were at all times inadequately supplied with materials of war, and at some periods were alarmingly weak in point of numbers. Washington had difficulties that seemed insurmountable. He was even obliged to disband one army and to enlist another, in the face of his veteran enemy. But he went triumphantly through them all. He drew his lines each month closer about Boston. He proposed each month, after his works permitted it, an assault on the British army. It was judged inexpedient, for want of the necessary means, and of that steady discipline that can only be relied on in veterans. But such was the spirit of the army, that it engaged in daring enterprise on the land and in the harbor. When an adequate supply of powder and of other military stores was received, Washington occupied a position that compelled the British general to hazard a battle or to evacuate the town. Such, then, became his critical position, that he willingly entered into an informal understanding, by which, to secure his unmolested departure, he agreed not to injure the town. These considerations were as mortifying to the British as they were gratifying to the colonists. The abandonment of Boston, under such circumstances, was regarded in England as a flight, and in America as a victory.[1]

The patriots now felt their strength. They saw what four only of the colonies had done, and they could calculate what thirteen colonies might do. They felt that the same power of endurance, exerted in a righteous cause, would insure its ultimate triumph. Every scene of carnage and of desolation roused the spirit of the country, and weakened attachment to Great Britain. Every trial of their strength gave firmness to their resistance and elevation to their demands. When the siege of Boston commenced, the colonies were hesitating on the great measure of war, were separated by local interests, were jealous of each others' plans, and appeared on the field, each with its independent army under its local colors:

[1] It may be interesting to state, that all the British generals lived to see America triumphant.

General Gage, on his return to England, held conferences with the ministers on American affairs, but appears to have lived mostly in private life. He died in April, 1787.

General Howe, after serving at the south with doubtful reputation, returned to England after the campaign of 1777, and went through the ordeal of a severe inquiry. He died in 1814.

General Clinton succeeded General Howe in the command of the British army, and served till 1782, when he was superseded by General Carleton. He died December 22, 1795.

General Burgoyne returned to Boston as a prisoner of war. After his return to England, he joined the opposition, and advocated in Parliament a discontinuance of the war. He died August 4, 1792.

Lord Percy was much praised for his generosity and chivalry. His regiment suffered severely at the battle of Bunker Hill. He was kind to the officers and soldiers who were wounded, and to the widows of those who fell. " He is daily doing something great and commendable," wrote a grateful officer.

when the siege of Boston ended, the colonies had drawn the sword and nearly cast away the scabbard; they had softened their jealousy of each other; they had united in a political association; and the union flag of the thirteen stripes waved over a continental army. When the siege of Boston commenced, the general object and the general desire were for a work of restoration, for a return to the halcyon days of a constitutional connection with the mother country: when the siege of Boston ended, a majority of the patriots had irrevocably decided, that the only just and solid foundation for security and liberty was the creation of AN INDEPENDENT AMERICAN EMPIRE.

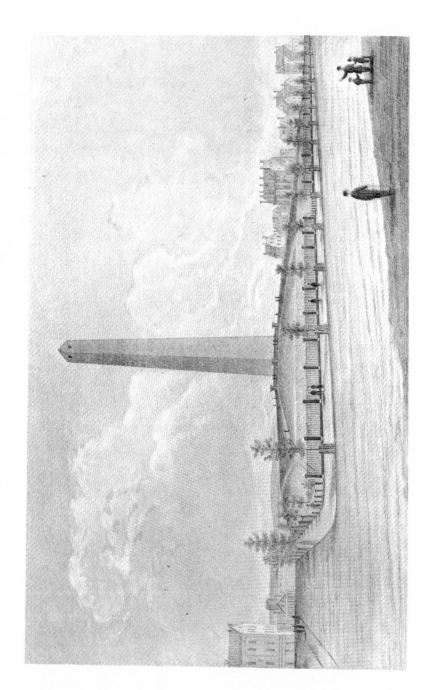

VIEW OF BUNKER HILL MONUMENT.

HISTORY

OF THE

BUNKER HILL MONUMENT.

It seems appropriate that a narrative of the early events of the war of the American Revolution should be accompanied with a history and description of the monument that gratitude and patriotism have raised to commemorate them. The account must, necessarily, be brief.[1]

It was contemplated early to erect a monument to the memory of General Warren. He presided over the Massachusetts grand lodge of Freemasons from its organization until his death. This lodge, after the evacuation of Boston, applied to the Massachusetts Council for permission to take up his remains, and bury them with the usual solemnities of the order. A committee of the Council reported (April 4, 1776) in favor of this petition, provided the design was carried out in such a manner that the government of the colony might have an opportunity to erect a monument to his memory. Though there was a procession, and an oration was delivered by Perez Morton, in honor of General Warren, no measures were taken to build a monument. The time of war, and the period immediately after it, were unfavorable for such a work.

The anniversary of the battle of Bunker Hill, for several years, passed unnoticed. The earliest general parade on this day was in 1786. It was, however, a celebration of the opening of Charles River Bridge. The toasts, songs, and

---

[1] The narrative in the text has been prepared from information derived from gentlemen who kindly communicated facts, from the records of associations, annual reports, letters, and newspapers. The documents in relation to the Bunker Hill Monument are voluminous.

speeches, which the occasion elicited, contain many allusions to the battle. The contrast presented in the celebration of one of the triumphs of peace, — the completion of the greatest enterprise of the kind undertaken in America, — with the terrific scene of war of eleven years previous, furnished themes of gratifying and patriotic remark.

The credit is due to the Charlestown Artillery of having been the first to celebrate the battle of Bunker Hill. The custom of parading on its anniversary has been kept up to the present time. In 1794 it celebrated the day with much parade. A portion of the military of Boston joined it; and, at its request, Dr. Bartlett delivered an oration in the meeting-house. There was also a procession. The whole proceedings gave great satisfaction.

King Solomon's Lodge was established in Charlestown in 1783; and the honor belongs to it of having first placed a monument on Breed's Hill. It appointed (November 11, 1794) a committee to erect such an one as would do honor to the lodge, and authorized it to draw on the treasurer to defray the expense. This work was promptly done, — the land being given for this purpose by Hon. James Russell. It was dedicated in the afternoon of the 2d of December. A procession was formed at Warren Hall, consisting of the members of the lodge, the municipal authorities of Charlestown, the ministers and military officers, the children of the public schools, and the citizens, which, accompanied by a band of music, "walked in solemn silence" to the hill. There a circle was formed round the pillar, and the master of the lodge, John Soley, Esq., delivered a neat and eloquent address. Minute-guns were then fired by a detachment of the Artillery, and the American flag was displayed at half-mast. The procession then returned to Warren Hall, where Dr. Josiah Bartlett delivered a eulogy on General Warren, and the ceremony was concluded by the following toast: "May the fragrance of a good report, like a sprig of cassia, bloom over the grave of every departed brother." The services throughout were impressive. The monument, and the dedication of it, reflect great credit on King Solomon's Lodge.

This monument, which stood a few rods west of the **present** monument, and on the spot where Warren fell, was a Tuscan pillar, built of wood, eighteen feet high, raised on a brick pedestal eight feet square, and rising ten feet from the ground. The pillar terminated in a gilt urn, bearing the inscription J. W., aged 35, — entwined with masonic emblems. The south side of the pedestal contained the following inscription:

Erected, A. D. MDCCXCIV.
By King Solomon's Lodge of Freemasons,
Constituted in Charlestown, 1783,
In Memory of
Major-general Joseph Warren,
And his Associates,
Who were slain on this memorable spot, June 17, 1775.

———

None but they who set a just value on the blessings of liberty are worthy to enjoy her.

In vain we toiled; in vain we fought; we bled in vain; if you, our offspring, want valor to repel the assaults of her invaders.

———

Charlestown settled, 1628.
Burnt, 1775.   Rebuilt, 1776.

———

The enclosed land given by the Hon. James Russell.

This monument cost about one thousand dollars. It was kept in repair by the lodge until 1825, when, with the land, it was presented to the Bunker Hill Monument Association.

The next celebration of this anniversary was by the Charlestown Artillery. At its request, William Austin, of Charlestown, delivered (June 17, 1801) an oration at the new meeting-house, which was published. On this occasion there was a procession, and, after the oration, a dinner at Warren Hall. The journals of the day contain full details of the proceedings. This celebration gave great gratification to those who participated in it, and reflected much credit on the company.

From the year 1801 to the year 1825, there appears to have been no general celebration of the day. The Charlestown Artillery continued its annual parade and salutes. Some years it was joined by a portion of the military of Boston, when the proceedings became sufficiently important to attract notice in the Boston journals. Occasionally there were dinners given, with the usual accompaniment of toasts and speeches. But no oration, during this period, appears to have been delivered.

Meantime the American revolution won more and more the admiration of the world. Public attention had been particularly called to its grand opening scene, the battle of Bunker Hill, and many regretted that no enduring memorial had been raised " to testify public gratitude, or do honor to national sentiment." [1] Among them was WILLIAM TUDOR, — an amiable man, an accomplished scholar, and a patriotic citizen. He desired to see on the battle-ground " the noblest column in the world ; " [2] and he was so ardent and persevering in urging such a project, that it has been stated that he first conceived the idea of it. [3] He watched this spot with great solicitude. Learning that a portion of it — about three acres — was to be sold, he conferred with several gentlemen as to the expediency of keeping it unoccupied. Dr. John C. Warren was one of them, who, with this object in view, purchased it, (November, 1822,) and held it until it was required by the Monument Association. Dr. Warren, thus energetic and early to promote this enterprise, continued to labor indefatigably in its behalf. Meetings of gentlemen friendly to it were held at his house. A party, who felt a deep interest in it, assembled also at Colonel Perkins' at breakfast, — among them Hon. Daniel Webster, Professor George Ticknor, Dr. John C. Warren, Hon. William

---

[1] The Massachusetts Legislature, February 1, 1818, instructed a committee to consider the expediency of building a monument of American marble to the memory of General Warren.

[2] The quotation is taken from a letter (1822) strongly urging that a monument should be built.

[3] Address of Hon. Edward Everett, May 28, 1833. " The idea was first conceived by an amiable and accomplished fellow-citizen, now no more, (the late William Tudor,) when the half century was near expiring since the occurrence of the event. It was by him communicated to a circle of friends, and by them to the public." He served as the first secretary, but soon sailed for South America. The records of the association contained the following : " June 7, 1825. — William Tudor, Esq., was chosen to fill the vacancy in the board of directors, as an acknowledgment of his services in promoting the objects of the association, he being at this time absent in South America." He was the author of the Life of Otis, Letters on the Eastern States Miscellanies, and Gebel Teir. He died at Rio Janeiro in 1830.

Sullivan, Hon. George Blake, and William Tudor, Esq. They then visited the battle-ground, and consulted in reference to building a monument. It was determined to commence the undertaking. Soon after, a circular, dated May 10, 1823, signed by Daniel Webster, William Tudor, and Theodore Lyman, Jr., invited the first meeting of a public nature of those friendly to it, to be held at the Merchants Exchange, Boston, on the following Tuesday.

The gentlemen who attended this meeting formed an association to procure an act of incorporation authorizing them, as trustees, to collect and hold subscriptions for the purpose of erecting an enduring monument "to the memory of those statesmen and soldiers who led the way in the American Revolution." Each one subscribed the sum of five dollars, and signed an agreement to this effect.[1] This meeting appointed H. A. S. Dearborn, William Tudor, and Theodore Lyman, Jr., to petition the legislature for an act of incorporation. Accordingly, an act was passed, — approved by the governor, June 7, 1823, — establishing the BUNKER HILL MONUMENT ASSOCIATION.

The Association held its first meeting June 13, 1823, and, on the 17th, made its first choice of officers. John Brooks, the governor of the state, was elected the president, and a code of by-laws was adopted. Many new members were elected by the original associates.[2] Little or no progress, however, was made this year in carrying forward the enterprise. At the

---

[1] The agreement was signed by the following persons : —

Daniel Webster,	Jesse Putnam,	Joseph Story,
Edward Everett,	Samuel D. Harris,	Samuel Swett,
Theodore Lyman, Jr.,	Stephen Gorham, Jr.,	William Tudor,
Thomas H. Perkins,	H. A. S. Dearborn,	Benjamin Gorham,
Franklin Dexter,	William Sullivan,	George Ticknor,
Charles R. Codman,	Warren Dutton,	Isaac P. Davis,
Thomas Harris,	Seth Knowles,	Benjamin Welles,
John C. Warren,	George Blake,	Francis C. Gray.
N. P. Russell,	Richard Sullivan,	

The names of all these persons, but two, appear in the act of incorporation.

[2] The Association elected 25 members, June 30, 1823 ; 65, August 21 1824 ; and 103, September 8, 1824.

next annual meeting, June 17, 1824, efficient measures were adopted. It was voted to have an annual celebration; and Hon. Daniel Webster was selected as the orator for 1825. A committee was appointed to gather memorials of the battle, and "to collect and arrange historically" all the documents relating to it. The directors were also instructed to prepare subscription papers. It was voted (September 3) that every person subscribing five dollars should belong to the Association, and be presented with an engraved diploma of his member-ship. The directors (September 20, 1824) issued a circular, from the pen of Hon. Edward Everett, — who, in preparing documents, and acting as secretary of the Association, labored most efficiently in its behalf, — which delineated the character of the battle and the object of the monument, and solicited the coöperation and interest of every member of the commu-nity. Another circular (October 1, 1824) was printed in sub-scription books, and sent to every town in Massachusetts. A third circular (January 19, 1825) repelled the charge that the directors desired to limit the subscriptions to Massachusetts. The other colonies, especially those of New England, had borne part in the great events designed to be commemorated, and its whole community were appealed to in behalf of the monument. The smallest sums were solicited, while the largest sums were not declined.

Circumstances proved favorable for the enterprise. It was a season of unusual prosperity, and the visit of LAFAYETTE, — his triumphal progress as the nation's guest, — made it a season of national enthusiasm. The directors invited him (August 21, 1824) to Bunker Hill. He accepted the invita-tion. On viewing the battle-ground, he expressed a lively interest in the proposed monument, and enrolled his name on a subscription list, — by special request of the directors, how-ever, with no sum set against it; and when Dr. Warren invited him to be present on the succeeding anniversary, he promptly acceded to the wishes of the Association. It was determined to celebrate the FIFTIETH JUBILEE with great splen-dor. The renown of the orator, the announcement (October 1, 1824) that the corner-stone would then be laid, and that Lafayette would take part in the ceremony, created high expectations of this celebration. An enthusiasm was kindled in behalf of the monument. The newspapers announced, from time to time, the state of the subscriptions. Their amount soon became large.

The directors, in the spring of 1825, had secured the title to the land, had purchased the slope of Breed's Hill, — about fifteen acres, — and made other necessary preparations; but had not matured the plan of the proposed monument. The first committee on the form consisted of Daniel Webster, Loammi Baldwin, George Ticknor, Gilbert Stewart, and Washington Allston. A premium of one hundred dollars was offered for the best design, when about fifty plans were presented, either in drawings or models. There was much discussion as to the most appropriate form to adopt. The debates in the board of directors were uncommonly able and learned; and, at length, at a special meeting, (May 19, 1825,) the choice was narrowed down to two forms, the column and the obelisk. A new committee (H. A. S. Dearborn, Edward Everett, Seth Knowles, S. D. Harris, T. H. Perkins) was appointed to procure designs of both, with estimates of the expense of each. This committee reported on the 7th of June. Hon. Daniel Webster presided at this meeting. There was then an animated discussion on the comparative merits of the two plans, which was prolonged to a late hour, when the question was decided. Sixteen of the directors voted. On a motion to adopt a column, five voted in the affirmative, and eleven in the negative. It was then voted to adopt the form of an obelisk, as being the most simple and imposing, the most congenial to our republican institutions, and the most appropriate to the character of the event to be commemorated. The following gentlemen were then appointed a committee to report a design : Loammi Baldwin, George Ticknor, Jacob Bigelow, Samuel Swett, and Washington Allston.

It was at this stage of the enterprise that the directors proposed to lay the corner-stone of the monument, and ground was broken (June 7) for this purpose. As a mark of respect to the liberality and patriotism of King Solomon's Lodge, they invited the grand master of the Grand Lodge of Massachusetts to perform the ceremony. They also invited General

Lafayette to accompany the president of the Association, Hon. Daniel Webster, and assist in it.

This celebration was unequalled in magnificence by anything of the kind that had been seen in New England. The morning proved propitious. The air was cool, the sky was clear, and timely showers the previous day had brightened the vesture of nature into its loveliest hue. Delighted thousands flocked into Boston to bear a part in the proceedings, or to witness the spectacle. At about ten o'clock a procession moved from the State House towards Bunker Hill. The military, in their fine uniforms, formed the van. About two hundred veterans of the revolution, of whom forty were survivors of the battle, rode in barouches next to the escort. These venerable men, the relics of a past generation, with emaciated frames, tottering limbs, and trembling voices, constituted a touching spectacle. Some wore, as honorable decorations, their old fighting equipments, and some bore the scars of still more honorable wounds. Glistening eyes constituted their answer to the enthusiastic cheers of the grateful multitudes who lined their pathway and cheered their progress. To this patriot band succeeded the Bunker Hill Monument Association. Then the masonic fraternity, in their splendid regalia, thousands in number. Then LAFAYETTE, continually welcomed by tokens of love and gratitude, and the invited guests. Then a long array of societies, with their various badges and banners It was a splendid procession, and of such length that the front nearly reached Charlestown Bridge ere the rear had left Boston Common. It proceeded to Breed's Hill, where the grand master of the Freemasons, the president of the Monument Association, and General Lafayette, performed the ceremony of laying the corner-stone, in the presence of a vast concourse of people.[1] The procession then moved to a spa-

---

[1] The plate contained the following

INSCRIPTION.

" On the XVII. day of June, MDCCCXXV., at the request of the Bunker Hill Monument Association, the Most Worshipful John Abbot, Grand Master of Masons in Massachusetts, did, in the presence of Gen. Lafayette, lay this Corner Stone of a Monument, to testify the gratitude of the present generation to their Fathers, who, on the 17th June, 1775, here fought in the cause

cious amphitheatre on the northern declivity of the hill, where
Hon. DANIEL WEBSTER delivered an address. It was at the
close of a dedicatory passage on the monument that he uttered
the words, "Let it rise till it meet the sun in its coming; let
the earliest light of the morning gild it, and parting day linger
and play on its summit." When the exercises here were concluded, a procession was escorted to Bunker Hill, where a tent
covering 38,400 square feet had been erected. Twelve tables
ran the entire length of it, which were set with four thousand
plates. Here speeches, toasts, and songs, concluded the ceremonies. Such is but a faint outline of a scene which those
who were so fortunate as to witness will not soon forget.

At a meeting of the directors (June 24) the committee on
laying the corner-stone reported that a stone had been prepared to receive a box; that one, containing a plate of silver
with inscriptions, had been deposited on the 17th; and that
stones, secured by iron clamps, had been placed over it. This
corner-stone, however, was subsequently rejected. On the
commencement of the work for the monument, the box was
taken out, put into the hands of Dr. Warren for safe keeping,
and placed in another stone, which now is in the north-eastern
angle of the structure.

of their country, and of free institutions, the memorable battle of Bunker
Hill, and with their blood vindicated for their posterity the privileges and happiness this land has since enjoyed. Officers of the Bunker Hill Monument
Association. — President, Daniel Webster; Vice-presidents, Thomas H. Perkins, Joseph Story; Secretary, Edward Everett; Treasurer, Nathaniel P.
Russell. [Here follows a list of twenty-five Directors.] Standing Committee
for collecting Subscriptions, — Henry A. S. Dearborn, John C. Warren,
Edward Everett, George Blake, and Samuel D. Harris. Committee on the
form of the Monument, — Daniel Webster, L. Baldwin, G. Stuart, Washington Allston, and G. Ticknor.

"President of the United States, John Quincy Adams. Governor of Mas-
sachusetts, Levi Lincoln; Governor of New Hampshire, David L. Morrell;
Governor of Connecticut, Oliver Wolcott; Governor of Vermont, C. P.
Van Ness; Governor of Rhode Island, James Fenner; Governor of Maine,
Albion K. Parris. Alexander Parris, Architect."

The architect here named was at this time employed by the Association
and had presented a plan of a monument. As his design was not adopted
the name of Solomon Willard ought to be on the inscription, if by "Architect" is to be understood the designer of the monument.

The directors soon decided upon a plan. The committee appointed for this purpose reported one on the 1st of July. It was then discussed, and the consideration of it was postponed until July 5th, when it was adopted. It was drawn by SOLOMON WILLARD. A building committee was not obtained, owing to the restrictions put upon it, until the 4th of October. It consisted of John C. Warren, Amos Lawrence, H. A. S. Dearborn, William Sullivan, and George Blake, — to all of whom great credit is due for well-directed and laborious effort. Dr. Warren was its chairman. This committee reported, October 4th, that Solomon Willard had been appointed the architect and superintendent of the monument. He had already rendered great service to the work. He had spent much time, and labor, and money, in exploring the country to ascertain the best place to procure the material; and it was his judgment that secured the quarry at Quincy. He desired that his services might be gratuitous, but to this the directors would not consent. A moderate compensation, his expenses, was all that he would accept. His name, in addition, appears as a donor of one thousand dollars. His design, under his own superintendence, has been faithfully carried out. James S. Savage was appointed the builder.

The earliest work was done at the granite quarry in Quincy, discovered by Mr. Willard, and secured by the Association for a trifling sum ($325). A railroad — the first one built in the country — was constructed by another corporation, to convey the stones to the wharf in Quincy, where they were put on board flat-bottomed boats, towed by steam-power to Deven's Wharf, Charlestown, and thence carried to the hill on teams. But this repeated transfer defaced the stones so much, that, after a few courses of the monument had been raised, they were teamed directly from the quarry to the hill. The building of the railroad delayed the prosecution of the work. It was not until December 1, 1826, that the building committee gave its instructions to Mr. Willard; and not until April 25, 1827, that a contract for teaming the stone from Deven's Wharf to the hill had been made with Thomas O. Nichols and John Pierce.

At length the community, in the spring of 1827, saw the

monument fairly under way, and watched its progress with interest and pride. The estimated cost of the obelisk was one hundred thousand dollars. The original subscription, with a grant of seven thousand dollars from the state, amounted to $64,010.55. After deducting the sums paid for the land, for laying the corner-stone, and for various necessary expenditures, the amount applicable to the building of the obelisk was only $33,576.40. This sum, and a loan of $23,400, supported it until January, 1829, and carried the obelisk fourteen courses — about thirty-seven feet — high. It was then suspended for the want of funds. During this period, Hon. Daniel Webster and Colonel Thomas H. Perkins were the presidents of the Association.

The work now encountered obstacles which it took years to overcome. It would require too much space to give the dark side of its history, — to detail the measures, in order to raise the required funds, that were suggested, attempted, and abandoned. In spite of the efforts of its friends, and of the appeals of the press, the work remained suspended. At length Amos Lawrence, Esq., who had taken a deep interest in its progress, and had rendered it essential financial aid, proffered a liberal conditional donation, in case the Massachusetts Charitable Mechanic Association would make an effort to finish the monument. This offer was made April 24, 1833, in a written communication to several of the members of this institution, — his object being to have the monument completed according to the original plan, and to keep the whole of the battle-field open to posterity.[1] It was laid before the

[1] This proposition was made in a letter addressed to Samuel T. Armstrong, Charles Wells, Joseph T. Buckingham, and J. P. Thorndike, members of the Mechanic Association. After stating his desire to see the monument completed, and the battle-field kept open, Mr. Lawrence stated that sixty thousand dollars would finish the monument, and do something towards ornamenting the grounds ; and that if the association would secure fifty thousand dollars within three months, he would pay five thousand dollars ; or he would pay ten per cent. on any less sum that should be in like manner secured. It is an interesting fact, also, that Mr. Lawrence, in his will, (made April 1, 1833,) had appropriated property to complete the monument, and preserve the whole battle-field open. His father, Deacon Samuel Lawrence, of Groton, was in the battle ; and also his uncle, Lieut. Faucett, who died of his wounds in Boston.

association May 2d, and acted upon at a special meeting, **May** 16, when the Association voted to make the effort. It called a public meeting in Faneuil Hall on the 28th, when Hon. Joseph T. Buckingham, its president, presided. George Blake, Edward Everett, Charles G. Greene, and Judge Story, spoke — the records say — with "an eloquence adapted to the occasion." The meeting was large and enthusiastic. The thrilling speech of Hon. Edward Everett was widely circulated in handbills, and through the press. A new diploma was prepared, in which the two Associations were connected, and which was given to those who contributed, and were members. The Monument Association voted that the president of the Mechanic Association, *ex officio*, should be its first vice-president. But still vigorous effort, from various causes, was delayed; and it was some time before subscription papers were returned.

Meantime the affairs of the Monument Association wore a more gloomy aspect. The debt, originally contracted in the purchase of the battle-field, had increased to about thirty thousand dollars. The Mechanic Association determined that the amount they collected should be applied to carrying up the obelisk. When the proposition was made to sell portions of the land to pay the debt, it met with much opposition, and effort was made to defeat it. At length a committee (May 5, 1834) made an elaborate report, which recommended a sale of the land. It estimated the cost of raising the monument to the height of 121 feet, at $28,967.36; to raise it to 159 feet 6 inches, at $42,922.40; and to raise it 220 feet, at $55,576.40. After long discussions, it was voted that, when the monument had been raised to the height of 159 feet it should be considered as completed! The association voted (June 17, 1834) to sell the land, which was done, and $25,000 were realized.

In the mean time the amount secured on the subscription list warranted a renewal of the work. The Monument Association (May 5, 1834) voted "to empower and request" the Mechanic Association to apply the moneys they had collected, or might collect, to complete the monument, "by raising the same to the elevation of 159 feet 6 inches," under "the

supervision of the executive committee of the corporation."
The Mechanic Association (June 4, 1834) authorized its own
executive committee to carry this vote into effect. Accordingly, Solomon Willard was again employed as the superintendent. Work was commenced on the 17th of June, 1834.
The Mechanic Association collected $19,073.03. They also
received the subscription known as "The Ladies' Fund,"
($2937.90,) which the Monument Association voted to pay
over to the Mechanic Association : total, $22,010.93. The
obelisk was raised to the height of eighty-two feet. Charles
Pratt was the master mason, though Mr. Savage, still employed by Mr. Willard, continued to render the work assistance. The Association expended, through Mr. Willard,
$18,321.77 ; and directly to the workmen, and for contingent
expenses, $2952.66. It invested the balance of its moneys
($736.50) in shares of the Tremont Bank, which were subse-
quently transferred to the Monument Association. Great
credit is due to this patriotic institution for making this timely
effort, and for the faithful manner in which it saw the funds
applied. The president was Joseph T. Buckingham; the
treasurer was Uriel Crocker; and the building committee
were Charles Wells, George Darracott, Jonathan Whitney,
Charles Leighton, and John P. Thorndike. They devoted to
this work much time and labor. The president of the Monument Association was Judge William Prescott.

Another interval was destined to elapse before it could be
said that "A DUTY had been performed." New schemes were
proposed to obtain the required means to finish the monument,
and the press contained indignant appeals. It was announced
at meetings of the directors, in 1839, that two gentlemen were
ready to give ten thousand dollars each, provided a sum necessary to complete the monument could be raised. One was
Amos Lawrence, Esq., of Boston, who thus again evinced
the deep interest he felt in this work ; the other was Judah
Touro, Esq., of New Orleans, who thus manifested a lib-

[1] The executive committee of the Monument Association consisted of Joseph
T. Buckingham, William Sullivan, George Darracott, Nathaniel Hammond,
John Skinner, W. W. Stone, J. P. Thorndike, Joseph Jenkins, Ebenezer
Breed.

eral patriotism, and his regard for the land of his early days. Stimulated by these offers, another subscription was proposed, but was deemed inexpedient; and the proposal of a fair was reasoned down or ridiculed down. So unpropitious, indeed, seemed the hour, that in the succeeding annual report (June 17, 1840) it is remarked that it was exceedingly doubtful whether the present generation would have the pleasure to see the monument completed. The remark was repeated in one of the sewing-circles of Boston, when several ladies proposed to get up a fair in its behalf. The proposal met with immediate favor. It received the sanction (June 25, 1840) of the board of directors, and met with the approving sentiment of the community. A circular, recommending the measure, was issued by a sub-committee of the directors, and stirring appeals were made through the press. The busy hands of woman, in the patriotic spirit of the women of the revolution, were soon "plying the needle with exquisite art" in the work of preparation. The fair was held in Quincy Hall, Boston, — commencing on the 5th, and closing on the 15th, of September. The scene that opened upon the delighted visiter, when the product of so much ingenuity was dispensed at the hands of so much grace and beauty, was brilliant and inspiring. Thousands from the city and the country flocked to the well-stored tables. The fair was conducted under the exclusive direction of the ladies.[1] A daily journal, "The Monument," printed in the hall, daily chronicled its success. It is but bare justice to state that it was one of the best devised and most admirably executed things of the kind ever attempted in the country. The result exceeded the expectations of its friends. It put an end to doubt and difficulty in relation to the completion of the monument. And thus "garlands of grace and beauty" crowned a work "which had its commencement in manly patriotism."

The net proceeds of the ladies' fair, ($30,035.53,) the donations of ten thousand dollars each from Amos Lawrence and Judah Touro, and the amount received from other sources, made the total sum realized at this effort (January 14, 1841)

[1] The executive committee were — Catherine G. Prescott, Sarah J. Hale, Lucinda Chapman, Susan P. Warren, Sarah Darracott, Abby L. Wales.

$55,153.27. Measures were promptly taken to complete the monument. The vote passed on the 5th of May, 1834, that it should be considered to be finished at the height of 159 feet, was rescinded. An able building committee was elected, — Charles Wells, George Darracott, J. P. Thorndike, and Charles Leighton. They had already done (1834) efficient service in the same capacity. Hon. Joseph T. Buckingham, at this time, was president of the Association. This committee contracted (November 4, 1840) with James S. Savage to complete the monument according to the original design of the architect, (Solomon Willard,) and under his superintendence. Mr. Savage was to receive for the work $43,800, and the apparatus that might be on hand at the close of it. By a subsequent arrangement, he was also to receive the fees taken at the monument until January, 1845, and agreed to do certain work not specified in the contract. Accordingly, work was recommenced May 2, 1841, and steadily prosecuted until its completion. The last stone was raised on the morning of July 23, 1842, in the presence of the government of the Association, — the American flag being waved from it during its ascent,[1] and salutes being fired from the Charlestown Artillery. Much additional work remained to be done, — such as grading the ground, making the walks, and building the fences. The Association took possession of the monument December 31, 1844.

Another splendid pageant is connected with the history of the monument, — the celebration, in 1843, in honor of its completion. On this anniversary a grand procession, composed of the military, various associations, delegations from the states, members of the national and state governments, including the President of the United States, moved from the State House to the monument-square. It contained about one hundred of the veterans of theRevolution, — only a few of whom, about eleven, were survivors of the battle. The same eloquent voice that was heard at the ceremony of laying the corner-stone, was heard, on this proud occasion, to proclaim, from the same spot,

[1] Mr. Edward Carnes, Jr., of Charlestown, accompanied the stone in its ascent, waving the American flag. A little time previous, a cannon had been raised to the top of it, and a salute fired from it.

"The monument is finished." The scene that presented itself defies description. Before the orator, (Hon. Daniel Webster,) and around him, was an immense concourse of people. A hundred thousand at least had gathered on the hallowed spot. And when, after remarking, "It is not from my lips, it could not be from any human lips, that that strain of eloquence is this day to flow most competent to move and excite the vast multitude around me : the powerful speaker stands motionless before us," — he paused, and pointed in silent admiration to the sublime structure, the audience burst into a long and loud applause. It was some moments before the speaker could go on with the address. The assembly dispersed at its conclusion. A dinner, in the evening, at Faneuil Hall, closed the proceedings of the day.

The receipts and expenditures connected with this work have been as follows : —

RECEIPTS.

The balance of the "capital stock" account of the Treasurer, being receipts from the following sources : —

Subscriptions to 1830, ...	$58,582.81
Grant of the State, ...	7,000.00
Ladies' Donation, ...	2,937.90
Proceeds of the Ladies' Fair, . . .	30,035.53
Subscriptions of Amos Lawrence and Judah Touro, ...	20,000.00
Other Subscriptions and Donations of 1840,	5,123.27
The Mechanic Association — Shares of the Tremont Bank, ...	800.00
Subscription of 1843, ...	3,550.00
Sundries, — rents, interest, fees at monument, to 1844, ...	2616.34

	$130,645.85
Balance of Real Estate account, profit of sale of land, . .	1,767.57
Fees received at the monument, 1845 and '46, . . .	2,473.96
Borrowed to finish the walks, conductor, &c., . . .	3,000.00
	$137,887.38
Collected by the Mechanic Association — deducting amount invested, ($736 50,) and accounted for above, . . .	18,330.76
	$156,218.14

EXPENDITURES.

Amount debited Bunker Hill Monument on the Treasurer's books, made up of the following items : —

Expended by the Building Committee to 1830,	$57,378.80
Paid James S. Savage, in 1841,	43,800.00
Grading, Engineering, &c., in 1843,	9,831.59
For Iron Fence,	5,760.00
Stone-work, Steps, &c.,	2,838.16
Paid to Mechanic Association, — Ladies' Donation,	2,937.90
	$122,546.45
Amount of Expense Account, including $4720.85 for laying the corner-stone,	10,398.89
Balance of Interest Account,	4,994.74
	$137,940.08
Amount expended by the Mechanic Association, out of the funds it collected,	18,336.53
	$156,276.61

The cost of the obelisk was about $120,000, the cost of fencing and grading about $19,000, and the contingent expenses about $17,000.[1]

The records of the Association contain many acknowledgments for services rendered in aid of this work. Among them are those to Hon. Daniel Webster, for early labors, and for his addresses; to Judge William Prescott, for serving six years as president; to Hon. Joseph T. Buckingham, for twelve years' labors as vice-president and president; to the Mechanic Association, for its timely effort; to Amos Lawrence and Judah Touro, Esquires, for their large donations; to the ladies engaged in the fair; and to the late Hon. Nathaniel P. Russell, the treasurer for twenty-five years. Mr. Russell's duties were important and laborious, and, besides giving them gratuitously, he was a liberal donor. Over three hundred and seventy thousand dollars passed through his hands. A vote of the Association (June, 1849) is expressive of the value of this

---

[1] A small balance is due to the treasurer. The Association have paid a large portion of the $3000 borrowed to complete the grounds, out of fees received at the monument.

long labor, and of the high respect entertained for his memory. There are also votes complimentary of the architect and the builder. Solomon Willard will be indissolubly connected with this structure, as its skilful designer and indefatigable and patriotic superintendent. James S. Savage, a skilful mechanic, and the last contractor, carried out this design accurately, and faithfully executed his contract. The thanks of the community are due to all those patriotic individuals who originated this work, or aided in carrying it to a successful result.[1]

In spite of the obstacles that were encountered, the work, as to economy, will bear a rigid investigation. Had means been provided at the outset to have completed it without sus-

---

[1] The officers of the Bunker Hill Monument Association, including the directors, have been too numerous to be given. Its presidents have been as follows : John Brooks, chosen in 1823 ; Daniel Webster, in 1825 ; Thomas H. Perkins, in 1827; Levi Lincoln, in 1829 ; William Prescott, in 1830 ; Abner Phelps, in 1831 ; William Prescott, in 1832 ; Joseph T. Buckingham, in 1836, who continued in office until 1847, when G. Washington Warren was chosen.

The secretaries have been — William Tudor, chosen in 1823 ; Franklin Dexter, in 1824 ; Edward Everett, in 1825 ; H. A. S. Dearborn, in 1829 ; E. G. Prescott, in 1830 ; William Marston, in 1831 ; E. G. Prescott, in 1832 ; Francis O. Watts, in 1836 ; G. Washington Warren, in 1839 ; J. H. Buckingham, in 1847.

Its vice-presidents have been — T. H. Perkins and Joseph Story, chosen in 1823 ; William Prescott and Joseph Story, in 1827 ; John C. Warren and Amos Lawrence, in 1829 ; John C. Warren and William Sullivan, in 1830 ; John D. Williams and George Odiorne, in 1831 ; John C. Warren and William Sullivan, in 1832. The number was then increased to five. The president of the Mechanic Association, S. T. Armstrong, Charles Wells, John C. Warren, and William Sullivan, were elected in 1833 ; the same, with Joseph Jenkins in the place of William Sullivan, in 1835 ; and the same until 1839, when the president of the Mechanic Association, Charles Wells, John C. Warren, Joseph Jenkins, and Leverett Saltonstall, were chosen. In 1840 the following were elected : — President of the Mechanic Association, Charles Wells, John C. Warren, George C. Shattuck, Leverett Saltonstall. This board continued to be elected until 1845, when Abbott Lawrence was elected in the room of Leverett Saltonstall. This board has continued up to the present time.

Hon. N. P. Russell was elected treasurer in 1823, and continued in office until his death. In 1849, his son, S. H. Russell, was chosen.

pension or embarrassment, it might, undoubtedly, have been built for less money. The apparatus to work with was expensive, and, after each suspension, became unfit for use, and required refitting; and there was loss in drilling new gangs of hands to do such difficult work properly. Still, the work has been done at a reasonable rate. It is estimated that, if the usual price of laying stone-work had been paid for it, the obelisk would have cost two hundred thousand dollars. The result is still favorable, if tested by the cost of other works. The Washington Monument, at Baltimore, which is only one hundred and sixty feet in height, and contains but half the number of cubic feet of material there is in the Bunker Hill obelisk, cost two hundred and twenty thousand dollars. The Boston Custom House, it is presumed, contains about an equal quantity of granite with the obelisk, and this cost about a million of dollars.[1] If these works have been executed at fair rates, the Bunker Hill Monument has been executed at a low rate. It is probable that simply with respect to economy in the execution, it will not suffer in comparison with any work of the kind constructed in modern times. That it is so must be ascribed to the skill of the architect who planned it, to the attention of the various committees who devoted to it so much time and labor, to the fidelity of the builder, and to the well-directed labor of the workmen. It is but bare justice that this fact of economy should be borne in mind. It is gratifying to know that the patriotic offerings of the community have not only not been wasted, but have been so faithfully applied.

Monument-square is four hundred and seventeen feet from north to south, and four hundred feet from east to west, and contains about four acres. It embraces the whole site of the redoubt, and a part of the site of the breastwork. According to the most accurate plan of the town and the battle, (Page's,) the monument stands where the south-west angle of the redoubt was; and the whole of the redoubt was between the monument and the street that bounds it on the west. The small mound in the north-east corner of the square is supposed to be the remains of the breastwork. Warren fell

---

[1] The authority for these statements is an elaborate description of the monument by its architect.

about two hundred feet west of the monument. An iron fence encloses the square, and another surrounds the monument. The square has entrances on each of its sides, and at each of its corners, and is surrounded by a walk and rows of trees.

The obelisk is thirty feet in diameter at the base, about fifteen feet at the top of the truncated part, and designed two hundred and twenty feet high; but the mortar and the seams between the stones make the precise height two hundred and twenty-one feet. Within the shaft is a hollow cone, with a circular stairway winding round it to the summit, which enters a circular chamber at the top. There are ninety courses of stone in the shaft, — six of them below the ground, and eighty-four above the ground. The cap-stone, or apex, is a single stone, four feet square at the base, and three feet six inches in height, weighing two and a half tons.

The foundation consists of six courses of stone of two feet rise. It is sunk twelve feet below the ground, and rests upon a bed of clay and gravel. The first course is fifty feet in diameter, and consists of forty-four stones, twelve feet long, two feet six inches wide, and two feet thick — each equal to five tons in weight. The blocks were rough-dressed, and covered the whole surface, except the corners. In this course there are twelve headers on each side. The second course consists of stretchers, which fall back three feet, and lap on to the centre of the blocks in the first course. The third course has headers going back into the body of the work, and the fourth course stretchers.

The obelisk contains four faces of dressed stone, besides the steps; namely, the outside and inside of the shaft, and the outside and inside of the cone. The outer wall is six feet thick at the bottom, and two feet thick at the top. There are twelve stones in the exterior, and six circling stones in the interior, of each course of the shaft; there are two courses of the cone, each of six stones, and four steps to each course of the shaft. Seventy-eight of the courses of the shaft are two feet eight inches rise; the next five courses, making the point, are one foot eight inches. In construction the courses are alike, except diminishing as they recede from the base upwards. In order to preserve the bond, the headers are shifted to opposite sides in each succeeding course ; namely, in the first course the headers show on the east and west sides, and in the second on the south, and so on. The corner-stone, about nine tons in weight, forms the quoin at the north-east angle. The accompanying cut of the monument will give an idea of its construction.

The cone commences at the top of the first course, and contains one hundred and forty-seven courses, having a rise of one foot four inches. Its exterior diameter, at the base, is ten feet, — at the top, six feet three inches ; its interior diameter, at the base, is seven feet, — at the top, four feet two inches. There are two hundred and ninety-four steps winding round it, of eight inches rise. There are several apertures to admit air and light.

The chamber, at the top, is circular, eleven feet in diameter, and seventeen feet high, with four windows, facing nearly the four cardinal points. The windows are two feet eight inches high, and two feet two inches broad. Here are the two brass field-pieces, — the Hancock and Adams, — which, in 1825, were presented by the state to the association.

Directly in front of the entrance-door of the monument, on a base of granite, is a model of the original monument erected by King Solomon's Lodge. It is made of Italian marble, and, with the pedestal, is about nine feet high.[1]

[1] After the model was placed in its present position, there was, June 24, 1845, a masonic celebration in honor of it. A procession moved from Charlestown-square to the monument at

Holmes' hoisting apparatus was used for setting the first fifty-five thousand feet of the stone. Its ingenious inventor, Almiran Holmes, had the entire charge of constructing the derrick, and of hoisting the first thirty-six thousand feet of the stone. He died before the work was recommenced in 1834. In the last contract, Mr. Savage removed the gearing which had been previously used, and substituted a steam-engine of six horse power, and an ingenious and improved boom derrick constructed by himself.[1]

But a detail of facts and figures does but poor justice to the Bunker Hill Monument. Fortunately, the pen that described the characteristics of the battle has supplied a description of the monument. Hon. Daniel Webster (Address of 1843) writes : "It is a plain shaft. It bears no inscriptions, fronting to the rising sun, from which the future antiquarian shall wipe the dust. Nor does the rising sun cause tones of music to issue from its summit. But at the rising of the sun and at the setting of the sun, in the blaze of noonday and beneath the milder effulgence of lunar light, it looks, it speaks, it acts, to the full comprehension of every American mind, and the awakening of glowing enthusiasm in every American heart. Its silent but awful utterance; its deep pathos, as it brings to our contemplation the 17th of June, 1775, and the conse-

---

about eleven o'clock in the forenoon. John Soley, Esq., delivered an address, which was responded to by Augustus Peabody, Esq., grand-master. An address was then delivered by G. Washington Warren, Esq. After the proceedings at the monument, the company partook of a dinner. This celebration was carried on by King Solomon's Lodge. An interesting account of it may be found in the Freemason's Monthly Magazine, August 1, 1845. The following inscription was put on this model. "This is an exact model of the first monument erected on Bunker Hill, which, with the land on which it stood, was given, A. D. 1825, by King Solomon's Lodge, of this town, to the Bunker Hill Monument Association, that they might erect upon its site a more imposing structure. The association, in fulfilment of a pledge at that time given, have allowed, in their imperishable obelisk, this model to be inserted, with appropriate ceremonies, by King Solomon's Lodge, June 24, A. D., 1845."

[1] The description of the monument in the text is compiled from a quarto volume, containing plans and sections of the obelisk, by Solomon Willard, and a description of the monument in "Sketches of Bunker Hill Battle and Monument," by Rev. G. E. Ellis.

quences which have resulted to us, to our country, and to the world, from the events of that day, and which we know must continue to rain influence on the destinies of mankind, to the end of time; the elevation with which it raises us high above the ordinary feelings of life, surpass all that the study of the closet, or even the inspiration of genius, can produce. To-day, it speaks to us. Its future auditories will be the successive generations of men, as they rise up before it, and gather around it. Its speech will be of patriotism and courage; of civil and religious liberty; of free government; of the moral improvement and elevation of mankind; and of the immortal memory of those, who, with heroic devotion, have sacrificed their lives for their country."

BREED'S HILL MONUMENT.

APPENDIX.

COLONIAL POLITICS.

No. 1. — CALL OF A MEETING HELD ON THE 26TH OF AUGUST, 1774, AT
FANEUIL HALL.

Boston, August 19, 1774.

Gentlemen, — The committee of the town of Worcester, having signified
their desire to the committee of correspondence of this town, to advertise our
brethren of the committees of sundry towns in Middlesex to convene on the
26th inst. at such place as we shall determine to be most convenient, that a
plan of operation may be agreed upon, to be adopted by the several counties
of this province, at this important crisis. In compliance with so wise and
salutary a proposal, the committee of Boston request the attendance of one
or more of your committee of correspondence at Faneuil Hall, in Boston, on
the 26th inst., at two o'clock, P. M., to consider and determine as above.

Per order of the committee of correspondence for this town,

JOHN SWEETSER, Jun

To the Committee of Correspondence
of the Town of Charlestown.

No. 2. — PROCEEDINGS OF A MEETING HELD AT FANEUIL HALL ON THE
26TH OF AUGUST, 1774.

At a meeting of delegates from the counties of Worcester, Middlesex, and
Essex, with the committee of correspondence of the town of Boston in
behalf of the county of Suffolk, holden at Boston on the 26th day of August,
1774, it was voted, that it is the opinion of· this body, the judges of the
superior court, judges of the inferior court of common pleas, commissioners
of oyer and terminer, attorney general, provost marshals, justices of the
peace, and other officers to the council and courts of justice belonging in this
province, are, by a late act of Parliament, entitled "An act for the better
regulation and government of Massachusetts Bay," rendered unconstitutional
officers.

And, thereupon, a committee was voted to consider and bring in a report of proper resolutions to be taken on this alarming occasion, at the adjournment, which was voted to be at 11, A. M., on the next day, being the 27th day of August aforesaid, which report was as follows : —

Whereas, the charter of this province, as well as laws enacted by virtue of the same, and confirmed by royal assent, have been, by the Parliament of Great Britain, without the least color of right or justice, declared in part null and void ; and, in conformity to an act of said Parliament, persons are appointed to fill certain offices of government in ways and under influences wholly unknown before in this province, incompatible with its charter, and forming a complete system of tyranny :

And whereas, no power on earth has a right, without the consent of this province, to alter the minutest tittle of its charter, or abrogate any act whatever, made in pursuance of it, and confirmed by the royal assent, or to constitute officers of government in ways not directed by charter, or so constituted as to put them under influence not known in our constitution ; and all such novel officers, attempting to act in such departments, are daring usurpers of power, by whomsoever commissioned, and ought to be deemed enemies to the province :

And whereas, we are entitled to life, liberty, and the means of sustenance, by the grace of Heaven, and without the king's leave, — of all which the Parliament of Great Britain, by the late act for shutting up the harbor of Boston, have cruelly, wantonly, and wickedly endeavored to deprive the inhabitants of the capital of this province :

And whereas, we are, by firm, and, in our opinion, irrefragable compacts, entitled to all the privileges of native Britons, — to the accumulated invasions of such privileges already experienced by this province, we find, to our surprise, we are robbed of the most essential rights of British subjects by the late iniquitous act, improperly entitled an act for the impartial administration of justice in this colony :

It is therefore the opinion of this body —

That a Provincial Congress is necessary for concerting and executing an effectual plan for counteracting the systems of despotism mentioned, as well as for substituting referee committees during the unconstitutionality of the courts of justice in the province ; and that, therefore, each county will act wisely by choosing members as soon as may be for said Congress, and by resolutely executing its measures when recommended :

That executive courts, whether superior or inferior, sessions of the peace, &c., by the late act of Parliament rendered unconstitutional, ought, previous to the Provincial Congress, to be properly opposed in the counties wherein they shall be attempted to be held :

That every officer belonging to the courts aforesaid, who shall attempt to exercise authority as such, will be a traitor cloaked with a pretext of law ; and so are all others to be considered, whether officers or private persons who shall attempt to execute the late act of Parliament for violating the constitution of this province :

That, therefore, all such officers and private persons ought to be held in the highest detestation by the people, as common plunderers; and that all who are connected with such officers and private persons ought to be encouraged to separate from them; — laborers to shun their vineyards; merchants, husbandmen, and others, to withhold their commerce and supplies:

That, on the other hand, every persecution of individuals asserting and maintaining the rights of this province and continent ought to be withstood by the whole county in which it may happen, and province, if necessary; and the interest as well as persons of such individuals defended from every attack of despotism:

That the military art, according to the Norfolk plan,[1] ought attentively to be practised by the people of this province, as a necessary means to secure their liberties against the designs of enemies, whether foreign or domestic.

The above report was repeatedly read, and voted paragraph by paragraph.

No. 3. — Extracts from the Diary of Thomas Newell, of Boston.[2]

1774. May 13. — Lively arrived, with Gen. Gage on board. Town-meeting called. Paul Revere despatched to York and Philadelphia.

May 17. — Hutchinson superseded by Gage.

June 1. — Governor Hutchinson, son and daughter, sailed for London.

Three transports, with troops on board, arrived at Nantasket Road from England.

June 14. — The 4th or king's own regiment landed at the Long Wharf, and marched to the common, where they encamped.

June 15, A. M. — 43d regiment landed at the Long Wharf, and marched to the common, and there encamped. Most of the stores on the Long Wharf are now shut up. Thus are we surrounded with fleet and army, the harbor shut, all navigation cease, and not one topsail vessel to be seen but those of our enemies.

June 22. — One transport arrived from Ireland.

July 1. — Admiral Graves[3] arrived with his fleet from London. More transports arrived from Ireland, with 5th and 38th regiments.

July 2, A. M. — Artillery from Castle William landed with eight brass cannon, and encamped on the common.

July 4. — 38th regiment landed at Hancock's Wharf, and encamped on the common.

July 5. — 5th regiment landed at the Long Wharf, and encamped on the common.

---

[1] This was a "Plan of Exercise for the Militia of the Province of the Massachusetts Bay: Extracted from the Plan of Discipline for the Norfolk militia." Published in a pamphlet in Boston, by Richard Draper, 1768.

[2] I am indebted to Thomas J. Whittemore, Esq., for this original diary.

[3] General Gage, as early as May 31, mentions a consultation "with the admiral.'

August 6. — The Scarboro man-of-war arrived, nine weeks from England P. M. Three transports from Halifax, with the 59th regiment on board, and company of artillery and brass cannon; eight days out. In the margin: The 59th regiment, some time in the next week, landed at Salem, and there encamped.

August 7 — Lord's Day — Fair — A. M. — Three transports from New York, with the royal regiment of Welsh Fusileers, and a detachment of royal artillery, and a quantity of ordnance stores, &c.

August 8. — Company of artillery landed, and encamped on common.

August 9. — This morning the regiment Welsh Fusileers (or 23d regt.) landed at Long Wharf. Encamped on Fort Hill.

August 27. — Governor Thomas Gage came to town from Salem.

September 3. — This afternoon four large field-pieces were (from the common) dragged by the soldiery and placed at the only entrance to this town by land.

September 13, P. M. — The 59th regiment arrived in town from Salem, and are now encamped on Boston Neck.

September 15. — Last night all the cannon in the North Battery were spiked up; it is said to be done by about one hundred men (who came in boats) from the men-of-war in the harbor.

September 17. — Last night town's people took four brass cannon from the gun-house very near the common.

September 19. — Most of our town carpenters, with a number from the country, are now employed in building barracks for the army.

—— hundred of the soldiery are now employed in repairing and mantling the fortification at the entrance of the town.

The 59th regiment, with a number of other soldiery, are now throwing up an intrenchment on the Neck.

September 20. — Some cannon removed by the men-of-war's men from the mill-pond.

September 26. — All the carpenters of the town and country (this morning) that were employed in building barracks for the soldiery left off work at the barracks, &c.

October 12. — The Rose man-of-war arrived here from Newfoundland, with three companies of the 65th regiment.

October 14. — The three companies of the 65th regiment landed, and now in barrack in King-street.

October 23. — This day four transports arrived here from New York, with a company of royal artillery, a large quantity of ordnance and stores for Castle William, three companies of the royal regiment of Ireland, or the 18th regiment, and the 47th regiment, on board.

October 29. — Arrived here several transports, with troops on board, from Quebec. The 10th and 52d regiments.

December 4. — Yesterday arrived the Scarborough man-of-war, which went express from hence to England the beginning of September last.

December 17. — This day the Boyne man-of-war, of sixty-four guns, and the Asia, of sixty guns, lately arrived, (below,) came up into the harbor, and are at anchor within musket-shot of the town.

December 19 — The Somerset man-of-war, of sixty-four guns, arrived in this harbor.

LEXINGTON AND CONCORD.

No. 1. — PUBLICATIONS ON THE EVENTS OF THE NINETEENTH OF APRIL.

The earliest accounts of the events of the nineteenth of April appeared in the newspapers of the day. Some of them were printed, soon after the battle, in a hand-bill, having forty coffins pictured over the top of it, over which were the names of the killed. It had, also, a wretched eulogy in verse, to their memory. The letters of this date are too numerous to be separately mentioned. A series of engravings of the battles appeared this year, made by Amos Doolittle, of New Haven. On hearing the news of the battle, he volunteered under Benedict Arnold. He visited the battle-ground, and on his return to New Haven made the engraving.

The Provincial Congress, April 22, 1775, ordered depositions to be taken in relation to the battle, and a narrative to be prepared. They were printed in the London Chronicle of 1774, and in the American newspapers ; and also by Isaiah Thomas, in pamphlet form, of twenty-two pages, entitled " A Narrative of the Incursions and Ravages of the King's Troops, under the Command of General Gage, on the nineteenth of April, 1775, together with the Depositions taken by order of Congress to support the truth of it."

Rev. William Gordon prepared a narrative, entitled " An Account of the Commencement of Hostilities between Great Britain and America, in the Province of the Massachusetts Bay, by the Reverend Mr. William Gordon, of Roxbury, in a Letter to a Gentleman in England, dated May 17, 1775." This is printed in Force's American Archives. This account, substantially, appeared in several almanacs of 1776, and, with additions and much abridgment, it was incorporated in his history.

Rev. Jonas Clark delivered a sermon at Lexington on the first anniversary of this battle, (1776,) to which, on its publication, he added " A Brief Narrative of the Principal Transactions of that Day." He was the minister of Lexington, and was an eye-witness of part of the events he describes.

Rev. William Emerson, minister of Concord, wrote at the time a brief account of the events in Concord, which was first printed in the Historical Discourse of Ralph Waldo Emerson, delivered at Concord in 1835.

General Gage, April 29, 1775, sent to Governor Trumbull a narrative entitled " A Circumstantial Account of an Attack that happened on the 19th of April, 1775, on His Majesty's Troops, by a Number of the People of the

Province of the Massachusetts Bay." This was also circulated in a hand-bill, and is printed in 2 Mass. Hist. Collections, vol. II., with the exception of the last paragraph, which is as follows : " Thus this unfortunate affair has happened through the rashness and imprudence of a few people who began firing on the troops at Lexington."

In 1779 a pamphlet was published in Boston, containing General Gage's instructions to Captain Brown and Ensign D'Bernicre, in relation to surveying the country, dated February 22, 1775 ; a narrative of their journey to Worcester and to Concord ; and an account of the " Transactions of the British Troops previous to and at the Battle of Lexington," &c. It was printed from Mss. left in Boston by a British officer. This is reprinted in 2 Mass. Hist. Collections, vol. IV.

In 1798 Colonel Paul Revere addressed to the corresponding secretary of the Massachusetts Historical Society a letter containing reminiscences chiefly connected with the events of the night of the 18th of April, which is printed in vol. v. of the first series of the society's collections.

In 1824 and 1825 several articles appeared on the battle in the Concord Gazette and Middlesex Yeoman, and also in the Boston Patriot.

In 1825 Hon. Edward Everett delivered at Concord an oration on the anniversary of the battle, which was published, and contains a sketch of the events of the day.

In 1825 Elias Phinney, Esq., published a " History of the Battle at Lexington, on the Morning of the 19th of April, 1775." This pamphlet contains ten depositions relating to the battle, taken in 1825, from the survivors.

In 1827 Dr. Ezra Ripley, with other citizens of Concord, published " A History of the Fight at Concord on the 19th of April, 1775, with a Particular Account of the Military Operations and Interesting Events of that ever memorable Day ; showing that then and there the first regular and forcible resistance was made to the British soldiery, and the first British blood was shed by armed Americans, and the Revolutionary War thus commenced." A second edition was published in 1832.

In 1835 Lemuel Shattuck, Esq. published a History of Concord, which contains a minute detail of the military transactions of the 19th of April, in Concord, and the depositions taken by authority of the Provincial Congress of 1775.

In 1835 Hon. Edward Everett delivered at Lexington an oration on the 19th of April, at the request of the citizens of that place, in which a sketch is given of the events that occurred there. This was published.

In 1835 Josiah Adams, Esq., delivered an address at Acton, being the first centennial anniversary of that town. This was published, and contains, in the appendix, a review of some of the transactions that occurred at Concord.

In 1835 Hon. Daniel P. King delivered " An Address, commemorative of Seven Young Men of Danvers, who were slain in the Battle of Lexington," at Danvers, on the occasion of laying a corner-stone to their memory.

No. 2. — DEPOSITION (1775) RELATIVE TO THE EVENTS ON THE MORNING OF THE NINETEENTH OF APRIL, AT LEXINGTON

We, Nathaniel Parkhurst, Jonas Parker, John Monroe, Jun., John Windship, Solomon Peirce, John Muzzy, Abner Meads, John Bridge, Jun., Ebenezer Bowman, William Monroe, 3d., Micah Hagar, Samuel Sanderson, Samuel Hastings, and James Brown, of Lexington, in the County of Middlesex, and Colony of the Massachusetts Bay, in New England, and all of lawful age, do testify and say, that on the morning of the nineteenth of April, instant, about one or two o'clock, being informed that a number of regular officers had been riding up and down the road the evening and night preceding, and that some of the inhabitants as they were passing had been insulted by the officers, and stopped by them ; and being also informed that the regular troops were on their march from Boston, in order (as it was said) to take the colony stores then deposited in Concord, we met on the parade of our company in this town : after the company had collected, we were ordered by Capt. John Parker (who commanded us) to disperse for the present, and to be ready to attend the beat of the drum ; and accordingly the company went into houses near the place of parade. We further testify and say, that about five o'clock in the morning we attended the beat of our drum, and were formed on the parade ; we were faced towards the regulars then marching up to us, and some of our company were coming to the parade, with their backs towards the troops, and others on the parade began to disperse, when the regulars fired on the company, before a gun was fired by any of our company on them ; they killed eight of our company, and wounded several, and continued their fire until we had all made our escape.

Lexington, 25th April, 1775.

No. 3. — DEPOSITION (1775) RELATIVE TO THE EVENTS IN CONCORD ON THE NINETEENTH OF APRIL.

We, Nathan Barret, Captain ; Jonathan Farrer, Joseph Butler, and Francis Wheeler, Lieutenants ; John Barret, Ensign ; John Brown, Silas Walker, Ephraim Melvin, Nathan Butterick, Stephen Hosmer, Jun., Samuel Barrett, Thomas Jones, Joseph Chandler, Peter Wheeler, Nathan Pierce, and Edward Richardson, all of Concord, in the County of Middlesex, in the Province of the Massachusetts Bay, of lawful age, testify and declare, that on Wednesday, the 19th instant, about an hour after sunrise, we assembled on a hill near the meeting-house in Concord aforesaid, in consequence of an information that a number of regular troops had killed six of our countrymen at Lexington, and were on their march to said Concord ; and about an hour after, we saw them approaching, to the number, as we imagine, of about twelve hundred, on which we retreated to a hill about eighty rods back, and the aforesaid troops then took possession of the hill where we were first posted. Presently after this, we saw them moving towards the North Bridge, about one mile from said meeting-house ; we then immediately went before them, and passed the bridge just before a party of them, to the number of about two hundred, arrived ; they there left about one half of those two hundred at the bridge, and proceeded with the rest towards Colonel Barrett's, about two miles from the said bridge ; we then, seeing several fires in the town, thought our houses were in danger, and immediately marched back towards said bridge ; and the troops who were stationed there, observing our approach, marched back over the bridge, and then took up some of the planks ; we then hastened our steps towards the bridge, and when we had got near the bridge, they fired on our men, first, three guns, one after the other, and then a considerable number more, upon which, and not before, (having orders from our commanding officers not to fire till we were fired upon,) we fired upon the regulars, and they retreated. At Concord, and on their retreat through Lexington, they plundered many houses, burnt three at Lexington, together with a shop and a barn, and committed damage, more or less, to almost every house from Concord to Charlestown.

Lexington, April 23d, 1775.

No. 4. — PETITION OF WILLIAM TAY, OF WOBURN, RELATIVE TO THE BATTLE.

Colony of the Massachusetts Bay in New England.

To the Honorable the Council of the Colony aforesaid, and the Honorable House of Representatives, in General Court assembled, the twentieth day of September, 1775.

Your petitioner, the subscriber, begs leave, humbly, to show :

That on the 19th day of April, 1775, being roused from his sleep by an alarm, occasioned by the secret and sudden march of the ministerial troops towards Concord, supposed to intend the destruction of the colony's magazine there deposited, — to prevent which, your petitioner, with about 180 of his fellow-townsmen, well armed, and resolved in defence of the common cause, speedily took their march from Woburn to Concord aforesaid, who, upon their arrival there, being reinforced by a number of their fellow-soldiers of the same regiment, smartly skirmished with those hostile troops, being deeply touched with their bloody massacre and inhuman murders in their march at Lexington, where we found sundry of our friends and neighbors inhumanly butchered on that bloody field ; and other salvage cruelties to our aged fathers, and poor, helpless, bed-ridden women under the infirmities of child-bearing ; together with their horrible devastations committed on their ignominious retreat the same day. (shocking to relate, but more so to behold,) to the eternal infamy of those British arms so frequently and so successfully wielded in the glorious cause of liberty through most of the European dominions, now made subservient to the ambitious purposes of a very salvage cruelty, inhuman butchery, and tyrannical slavery.

These shocking scenes continually opening to view, served to heighten resentment, and warm endeavors to reap a just revenge upon those inhuman perpetrators, and to risk our lives in defence of the glorious cause, as the heroic deeds of our troops through the whole series of the tragical actions of that memorable day abundantly testify.

In which your petitioner, by the joint testimony of all his fellow-soldiers, lent, at least, an equal part through the whole stretch of way from Concord to Charlestown aforesaid, where your petitioner, with several others, passing by an house, were fired upon by three of the ministerial troops planted within, who, returning the fire, killed two of them ; thereupon your petitioner rushed into the house, seized the survivor, a sergeant, in his arms, gave him sundry cuffs, who then resigned himself and arms to your petitioner, none others being then within said house.

But so it happened, that while your petitioner was busied in securing his prisoner, others coming up and rushing into said house, those arms were carried off by some person to your petitioner unknown, which arms are since found in the hands of Lieut. Joseph Howard, of Concord ; of all which your petitioner informed the committee of safety for this colony, who, on the 24th day of May, 1775, gave it as their opinion that these arms were fairly the property of your petitioner.

Nevertheless, the said Joseph (though duly requested) refuses to deliver the same, under pretext of his own superior right.

Wherefore your petitioner earnestly prays that your honors would take his cause under due consideration, and make such order thereon as to your honors, in your great wisdom, shall seem just and reasonable, which that he may obtain he as in duty bound shall ever pray, &c.

WILLIAM TAY, Jr.

No. 5.— PETITION OF MARTHA MOULTON, RELATIVE TO EVENTS IN CONCORD.

To the Honorable General Court of the Province of the Massachusetts Bay, in New England, in their present session at Watertown.

The petition of Martha Moulton, of Concord, in said Province, widow-woman,

Humbly sheweth :

That on the 19th day of April, 1775, in the forenoon, the town of Concord, wherein I dwell, was beset with an army of regulars, who, in a hostile manner, entered the town, and drawed up in form before the door of the house where I live ; and there they continued on the green, feeding their horses within five feet of the door ; and about fifty or sixty of them was in and out the house, calling for water and what they wanted, for about three hours. At the same time, all our near neighbors, in the greatest consternation, were drawn off to places far from the thickest part of the town, where I live, and had taken with them their families and what of their best effects they could carry, — some to a neighboring wood, and others to remote houses, for security.

Your petitioner, being left to the mercy of six or seven hundred armed men and no person near but an old man of eighty-five years, and myself seventy-one years old, and both very infirm. It may easily be imagined what a sad condition your petitioner must be in. Under these circumstances, your petitioner committed herself, more especially, to the Divine Protection, and was very remarkably helpt with so much fortitude of mind, as to wait on them, as they called, with water, or what we had, — chairs for Major Pitcairn and four or five more officers, — who sat at the door viewing their men. At length your petitioner had, by degrees, cultivated so much favor as to talk a little with them. When all on a sudden they had set fire to the great gun-carriages just by the house, and while they were in flames your petitioner saw smoke arise out of the Town House higher than the ridge of the house. Then your petitioner did put her life, as it were, in her hand, and ventured to beg of the officers to send some of their men to put out the fire ; but they took no notice, only sneered. Your petitioner seeing the Town House on fire, and must in a few minutes be past recovery, did yet venture to expostulate with the officers just by her, as she stood with a pail of water in her hand, begging of them to send, &c. When they only said, " O, mother, we won't do you any harm ! " " Don't be concerned, mother," and such like talk. The house still burning, and knowing that all the row of four or five houses, as well as the school-house, was in certain danger, your petitioner (not knowing but she might provoke them by her insufficient pleading) yet ventured to put as much strength to her arguments as an unfortunate widow could think of ; and so your petitioner can safely say that, under Divine Providence, she was an instrument of saving the Court House, and how many more is not certain, from being consumed, with a great deal of valuable furniture, and at the great risk of her life. At last, by one pail of water after another, they sent and did extinguish the fire. And now, may it please this honored Court, as several people of note in the town have advised your petitioner thus to inform the public of what she had done, and as no notice has been taken of her for the same, she begs leave to lay this her case before your honors, and to let this honored Court also know that the petitioner is not only so old as to be not able to earn wherewith to support herself, is very poor, and shall think her highly honored in the favorable notice of this honored Court. As what the petitioner has done was of a public as well as a private good, and as your honors are in a public capacity, your petitioner begs that it may not be taken ill, in this way, to ask in the most humble manner something, as a fatherly bounty, such as to your great wisdom and compassion shall seem meet ; and your petitioner, as in duty bound, for the peace and prosperity of this our American Israel, shall ever pray.

MARTHA MOULTON.[1]

Concord, February 4, 1776.

[1] The committee reported a resolve in favor of paying this heroine three pounds for her good services in so boldly and successfully preventing the army from burning the Town House in Concord, as set forth in her petition.

No. 6. — Extract from a Petition of Jacob Rogers, of Charlestown dated Cambridge, October 10, 1775, relating to Events in Charles-town.

As to my conduct the 19th of April : We were alarmed with various reports concerning the king's troops, which put everybody in confusion About ten in the morning I met Doctor Warren riding hastily out of town and asked him if the news was true of the men's being killed at Lexington ; he assured me it was. I replied I was very glad our people had not fired first, as it would have given the king's troops a handle to execute their project of desolation. He rode on.

In the afternoon Mr. James Russell received a letter from General Gage, importing that he was informed the people of Charlestown had gone out armed to oppose his majesty's troops, and that if one single man more went out armed, we might expect the most disagreeable consequences.

A line-of-battle ship lying before the town ; a report that Cambridge bridge was taken up ; no other retreat but through Charlestown : numbers of men, women, and children, in this confusion, getting out of town. Among the rest, I got my chaise, took my wife and children ; and as I live near the school-house, in a back street, drove into the main street, put my children in a cart with others then driving out of town, who were fired at several times on the common, and followed after. Just abreast of Captain Fenton's, on the neck of land, Mr. David Waitt, leather-dresser, of Charlestown, came riding in full speed from Cambridge, took hold of my reins, and assisted me to turn up on Bunker's Hill, as he said the troops were then entering the common. I had just reached the summit of the hill, dismounted from the chaise, and tied it fast in my father-in-law's pasture, when we saw the troops within about forty rods of us, on the hill. One Hayley, a tailor, now of Cambridge, with his wife, and a gun on his shoulder, going towards them, drew a whole volley of shot on himself and us, that I expected my wife, or one of her sisters, who were with us, to drop every moment.

It being now a little dark, we proceeded with many others to the Pest House, till we arrived at Mr. Townsend's, pump-maker, in the training-field ; on hearing women's voices, we went in, and found him, Captain Adams, tavern-keeper, Mr. Samuel Carey, now clerk to Colonel Mifflin, quartermaster-general, and some others, and a house full of women and children, in the greatest terror, afraid to go to their own habitations. After refreshing ourselves, it being then dark, Mr. Carey, myself, and one or two more, went into town, to see if we might, with safety, proceed to our own houses. On our way, met a Mr. Hutchinson, who informed us all was then pretty quiet ; that when the soldiers came through the street, the officers desired the women and children to keep in doors for their safety ; that they begged for drink, which the people were glad to bring them, for fear of their being ill-treated. Mr. Carey and I proceeded to the tavern by the Town House, where the officers were ; all was tumult and confusion ; nothing but drink called for everywhere. I stayed a few minutes, and proceeded to my own house, and finding things pretty quiet, went in search of my wife and sisters, and found them coming up the street with Captain Adams. On our arrival at home, we found that her brother, a youth of fourteen, was shot dead on the neck of land by the soldiers, as he was looking out of a window. I stayed a little while to console them, and went into the main street to see if all was quiet, and found an officer and guard under arms by Mr. David Wood's, baker, who continued, it seems, all night; from thence, seeing everything quiet, came home and went to bed, and never gave assistance or refreshment of any kind whatever. Neither was any officer or soldier near my house that day or night. The next morning, with difficulty, I obtained to send for my horse and chaise from off the hill, where it had been all night, and found my cushion stole, and many other things I had in the box. Went to wait on Gen. Pigot, the commanding officer, for leave to go in search of my children; found Doctor Rand, Captain Cordis, and others, there for the same purpose, but could not obtain it till he had sent to Boston for orders, and could not find them till next night, having travelled in fear from house to house, till they got to Captain Waters', in Malden.[1]

BUNKER HILL BATTLE.

No. 1. — THE AUTHORITIES ON THE BATTLE OF BUNKER HILL.[2]

1775. June 17. — The American Orderly Books contain meagre references to the battle. General Ward's has, in the margin, only a record of the loss, — calling it " The Battle of Charlestown." Fenno's contains the order for the three Massachusetts regiments to parade, and a brief account of the action. The British Orderly Books — General Howe's and Adjutant Waller's — have the British orders in full.

June 19. — Colonel John Stark, in a letter to the New Hampshire Con gress, dated at Medford, says that the Americans intrenched on " Charlestown Hill," and that he went on by order of General Ward.

June 20. — The Massachusetts Provincial Congress sent an account to the Continental Congress, which was prepared by a committee appointed June 18, — Major Hawly chairman, who reported it June 20. It describes the place of intrenchment as " A small hill south of Bunker Hill." This Congress sent another account to Albany, June 28, designating the place as " A hill in Charlestown."

[1] The committee of safety, July 7, 1775, ordered a circular to be sent to the town of Reading, desiring "all the inhabitants of this colony" to behave peaceably and quietly towards Captain Rogers. Tay's, Moulton's, and Rogers' petitions are from Mss.

[2] This notice of the authorities does not include many letters of an early date, some which appeared in the newspapers, giving general descriptions of the battle. A large number of them will be found collected in Force's American Archives.

June 20. — William Williams, in a letter dated Lebanon, Conn., **June 20, 1775,** ten o'clock at night, and sent to the Connecticut delegation in **Congress,** says : " I receive it that General Putnam commanded our troops, perhaps not in chief."

June 22. — Isaac Lothrop, member of the Provincial Congress, sent to General Wooster a letter dated Watertown, June 22, 1775, which was printed in the newspapers. He designates the place of the action " Breed's Hill."

June 23. — Rev. Ezra Stiles, of Newport, records in his diary details he gathered from persons who obtained information from General Putnam in the camp, who stated, " That Putnam was not on Bunker Hill at the beginning, but soon repaired thither, and was in the heat of the action till towards night, when he went away to fetch across reinforcements ; and, before he could return, our men began to retreat."

June 25. — Letter from Peter Brown to his mother, dated " Cambridge, June 25, 1775." He was clerk of a company in Prescott's regiment, and he gives a general account of the proceedings until the retreat. It is the only important contemporary letter, written by a private in the battle, I have seen. He calls the place of the battle " Charlestown Hill." It is preserved in Stiles' Diary.

June 25. — Letter written by General Burgoyne, who saw the action from Copp's Hill, to Lord Stanley, printed in the newspapers of 1775, and dated " Boston, June 25." The British journals contain comments on this letter.

June 25. — Official Letter of General Gage, addressed to the Earl of Dartmouth, and sent by the Cerberus, dated Boston, June 25. Severe strictures appeared in the British journals on this account, which were collected in the Remembrancer of 1775. General Gage sent substantially the same account to the Earl of Dunmore, at Virginia, dated June 26. It was also printed in a hand-bill substantially as it appears officially, and circulated in Boston, dated also June 26.

June 30. — Rev. John Martin related to President Stiles an account of the battle, who recorded it in his diary, with a rude plan of the battle. **He was** in the hottest of it, and supplies much interesting detail. He states the Americans " took possession of Bunker Hill, under the command of Colonel Prescott ; " that application to General Ward for aid " brought Colonel Putnam and a large reinforcement about noon ; " and that Putnam was deeply engaged with the enemy.

July 5 — A letter (British) from Boston gives a detail of the action. It was one of the " celebrated fugitive pieces " that occasioned the inquiry into the conduct of General Howe, and reprinted in " The Detail and Conduct of the American War." It is an excellent British authority.

July 12. — A letter of Samuel Gray, dated Roxbury, July 12, gives inter-esting facts relative to the battle. It calls the place "Charlestown Hill," and states that two generals and the engineer were on the ground on the night of June 16, at the consultation as to the place to be fortified.

July 13. — An article in Rivington's New York Gazette (Tory) gives a brief view of the action.

July 20. — In a letter addressed to Samuel Adams, dated "Watertown, July 20, 1775," J. Pitts writes, that no one appeared to have any command but Colonel Prescott, and that General Putnam was employed in collecting the men.

July 22. — John Chester, who commanded a Connecticut company, wrote a letter on the battle, dated "Camp at Cambridge, July 22, 1775," and ad-dressed to a clergyman. It gives first a general view of the battle, and then details his own agency in it. It is an excellent authority. He gives the fact that, after the British landed, General Putnam ordered all the Connecticut troops to march to oppose the enemy.

July 25. — The committee of safety appointed Rev. Messrs. Cooper, Gardner, and Thatcher, to draw up a narrative of the battle. This was sent to London to Arthur Lee. It states that "The commander of party" gave the word to retreat from the redoubt, but does not state his name. I found, at the Antiquarian Hall, Worcester, a Ms. copy of this account, with the erasures and interlineations preserved. It was written by Rev. Peter Thatcher, who states that he saw the action from the north side of Mystic River. It contains passages not in the printed copy. This is the account that states Breed's Hill was chosen "by some mistake."

August 20. — Rivington's New York Gazette has a graphic sketch of the battle, with a rude plan of it. It does not, however, name an American officer engaged.

A Voyage to Boston, a poem. By the author of American Liberty, a poem ; General Gage's Soliloquy, &c. Philadelphia, 1775. This contains several pages of satire on the British generals, and the result of the battle of Bunker Hill. It was probably written by Phillip Freneau. See page 38 for an extract.

The British Annual Register contains a narrative of the battle, in which it is stated that "Doctor Warren, acting as major-general, commanded." The Gentleman's Magazine, London, has a wood engraving, purporting to be a view of the redoubt ; see page 198. The Pennsylvania Magazine for Sep-tember has a picture of the battle.

John Clark, first lieutenant of the marines, who was in the battle, pub-lished in London "An Impartial and Authentic Narrative of the Battle," &c.

"on Bunker's Hill, near Charlestown, in New England," &c., with anecdotes. The whole collected and written on the spot. It gives Howe's speech to his army. It states that Doctor Warren was supposed to be the commander ; and that General Putnam was about three miles distant, and formed an ambuscade with about three thousand men. A second edition of this pamphlet was printed in 1775.

1776. — George's Cambridge Almanack, or Essex Callender, for 1776, contains a brief narrative of the battle, in which it is stated that Joseph Warren " was commander-in-chief on this occasion."

Colonel James Scamman published in the New England Chronicle, Feb. 29, 1776, a report of the court-martial that tried him, July 13, 1775, which was interspersed with notes. In one of them it is casually remarked, that " There was no general officer who commanded on Bunker Hill."

A pamphlet was published in Philadelphia, entitled " Battle of Bunker Hill. A Dramatic Piece, of five acts, in Heroic Measure. By a Gentleman of Maryland," — Hugh Henry Brackenridge. It names Putnam, Warren, and Gardner. An extract from this piece will be found on page 181.

A plan of the battle was published in England, entitled " A Plan of the Action on Bunker's Hill, on the 17th of June, 1775, between His Majesty's Troops, under the command of General Howe, and the Rebel Forces. By Lieut. Page, of the Engineers, who acted as Aid-de-camp to General Howe in that action. N. B. — The Ground Plan is from an actual survey by Captain Montresor." The plate of this was used by Stedman in 1794, for his history, with the names of the engineer and surveyor suppressed, and with a few verbal alterations.

1778. — Rev. James Murray, of Newcastle-upon-Tyne, published in London, July 29, 1778, a history of the war, in which he gives a full account of the battle, and states that " Doctor Warren acted as major-general and commander on this occasion."

General Charles Lee, in his Vindication, published in 1778, alludes to the battle, praises the bravery of several of the colonels, and says : " The Americans were composed in part of raw lads and old men, half armed, with no practice or discipline, commanded without order, and God knows by whom."

1779. — The London Chronicle contained an interesting review of the action, embracing many curious details, written by Israel Mauduit.

Governor Trumbull, in his letter, printed in vol. VI. of the Mass. Historical Collections, and dated August 31, 1779, gives a sketch of the battle, and names General Warren as the commanding officer.

A pamphlet was published, entitled " America Invincible : An Heroic

Poem. By an Officer of Rank in the Army." It contains a description of the battle. It alludes only to General Warren.

1781. — " An Impartial History of the War in America" was published in Boston, by Nathaniel Coverly and Robert Hodge. Its " authors " profess to have had " the best opportunities " for procuring facts ; but they adopt, with few variations, and without acknowledgment, Murray's account, word for word, and give General Warren the command. The only other American officer named is Lt.-col. Parker.

" The American War, a Poem ; in Six Books," was published in London. It has a poor picture of the battle, and a sketch of it in rhyme. A few lines will suffice to indicate the quality of the verse : —

> About two thousand were embarked to go
> 'Gainst the redoubt, and formidable foe :
> The Lively's, Falcon's, Fame's, and Glasgow's roar,
> Covered their landing on the destined shore.

" An Eulogium on Major-general Joseph Warren, who fell in the Action at Charlestown, June 17, 1775. By a Columbian. *Arma virumque cano.* — Virgil. Boston : Printed by John Boyle, in Marlborough-street. 1781." This tract contains a poetic description of the battle, but mentions only the names of Warren and Chester. Extracts from it may be found on pages 77, 144, and 172.

1788. — General David Humphries published an Essay on the Life of General Putnam, dated Mount Vernon, July 4, 1788, — the general being living. He says : " In this battle the presence and example of General Putnam, who arrived with the reinforcement, were not less conspicuous than useful."

The History of the American War, by Rev. William Gordon, was printed in London, the preface to which is dated October 23, 1788. It adopts the greater part of the language of the account of the committee of safety, (Thatcher's,) and defines the positions of Putnam, Warren, and Pomeroy. This is the first time Colonel Prescott appears, in print, as the commander of the intrenching party.

1789. — Ramsay's History of the American Revolution was published, and has a narrative of the battle. It does not specify a regiment engaged, or designate an officer in command ; and in a eulogy on Warren, does not assign to him any special agency in the battle.

1790. — Rev. Josiah Whitney preached a sermon at the funeral of General Putnam, who died May 29, 1790. Mr. Whitney, in a note, in commenting on Humphries' account of the battle, says : " The detachment was first put under the command of General Putnam. With it he took possession of the hill, and ordered the battle from the beginning to the end." This is the first time I have met, in print, with the statement that General Putnam was the commander.

1794. — Stedman's History of the American War was published in England. The only American officer named is "Doctor Warren, who commanded in the redoubt." It adopts, without acknowledgment, Page's plan, and uses the same plate, with a few verbal alterations.

"An Oration, delivered at the Meeting-house in Charlestown, June 17, by Josiah Bartlett." Doctor Bartlett was invited by the artillery company, and his address is dedicated to Major William Calder, and the officers and members of that company. It contains but few allusions to the battle. On the dedication of the monument on Breed's Hill, built by King Solomon's Lodge, in December, Doctor Bartlett delivered a eulogy on General Warren, and John Soley, Esq., a brief address.

1796. — Colonel Trumbull's engraving of the battle was published about this time. He began his picture in London in 1786, and issued a subscription paper for his engraving April, 1790. An account of the battle is printed in the appendix to Colonel Trumbull's Autobiography, printed in 1841.

1798. — General Heath's Memoirs were printed, which contain a brief account of the battle. He states that Colonel William Prescott, notwithstanding anything that may have been said, "was the proper commanding officer at the redoubt."

1801. — "An Oration, pronounced at Charlestown, at the Request of the Artillery Company, on the seventeenth of June ; being the Anniversary of the Battle of Bunker Hill, and of that Company," &c., by William Austin, A. B. It contains a brief general description of the battle, and regards General Putnam as the commander.

1804. — Marshall, in his Life of Washington, states that Colonel Prescott commanded the original detachment ; and that, previous to the action, the Americans were reinforced by a body of troops, under Generals Warren and Pomeroy. He does not mention General Putnam's name.

1805. — Hubley, in his History of the Revolution, follows chiefly the committee of safety's account, — adopting Gordon's language respecting Prescott, Warren, and Putnam.

1808. — James Allen, who died in 1808, wrote an Epic, with the title of "Bunker Hill." A portion of it may be found in the notes to Colonel Swett's History of the battle of Bunker Hill.

1812. — Lee's Memoirs of the War in the Southern Department contain a train of reflections on Howe's campaigns, in which the influence of the battle of Bunker Hill is dwelt upon, and a sketch of it given. Lee states

that the Americans were commanded by Colonel Prescott. He does not
mention Putnam's name.

1816. — General James Wilkinson, in his memoirs, chapter xix., gives
what is called "A rapid sketch of the Battle of Breed's Hill." He went
over the field, March 17, 1776, with Colonels Stark and Reed ; and October
27, 1815, addressed a letter, with a series of queries, to Major Caleb Stark,
on this subject. He gives reminiscences of his own, and details he received
from others ; and presents a fresh history of the battle. He states there was
no general command exercised on the field ; that Colonel Prescott, seconded
by a Colonel Brewer, was ordered to take possession of Bunker Hill ; that
Prescott commanded at the redoubt, and Stark at the rail fence, between
which "there was no preconcert or plan of coöperation." He stations Put
nam, with intrenching tools slung across his horse, out of the action, on
Bunker Hill, with Colonel Gerrish, and affirms that all the reinforcements which arrived here, after Colonel Stark had passed, halted, and kept
company with them. This work contains the earliest reflections on General
Putnam's conduct on this occasion, either printed or in manuscript, that I
have met. It is worthy of remark, that, in the review of this work, in the
North American Review, October, 1817, no fault is found with the account
of the Battle of Bunker Hill.

1818. — The Analectic Magazine for February contains a history of the
battle, chiefly in Thatcher's and Gordon's language, without acknowledgment, but with important variations. It states that the original detachment
was under Colonel Prescott ; that General Warren, the "leader," was
"everywhere aiding and encouraging his men ;" that General Pomeroy "commanded a brigade ;" and that General Putnam "directed the whole on the
fall of General Warren." It is accompanied by an engraving of Henry
De Berniere's plan of the battle, from a sketch found in the captured baggage
of a British officer in 1775. This is the first American engraving of a full
plan of the battle.

The Analectic Magazine for March contains an additional article, with
many interesting and correct details gathered from actors in it, and several
documents in relation to it.

The Port Folio for March has another engraving of Berniere's plan, with
corrections of the original in red color, by General Henry Dearborn, (who
commanded a company, during the action, of Stark's regiment,) and an account of the battle by him, written for this journal, at the request of the
editor. In this account it is stated that General Putnam remained at or near
the top of Bunker Hill during the whole action ; that Colonel Prescott commanded in the redoubt ; that during the action no officer but Colonel Stark
gave any orders ; that no reinforcement of men or of ammunition was sent
to those engaged ; and that General Putnam rode off with a number of spades
and pickaxes in his hand.

Daniel Putnam, son of General Putnam, published "A Letter to Major-general Dearborn," dated May 4, 1818. It contains a defence of General Putnam, and interesting anecdotes of the battle.

The Boston Patriot of June 13, 1818, contained a brief letter from Gen eral Dearborn, dated June 10, 1818, and fourteen documents relating to the battle ; the whole entitled "Major-general H. Dearborn's Vindication."

The Columbian Centinel, July 4, 1818, has the first of a series of elaborate numbers, entitled "General Putnam defended. Review of General Dearborn's Defence of his Attack on General Putnam." It takes the ground that, though "It is certainly true that there could not, in the nature of the case, have been any authorized commander," yet that General Putnam was in fact the commander of the detachment. This review was written by Hon. John Lowell, and embodies many depositions.

The North American Review for July, 1818, has an article, entitled "Battle of Bunker Hill — General Putnam," in which General Putnam is defended, and an interesting view of the battle is given. It contends that General Putnam commanded at the rail fence and on Bunker Hill, while Prescott commanded in the redoubt ; and that, "In truth, if there was any commander-in-chief in the action, it was Prescott ; " or that "if it were proper to give the battle a name, from any distinguished agent in it, it should be called Prescott's Battle." This article was written by Hon. Daniel Webster.[1]

In October, Colonel Samuel Swett published, as an appendix to a new edition of Humphrey's Life of Putnam, an "Historical and Topographical Sketch of Bunker Hill Battle." A second edition of this work was published, in pamphlet form, in 1826, with a plan and notes ; and a third edition, with additional notes, in 1827. Colonel Swett's indefatigable labors preserved many interesting facts from oblivion. He states that Colonel Prescott "was ordered to proceed with the detachment at Charlestown," "Genera Putnam having the principal direction and superintendence of the expeditior accompanying it."

The Boston Patriot, November 17, 1818, contains the first number of a series of articles reviewing Colonel Swett's history, — subsequently published in a pamphlet form, — and entitled "Enquiry into the Conduct of General Putnam," &c. Its main object is to establish the point, "that General Putnam was not in any part of the battle of Bunker or Breed's Hill." It was written by David Lee Child, Esq.

Hon. William Tudor, judge-advocate in most of the trials of the officers after the battle, in a statement published in the Columbian Centinel, July 11 1818, says : General Putnam appeared to have been on Breed's Hill withou

---

[1] An extract from this article will be found on pages 204—206.

any command, for there was no authorized commander ; Colonel **Prescott** appeared to have been the chief.

John Adams, ex-president, in a letter published also in the Centinel, and dated June 19, 1818, states that the army had no commander-in-chief, — that he always understood that General Pomeroy was the first officer of Massachusetts on Bunker or Breed's Hill.

The newspapers of 1818 abound with letters, depositions, and articles in relation to the battle. I have files of the Boston Patriot, Columbian Centinel, and Salem Gazette, and have consulted all they contain. Of the Ms. documents quoted, are the statements of Governor Brooks, Joseph Pearce, and General Winslow, taken down by Colonel Swett in 1818.

1823. — Thatcher's Military Journal contains a narrative of the battle, purporting to be written in July, 1775. Thatcher states that, though several general officers were present, Colonel Prescott retained the command during the action.

Tudor's Life of Otis contains a brief description of the battle, with inter esting anecdotes of Warren and Prescott. It is stated that the Americans were commanded by Colonel Prescott.

1825. — Alden Bradford published, in pamphlet form, a concise narrative of the battle, with copious notes. He maintains that, in fact, " General Putnam was considered and acted as commander-in-chief."

An Address, delivered at the laying of the corner-stone of the Bunker Hill Monument. By Daniel Webster. This address was delivered at the request of the Bunker Hill Monument Association, and in the presence of Lafayette.

This year the ceremonies of the laying of the corner-stone of the monu ment occasioned renewed attention to the details of the battle ; and numerous Ms. depositions, then taken from the actors in it, are extant. A long narrative of the battle appeared in the Columbian Centinel, December, 1824, and January, 1825.

1831. — A pamphlet was published by Charles Coffin, at Saco, entitled " History of the Battle of Breed's Hill." It contains the accounts of Heath, Lee, Wilkinson and Dearborn, a few depositions, and a few pages of remarks.

1836. — An Address, delivered at Charlestown, Mass., on the 17th of June, 1836, at the request of the young men, without distinction of party, in commemoration of the Battle of Bunker Hill. By Alexander H. Everett. This address contains a graphic description of the battle.

1838. — Judge William Prescott, son of Colonel Prescott, prepared a memoir of the battle, (see page 121,) which contains much detail not else**where** to be found. Copious extracts from it, taken from the original, **in the** hand-writing of Judge Prescott, will be found in the preceding pages Appended to the memoir is a letter, dated in 1838, and hence it is placec under this year.

1841. — "An Oration, delivered at Charlestown, Massachusetts, on the 17th of June, 1841, in commemoration of the battle of Bunker Hill. By George E. Ellis." This oration was delivered at the request of the officers and members of the Warren Phalanx. It contains a full narrative of the battle. It was prepared into a small volume, with illustrative documents, and published by C. P. Emmons, of Charlestown.

1843. — Address, delivered at Bunker Hill, June 17, 1843, on the completion of the Monument. By Daniel Webster. This address is not of an historical character.

The Veil Removed : Reflections on the Lives of Putnam, and the Histories of the Battle. By John Fellows. Printed in New York. He renews the charges against General Putnam, and reprints, often very incorrectly, many revolutionary depositions.

No. 2. — NARRATIVE OF THE BATTLE, PREPARED BY ORDER OF THE MAS-SACHUSETTS COMMITTEE OF SAFETY.

The committee of safety, on the 6th of July, 1775, passed the following vote : —

July 6, 1775.

This Committee have, with great concern, considered the advantages our enemies will derive from General Gage's misrepresentations of the battle of Charlestown, unless counteracted by the truth of that day's transactions being fairly and honestly represented to our friends and others in Great Britain ; therefore,

Resolved, That it be humbly recommended to the honorable Congress, now sitting at Watertown, to appoint a committee to draw up and transmit to Great Britain, as soon as possible, a fair, honest, and impartial account of the late battle of Charlestown, on the 17th ultimo, so that our friends, and others in that part of the world, may not be, in any degree, imposed upon by General Gage's misrepresentations of that day's transactions ; and that there also be a standing committee for that purpose.

In compliance with this recommendation, the Provincial Congress, July 7 ordered the committee of safety to be a committee for this purpose, and alsc to be a standing committee for like purposes. This committee (11th) " being exceedingly crowded with business," requested " Rev. Dr. Cooper, Rev. Mr Gardner, and the Rev. Mr. Peter Thatcher," to draw up a true state of thit action, as soon as might be, and lay it before them. The following accrur was accordingly prepared : —

In obedience to the order of the Congress, this committee have inquired
into the premises, and, upon the best information obtained, find that the commanders of the New England army had, about the 14th ult., received advice
that General Gage had issued orders for a party of the troops under his command to post themselves on Bunker's Hill, a promontory just at the entrance
of the peninsula at Charlestown, which orders were soon to be executed.
Upon which it was determined, with the advice of this committee, to send a
party, who might erect some fortifications upon the said hill, and defeat this
design of our enemies. Accordingly, on the 16th ult., orders were issued,
that a detachment of 1000 men should that evening march to Charlestown,
and intrench upon that hill. Just before nine o'clock they left Cambridge,
and proceeded to Breed's Hill, situated on the further part of the peninsula
next to Boston, for, by some mistake, this hill was marked out for the
intrenchment instead of the other. Many things being necessary to be done
preparatory to the intrenchments being thrown up, (which could not be done
before, lest the enemy should discover and defeat the design,) it was nearly
twelve o'clock before the works were entered upon. They were then carried
on with the utmost diligence and alacrity, so that by the dawn of the day
they had thrown up a small redoubt about eight rods square. At this time a
heavy fire began from the enemy's ships, a number of floating batteries, and
from a fortification of the enemy's upon Copp's Hill in Boston, directly opposite to our little redoubt. An incessant shower of shot and bombs was rained
by these upon our works, by which only one man fell. The provincials continued to labor indefatigably till they had thrown up a small breastwork,
exténding from the east side of the redoubt to the bottom of the hill, but
were prevented completing it by the intolerable fire of the enemy.

Between twelve and one o'clock a number of boats and barges, filled with
the regular troops from Boston, were observed approaching towards Charlestown ; these troops landed at a place called Moreton's Point, situated a little
to the eastward of our works. This brigade formed upon their landing, and
stood thus formed till a second detachment arrived from Boston to join them ;
having sent out large flank guards, they began a very slow march towards
our lines. At this instant smoke and flames were seen to arise from the
town of Charlestown, which had been set on fire by the enemy, that the
smoke might cover their attack upon our lines, and perhaps with a design to
rout or destroy one or two regiments of provincials who had been posted in
that town. If either of these was their design, they were disappointed, for
the wind shifting on a sudden, carried the smoke another way, and the regiments were already removed. The provincials, within their intrenchments,
impatiently waited the attack of the enemy, and reserved their fire till they
came within ten or twelve rods, and then began a furious discharge of small-
arms. This fire arrested the enemy, which they for some time returned,
without advancing a step, and then retreated in disorder, and with great precipitation, to the place of landing, and some of them sought refuge even

within their boats.   Here the officers were observed, by the spectators on the opposite shore, to run down to them, using the most passionate gestures, and pushing the men forward with their swords.   At length they were rallied, and marched up, with apparent reluctance, towards the intrenchment ; the Americans again reserved their fire until the enemy came within five or six rods, and a second time put the regulars to flight, who ran in great confusion towards their boats.   Similar and superior exertions were now necessarily made by the officers, which, notwithstanding the men discovered an almost insuperable reluctance to fighting in this cause, were again successful. They formed once more, and having brought some cannon to bear in such a manner as to rake the inside of the breastwork from one end of it to the other, the provincials retreated within their little fort.   The ministerial army now made a decisive effort.   The fire from the ships and batteries, as well as from the cannon in the front of their army, was redoubled.   The officers, in the rear of their army, were observed to goad forward the men with renewed exertions, and they attacked the redoubt on three sides at once.   The breast-work on the outside of the fort was abandoned ; the ammunition of the pro-vincials was expended, and few of their arms were fixed with bayonets.   Can it then be wondered that the word was given by the commander of the party to retreat ?   But this he delayed till the redoubt was half filled with regulars, and the provincials had kept the enemy at bay some time, confronting them with the butt ends of their muskets.   The retreat of this little handful of brave men would have been effectually cut off, had it not happened that the flanking party of the enemy, which was to have come upon the back of the redoubt, was checked by a party of the provincials, who fought with the utmost bravery, and kept them from advancing further than the beach ; the engagement of these two parties was kept up with the utmost vigor ; and it must be acknowledged that this party of the ministerial troops evidenced a courage worthy a better cause.   All their efforts, however, were insufficient to compel the provincials to retreat till their main body had left the hill.   Per-ceiving this was done, they then gave ground, but with more regularity than could be expected of troops who had no longer been under discipline, and many of whom had never before seen an engagement.

In this retreat the Americans had to pass over the neck which joins the peninsula of Charlestown to the main land.   This neck was commanded by the Glasgow man-of-war, and two floating batteries, placed in such a manner as that their shot raked every part of it.   The incessant fire kept up across this neck had, from the beginning of the engagement, prevented any con-siderable reinforcements from getting to the provincials on the hill, and it was feared it would cut off their retreat, but they retired over it with little or no loss.

With a ridiculous parade of triumph the ministerial troops again took possession of the hill which had served them as a retreat in flight from the battle of Concord.   It was expected that they would prosecute the supposed advantage they had gained by marching immediately to Cambridge, which was distant but two miles, and which was not then in a state of defence. This they failed to do.   The wonder excited by such conduct soon ceased

when, by the best accounts from Boston, we are told that, of 3000 men who marched out upon this expedition, no less than 1500 (92 of which were commissioned officers) were killed or wounded ; and about 1200 of them either killed or mortally wounded. Such a slaughter was, perhaps, never before made upon British troops in the space of about an hour, during which the heat of the engagement lasted, by about 1500 men, which were the most that were any time engaged on the American side.

The loss of the New England army amounted, according to an exact return, to 145 killed and missing, and 304 wounded ; thirty of the first were wounded and taken prisoners by the enemy. Among the dead was Major-general Joseph Warren, a man whose memory will be endeared to his counrymen, and to the worthy in every part and age of the world, so long as virtue and valor shall be esteemed among mankind. The heroic Colonel Gardner, of Cambridge, has since died of his wounds ; and the brave Lieutenant-colonel Parker, of Chelmsford, who was wounded and taken prisoner, perished in Boston jail. These three, with Major Moore and Major M'Clary, who nobly struggled in the cause of their country, were the only officers of distinction which we lost. Some officers of great worth, though inferior in rank, were killed, whom we deeply lament. But the officers and soldiers in general, who were wounded, are in a fair way of recovery. The town of Charlestown, the buildings of which were, in general, large and elegant, and which contained effects belonging to the unhappy sufferers in Boston, to a very great amount, was entirely destroyed, and its chimneys and cellars now present a prospect to the Americans, exciting an indignation in their bosoms which nothing can appease but the sacrifice of those miscreants who have introduced horror, desolation, and havoc, into these once happy abodes of liberty, peace, and plenty.

Though the officers and soldiers of the ministerial army meanly exult in having gained this ground, yet they cannot but attest to the bravery of our troops, and acknowledge that the battles of Fontenoy and Minden, according to the numbers engaged, and the time the engagement continued, were not to be compared with this ; and, indeed, the laurels of Minden were totally blasted in the battle of Charlestown. The ground purchased thus dearly by the British troops affords them no advantage against the American army, now strongly intrenched on a neighboring eminence. The Continental troops, nobly animated from the justice of their cause, sternly urge to decide the contest by the sword ; but we wish for no further effusion of blood, if the freedom and peace of America can be secured without it : but if it must be otherwise, we are determined to struggle. We disdain life without liberty.

Oh, Britons ! be wise for yourselves, before it is too late, and secure a commercial intercourse with the American colonies before it is for ever lost ; disarm your ministerial assassins, put an end to this unrighteous and unnatural war, and suffer not any rapacious despots to amuse you with the unprofitable ideas of your right to tax and officer the colonies, till the most profitable and advantageous trade you have is irrecoverably lost. Be wise for yourselves, and the Americans will contribute to and rejoice in your prosperity.

J. PALMER, per order.

In regard to what I know of the setting fire to Charlestown, on the 17th of June, is — I was on Copp's Hill, at the landing of the troops in Charles town ; and about one hour after the troops were landed, orders came down to set fire to the town, and soon after a carcass was discharged from the hill, which set fire to one of the old houses, just above the ferry-ways ; from that the meeting-house and several other houses were set on fire by carcasses ; and the houses at the eastern end of the town were set on fire by men landed out of the boats.

WILLIAM COCKRAN.

Middlesex ss., August 16, 1775.

Then William Cockran personally appeared before me, the subscriber, and made solemn oath to the truth of the within deposition.

JAMES OTIS,

A Justice of the Peace through the Province of
Massachusetts Bay, in New England.

This account was sent to London, with the following letter to Arthur Lee : —

In Committee of Safety, Watertown, July 25, 1775.

Sir, — The committee of safety of this colony, having been ordered by the honorable Provincial Congress to draw up and transmit to Great Britain a fair and impartial account of the late battle of Charlestown, beg leave to enclose the same to you, desiring you to insert the same in the public papers, so that the European world may be convinced of the causeless and unexampled cruelty with which the British ministry have treated the innocent American colonies.

We are, sir, with great respect,
Your most humble servant,

J. PALMER, per order.

To ARTHUR LEE, Esq., at London.

There is among the manuscripts of the American Antiquarian Society, at Worcester, a copy of this account, with the interlineations and corrections preserved. It contains passages not in the printed copy. It is enclosed in a paper having the following statement, without a date : —

The following account was written by a person who was an eye-witness of the battle of Bunker's Hill. Some of the circumstances the intervention of the hill prevented him from seeing, for he stood on the north side of Mystic River. What facts he did not see himself were communicated to him from Colonel Prescott, (who commanded the provincials,) and by other persons, who were personally conversant in the scenes which this narrative describes. It was drawn up within one fortnight after the seventeenth of June, 1775, while events were recent in the minds of the actors ; and it is now faithfully copied from the draught then made in a great hurry. This must serve as an excuse for those inaccuracies and embarrassments of the style, which would have been altered, had not the author felt himself obliged to give a copy a the account precisely as it was then written. It was transmitted by the committee of safety of Massachusetts to their friends in England, and may now, possibly, be in the hands of some person there. The author signs his name, which, though it may give no other celebrity to the account, will, he hopes, convince those who know him that the account is true ; for he flatters himself that they, none of them, can believe him to be guilty of the baseness and wickedness of a falsehood.

PETER THATCHER.

No. 3. — OFFICIAL ACCOUNT OF GENERAL GAGE, PUBLISHED IN THE LONDON GAZETTE.

Whitehall, July 25, 1775.

This morning, arrived Capt. Chadds, of his majesty's ship Cerberus, with the following letter from the Honorable Lieutenant-general Gage to the Earl of Dartmouth, one of his majesty's principal secretaries of state.

Copy of a Letter from the Honorable Lieutenant-general Gage to the Earl of Dartmouth. Dated Boston, June 25, 1775.

My Lord, — I am to acquaint your lordship of an action that happened on the 17th instant between his majesty's troops and a large body of the rebel forces.

An alarm was given at break of day, on the 17th instant, by a firing from the Lively ship of war ; and advice was soon afterwards received, that the rebels had broke ground, and were raising a battery on the heights of the peninsula of Charlestown, against the town of Boston. They were plainly seen at work, and, in a few hours, a battery of six guns played upon their works. Preparations were instantly made for landing a body of men to drive them off, and ten companies of the grenadiers, ten of light-infantry, with the 5th, 38th, 43d, and 52d battalions, with a proportion of field artillery, under the command of Major-general Howe and Brigadier-general Pigot, were embarked with great expedition, and landed on the peninsula without opposition, under the protection of some ships of war, armed vessels, and boats, by whose fire the rebels were kept within their works.

The troops formed as soon as landed ; the light-infantry posted on the right, and the grenadiers upon their left. The 5th and 38th battalions drew up in the rear of those corps, and the 43d and 52d battalions made a third line. The rebels upon the heights were perceived to be in great force, and strongly posted. A redoubt, thrown up on the 16th, at night, with other works, full of men, defended with cannon, and a large body posted in the houses in Charlestown, covered their right flank ; and their centre and left were covered by a breastwork, part of it cannon-proof, which reached from the left of the redoubt to the Mystic or Medford River.

This appearance of the rebels' strength, and the large columns seen pouring in to their assistance, occasioned an application for the troops to be reinforced with some companies of light-infantry and grenadiers, the 47th battalion, and the 1st battalion of marines; the whole, when in conjunction, making a body of something above 2000 men. These troops advanced, formed in two lines, and the attack began by a sharp cannonade from our field-pieces and howitzers, the lines advancing slowly, and frequently halting to give time for the artillery to fire. The light-infantry was directed to force the left point of the breastwork, to take the rebel line in flank, and the grenadiers to attack in front, supported by the 5th and 52d battalion. These orders were executed with perseverance, under a heavy fire from the vast numbers of the rebels; and, notwithstanding various impediments before the troops could reach the works, and though the left, under Brigadier-general Pigot, who engaged also with the rebels at Charlestown, which, at a critical moment, was set on fire, the brigadier pursued his point, and carried the redoubt.

The rebels were then forced from other strongholds, and pursued till they were drove clear off the peninsula, leaving five pieces of cannon behind them.

The loss the rebels sustained must have been considerable, from the great numbers they carried off during the time of action, and buried in holes, since discovered, exclusive of what they suffered by the shipping and boats; near one hundred were buried the day after, and thirty found wounded, in the field, three of which are since dead.

I enclose your lordship a return of the killed and wounded of his majesty's troops.

This action has shown the superiority of the king's troops, who, under every disadvantage, attacked and defeated above three times their own number, strongly posted, and covered by breastworks.

The conduct of Major-general Howe was conspicuous on this occasion, and his example spirited the troops, in which Major-general Clinton assisted, who followed the reinforcement. And, in justice to Brigadier-general Pigot, I am to add, that the success of the day must, in great measure, be attributed to his firmness and gallantry.

Lieutenant-colonels Nesbit, Abercrombie, and Clarke; Majors Butler, Williams, Bruce, Spendlove, Small, Mitchell, Pitcairn, and Short, exerted themselves remarkably; and the valor of the British officers and soldiers in general was at no time more conspicuous than in this action.

I have the honor to be, &c.,

THO. GAGE.

Return of the Officers, Non-commission Officers, and Privates, killed and wounded, of His Majesty's Troops, at the Attack of the Redoubts and Intrenchments on the Heights of Charlestown, June 17, 1775.

Royal Regiment Artillery. — Capt. Huddleton, Capt. Lemoin, Lieut. Shuttleworth, 1 sergeant, 8 rank and file, wounded.

4th Foot. — Capt. Balfour, Capt. West, Lieut. Barron, Lieut. Brown, wounded; 1 sergeant, 13 rank and file, killed; 1 sergeant, 1 drummer and fifer, 29 rank and file, wounded.

5th. — Capt. Harris, Capt. Jackson, Capt. Downes, Capt. Marsden, Lieut. M'Clintock, Lieut. Croker, Ensign Charleton, Ensign Balaguire, wounded ; 22 rank and file, killed ; 10 sergeants, 2 drummers and fifers, 110 rank and file, wounded.

10th. — Capt. Parsons, Capt. Fitzgerald, Lieut. Pettigrew, Lieut. Verner, Lieut. Hamilton, Lieut. Kelly, wounded ; 2 sergeants, 5 rank and file, killed : 1 drummer and fifer, 39 rank and file, wounded.

18th. — Lieut. Richardson, wounded ; 3 rank and file, killed ; 7 rank and file wounded.

22d. — Lieut.-col. Abercrombie, wounded, and since dead.

23d. — Capt. Blakeney, Lieut. Beckwith, Lieut. Cochrane, Lieut. Lenthall, wounded ; 2 sergeants, 1 drummer, 11 rank and file, killed ; 2 sergeants, 1 drummer and fifer, 35 rank and file, wounded.

35th. — Lieut. Baird, killed ; Captain Drew, Capt. Lyon, Lieut. Massay, Lieut. Campbell, wounded ; 18 rank and file, killed ; 3 sergeants, 2 drummers, 41 rank and file, wounded.

38th. — Lieut. Dutton, killed ; Capt. Coker, Capt. Boyd, Lieut. Christie, Lieut. House, Lieut. Myres, Ensign Sergeant, Ensign Sweney, Quartermaster Mitchell, wounded ; 2 sergeants, 23 rank and file, killed ; 4 sergeants, 1 drummer and fifer, 69 rank and file, wounded.

43d. — Major Spendlove, Capt. M'Kenzie, Lieut. Robinson, Lieut. Dalrymple, wounded ; 2 sergeants, 20 rank and file, killed ; 3 sergeants, 2 drummers and fifers, 77 rank and file, wounded.

47th. — Major Small, Capt. Craig, Capt. England, Capt. Alcock, Lieut. England, wounded ; Lieut. Hilliard, Lieut. Gould, wounded, since dead ; 1 sergeant, 15 rank and file, killed ; 3 sergeants, 47 rank and file, wounded.

52d. — Major Williams, wounded, since dead ; Capt. Addison, Capt. Smith, Capt. Davidson, killed ; Capt. Nelson, Lieut. Higgins, Lieut. Thompson, Lieut. Crawford, Ensign Chetwynd, Ensign Græme, wounded , 1 sergeant, 20 rank and file, killed ; 7 sergeants, 73 rank and file, wounded.

59th. — Lieut. Haynes, wounded ; 6 rank and file, killed ; 25 rank and file, wounded.

63d. — Lieut. Dalrymple, killed ; Capt. Folliot, Capt. Stopford, wounded ; 1 sergeant, 7 rank and file, killed ; 2 sergeants, 1 drummer, 25 rank and file, wounded.

65th. — Capt. Hudson, killed ; Major Butler, Capt. Sinclair, Lieut. Paxton, Lieut. Hales, Lieut. Smith, wounded ; 1 sergeant, 8 rank and file, killed ; 1 sergeant, 1 drummer, 25 rank and file, wounded.

1st battalion marines. — Major Pitcairn, wounded, since dead ; Capt. Ellis, Lieut. Shea, Lieut. Finnie, killed ; Capt. Averne, Capt. Chudleigh, Capt. Johnson, Lieut. Ragg, wounded ; 2 sergeants, 15 rank and file, killed ; 2 sergeants, 55 rank and file, wounded.

2d battalion marines. — Capt. Campbell, Lieut. Gardiner, killed ; Capt. Logan, Lieut. Dyer, Lieut. Brisbane, wounded ; 5 rank and file, killed ; 1 sergeant, 29 rank and file, wounded.

OFFICERS ATTENDING ON GENERAL HOWE.

67th. — Capt. Sherwin, aid-de-camp, killed.

14th. — Lieut. Bruce, killed ; Ensign Hesketh, wounded.

Royal Navy. — Lieut. Jorden, wounded.

Engineer Lieut. Page, wounded.

Volunteers, late Barre's, Lieut. Alex. Campbell, on half-pay, wounded.

Royal Artillery. — Mr. Uance, wounded.

4th Foot. — Mr. Dorcus, wounded.

35th. — Mr. Maden, wounded.

52d. — Mr. Harrison, wounded.

59th. — Mr. Clarke, wounded.

2d Battalion Marines. — Mr. Bowman, wounded.

Total. — 1 lieutenant-colonel, 2 majors, 7 captains, 9 lieutenants, 15 sergeants, 1 drummer, 191 rank and file, killed ; 3 majors, 27 captains, 32 lieutenants, 8 ensigns, 40 sergeants, 12 drummers, 706 rank and file, wounded.

N. B. — Capt. Downes, of the 5th regiment, and Lieut. Higgins, of the 52d, died of their wounds on the 24th instant.

No 4. — LETTER OF CAPTAIN JOHN CHESTER, SUPPOSED TO BE ADDRESSED TO REV. JOSEPH FISH, OF STONINGTON, CONNECTICUT.[1]

Camp at Cambridge, July 22d, 1775.

Rev. and Much Respected Sir, — Your favor of the 4th instant I received the day before the Fast, and should have answered it by the bearer, Mr. Niles, had I not been that day on fatigue duty. The day after Fast Mr. Niles set off for home, from Roxbury. I want words to express my gratitude for your religious advice, your many useful and important hints, your arguments and reasons for our animation and support in the glorious struggle for freedom, and your tender expressions of friendship for my family, as well as your anxious concern for my own personal safety.

I shall endeavor, as far as my time and business will permit, to give you, sir, the particulars of the battle of Charlestown. Though, as to the greater part of account published, I may not be able to mend it.

In the latter part of the day before the battle, our adjutant informed me that orders were issued from head-quarters that 1800 province men, and 200 Connecticut men, parade themselves [* * * *] clock, with provisions for twenty-four hours, blankets [* * *] there wait for further orders. About nine o'[clock t]hey were ordered to march to Bunker Hill, a nu[mbe]r of wagons accompanying them with intrenching tools, &c. Just about twelve o'clock at night they began intrenching, and went on with great vigor till day-break,

---

[1] I am indebted to Gurdon Trumbull, Esq., for this letter, who has the original. The conclusion of it is lost. J. Hammond Trunbull, Esq , has also kindly furnished matter for this work. See p. 415 for Letter, dated June 19, by Chester and Webb.

and were then discovered by the regulars, who were heard to swear most terribly about the Yankees ; and they began a heavy fire before sunrise from the ships and Cops Hill, which was kept up with little or no cessation till afternoor. But finding our people paid little regard to their cannon, and knowing the great importance of the post, they landed, (I believe it was about two o'clock,) and formed in three or four solid columns, and advanced towards the fort. Those on their right soon changed their position into a line for battle, and marched on very regularly, rank and file. They were very near Mystic River, and, by their movements, had determined to outflank our men, and surround them and the fort. But our officers in command, soon perceiving their intention, ordered a large party of men (chiefly Connecticut) to leave the fort, and march down and oppose the enemy's right wing. This they did ; and had time to form somewhat regularly behind a fence half of stone and two rayles of wood. Here nature had formed something of a breast-work, or else there had been a ditch many years agone. They grounded arms, and went to a neighboring parallel fence, and brought rayles and made a slight fortification against musquet-ball. Here they received the enemy to very tolerable advantage. Our officers ordered their men not to fire till the word was given. Lieut. Dana tells me he was the first man that fired, and that he did it singly, and with a view to draw the enemy's fire, and he obtained his end fully, without any damage to our party. Our men then returned the fire, well-directed, and to very good effect, and so disconcerted the enemy that they partly brok[e and re]treated. Many of our men were for pursuing, [but by] the prudence of the officers they were prevented lea[ving s]o advantageous a post. The enemy again rallied and ad[vanc]ed, and in the same manner were repulsed a second, and some say, a third time. But at last they stood their ground, and the action was warm, till the enemy carried the fort which was on their left wing, and soon there was a retreat of the whole of the pro-vincials. I am told that a gentleman on Chelsea side saw the whole engage-ment, and that he said it lasted thirty-five minutes with the musquetry, and that our first firings swept down the enemy most amazingly. The men that went to intrenching over night were in the warmest of the battle, and, by all accounts, they fought most manfully. They had got hardened to the noise of cannon ; but those that came up as recruits were evidently most terribly frightened, many of them, and did not march up with that true courage that their cause ought to have inspired them with. And to this cause, I conceive, was owing our retreat. Five hundred men more, that might easily have been there, if they were in any tolerable order and spirits, might have sent the enemy from whence they came, or to their long homes.

I wish it was in my power to give you a satisfactory reason " why our intrenchments were not supported with fresh recruits from Cambridge, and why that important pass over Charlestown Neck was not guarded against annoyance from Mystic River, as well as the other side from the fire of the ships and floating batteries, and our retreat secured," &c. &c. Possibly the whole attempt was rather premature, and not thoroughly well planned. If we might again attempt it, we should, undoubtedly, have contrived and executed much better. Perhaps it may be better, however, to prepare ourselves well for some future attempt, than to lament the unfortunate success of the last, which we cannot now possibly mend.

As to my own concern in it, with that of my company, would inform, that one subaltern, one sergeant, and thirty privates, were draughted out over night to intrench. They tarried, and fought till the retreat. Just after dinner, on Saturday, 17th ult., I was walking out from my lodgings, quite calm and composed, and all at once the drums beat to arms, and bells rang, and a great noise in Cambridge. Capt. Putnam came by on full gallop. What is the matter? says I. Have you not heard? No. Why, the regulars are landing at Charlestown, says he ; and father says you must all meet, and march immediately to Bunker Hill to oppose the enemy. I waited not, but ran, and got my arms and ammunition, and hasted to my company, (who were in the church for barracks,) and found them nearly ready to march. We soon marched, with our frocks and trowsers on over our other clothes, (for our company is in uniform wholly blue, turned up with red,) for we were loath to expose ourselves by our dress, and down we marched. I imagined we arrived at the hill near the close of the battle. When we arrived there was not a company with us in any kind of order, although, when we first set out, perhaps three regiments were by our side, and near us ; but here they were scattered, some behind rocks and hay-cocks, and thirty men, perhaps, behind an apple-tree, and frequently twenty men round a wounded man. retreating, when not more than three or four could touch him to advantage. Others were retreating, seemingly without any excuse, and some said they had left the fort with leave of the officers, because they had been all night and day on fatigue, without sleep, victuals, or drink ; and some said they had no officers to head them, which, indeed, seemed to be the case. At last I met with a considerable company, who were going off rank and file. I called to the officer that led them, and asked why he retreated? He made me no answer. I halted my men, and told him if he went on it should be at his peril. He still seemed regardless of me. I then ordered my men to make ready. They immediately cocked, and declared if I ordered they would fire. Upon that they stopped short, tried to excuse themselves ; but I could not tarry to hear him, but ordered him forward, and he complied.

We were then very soon in the heat of action. Before we reached the summit of Bunker Hill, and while we were going over the Neck, we were in imminent danger from the cannon-shot, which buzzed around us like hail. The musquetry began before we passed the Neck ; and when we were on the top of the hill, and during our descent to the foot of it on the south, the small as well as cannon shot were incessantly whistling by us. We joined our army on the right of the centre, just by a poor stone fence, two or three feet high, and very thin, so that the bullets came through. Here we lost our regularity, as every company had done before us, and fought as they did, every man loading and firing as fast as he could. As near as I could guess, we fought standing about six minutes, my officers and men think * * * *

No. 5. — Extract from Letter, dated Cambridge, June 25, 1775, from Peter Brown, of Westford, to his Mother in Newport.[1]

Friday, 16th of June, we were ordered, &c.   The whole that was called for was these three — Colonels Prescott's, Fry's, and Nickson's regiments. About nine o'clock at night we marched down to Charlestown Hill, against Cops Hill, in Boston, where we intrenched, and made a fort of about ten rod long and eight wide, with a breastwork of about eight more.   We worked there undiscovered until about five in the morning, before we saw our danger, being against eight ships of the line, and all Boston fortified against us.

The danger we were in made us think there was treachery, and that we were brought here to be all slain.   And I must and will venture to say there was treachery, oversight, or presumption, in the conduct of our officers. And about half-after five in the morning, we not having one half of the fort done, they began to fire (I suppose as soon as they had orders) pretty briskly for a few minutes, then stopt, then again to the number of twenty or more. They killed one of us, then ceased until about eleven o'clock, when they began to fire as brisk as ever, which caused some of our young country people to desert, apprehending danger in a clearer manner than the rest, who were more diligent in digging and fortifying ourselves against them, &c. &c. They fired very warm from Boston, and from on board, till about two o'clock, when they began to fire from the ships in the ferry-way, and from the ship that lay in the river, against to stop our reinforcements, which they did in some measure ; one cannon cut off three men in two on the Neck.   Our officers sent time after time after the cannon from Cambridge, in the morning, and could get but four ; the captain of which fired but a few times, and then swung his hat round three times to the enemy, then ceased to fire, it being about three o'clock, cessation of the cannons' warring.   Soon after we espied forty boats or barges coming over full of regulars, — it is supposed there were about three thousand of them, — and about seven hundred of us left, not deserted, besides five hundred reinforcement, that could not get nigh to do us any good, till they saw that we must all be cut off, or some of them, so they advanced.   When our officers saw that the regulars intended to land, they ordered the artillery to go out of the fort and prevent their landing, if possible ; from whence the artillery captain took his field-pieces, and went right home to Cambridge fast as he could, — for which he is now confined, and we expect he will be shot for it.   The enemy landed and fronted before us, and formed themselves into an oblong square, so as to surround us, which they did in part.   After they were well formed they advanced toward us, in order to swallow us up ; they found a choaky mouthful of us, though we could do nothing with our small arms as yet for distance, and had but two cannon and no gunner.   And they from Boston, and from the ships, firing and throwing bombs, keeping us down till they got almost around us.   But God, in mercy to us, fought our battle for us ; and though we were but a

---

[1] Peter Brown was in the battle of the nineteenth of April ; enlisted under Colonel Prescott, and was clerk of a company.   This is taken from Stiles' Ms. Diary.

few, and so was suffered to be defeated by the enemy ; yet we were preserved in a most wonderful manner, far beyond our expectation, and to our admiration, — for out of our regiment there was but thirty-seven killed, four or five taken captive, and forty-seven wounded. If we should be called to action again, I hope to have courage and strength to act my part valiantly in defence of our liberty and country, trusting in Him who hath yet kept me, and hath covered my head in the day of battle ; and though we have left four out of our company, and some taken captives by the cruel enemies of America, I was not suffered to be touched, although I was in the fort when the enemy came in, and jumped over the walls, and ran half a mile, where balls flew like hail-stones, and cannon roared like thunder.

Signed,   PETER BROWN.

No. 6. — EXTRACT FROM A LETTER WRITTEN BY SAMUEL GRAY TO MR. DYER, DATED ROXBURY, JULY 12, 1775.[1]

To give you a clear and distinct account of a very confused transaction, — the causes and reasons of the proceedings of the late battle of Charlestown, and of our defeat, as 't is called, — will be impossible for me, who am not personally knowing to every fact reported about the transactions of that and the preceding day. As far as I am able to give the facts, I will do it, and choose to leave conclusions to you. Some reports, which I have from good characters, must make part of the history.

Friday night, after the 16th of June, a large part of the Continental army intrenched on the southerly part of Charlestown Hill, on the height toward Charles River. North of this hill lies Bunker Hill, adjoining East or Mystic River. Between these two is a valley. North of Bunker Hill is a low, flat, narrow neck of land, the only avenue to the hill and town. The low neck and the valley (both which must be passed in advancing to or retreating from the intrenchment) are exposed to a cross fire from the ships and floating batteries on each side, and the valley to the fire of the battery on Copps Hill, in Boston. About sunrise, the 17th, our intrenchment was discovered, and a heavy fire immediately began from the ships and batteries, which continued with very little cessation till about one o'clock, when a large party of the ministerial troops landed on a point of land S. E. from the intrenchment, about 4 o'clock. The savages set fire to the town, beginning with the meeting-house. A heavy fire from the cannon and musketry was kept up on both sides till about five o'clock, when our men retreated : — thus far my own knowledge. I am informed that, in a council of war, it was determined to intrench on Charlestown Hill and on Dorchester Hill the same night, but not till we were so supplied with powder, &c., as to be able to defend the posts we might take, and annoy the enemy ; that on Friday a resolution was suddenly

1 I am indebted for this letter to Henry Stevens, Esq.

taken to intrench the night following, without any further council thereon; that the engineer and two generals went on to the hill at night and reconnoitered the ground; that one general and the engineer were of opinion we ought not to intrench on Charlestown Hill till we had thrown up some works on the north and south ends of Bunker Hill, to cover our men in their retreat, if that should happen, but on the pressing importunity of the other general officer, it was consented to begin as was done. The Europeans suffered greatly from the fire of our men in their ascending the hill. A party of about 400, under the command of Capt. Knowlton, of Ashford, lay under cover of a fence thrown together, and reserved their fire until the enemy came within twelve or fifteen rods, when they gave them a well-aimed fire, and killed and wounded multitudes of them. The particular account of their loss cannot be known with certainty; but we generally give credit to the report, confirmed so many various ways, that their loss is about 1500 in killed and wounded, — the particulars of which you are before this made acquainted with. Our loss in killed, wounded, prisoners, and missing, I think, cannot exceed 200, by the best information I am able to get. I think our loss can never be ascertained with precision, as the order, regularity, and discipline, of the troops from this province, is so deficient that no return can be made which is to be relied upon. However, the returns, for many reasons, (which you may easily divine when I have told you what their state is,) will exceed rather than fall short of the real loss. The officers and soldiers [torn out " drafted? "] under command of Major Durkee, Captains Knowlton, Coit, Clark, and Chester, and all the continental troops ordered up, and some from this province, did honor to themselves and the cause of their country, and gave the lie to Colonel Grant's infamous assertion on our countrymen, that they have no one quality of a soldier. A little experience will, I hope, make us possessed of all those qualifications of the most regular troops, which, in this country, are worth our pursuit or imitation. The reason why our men on fatigue all night were not relieved, or attempted to be relieved, I cannot assign; had they been supported in a proper manner, there can't remain a question but that the enemy must have been totally defeated. This battle has been of infinite service to us; made us more vigilant, watchful, and cautious. We are fortified from Prospect Hill to Mystic River, and on the other hand to Cambridge River, I hope so as to secure us in case of an attack : our lines are very extensive, and will require a large force to defend them properly on that side. On this side we have a fort upon the hill westward of the meeting-house. An intrenchment at Dudly House, including the garden, and extended to the hill E. of the meeting-house. A small breastwork across the main street, and another on Dorchester road, near the burying-ground. One on each side the road, through the lands and meadows a little south of the George Tavern. Across the road are trees, the top toward the town of Boston, sharpened and well pointed, to prevent the progress of the light horse.

A redoubt near Pierpont's or Williams' Mill, and another at Brookline, the lower end of Sewall's Farm, to obstruct their landing, and another breastwork at Dorchester. Our works are not yet completed, but I think we are able to repulse them if they are not more than three-fold our numbers; and then, I believe, our people will not quit their ground.

No. 7. — LETTER OF COLONEL WILLIAM PRESCOTT, ADDRESSED TO JOHN ADAMS, AT THAT TIME A DELEGATE TO THE CONTINENTAL CONGRESS.[1]

Camp at Cambridge, August 25, 1775.

SIR,

I have received a line from my brother, which informs me of your desire of a particular account of the action at Charlestown. It is not in my power, at present, to give so minute an account as I should choose, being ordered to decamp and march to another station.

On the 16 June, in the evening, I received orders to march to Breed's Hill in Charlestown, with a party of about one thousand men, consisting of three hundred of my own regiment, Colonel Bridge and Lieut. Brickett, with a detachment of theirs, and two hundred Connecticut forces, commandèd by Captain Knowlton. We arrived at the spot, the lines were drawn by the engineer, and we began the intrenchment about twelve o'clock; and plying the work with all possible expedition till just before sun-rising, when the enemy began a very heavy cannonading and bombardment. In the interim, the engineer forsook me. Having thrown up a small redoubt, found it necessary to draw a line about twenty rods in length from the fort northerly, under a very warm fire from the enemy's artillery. About this time, the above field officers, being indisposed, could render me but little service, and the most of the men under their command deserted the party. The enemy continuing an incessant fire with their artillery, about two o'clock in the afternoon, on the seventeenth, the enemy began to land a north-easterly point from the fort, and I ordered the train, with two field-pieces, to go and oppose them, and the Connecticut forces to support them; but the train marched a different course, and I believe those sent to their support followed, I suppose to Bunker's Hill. Another party of the enemy landed and fired the town. There was a party of Hampshire, in conjunction with some other forces, lined a fence at the distance of three score rods back of the fort, partly to the north. About an hour after the enemy landed, they began to march to the attack in three columns. I commanded my Lieut.-col. Robinson and Major Woods, each with a detachment, to flank the enemy, who, I have reason to think, behaved with prudence and courage. I was now left with per-

---

[1] Hon. Charles Francis Adams kindly loaned me a collection of letters addressed to John Adams, dated in various towns during the siege, among them Prescott's letter and the extracts in this Number. I did not receive them until the preceding pages were in type — a few of which were altered to get in important facts.

Prescott certainly was ordered to Bunker Hill, for there was no place in Charlestown then called "Breed's Hill" (see p. 119). He inadvertently used the name given after the battle.

haps one hundred and fifty men in the fort. The enemy advanced **and fired very** hotly on the fort, and meeting with a warm reception, there was a very smart firing on both sides. After a considerable time, finding our ammunition was almost spent, I commanded a cessation till the enemy advanced within thirty yards, when we gave them such a hot fire that they were obliged to retire nearly one hundred and fifty yards before they could rally and come again to the attack. Our ammunition being nearly exhausted, could keep up only a scattering fire. The enemy being numerous, surrounded our little fort, began to mount our lines and enter the fort with their bayonets. We was obliged to retreat through them, while they kept up as hot a fire as it was possible for them to make. We having very few bayonets, could make no resistance. We kept the fort about one hour and twenty minutes after the attack with small arms. This is nearly the state of facts, though imperfect and too general, which, if any ways satisfactory to you, will afford pleasure to your most obedient humble servant.   WILLIAM PRESCOTT.

To the Hon. JOHN ADAMS, Esq.

William Tudor to John Adams, 26th June, 1775.

The ministerial troops gained the hill, but were victorious losers. A few more such victories, and they are undone. I cannot think our retreat an unfortunate one. Such is the situation of that hill, that we could not have kept it, exposed to the mighty fire which our men must have received from the ships and batteries that command the whole eminence. Eight hundred provincials bore the assault of two thousand regulars, and twice repulsed them ; but the heroes were not supported, and could only retire. Our men were not used to cannon-balls, and they came so thick from the ships, floating batteries, &c., that they were discouraged advancing. They have since been more used to them, and dare encounter them.

General William Heath to John Adams, Oct. 23, 1775.

A publication in one of the Connecticut papers, some time since, ascribed the honor of the noble resistance made at Bunker's Hill, on the 17th of June last, to a number of officers by name, belonging to that colony, some of whom, as I am informed, were not on the hill ; whilst other brave officers belonging to our colony, such as Colonels Prescott, Brewer, Gardner, Parker, &c., who nobly fought, and some of whom fell, are not even mentioned. But this account was detested by the brave Putnam, and others of that colony.

General Artemas Ward to John Adams, Oct. 30, 1775.

It is my opinion we should have began a month ago to engage men for another campaign. If the present army's time should be out, and no other secured, I fear the enemy will take advantage thereof. I wish Gen. Frye might be provided for. I think him a good man for the service, and am very sorry he has not been provided for by the Continental Congress before this time. Some have said hard things of the officers belonging to this colony, and despised them ; but I think, as mean as they have represented them to l e, there has been no one action with the enemy which has not been conducted by an officer of this colony, except that at Chelsea, which was conducted by General Putnam.

No. 8. — ACCOUNT OF THE BATTLE IN RIVINGTON'S GAZETTE, NUMBER 120, AUGUST 3, 1775.

As to camp news, I was there for the first time last Saturday. Our people appear hearty, and very happy. The great numbers who crowd to view it, and see their friends, and the parading of the regiments upon the commons, make a grand appearance. The famous Prospect Hill is just by the stone house on the left hand, as you go to Charlestown. I believe the regulars will hardly venture out, for they must lose a vast many men if they should; and they cannot afford to purchase every inch of ground, as they did at Charlestown. The number of the regulars lost and had wounded you have seen in the account taken from the orderly sergeant, which agrees pretty nearly with a variety of accounts we have received from people who have come here from Boston in fishing-boats. They must have suffered greatly, for the fire continued with small arms sixty-one minutes, and great part of the time very close fighting. My class-mate, Col. ———, was in the intrenchment, and was wounded in the head and leg. He says there was no need of waiting for a chance to fire, for, as soon as you had loaded, there was always a mark at hand, and as near as you pleased. His description of the intrenchment, &c., was this : —

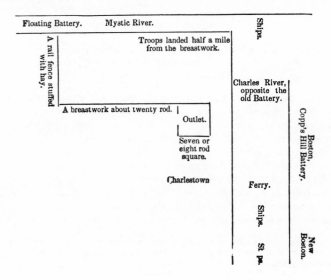

The square or fort had about 150 men in it. The breastwork, about **200.** The rail fence stuffed with straw, 400 or 500. The reason why the square was so thinly manned on the side toward Boston was, because the fire from Copp's Hill poured in so thick that there was no living in it. The regulars, when they found the fire slacken for want of ammunition, pushed over the walls, with their guns in their left hand, and their swords in their right, for it was such an unfinished piece of work that they ran over it. Part of them had come round on the side next Charlestown, so as to fire on the back of our people when they began to leave the intrenchment, and it was then we lost our men. The ships and floating batteries prevented any assistance or support of consequence being given to our men. The fire from Copp's Hill ceased when that with small arms began ; but that from a ship off New Boston killed and raked our men quite up to the Sun Tavern. ———— thinks there was more than 3000 of the regulars landed. They advanced in open order, the men often twelve feet apart in the front, but very close after one another, in extraordinary deep or long files. As fast as the front man was shot down, the next stepped forward into his place, but our men dropped them so fast they were a long time coming up. It was surprising how they would step over their dead bodies, as though they had been logs of wood. Their officers, it is said, were obliged to push them on behind, notwithstanding which, they once ran and filled some of the boats, the fire was so hot. One of ——— captains told me he fired about 35 times, and after that threw stones. ——— says when they pushed over the breastwork, what with the smoke and dust, it was so dark in the square that he was obliged to feel about for the outlet ; the earth, which they threw up for a breastwork, being very dry and loose for they had only one of these short nights to execute it in.

No. 9. — CRITICISM ON THE BATTLE PRINTED IN THE LONDON CHRONICLE, AUGUST 3, 1779.[1]

To the Printer of the London Chronicle:

If the English general had had his choice given him of the ground upon which he should find his enemy, he could not have wished to place the rebels in a situation for more certain ruin than that in which they had placed themselves at Bunker's Hill. And yet, from some fatality in our counsels, or rather, perhaps, from the total absence of all timely counsel, what ought to have been destructive to them proved only so to the royal army.

Every one knows that the ground on which stood Charlestown and Bunker's Hill was a peninsula. The isthmus which joined it to the continent used originally to be covered at high water ; but, for the convenience of the inhabitants, had a causeway raised upon it, which answered all the purposes

---

[1] Many criticisms on the battle appeared in the British journals. The one in the text forms one of a series on the conduct of General Howe. It was subsequently printed in pamphlet form.

of a wharf for landing upon. And the land adjoining was firm, good ground, having formerly been an apple orchard.

Nothing can be more obvious, especially if the reader will look upon the plan, than that the army, by landing at the neck or isthmus, must have entirely cut off the rebels' retreat, and not a man of them could have escaped.

The water in the Mystic River was deep enough for the gun-boats and smaller vessels to lie very near to this causeway, to cover and protect the landing of our own army, and to prevent any further reinforcements being sent to the enemy, as well as to secure the retreat and reëmbarkation of our own army, if that could have become necessary.

The ambuscade which flanked our troops in their march up to Bunker's Hill, and did so much mischief, had by this means been avoided.

Instead of shutting up the rebels, by landing at the isthmus, which was the place the most commodious for the descent, and for beginning the attack, the general unhappily chose to land in the face of the rebel intrenchments, and at the greatest possible distance from the neck or isthmus, and thereby left the way open for their escape ; and, still more unhappily, knowing nothing of the ground, attempted to march the troops in a part where they had ten or twelve rows of railing to clamber over ; the lands between Charles town and the beach being, for the convenience of the inhabitants, divided into narrow slips, not more than from ten to thirty rods over.

These posts and rails were too strong for the column to push down, and the march was so retarded by the getting over them, that the next morning they were found studded with bullets, not a hand's breadth from each other.

All this was well known to the inhabitants of Boston ; but they thought that military men, and such a great English general as Mr. Howe, must know better than they. And all this might have been known, and ought to have been known, to the English commander.

Had the rebels' coming into this peninsula been a thing utterly unexpected and never before thought of, the suddenness of the event might have been an apology for their not instantly thinking of the measures most proper to be taken upon such an occasion. But, far from unexpected, this was an event which they had long been apprehensive of, — the possibility of which had been in contemplation for two months before. The action at Bunker's Hill was on the 17th of June ; and so long before as the 21st of April, a message had been sent to the selectmen of Charlestown, that if they suffered the rebels to take possession of their town, or to throw up any works to annoy the ships, the ships would fire upon them. The message giving them this warning doubtless was very proper. But it was easy to foresee, that if the rebels chose to possess themselves of any part of the peninsula, the inhabitants of Charlestown could not prevent it. In all these eight weeks, therefore, it might have been hoped that the general and admiral should have concerted the proper measures for them to take, in case the enemy should come thither. It might have been hoped that the admiral should have perfectly informed himself of the depth of water in the Mystic River, and how near at the several times of the tide the vessels could come to the causeway. We might have hoped that the general would have informed himself of every inch of ground in so small a peninsula; and have previously concerted what he ought to do, and where he ought to land, upon every appearance of an enemy. And yet we do not seem to have given ourselves the trouble of a single thought about viewing the ground, or of considering before-hand what would be the proper measures to be taken in case the enemy should appear there. Instead of this, the morning on which the enemy was discovered, at three o'clock, a council of war was to be called, which might as well have been held a month before, and many hours more given to the rebels for carrying on their works, and finishing their redoubt.

The map will show us that Charlestown Neck lies at the utmost passable distance from the rebel quarters at Cambridge and Boston Neck; so that the troops had every possible advantage in landing at the causeway, and not a single man of the rebels could have escaped.

Is it necessary for a gentleman to be a soldier to see this? Will not every man's common sense, upon viewing the map, be convinced of it?

Whether, after the rebels were fled, General Clinton's advice to pursue was right or not, may be made a doubt. But if, instead of having sacrificed the lives of a thousand brave men by the want of all previous concert, and never having surveyed the ground; if, instead of this negligence and inattention, we had shut up the whole rebel force in the peninsula, and destroyed and taken that whole army, there can be no doubt but that we might then have pursued our advantage; and that if then we had marched to Roxbury and Cambridge, the troops would probably have not found a man there to oppose them; at least, in that general consternation, they might very easily have been dispersed; and the other provinces not having then openly joined them, we should probably have heard nothing more of the rebellion.

It was said at the time, I have heard, that we were unwilling to make the rebels desperate; but I hope no military man would offer to give such a reason. Veteran troops, long possessed with a very high sense of honor, like the old Spanish infantry at Rocroy, might possibly resolve to die in their ranks, and sell their lives as dearly as they could, though I know no instance in modern war of this Spanish obstinacy. But for regular British troops to be afraid of shutting up a rabble of irregular new-raised militia, that had never fired a gun, and had no honor to lose, lest they should fight too desperately for them, argues too great a degree of weakness to be supposed of any man fit to be trusted in the king's service. Happy had it been for Mr. Burgoyne if Mr. Gates had reasoned in this manner, and left the king's troops a way open for their escape, for fear of making them desperate. And yet Mr. Gates, when he lived with his father in the service of Charles Duke of Bolton. was never thought to possess an understanding superior to other men; and the letters of some of the most sensible and best informed men among the rebels show, that they thought him scarce equal to the command.

But what was it we had to fear by this notion of making them desperate? The rebels could not but see the execution they had done upon the royal army in their march; and yet they ran away the instant our troops were got up to them : — was this their point of honor? Had they found themselves cut off from all possibility of retreat, by our army's landing at the isthmus, in all probability they would have instantly thrown down their arms and submitted. If they had not, they must then have come out of their intrenchments, and fought their way through our army to get to the isthmus ; that is to say, we chose to land, and march up to their intrenchments, and fight under every possible disadvantage, for fear that by landing at the Neck we should have obliged them to come out of their intrenchments, and fight us upon equal terms, or even upon what disadvantages the general should please to lay in their way. But the innumerable errors of that day, if they had been known in time, might have sufficiently convinced us how little was to be expected from an army so commanded.

T. P.

No. 10.— List of the Regiments Portions of which were in the Bunker Hill Battle,

—

PRESCOTT'S REGIMENT.[1]

Captains.	Lieutenants.	Ensigns.	Number.
Henry Farwell,	Levi Whitney,	Benjamin Bass,	69.
Joshua Parker,	Amaziah Faucett,	Thomas Rogers,	63.
Samuel Patch,	Zachary Walker,	Joshua Brown,	26.
Hugh Maxwell,	Joseph Stebbins,		52.
Asa Lawrence,	Joseph Spaulding,	Thomas Spaulding,	55.
Oliver Parker,	Ephraim Corey,	John Williams,	26.
John Nutting,	Nathaniel Lakin,	John Mosher,	61
Samuel Gilbert,	Joseph Gilbert,	Joseph Baker,	51.
Abijah Wyman,	Joshua Brown,	Thomas Cummings,	29.
Reuben Dow,	John Goss.		

FRYE'S REGIMENT.

Benjamin Varnum,	Samuel Johnson,	Cyrus Marple,	63.
John Davis,	Nathaniel Herrick,	Eliphalet Bodwell,	56.
Benjamin Ames,	David Chandler,	Isaac Abbott,	53.
William Perley,	John Robinson,	Benjamin Perley,	57.
Nathaniel Gage,	Thomas Stickney,	Eliphalet Hardy,	51.

[1] The imperfect character of the returns of the regiments has already been remarked upon. See Chapter VII. It is impossible to ascertain even all the companies that were in the battle, much less the officers. The letter of Col. Prescott makes it uncertain whether the whole of his own regiment were in it, as only three hundred of it went on with him on the evening of June 16. Some of the officers, in the returns in the text, were commissioned immediately after the battle. This list is made up, mostly from copies of original returns in the Massachusetts archives.

Captains.	*Lieutenants.*	*Ensigns.*	*Number.*
James Sawyer,	Timothy Johnson,	Nathaniel Eaton,	63.
William H. Ballard,		—— Foster,	40.
John Currier,	—— Wells,	—— Chase,	60.
Jonas Richardson,	—— Reed,	—— Fox,	45.
Jonathan Evans,	John Merrill,	Reuben Evans.	

BRIDGE'S REGIMENT.

Jonathan Stickney,	Elijah Danforth,	John Lewis,	66.
Benjamin Walker,	John Flint,	Ebenezer Fitch,	78.
John Bachelor,	Ebenezer Damon,	James Bancroft,	69.
Ebenezer Bancroft,	Nathaniel Holden,	Samuel Brown,	50.
Peter Coburn,	Josiah Foster,	Ebenezer Farnum,	51.
Ebenezer Harnden,	William Blanchard,	Eleazor Stickney,	47.
John Ford,	Isaac Parker,	Jonas Parker,	59.
John Rowe,	Mark Pool,	Ebenezer Cleaveland,	40.
Jacob Tyler,	Charles Forbush.		

LITTLE'S REGIMENT.

Jacob Gerrish,	Silas Adams,	Thomas Brown,	45.
Ezra Lunt,	Paul Lunt,	Nath'l Montgomery,	45.
Benjamin Perkins,	Joseph Whittemore,	William Stickney,	59.
Nathaniel Wade,	Joseph Hodgskins,	Aaron Parker,	51.
Nathaniel Warner,	John Burnham,	Daniel Collins,	47.
John Baker,	Caleb Lamson,	Daniel Draper,	47.
James Collins,			46.
Gideon Parker,	Joseph Everly,	Moses Trask,	57.
Abraham Dodge,	Ebenezer Low,	James Lord,	59.

DOOLITTLE'S REGIMENT.

Joel Fletcher,	John Wheeler,	John Proctor.
Adam Wheeler,	Elijah Stearns,	Adam Maynard.
John Holman,	John Bowker,	David Pair.
John Jones,	Samuel Thompson.	
Robert Oliver,	Thomas Grover,	Abraham Pennel.
Abel Wilder,	Jonas Allen,	Daniel Pike.
John Leland,	Samuel Burbank.	

GERRISH'S REGIMENT.

Richard Dodge,	Robert Dodge,	Paul Dodge.
Barnabas Dodge,	Matthew Fairfield,	Joseph Knight.
Thomas Cogswell,	Moses Danton,	Amos Cogswell
Timothy Corey,	Thomas Cummings,	Jonas Johnson.
Samuel Sprague,	Joseph Cheever,	William Oliver.
John Baker, Jr.,	Joseph Pettingill,	Mark Cressy.
Thomas Mighill,	Thomas Pike.	
Isaac Sherman,	Caleb Robinson.	

GARDNER'S REGIMENT.

Captains.	Lieutenants.	Ensigns.	Number
Thomas Downing,	William Maynard.		
Phineas Cook,	Josiah Warren,	Aaron Richardson.	
Nathan Fuller,	Nathan Smith,	John George.	
Isaac Hall,	Caleb Brooks,	Samuel Cutter.	
Josiah Harris,	Bartholomew Trow,	Thomas Miller.	
Abner Craft,	Josiah Swan,	John Child.	
Abijah Child,	Solomon Bowman,	Jedediah Thayer.	
Benjamin Lock,	Ebenezer Brattle,	Stephen Frost.	
Moses Draper.			
Naylor Hatch.			

WARD'S REGIMENT.

Josiah Fay.			
Seth Washburn,	Joseph Livermore,	Loring Lincoln.	
Job Cushing,	Ezra Beaman,	Asa Rice.	
Daniel Barnes,	William Morse,	Paul Brigham.	
James Miller,	Abel Perry,	Aaron Abby.	
Luke Drury,	Asaph Sherman,	Jonas Brown.	
Jonas Hubbard,	John Smith,	William Gates.	
Samuel Wood,	Timothy Brigham,	Thomas Seaver.	
Moses Wheelock,	Thomas Bond,	Obadiah Mann.	

BREWER'S REGIMENT.

Isaac Gray,	Thomas Willington,	—— Wilson,	59.
Edward Blake,	Abraham Tuckerman,	John Eames,	55.
John Black,	Benjamin Gates,	John Patrick,	59.
Aaron Haynes,	Elisha Brewer,		53.
Daniel Whiting,	Obadiah Dewey,		51.
Benjamin Bullard,	Aaron Gardner,		45.
Thaddeus Russell,	Nathaniel Maynard,	Nathaniel Reeves,	53.
Joseph Stebbins,			22

NIXON'S REGIMENT.

Thomas Drury,	William Maynard,	Joseph Nixon.	
Samuel McCobb,	Benjamin Pattee,	John Riggs.	
Ebenezer Winship,	William Warren,	Richard Buckminister.	
David Moore,	Micah Goodenow,	Jona. Hill.	
Micajah Gleason,	James Kimball,	William Ryan.	
Moses McFarland,	David Bradley,	Jacob Quimby.	
Alisha Brown,	Daniel Taylor,	Silas Mann.	
	Silas Walker,	Edward Richardson.	
	John Heald,	John Hartwell.	

WOODBRIDGE'S REGIMENT. 00

Reuben Dickenson,	Zaccheus Crocker,	Daniel Shay,	60
Noadiah Leonard,	Josiah Smith,	Samuel Gould,	54

Captains.	*Lieutenants.*	*Ensigns.*	*Number*
Stephen Gearl,	Aaron Rowley,	Abner Pease,	**43.**
David Cowden,			**30.**
John Cowls,			**35.**
Ichabod Dexter,	Ithamer Goodnough,	John Mayo,	**52.**
John King,			**39.**
Seth Murray,			**50**
00			

GRIDLEY'S REGIMENT.

Samuel Gridley,	Wm. Smith, R. Woodward,	D. Ingersol,	**49.**
Samuel R. Trevett,	Jos. O. Swasey, R. Gardner,	Thomas Bowden,	37
John Callender,	Wm. Perkins, David Allen,	Samuel Treat,	**47.**

STARK'S REGIMENT.

Isaac Baldwin,	John Hale,	Stephen Hoyt.
Elisha Woodbury,	Thomas Hardy,	Jona. Corlis.
Samuel Richards,	Moses Little,	Jesse Carr.
John Moore,	Jonas McLaughlin,	Nathaniel Boyd.
Joshua Abbott,	Samuel Atkinson,	Abiel Chandler.
Gordon Hutchins,	Joseph Soper,	Daniel Livermore.
Aaron Kinsman,	Ebenezer Eastman,	Samuel Dearborn.
Henry Dearborn,	Amos Morrill,	Michael Mc'Clary.
Daniel Moore,	Ebenezer Frye,	John Moore.
George Reid,	Abraham Reid,	James Anderson.

REED'S REGIMENT.

John Marcy,	Isaac Farwell,	James Taggart,	**48.**
Benjamin Mann,	Benjamin Brewer,	Samuel Pettingill,	**49.**
Josiah Crosby,	Daniel Wilkins,	Thomas Maxwell,	**44.**
William Walker,	James Brown,	William Roby,	**46.**
Philip Thomas,	John Harper,	Ezekiel Rand,	**46.**
Ezra Towne,	Josiah Brown,	John Harkness,	**52.**
Jona. Whitcomb,	Elijah Clayes,	Stephen Carter,	**59.**
Jacob Hinds,	Isaac Stone,	George Aldrich,	**54.**
Levi Spaulding,	Joseph Bradford,	Thomas Buffe,	**44.**
Hezekiah Hutchins,	Amos Emerson,	John Marsh,	**44.**

PUTNAM'S REGIMENT.

Brig.-Gen. I. Putnam,	Jona. Kingsley,	Thos. Grosvenor,	Elijah Loomis.
Lt.-Col. E. Storrs,	James Dana,	Ebenezer Gray,	Isaac Farewell.
Maj. John Durkee,	J. Huntingdon,	Jacobus Delbit,	Lemuel Bingham.
Maj. Obadiah Johnson,	Ephraim Lyon,	Wells Clift,	Isaac Hyde, Jr.
Thos. Knowlton, Jr.,	Reuben Marcy,	John Keyes,	Daniel Allen, Jr.
James Clark,	Daniel Tilden,	Andrew Fitch,	Thomas Bill.
Ephraim Manning,	Stephen Lyon,	Asa Morris,	William Irissell.
Joseph Elliott,	Benoni Cutter,	Daniel Waters,	Comfort Day.
Ebenezer Mosely,	Steph. Brown,	M. Bingham,	Nath'l Wales.
Israel Putnam Jr.,	S. Robbins, Jr.,	Amos Avery,	Caleb Stanley.

SPENCER'S REGIMENT.

John Chester,	Barnabas Dean,	Steph. Goodrich,	Charles Butler.
William Coit,	Jedediah Hyde,	James Day,	Wm. Adams, Jr.

SIEGE OF BOSTON.

No. 1.—RETURN OF THE AMERICAN ARMY.

General Return of the Army of the United Colonies, March 2, 1776.

	Regiments.	Fit for Duty.	Total.		Regiments.	Fit for Duty.	Total.
1.	Riflemen,	591	750	15. Col. Patterson's,		288	413
2.	Col. Reed's,	321	407	16.	Sargent's,	209	428
3.	Learned's,	386	539	17.	Huntington's,	356	498
4.	Nixon's,	315	447	18.	Phinney's,	285	413
5.	Stark's,	312	379	19.	Webb's,	399	513
6.	Whitcomb's,	260	359	20.	Arnold's,	325	444
7.	Prescott's,	313	402	21.	Ward's,	396	485
8.	Poor's,	354	512	22.	Wyllys',	336	495
9.	Varnum's,	292	377	23.	Bayley's,	427	550
10.	Parsons',	426	509	24.	Greaton's,	269	359
11.	Hitchcock's,	295	348	25.	Bond's,	393	475
12.	Little's,	354	476	26.	Baldwin's,	417	498
13.	Reed's,	399	537	27.	Hutchinson's,	452	624
14.	Glover's,		273				

Total fit for duty, 9170.   Total of the regular army, 12,510.

General Return of the Militia of Massachusetts, March 2, 1776.

Regiments.	Fit for Duty.	Total.	Regiments.	Fit for Duty.	Total.
Col. Waldron's,	547	655	Col. L. Robinson's,	467	555
French's,	555	695	Carey's,	654	749
Wolcott's,	467	573	Smith's,	463	517
Wadsworth's,	448	548	J. Robinson's,	429	499
Whitney's,	503	617	Douglass',	437	610

Total fit for duty, 4970.   Total of the militia, 6018.

Total of the regular army and militia fit for duty, **14,140**.   Total of the army, 18,528.   A return of the regiment of artillery, commanded by Col. Knox, dated March 3, gives 635 men.

No. 2. — RETURNS OF THE ARMY DURING THE SIEGE.

Table exhibiting a Summary of the Returns of the Army under the Command of General Washington, during the Siege of Boston.[1]

	Commissioned officers and staff	Non-commissioned officers.	Rank and File.						Artillery.	Militia of Massachusetts.
			Present fit for duty.	Sick present.	Sick absent.	On furlough.	On command.	Total.		
1775.										
July 19,	1,119	1,768	13,743	1,108	490	376	1,053	16,770	585	
July 29,	1,117	1,823	13,899	1,330	690	287	692	16,898		
August 5,	1,178	1,910	13,735	1,943	750	255	1,011	17,694	586	
August 12,	1,234	2,023	14,544	2,131	977	187	1,124	18,963		
August 18,	1,231	2,007	14,442	2,218	1,006	220	1,174	19,060		
August 26,	1,242	2,018	14,701	2,179	1,071	225	1,127	19,303	596	
Sept. 2,	1,226	2,028	14,868	2,221	985	262	1,043	19,379		
Sept. 9,	1,303	2,107	14,766	2,026	988	342	1,410	19,532		
Sept. 23,	1,225	2,034	14,330	1,886	931	468	1,750	19,365	590	
Oct. 17,	1,191	1,988	13,923	1,476	952	746	2,400	19,497		
Nov. 18,	1,128	1,925	12,741	1,472	790	1,012	3,063	19,078	579	
Nov. 25,	1,068	1,866	12,065	1,464	805	1,626	2,990	18,950		
Dec. 30,	1,088	1,736	11,752	1,206	542	1,013	2,273	16,786	590	3,231
1776.										
Jan. 8,	979	1,150	10,209	705	233	1,044	1,318	13,509		
Jan. 21,	861	1,167	9,424	1,174	194	714	1,171	12,677		
Jan. 28,	850	1,194	9,799	1,422	245	420	1,248	13,134		
Feb. 4,	896	992	8,863	1,153	270	99	1,233	11,618		
Feb. 18,	1,245	1,452	13,396	1,687	364	49	1,569	17,065	622	
Feb. 25.	1,228	1,515	14,123	2,056	389	63	1,845	18,276		6,287
March 2,	1,217	1,521	14,140	2,398	367	49	1,574	18,528	635	6,869
March 9,	1,254	1,535	14,232	2,445	330	29	1,374	18,410	640	6,838

No. 3. — INVENTORY OF THE STORES, ORDNANCE, AND VESSELS, LEFT IN BOSTON BY THE BRITISH.

The following inventory was made by order of Thomas Mifflin, quartermaster-general of the continental army, March 18 and 19, 1776.

A brigantine, about 120 tons burden, loaded with oil and pearl.

A schooner, about 80 tons, scuttled, with 200 hogsheads of salt on board. 150 hhds. of salt in a store. 100 bundles of iron hoops.

Long Wharf. — 157 pack saddles. 123 water-casks. A brigantine, scuttled, about 140 tons. A sloop, scuttled, about 70 tons. A schooner, scuttled, about 40 tons. 1000 chaldrons of sea coals. 52 iron grates. General

[1] This table is copied from Sparks' Writings of Washington, vol. 3, p. 493.

Gage's chariot taken out of the dock, broken. A quantity of cordage and old cable, broken. Five anchors.

Green's Wharf. — About 200 blankets. Four and two thirds jars (large) of sweet oil.

Hatch's Wharf. — Three cannon, double charged and spiked.

Hancock's Wharf. — A new ship, about 300 tons, scuttled. About 1000 bushels salt. 3000 blankets. 30 water-casks.

Tudor's Wharf. — A ship, about 350 tons, scuttled.

Dummet's Wharf. — 5000 bushels wheat in store. A sloop, about 60 tons, scuttled. A fishing-boat.

Webb's Wharf. — A sloop, about 60 tons, scuttled.

Fuller's Wharf. — About 500 bushels of salt.

Fitch's Wharf. — A schooner, 70 tons, scuttled.

B. M. General's Office. — About 1000 bushels sea coal, and one clock; also lumber. About 150 hogsheads of lime; four barrels of flour; 100 empty iron-bound casks, carried to Fort Hill by Gen. Putnam's order. Ten 24 pound cannon cartridges.

Tileston's Wharf. — 300 hogsheads of salt. Three brigantines: — one, 150 tons; one, 120 tons; and one, 130 tons. The brig Washington, commanded by Captain Martindale, with all her guns, in the dock. One and a half hogsheads of sugar. A quantity of pickets, fascines and gabions, in store. About 5000 feet of boards.

Griffin's Wharf. — A number of iron grates.

Hubbard's Wharf. — About 1500 rugs and blankets. 50 water-casks, iron bound, carried to Fort Hill by Gen. Putnam's order. One cask of deck nails. About 200 cords of wood. About 200 chaldrons of sea coal.

South Battery, or Laboratory. — 52 pieces of cannon, trunnions broken off and spiked. 600 feet of boards. About 30 iron-bound casks, carried to Fort Hill by order of Gen. Putnam. A number of ball and empty shells. A brigantine, 120 tons; a schooner, 60 tons.

Wheelwright's Wharf. — 14 anchors. Three and a half hogsheads of brimstone. 300 hogsheads of sea coal. One 13 inch mortar, with an iron bed; a number of shells, carcasses, and cannon-shot, in the dock.

Hall's Wharf, and in his possession. — 600 bushels of corn and oats; 100 sacks of bran; 8 hhds. of molasses; 100 empty iron-bound casks. Two schooners, about 60 tons each. One sloop, about 40 tons. Ten horses, teams and harness.

Hutchinson's Wharf. — A new ship, about 350 tons, scuttled. Two brigs, about 120 tons each, scuttled. Two sloops, about 60 tons each, scuttled.

Winnisimet. — A new ship, building, thrown off the stocks, 200 tons. About 100 bushels salt. Store pulled down.

Peck's Wharf. — About 100 hhds. essence of spruce. 10 hhds. of beef. 6 hhds. of molasses, not quite full. 5 bbls. of molasses. A sloop, about 50 tons, two thirds full of molasses.

At Mr. Lovell's. — General Gage's coach, a phaeton and harness complete. 20 iron pots and kettles.

Joy's Yard. — A parcel of lumber, tools and joists.

Hill's Bakehouse. — 20 bbls. of flour.

North and South Mills. — 10,000 bushels of wheat and flour, not bolted; 1500 bushels of bran.

King's Brewery. — 13 empty bound butts; 14 hhds. spruce beer; two iron-tierced trucks.

Town Granary. — 1000 bushels beans; 100 bushels horse beans.

Vincent's Stable. — 10 tons hay.

Love's Lumber-yard, — 50,000 shingles; 35,000 feet of boards: 1000 clap-boards: 20 hand-barrows.

Henderson Inches' Store, near Beacon Hill. — About 6 tons of hay.

Stable at the Ropewalks. — About 10 tons of hay; 110 horses.

By return this day,

Boston, March 20, 1776.   JOHN G. FRAZER, D. Q. M. General.

The Commissary of Artillery, Ezekiel Cheever, in a return dated March 22, 1776, gives an account of the ordnance stores left by the British. There were, at the

North Battery. — Seven 12 pounders, two 9 pounders, and four 6 pound-ers — all useless.

On Copp's Hill. — Three 28 pounders, one 8 inch shell, one hundred and seventy-seven 28 pound shot, 273 wads, 2 hand-barrow levers, 2 drag ropes, half a side of leather.

At West Boston. — Three 32 pounders, 39 shot, 154 wads, one 13 inch mortar, 1 large chain.

On Beacon Hill. — Two 12 pounders, 23 shot, 23 wads.

Besides these, there were 82 cannon in different places, ten swivels in the Washington, a lot of shot and shells, and cannon-wheels.

The assistant Quartermaster-general, John G. Frazer, employed two com-panies, of ten men each, to take out of the dock and harbor articles thrown over by the British. An inventory, dated May 10, names large quantities of anchors, cannon, gun-carriages, shot, shells and tools. There were two 13 inch mortars, three hundred and ninety 24 pound shot, six hundred and forty-five 12 pound shot, eighty 6 pound shot, three hundred and fifty-eight 32 pound shot, four hundred and two 18 pound shot, 271 grape shot, and 162 shells.

The same officer reported, April 14, 1776, the names of forty-five vessels remaining in the harbor after the British evacuated the town.

Dr. John Warren, in a deposition read to the Massachusetts Council, April 9, 1776, states that he found at the workhouse, used by the British as a hospital, particularly in one room used as a medicinal store-room, large quantities of medicine, in which were small quantities of white and yellow arsenic intermixed. And also that he was informed by Dr. Samuel Scott that he had found a large quantity of arsenic.

No. 4. — Account of the Forts erected during the Siege.

The works erected in Boston and around Boston, during the siege, have become so obliterated by time and improvement as to render it almost a hopeless work to endeavor to indicate their localities by existing landmarks. The following article, which appeared in Silliman's Journal in 1822, shows how difficult it was to trace them, even at that time. The map referred to in the article as Marshall's is merely a copy of the one in Gordon's History, which was undoubtedly made from two others : Pelham's map of Boston and vicinity, for the country, and Page's plan of the environs and harbor of Boston, for the islands and harbor.

On the Forts around Boston, which were erected during the War of Independence. By J. Finch, F.B.S., &c.

Every fort made use of to defend the heroes of the Revolutionary War has acquired a title to the respect, the gratitude, and the veneration of all friends to liberty, in every part of the world. In future ages, they will inquire where the fortifications are, which were thrown up around the town of Boston, which held a British army besieged during eleven months, and finally compelled them to carry their arms and their warfare to other lands. Impelled by curiosity, let us visit these lines, which will be so celebrated in history — where the standards of liberty were unfurled, and freedom proclaimed to the vast continent of America — where the first intrenchments were raised against the forces of Britain — and from which, as from a barrier of iron, their armies recoiled. There cannot be any nobler monuments than these on the earth ; if they do not yet boast

"La Gloria di una remotissima antichita,"

every passing day, every hour, every moment, is conferring this quality upon them.

Nearly half a century has elapsed since these lines were erected, and it is desirable to have some record by which posterity may know how much they have suffered, during that period, by the war of the elements, and by the hands of men. The first cause of destruction has been trifling, but the storms of a thousand years would not have achieved the injury which has been committed by the industrious farmers. Wherever these works were an impediment to cultivation, they have been levelled to the ground, and fortresses which were directed by a Washington, or built by a Putnam, or a Greene, have been destroyed, to give room for the production of Indian corn, or to afford a level pasture for cattle. It would redound to the high honor of the State of Massachusetts, if some plan were devised by which the forts which sti l remain could be saved from the oblivion which apparently menaces them.

Annexed to Marshall's Life of Washington is a map of the country around Boston, in which the situation of the various forts and batteries is represented, and a stranger will find it a guide to many of the positions ; but or an attentive examination he will perceive that the map is rather inaccurate in some of the details.

1. At *Breed's Hill*, that blood-stained field, the redoubt thrown up by the Americans is nearly effaced ; scarcely the slightest trace of it remains ; but the intrenchment, which extended from the redoubt to the marsh, is still marked by a slight elevation of the ground. The redoubt thrown up by the British on the summit of the hill may be easily distinguished.

2. *Bunker Hill.* The remains of the British fort are visible ; the works must have been very strong, and occupied a large extent of ground ; they are on the summit and slope of the hill looking towards the peninsula.

3. *Ploughed Hill.* The works upon this hill were commenced by the Americans on the night of August 26th, 1775, and received more fire from the British than any of the other forts ; in a few days more than three hundred shells were fired at these fortifications. A small part of the rampart remains, but the whole hill is surrounded by the mounds and fosse of the ancient fort, which has been nearly obliterated.

4. *Cobble* or *Barrell's Hill* was fortified, and occupied as a strong post, in the war of the Revolution, by General Putnam, and, in consequence of its strength, was called Putnam's impregnable fortress. Every fort which was defended by that general might be considered as impregnable, if daring courage and intrepidity could always resist superior force ; yet this title seems to have been more exclusively given to the one noticed above. It was commenced on the night of November 22d ; and the activity of its fire is well known to those who have studied the details of the siege of Boston. This fort has been destroyed, but the position is easily identified. In Marshall's map, the intrenchment, which is placed between this hill and the creek, should be removed to the southern shore.

5. *Lechmere Point Redoubt*, one hundred yards from West Boston Bridge, displays more science in its construction, and has a wider and deeper fosse, than most of the other fortifications. It was commenced on December 11th, 1775, and it was several days before it was completed, during which time it was much exposed to the fire of the English in Boston. Two or three soldiers of the revolutionary army were killed at this redoubt, and the Prunus virginiana, with its red berries, marks the spot where they were probably interred. Upon one angle of the fort, where the cannon were pointed with most destructive effect, a church is now erecting ; and when I visited the spot, the carpenters were busily engaged in preparing the wood-work in one of the bastions. The glacis, the counterscarp, the embrasures, the covered way, and the batteries, are fast disappearing. Diggers of gravel on one side, and builders on the other, were busily employed in completing the destruction of the strongest battery erected by the army of America, and were thus achieving, without opposition, that which an enemy could not effect.

A causeway made across the marsh, the covered way which crosses the brow of the hill, and the lines which flanked Willis' Creek, are still perfect, and may be traced with great facility.

6. *Winter Hill Fort* appears to have been the most extensive, and the intrenchments more numerous than any of the other positions of the American army. The fort on the hill is almost entirely destroyed; only a small part of the rampart still remains perfect.

A redoubt situated upon Ten Hill Farm, which commanded the navigation of the Mystic River, is complete, as are also some slight intrenchments near.

A redoubt situated between Winter and Prospect Hill has been completely carried away, and a quarry has been opened on the spot. In the general orders, issued at Cambridge, guards were directed to be stationed at White House Redoubt, and this, I believe, was the post intended. General Lee is said to have had his head-quarters in a farm-house immediately in the rear of this redoubt.

7. *Prospect Hill* has two eminences, both of which were strongly fortified, and connected by a rampart and fosse. About two hundred yards are quite entire; they are ornamented with the Aster, Solidago, Rosa, &c.; and those who feel any curiosity about these lines will be much gratified by the view here afforded. The forts on these hills were destroyed only a few years ago, but their size can be distinctly seen. On the southern eminence a part of the fort is still entire, and the south-west face of the hill is divided into several platforms, of which I cannot exactly ascertain the use. There are also evident marks of the dwellings of the soldiers. The extensive view from this hill, the walk on the ancient ramparts, and the sight of the various stations occupied by the American army, will render this hill, at a future period, a favorite resort.

8. *Forts* marked No. 3, on Marshall's map, near the south-west of Prospect Hill, have some of their bastions entire, but the surface is cultivated, and part of the outline destroyed.

9. *The Cambridge Lines*, situated upon Butler's Hill, appear to have consisted of six regular forts, connected by a strong intrenchment. The most northerly of these forts is perfect, with the exception of one of its angles destroyed by the road; it appears as if just quitted by the army of America; its bastions are entire, the outline is perfect, and it seems a *chef d'œuvre* of the military art. The state of preservation in which it is found, and the motives which led to its erection, all confer a high degree of interest upon this fortification. May it continue uninjured for a long period of years, with no other foe but the assaults of time !

A square fort may be seen near the southern extremity of these lines, in fine preservation; it is in a field within two hundred yards of the road to Cambridge. As it was near the head-quarters of the army, it must have been often visited by General Washington, and this circumstance alone would render it an object of interest; but the proprietor appears to have wanted no inducement but his own mind to preserve this monument of times which are gone. The eastern rampart is lower than the others, and the gateway, with its bank of earth, still remains.

The other forts and batteries of this line of defence, which constituted the firmest bulwark of the American army, are all levelled with the ground.

and the intrenchments which were raised and defended by warriors are **now** employed in the peaceful pursuits of agriculture.

10. *The Second Line of Defence* may be traced on the College Green **at** Cambridge, but its proximity to the public halls may have produced **some** inconvenience, and it has been carefully destroyed.

11. *A Semi-circular Battery*, with three embrasures, on the northern shore of Charles River, near its entrance into the bay, is in a perfect state of preservation. It is rather above the level of the marsh, and those who would wish to see it should pass on the road to Cambridge, until they arrive at a cross-road, which leads to the bank of the river ; by following the course of the stream, they may arrive at this battery without crossing the marsh, which is its northern boundary and difficult to pass. Marshall places two batteries in this situation, but I could find only the one noticed above.

12. *Brookline Fort*, or, as it is called in the annals of the Revolution, the Fort on Sewall's Point, was very extensive, and would be still perfect, were it not for the road, which divides it into two nearly equal parts, with this exception, — the ramparts, and an irregular bastion, which commanded the entrance of Charles River, are entire. The fort was nearly quadrangular, and the fortifications stronger than many of the other positions of the American army.

13. *A Battery*, on the southern shore of Muddy River, with three embrasures, is only slightly injured. The ramparts and the fosse were adorned, when I saw them, with the beautiful leaves and the red fruit of the sumach, and with the dark-red foliage of the oak.

14. *A Redoubt*, placed by Marshall to the westward of this position, could not be discovered, nor three others, placed on the map between Stony Brook and the forts at Roxbury : perhaps the researches were not sufficiently accurate.

Two hundred yards north of the lower fort at Roxbury, near the spot on which the meeting-house now stands, was an intrenchment, which, I am informed by Gen. Sumner, was levelled many years ago.

15. *Forts at Roxbury*. If it is possible that any person should feel indifferent about the fortresses which achieved the independence of the eastern states of America, a visit to these forts will immediately recall to his mind all those associations which are so intimately combined with that proud period of American history. The lower fort at Roxbury appears to have been the earliest erected, and by its elevation commanded the avenue to Boston over the peninsula, and prevented the advance of the English troops in that direction. It is of the most irregular form ; the interior occupies about two acres of ground, and as the hill is bare of soil, the places may still be seen whence the earth was taken to form the ramparts. This fortification has not been at all injured, and the embrasures may still be noticed where the cannon were placed which fired upon the advanced lines of the enemy.

On a higher eminence of the same hill is situated a quadrangular fort, built on the summit of the rock ; and being perhaps their first attempt at regular fortification, it was considered by the militia of unparalleled strength, and excited great confidence in that wing of the army stationed at Roxbury.

*　*　*　*　*　*　*　*　*　*　*　*　*

16. *The Roxbury Lines*, about three quarters of a mile in advance of the forts, and two hundred yards north of the town, are still to be seen on the eastern side of the peninsula, and may be distinguished by any person going by the nearest road to Dorchester, over Lamb's Dam.

17. At this period it may be proper to mention the British fortifications. The lines situated upon the neck are almost as perfect at the present day as when first erected, with the exception of that part destroyed by the road. They may be seen to great advantage on the western side of the isthmus, about a quarter of a mile south of the green stores. There appear to have been two lines of intrenchments carried quite across the peninsula, and the fosse, which was filled at high water, converted Boston into an island. The mounds, ramparts and wide ditches, which remain, attest the strength of the original works. The small battery on the common, erected by the British, may perhaps remain for a long period of years, as a memorial of ancient times.

18. *The Dorchester Lines.* Of these, some very slight traces may be distinguished.

19. *Forts on Dorchester Heights.* We now hasten to the last forts, the erection of which terminated the contest in this portion of the eastern states of America.

*　*　*　*　*　*　*　*　*　*　*　*　*

It is to be regretted that the intrenchments thrown up by the army of the Revolution, on the Heights of Dorchester, are almost entirely obliterated by the erection of two new forts in the late war. But some traces of the ancient works may be seen on both hills; the old forts were constructed with more skill, and display more science, than the recent works, the ramparts of which are even now falling down; and we would gladly see them destroyed, if from their ruins the ancient works could reäppear.

20. A noble octagonal fort and two batteries, which may be seen in perfect preservation upon the promontory, were erected after the departure of the English from Boston, and do not require a place in the present essay. The fort is situated at the point; one battery is in the rear of the House of Industry, whose inmates will probably soon destroy it, and the other upon a rising ground immediately below the Heights of Dorchester.

21. At *Nook Hill*, near South Boston Bridge, may be seen the last breastwork which was thrown up by the forces of America, during this arduous contest. Its appearance, on the morning of March 17, 1776, induced the departure of the British troops from Boston in a few hours, and thus placed the seal to the independence of the New England States. But those who would wish to see this intrenchment must visit it soon. The enemy have attacked it on three sides, and are proceeding by sap and by mine; part of the fosse is already destroyed, and the rampart nods to its fall.

If these fortresses should be regarded with indifference, let us consider that the siege of Boston was one of the most prominent features in the war of the Revolution. The forces of England were, in the commencement of the contest, besieged, and the plans for the independence of America were matured, under the shelter of these ramparts.

In a military point of view it presents conspicuous features : an island, or rather a peninsula, besieged from the continent ; accomplished generals and brave and disciplined troops on one side, and undisciplined but numerous forces on the other. At the same time, the army of England did all that men in such a situation could attempt. If they had obtained possession of any part of the lines, by the sacrifice of an immense number of lives, still no advantage could have been gained by advancing into a country where every man was a foe, every stone wall a rampart, and every hill a fortress. When we examine the extent of the lines, (more than twelve miles,) the numerous forts covering every hill, redoubts and batteries erected upon every rising ground, ramparts and intrenchments defending every valley, we are surprised at the immensity of the works constructed, and the labor required to complete them. Nothing but the enthusiasm of liberty could have enabled the men of America to construct such works. In history they are equalled only by the lines and forts raised by Julius Cæsar to surround the army of Pompey, of which the description in Lucan's Pharsalia will justly apply to the lines before Boston :

> Franguntur montes, planumque per ardua Cæsar
> Ducit opus ; pandit fossas, turritaque summis
> Disponit castella jugis, magno que recessû
> Amplexus fines ; saltus nemorosaque tesqua
> Et silvas, vestaque feras indagine claudit. Lib. VI. 38—43.

Or the relation of the same siege in Cæsar De Bello Civili, Lib. 3, may be considered as more applicable.

Should the inhabitants of New England, at some future day, take a pleasure in preserving the forts which were erected by their ancestors, defended by their valor, and which they would have laid down their lives to maintain, the hills on which they are situated should be adorned with trees, shrubs, and the finest flowers. The laurel, planted on the spot where Warren fell, would be an emblem of unfading honor ; the white birch and pine might adorn Prospect Hill ; at Roxbury, the cedar and the oak should still retain their eminence ; and upon the Heights of Dorchester, we would plant the laurel, and the finest trees which adorn the forest, because there was achieved a glorious victory, without the sacrifice of life.

Many centuries hence, if despotism without, or anarchy within, should cause the republican institutions of America to fade, then these fortresses ought to be destroyed, because they would be a constant reproach to the people ; but until that period, they should be preserved as the noblest monu ments of liberty.

COPY OF A PORTION OF A LETTER WRITTEN BY CAPTAIN CHESTER AND LIEUTENANT SAMUEL B. WEBB, AND ADDRESSED TO JOSEPH WEBB, WHO WAS BROTHER TO LIEUTENANT WEBB AND BROTHER-IN-LAW TO CAPTAIN CHESTER.[1]

Cambridge, June 19th, 1775,
Monday morn., 9 o'clock.

My dear Brother, — The horrors and devastations of war now begin to appear with us in earnest. The generals of the late engagement and present manouvers you will doubtless hear before this can reach you. However, as you may be in some doubt, I shall endeavor to give you some particulars, which I hope will not be disagreeable, tho' it may be repeating. Know then that last Fryday afternoon orders were issued for about 1800 of the province men and 200 of Connecticut men, to parade themselves at 6 o'clock, with one day's provisions, blankets, &c., and then receive their order (nearly the same order in Roxbury Camp also). Near 9 o'clock they marched (with intrenching tools in carts by their side) over Winter's Hill[2] in Charlestown, and passed the intrenchments the regulars began when they retreated from Concord, and went to intrenching on Bunker's Hill,[3] which is nearer the water, castle, and shipping. Here they worked most notably, and had a very fine fortification, which the enemy never knew 'till morning. They then began a most heavy fire, from the Copp's Hill, near Dr. Cutler's church, and from all the ships that could play, which continued till near night. About 1 o'clock, P.M. we that were at Cambridge heard that the regulars were landing from their floating batteries, and the alarm was sounded, and we ordered to march directly down to the fort at Charlestown. Before our company could get there, the battle had begun in earnest, and cannon and musket balls were flying about our ears like hail, and a hotter fire you can have no idea off. Our men were in fine spirits. Your brother and I led them, and they kept their order very finely, two and two.

My dear brother, you'll see by this the amazing hurry we are in. Capt. Chester is called of, and begs me to go on with this letter, which I'll endeavor to do; tho', if it appears incorrect and unconnected, you must make proper allowance.

After the alarm, on our march down, we met many of our worthy friends, wounded, sweltering in their blood, carried on the shoulders by their fellow soldiers. Judge you what must be our feelings at this shocking spectacle; the orders were, *press on, press on,* our brethren are suffering, and will be cut off. We pushed on, and came into the field of battle, thro' the cannonading of the ships, — bombs, chain-shot, ring-shot, and double-headed shot, flew as thick as hailstones, but thank Heaven few of our men suffered by them; but when we mounted the summit, where the engagement was, — Good God, how the balls flew, — I freely acknowledge I never had such a

---

[1] See page 389.   [2] This was Bunker Hill.   [3] This was what is now called Breed's Hill.

tremor come over me before. We descended the hill, into the field of battle, and began our fire very briskly; the regulars fell in great plenty, but to do them justice, they keep a grand front, and stood their ground nobly. Twice before this time they gave way, but not long before we saw numbers mounting the walls of our fort, — on which our men in the fort were ordered to fire, and make a swift retreat. We covered their retreat till they came up with us, by a brisk fire from our small-arms. The dead and wounded lay on every side of me; their groans were piercing, indeed, tho' long before this time, I believe, the fear of death had quitted almost every breast. They now had possession of our fort and four field-pieces, and by much the advantage of the ground.

[The copyist remarks: The half-sheet of "foolscap" containing the above ends abruptly, as you see; a half-sheet of heavy laid paper, like a leaf from an account-book, contains the remainder of the letter, and is signed by both Samuel B. Webb and John Chester, — 4 o'clock, P.M., — from which the following sentences are extracted: —]

Lieut. Webb says: for God's sake, to urge Gen. Lee and Col. Washington to join, head-officers is what we stand greatly in need of; we have no acting head here but Putnam, — he acts nobly in every thing * * * * by the by, in the Saturday's battle, our gunner to the field-pieces quitted his post, &c., &c., and is now under confinement for it, and to be tryed by a general court martial; so that we fought against eight or ten capital ships' fire, — the fire from Cop's Hill, in Boston, of 24-pounders, and the regulars' field-pieces, — together with shells; when on our side nothing but small-arms was fired, except four guns fired by Gen. Putnam after the gunner quitted the field-pieces.

Chester writes: Our men that were draughted out to entrench last Fryday night have lost blankets, guns, coats, a few shirts, knapsacks, &c., &c.; we want supplies, but know not how to get them. * * * * You'll see by the handwriting which I wrote, and which Lieut. Webb wrote * * * *

NOTE. — I regret that I cannot recall the name of the gentleman who kindly showed me the original, and gave me the copy of this important letter.

INDEX.